The **Rough Guide** to

Cape Town
the Winelands & the Garden Route

written and researched by

Tony Pinchuck and Barbara McCrea

ROUGH
GUIDES

www.roughguides.com

Contents

Introduction to

Cape Town

the Winelands & the Garden Route

Cape Town is southern Africa's most beautiful, most romantic and most visited city. Its physical setting is extraordinary, something its pre-colonial Khoikhoi inhabitants recognized when they referred to Table Mountain, the city's emblematic landmark, as Hoerikwaggo – the mountain in the sea. If the landscape doesn't take your breath away, its high-octane activities, from paragliding to shark-cage diving should do the trick, and that's before you've sampled the nightlife. Which isn't to say Cape Town is just about adrenaline. Away from the thrills and pumping party scene, you'll find a city boasting breathtaking beaches, rolling vineyards and fine museums – enough to keep you busy over an extended visit. Despite this, most visitors find the time to escape the city – to the Winelands, to sample South Africa's celebrated wines and further east along the Garden Route, whose draw includes unparalleled whale-watching, crashing seascapes, dappled forests and – at its culmination – lions, leopards and elephants in the best game reserve in the southern half of the country.

Cape Town has a rich urban texture too, etched in its diverse **architecture**. In the suburbs, shimmering white Cape Dutch homesteads, rooted in seventeenth-century northern European traditions, characterize the grand estates of the Constantia Winelands; in the city, Muslim slaves, freed in the nineteenth century, added their minarets to the centre's skyline; and the English, who invaded and freed these slaves, introduced Georgian and Victorian buildings. In the tight terraces of the Bo-Kaap quarter and the tenements of District Six, the coloured descendants of slaves evolved a unique, evocatively Capetonian brand of jazz, which is well worth catching live. Indeed

ABOVE KOOPMAN'S DE-WET HOUSE; STREET VENDOR IN KHALITSHA TOWNSHIP; DUNG BEETLE

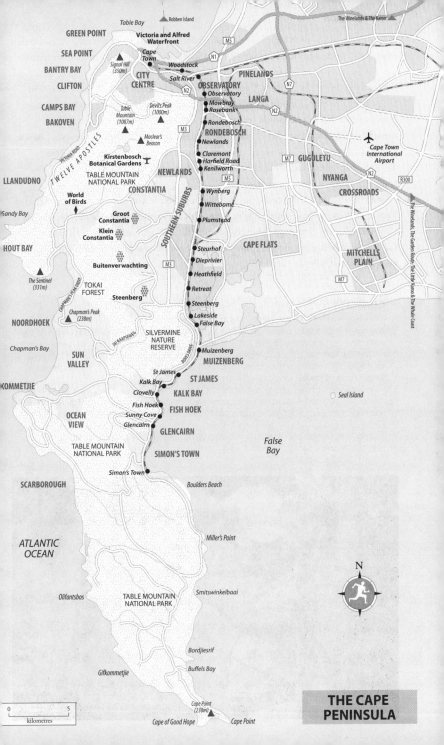

THE CAPE PENINSULA

great sounds, along with high standards of accommodation, smart restaurants, laidback cafés and a vibrant gay scene, make visiting Cape Town a truly cosmopolitan experience.

But despite a reputation for greater **liberalism** and racial tolerance during the apartheid era than the rest of the country, Cape Town has paradoxically been the slowest city in South Africa to embrace post-apartheid multiracialism. Ever since the mid-seventeenth century when Jan van Riebeeck, leader of the first whites to settle in South Africa, thought of digging a canal across the Cape Peninsula to cut it off from the rest of Africa, Cape Town has stood aloof from the rest of the country. For 350 years Cape Town's white establishment endeavoured to maintain an illusion that the city was somehow really European, despite its location.

Under apartheid, black (as opposed to coloured) South Africans were actively excluded from the Western Cape, which is why today **Africans** are still a minority in the Mother City, though they constitute the overwhelming majority in South Africa. For most Capetonians, living in crowded **townships** and **shantytowns**, poverty and sky-high crime rates are part of everyday life.

CINE CITY

Following the success of *U-Carmen eKhayelitsha* at the Berlin Film Festival in 2005, Cape Town was not only lauded for showing its grittier face on film, but Hollywood directors began to realize the city's **chameleon-like** ability to re-create anything from French boulevards to hectic New York traffic. Cape Town was subsequently able to stand in for 35 diverse locations for the 2005 Nicolas Cage movie *Lord of War*, including Bolivia, Beirut, Berlin, the Caribbean, Sierra Leone, Indonesia, Odessa and New York City.

Pre *U-Carmen eKhayelitsha*, feature films shot here were forgettable affairs involving equally unmemorable actors. Nowadays, Capetonians are increasingly spotting major **Hollywood names** in bars along the Atlantic seaboard beaches, as *24* starring Kiefer Sutherland, *Blood Diamond* with Leonardo DiCaprio and Jennifer Connolly, and Clint Eastwood-directed *Invictus*, starring Matt Damon and Morgan Freeman, have been shot in the city. Indeed, star-gazing is likely to become a common pastime on the peninsula with the arrival of the R350m Cape Town Film Studios in 2011.

What to see

Table Mountain, frequently mantled by its "tablecloth" clouds, is the solid core of Cape Town, dividing the city into distinct zones, with public gardens, wilderness, forests, hiking routes, vineyards and desirable residential areas. To its north lies the **city centre**, home to the city's most important museums and galleries, and with a buzzing street life – buskers, hawkers and market traders. In the adjacent **Bo-Kaap** Muslim quarter, colourful terraces and restaurants serving local curries add piquancy to the city's heart. A stone's throw from the centre, the **V&A Waterfront** is Cape Town's most popular spot for shopping, eating and drinking in a highly picturesque setting among the piers and quays of a working harbour. It's also the embarkation point for catamarans to **Robben Island**, the site of Nelson Mandela's notorious incarceration. The rocky shore west of the Waterfront is occupied by the inner-city suburbs of **Green Point**, **De Waterkant** and **Sea Point**, home to some of the peninsula's oldest and best restaurants, their back-streets crammed with backpacker lodges, B&Bs and hotels. Equally good for accommodation, but more leafy and upmarket in comparison, the **City Bowl suburbs** gaze down from the Table Mountain foothills across the central business district to the ships in Duncan Dock.

South from Sea Point, a coastal road traces the chilly **Atlantic seaboard** under the heights of the Twelve Apostles and past some of Cape Town's most expensive suburbs and spectacular beaches to Hout Bay. From here, the road merges with the precipitous **Chapman's Peak Drive**, ten dramatically snaking kilometres of Victorian engineering carved into the western cliffsides of the Table Mountain massif, high above the crashing waves. To the east, across Table Mountain, the exceptionally beautiful **Kirstenbosch National**

LEFT ON THE SET OF BLOOD DIAMOND **ABOVE** SUNDOWNERS AT CAMPS BAY

Botanical Gardens creep up the lower slopes, as do the **Constantia Winelands** a little further south, while the middle-class **southern suburbs** stretch down the peninsula as far as Muizenberg. The scenic Metrorail train line cuts through these suburbs and continues along the **False Bay seaboard**, passing through village-like **Kalk Bay**, with its intact harbour and working fishing community, and **Fish Hoek**, which has the best bathing beach along the eastern peninsula, before the final stop at the historic settlement of **Simon's Town**.

Most visitors see only the areas that were classified under apartheid as "white" and which still remain relatively safe and salubrious. But the townships of the **Cape Flats** to the east of the city can be visited on guided tours, and if you really want to get under the skin of the African areas, you can enjoy the hospitality of any of several B&Bs in **Xhosa homes.**

Beyond the city, the beautiful **Winelands** lie just an hour east of the Cape Flats, rich in elegant examples of Cape Dutch architecture, wonderful wines and excellent restaurants. Southeast of Cape Town you can take the picturesque coastal route, winding around massive sea-cliffs, to reach Hermanus, the largest settlement on the **Whale Coast**, and a fabulous spot for shore-based whale-watching.

After Cape Town, the best-known tourist feature of the Western Cape is the **Garden Route**, a drive along the N2 from Cape Town all the way to Port Elizabeth in the Eastern Cape. The Garden Route can be driven in a day, but to cover it so quickly would mean missing its essence, which lies off the road in its coastal towns, lagoons, mountains and ancient forests on the stretch between **Mossel Bay** and **Storms River Mouth**. The highlight along here is the **Tsitsikamma National Park**, where the dark Storms River opens spectacularly into the Indian Ocean. Public transport along the Garden Route is better than anywhere in the country, partly because the route is a single stretch of freeway, and tour operators along the way have begun turning it into the country's most concentrated strip for packaged **adventure sports** and **outdoor activities**. Parallel to the Garden Route, Route 62 provides a thoroughly rewarding inland alternative, traversing some of the most dramatic mountain passes in the region and taking in a number of picturesque Little Karoo *dorps*.

But the ultimate destination at the eastern end of the region, to which both the Garden Route and Route 62 lead, is **Addo Elephant National Park**, where sightings of elephants are virtually guaranteed, and there's a chance of seeing lions, buffalo and rhinos, among other wildlife.

When to visit

Cape Town has a **Mediterranean climate**, the warm, dryish summers balanced by cool wet winters. Come prepared for hot days in winter and cold snaps in summer, and pack a jumper and jacket whatever time of year you come. The **southeaster**, the cool summer wind that blows in across False Bay, forms a major obsession for Capetonians. Its fickle moods can singlehandedly determine what kind of day you're going to have, and when it gusts at over 60kph you won't want to be outdoors, let alone on the beach. Conversely,

ANIMAL ATTRACTIONS

In Cape Town you're never far from the Table Mountain National Park and although this is no longer lion country (the last one was shot in the 1720s), you can still see countless varieties of animals, birds and reptiles here and along the city's coastline.

Commonest of the peninsula's large mammals are **baboons**, which number between three hundred and four hundred and are mostly seen in the Cape of Good Hope section of the park. Another common species are **dassies**, or rock hyraxes, the fluffy beasts that resemble large guinea pigs and routinely sun themselves around the Upper Cable Station on Table Mountain. Of the scores of other mammals present, including **caracals**, **genets**, **polecats**, **Cape foxes** and some twenty species of **mice**, among the ones you'll most likely see are **Cape Mountain zebras**, **bontebok** (a large antelope) and **mongooses**.

Moving offshore, **African penguins** can be seen in high numbers at the colony in Boulders Bay and along the coastline to Hermanus. The city's most famous and glorious marine mammals, however, are the hefty **southern right whales** that arrive in False Bay during their calving season (peak period mid-Aug and mid-Oct), while **dolphins** are commonly spotted off the coast. And if you're willing to go under, you'll discover that False Bay is one of the best places in the country to meet a **great white shark** face to face on a shark-diving excursion.

its gentler incarnation as the so-called **Cape Doctor** brings welcome relief on humid summer days, and lays the famous cloudy tablecloth on top of Table Mountain. The **Garden Route** falls within overlapping weather systems and as a result has rain throughout the year, falling predominantly at night, which brings forth the verdure from which the region draws its name.

For sun and swimming, the best time to visit is from **October to mid-December** and **mid-January to Easter**, when it's light long into the evening and there's an average of ten hours of sunshine a day. Between mid-December and mid-January, the whole region becomes congested as the nation takes its annual seaside holiday. In Cape Town, this is major party time, with plenty of **major festivals** and events; if this is when you plan to visit, arrange accommodation and transport well in advance, and expect to pay considerably more for your bed than during the rest of the year.

Despite its shorter daylight hours, the **autumn** period, from April to mid-May, has a lot going for it: the southeaster drops and air temperatures remain pleasantly warm and the light is sharp and bright. For similar reasons the **spring** month of September can be very agreeable, with the added attraction that following the winter rains the peninsula tends to be at its greenest. Although spells of heavy rain occur in **winter** (June and July), it tends to be relatively mild, with temperatures rarely falling below 6°C. Glorious sunny days with crisp blue skies are common, and you won't see bare wintry trees either: indigenous vegetation is evergreen and gardens flower year-round. It's also in July that the first migrating **whales** begin to appear along the Southern Cape coast, usually staying till the end of November.

TOP SUNBIRD IN KIRSTENBOSCH GARDENS **OPPOSITE FROM TOP** DIE ANTWOORD; DE HOOP NATURE RESERVE; KOOPMAN'S DE-WET HOUSE

Author picks

Although he's lived there for over a decade, our author is constantly amazed by Cape Town, where he's watched a whale breach during his morning coffee, trodden grapes with a high court judge and run into a baboon during a morning jog. Chance encounters aside, here are some of the other things that make his adopted home so special...

Best Table in town No café in Cape Town offers better views of Table Mountain, or better coffee, than *Common Ground* **p.120**.

Top wildlife experience The five-day Whale Trail in De Hoop Nature Reserve is stunningly beautiful throughout the year – and sublime in season when there are whales around every corner **p.180**.

Most spine chilling artwork It's hard to remain unmoved in the face of Jane Alexander's powerful sculpture *Butcher Boys* at the National Gallery **p.52**.

Foulest-mouthed musicians Zef-rap crew Die Antwoord have stormed the world with Cape Flats slang, but still perform at home **p.269**.

Tree-hugging overnight stay Hide out in the boughs of virgin forest at *Teniqua Treetops*, a romantic experiment in sustainable living. **p.201**.

Wettest seafood The small deck at *Harbour House Restaurant* in Kalk Bay, jetties out over the crashing surf, with the risk of a drenching at high tide **p.122**.

Hidden history The lantern in the fanlight at Koopman's De Wet House was designed to light the street and prevent plotting slaves from congregating **p.58**.

Safari style The glass bedroom walls at boutique-hotel-in-the-bush *Kwandwe Ecca Lodge* are all that separates you from the Big Five **p.253**.

> Our author recommendations don't end here. We've flagged up our favourite places – a perfectly sited hotel, an atmospheric café, a special restaurant – throughout the guide, highlighted with the ★ symbol.

18

things not to miss

It's not possible to see everything that Cape Town and the Garden Route have to offer in one trip – and we don't suggest you try. What follows is a selective and subjective taste of the highlights, including outstanding national parks, spectacular wildlife, thrilling adventure sports and beautiful architecture. They're arranged in five colour-coded categories to help you find the very best things to see, do and experience. All entries have a page reference to take you straight into the Guide, where you can find out more.

1 TABLE MOUNTAIN CABLEWAY
Page 69
The cable car is the most spectacular way to ascend Cape Town's famous peak.

2 OCEAN SAFARIS
Page 194
Take to the waves for incomparable encounters with South Africa's whale and dolphin species.

3 SUNDOWNERS
Page 127
Relax with a tipple at Clifton as the sun turns into a glowing orb and sinks into the ocean.

4 TOWNSHIP TOURS
Page 82
Touch the reality of daily life for most Capetonians in one of the city's sprawling townships.

9

10

11

12

 CAPE MINSTRELS
Page 30
Every January 2, minstrel bands hold an unmissable carnival through the streets of Cape Town.

13

13 CHAPMAN'S PEAK DRIVE
Page 91
Take a spin along the precipitous cliff edge of the Atlantic seaboard for the most sublime views on the peninsula.

14 CANOPY TOURS
Page 188
Swing through the treetops among the arboreal giants of South Africa's tallest indigenous forest.

15 DE HOOP NATURE RESERVE
Page 180
Monumental dunes, zebras, bontebok and whales by the dozen make this one of the most compelling reserves in the Western Cape.

16 ROBBEN ISLAND
Page 64
Visit the notorious offshore jail where some of South Africa's most famous figures, including Nelson Mandela, were incarcerated.

17 CAPE TOWN INTERNATIONAL JAZZ FESTIVAL
Page 30
Local musos come into their own at the most important jazz event of the year.

18 V&A WATERFRONT
Page 61
Find out why a huge harbourside shopping mall is Cape Town's most popular tourist destination.

14

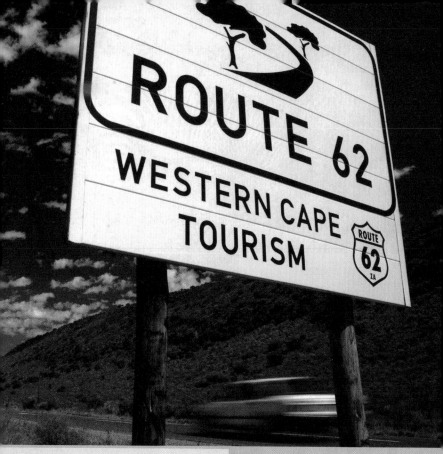

ROUTE 62 THROUGH THE LITTLE KAROO

Basics

Getting there

Most overseas visitors to Cape Town travel there by air, either on a direct flight or via Johannesburg, which is connected to Cape Town by frequent domestic flights (see p.24). There are no direct services from North America, but a nonstop flight from the UK makes the twelve-hour-plus journey a little more bearable. It can be cheaper, however, to fly via mainland Europe or Africa.

Airfares always depend on the **season**, with the highest prices and greatest demand occurring in June, July, August, December and the first week of January. Prices drop during the "shoulder" season in May and September. You get the best prices during the low season in October, November and the last three weeks of January till March.

Flights from the UK and Ireland

From London there are nonstop flights with British Airways (Ⓦ ba.com), South African Airways (Ⓦ flysaa.com) and Virgin Atlantic (Ⓦ virgin-atlantic .com) to Cape Town. **Flying time** from the UK to Cape Town is around twelve hours and average high/low-season scheduled direct fares from London start at £800/500. You can save up to £200 by flying via mainland Europe, Africa or Asia, and enduring at least one change of plane, often in Johannesburg.

There are no direct flights from **Ireland**, but a number of European and Middle Eastern carriers fly to Cape Town via their hub airports.

Flights from the US and Canada

There are no direct flights **from the US**, but there are three nonstop **flights** a week from New York (JFK) to Johannesburg operated by South African Airways (SAA) in partnership with United Airlines (Ⓦ united.com). These take between fifteen and sixteen hours. Most other flights stop off in Europe, the Middle East or Asia and involve a change of plane. On the flights from the US to Cape Town via Jo'burg, expect the high/low-season fare to start from $2600/1700 for a return trip, depending on season; you might save from $100 to as much as $700 if you fly **via Europe**.

From Canada, you'll have to change planes in the US, Europe or Asia on hauls that can last up to thirty hours. Fares from Vancouver to Cape Town start at Can$2200.

Flights from Australia and New Zealand

There are nonstop flights **from Sydney** (which take 12hr) and **Perth** (just under 10hr) to **Johannesburg**, with onward connections to **Cape Town**; New Zealanders also tend to fly via Sydney. South African Airways (SAA) and Qantas (Ⓦ quantas.com) both serve South Africa from Australia. Several Asian, African and Middle Eastern airlines fly to Cape Town via their hub cities, and tend to be less expensive, but their routings often entail long stopovers.

Cape Town is not a cheap destination for travellers from Australia and New Zealand; high/low-season fares start at around Aus$2800/1800 for a return flight **from Sydney** to Cape Town via Johannesburg, and a flight to Europe with a stopover in South Africa, or even an RTW ticket, may represent better value than a straightforward return.

AGENTS AND OPERATORS

Abercrombie & Kent Australia ☎ 1300 851 800, Ⓦ abercrombiekent.com.au; UK ☎ 0845 618 2202, Ⓦ abercrombiekent.co.uk; US ☎ 1 800 554 7016, Ⓦ abercrombiekent.com. Classy operator whose packages feature Cape Town, Johannesburg, Kruger and luxury rail travel.
Adventure Center US ☎ 1 800 228 8747, Ⓦ adventurecenter .com. Wide variety of affordable packages, including luxury rail journeys from Victoria Falls or Johannesburg to Cape Town.
Africa Travel Centre UK ☎ 0845 450 1520, Ⓦ africatravel.co.uk. Experienced Africa specialists, who are agents for many South Africa-based overland operators.
Bales Worldwide UK ☎ 0845 057 1819, Ⓦ balesworldwide .com. High-quality escorted tours.
Cox & Kings UK ☎ 020 7873 5000, Ⓦ coxandkings.co.uk; US ☎ 1 800 999 1758. Stylish operator with classic luxury journeys and deluxe safaris, including a twelve-day Cape Town to Johannesburg excursion and deluxe safaris.
Destinations Ireland ☎ 01 435 0092, Ⓦ destinations.ie. Specialists in long-haul destinations, including South Africa.
Exodus UK ☎ 020 8675 5550, Ⓦ exodus.co.uk. Small-group adventure tour operator with trips in and around Cape Town, excursions to the country's wildlife reserves and activity packages such as horseriding, kloofing (canyoning), mountain biking and surfing.
Expert Africa UK ☎ 020 8232 9777, Ⓦ expertafrica.com. Small-group tours for independent travellers, as well as tailor-made trips. Strong on Cape Town and the Western Cape.
Explore Worldwide UK ☎ 0845 013 1537, Ⓦ explore .co.uk. Good range of small-group tours, expeditions and safaris, staying mostly in small hotels and taking in Cape Town and around
Goway Travel Experiences US ☎ 1 800 387 8850, Ⓦ goway .com. Wide range of packages from three to fourteen days taking in the Western Cape and Eastern Cape game reserves.

A BETTER KIND OF TRAVEL

At Rough Guides we are passionately committed to travel. We feel that travelling is the best way to understand the world we live in and the people we share it with – plus tourism has brought a great deal of benefit to developing economies around the world over the last few decades. But the growth in tourism has also damaged some places irreparably, and climate change is exacerbated by most forms of transport, especially flying. All Rough Guides' trips are carbon-offset, and every year we donate money to a variety of charities devoted to combating the effects of climate change.

Joe Walsh Tours Ireland ☎ 01 241 0800, ⓦ www .joewalshtours.ie. Budget fares as well as beach and safari packages in the Western and Eastern Cape provinces.

Journeys International US ☎ 1 800 255 8735, ⓦ www .journeys-intl.com. Small-group trips with a range of packages in the Western Cape, several of which are specifically tailored to families.

Kumuka Expeditions Australia ☎ 1300 667 277, ⓦ kumuka .com.au; UK ☎ 0800 092 9595, ⓦ kumuka.co.uk; US ☎ 1 800 517 0867, ⓦ kumuka.com. Five-week journeys from Nairobi to Cape Town and short tours around South Africa, using local operators.

Kuoni Travel UK ☎ 01306 747 002, ⓦ kuoni.co.uk. Flexible package holidays, including safaris, escorted tours and golfing packages along the Garden Route. Good deals for families.

North South Travel UK ☎ 01245 608 291, ⓦ northsouthtravel .co.uk. Discounted fares worldwide. Profits are used to support projects in the developing world, especially the promotion of sustainable tourism.

Okavango Tours and Safaris UK ☎ 020 8347 4030, ⓦ okavango.com. Top-notch outfit with on-the-ground knowledge of sub-Saharan Africa, offering fully flexible and individual tours across the country, including the Western Cape.

Rainbow Tours UK ☎ 020 7226 1004, ⓦ rainbowtours.co.uk. Knowledgeable and sensitive South Africa specialists whose trips emphasize eco-friendly and community-based tourism, whether you want to take in penguins, the Winelands or whales.

STA Travel Australia ☎ 134 782, NZ ☎ 0800 474 400, SA ☎ 0861 781 781, UK ☎ 0871 230 0040, US ☎ 1 800 781 4040; ⓦ statravel .com. Worldwide specialist in independent travel; also student IDs, travel insurance, car rental, rail passes and more. Good discounts for students and under-26s.

Trailfinders Australia ☎ 1300 780 212, Ireland ☎ 01 677 7888, UK ☎ 0845 058 5858; ⓦ trailfinders.com. One of the best-informed and most efficient agents for independent travellers offering deals on flights to Cape Town and on hotels.

Tribes UK ☎ 01728 685 971, ⓦ tribes.co.uk. Unusual and off-the-beaten-track fair-trade safaris and cultural tours, including Alternative Cape Town.

Twohigs Ireland ☎ 01 648 0800, ⓦ twohigs.com. Long-haul specialist offering South Africa packages.

USIT Northern Ireland ☎ 028 9032 7111, Ireland ☎ 01 602 1906, ⓦ www.usit.ie. Specialist in student, youth and independent travel, offering flights and online hostel room bookings.

Wilderness Travel US ☎ 1 800 368 2794, ⓦ wildernesstravel .com. Hiking, cultural and wildlife adventures with a sixteen-day package taking in Cape Town and the Garden Route.

Wildlife Worldwide UK ☎ 0845 130 6982, ⓦ wildlifeworldwide .com. Tailor-made trips for wildlife and wilderness enthusiasts, including a Garden Route self-drive package and excursions taking in national parks and the Winelands.

Arrival

Cape Town International Airport, Cape Town's international and domestic airport (CPT; ⓦ www.acsa.co.za) lies 22km east of the city centre. A bureau de change is open to coincide with international arrivals; there are also ATMs here and a tourist information desk. The major car rental firms have desks inside the international terminal. Pre-booking a vehicle is essential, especially during the week when there is a big demand from domestic business travellers, and over the mid-December to mid-January and Easter peak seasons.

Metered 24-hour taxis operated by Touch Down Taxis (☎ 021 919 4659), an association of independent **cab companies** officially authorized by the airport, rank in reasonable numbers outside both terminals and charge around R250 for the trip into the city.

The cheapest transport from the airport is the **MyCiTi bus** (every 20min; 4.20am–9pm; R50; ☎ 0800 65 64 63, ⓦ www.capetown.gov.za/myciti) operated by the city, which goes to the Civic Centre on Hertzog Boulevard, opposite the central train and bus station. More expensive but considerably more convenient are the door-to-door **shuttle services** which offer transport around Cape Town, including airport transfers (see "City Transport").

Mobile phone rental is available at the international and domestic terminals from Vodashop Rentafone (ⓦ www.rentafone.net) or Cellucity (ⓦ www.cellucity.co.za) and can be organized beforehand for collection on arrival. Several car rental companies include free mobile rental (you only pay for calls) in their deals, and you can also rent GPS systems.

Getting around

At the time of writing, Cape Town's public bus system was in the process of transformation, expanding from a not-very-useful collection of routes to a pretty comprehensive network serving the city centre, its surrounding suburbs and the Atlantic seaboard. This should bring the buses in line with the False Bay seaboard and southern suburbs, which have had a well-used train line for as long as anyone can remember.

Until the new system comes on stream, though, public transport options are limited to the train, some lumbering buses on a handful of routes and an interim rapid bus service restricted to the centre. For some attractions, you'll still need a **car** or else to rely on tours, or **minibus** and **metered taxis**. For getting further afield, there are several decent **intercity bus** lines as well as the **Baz Bus** backpacker service that gets to some places the intercity buses don't reach.

City transport

Although Cape Town's city centre is compact enough to get around on foot, many of the major attractions are spread along the considerable length of the peninsula and require transport to get there. Viable public transport is limited, but should improve with the phasing in of the **MyCiTi rapid bus service** from 2011 and its further expansion in

mid-2012. Apart from that, the only recommended system is **Metrorail**, a single train line down the peninsula. It's easy, well used and reasonably safe during the day, but should be avoided after dark. With the exception of a couple of specific routes, forget about Golden Arrow buses, whose services are limited, slow and irregular.

The **Golden Acre** shopping complex, at the junction of Strand and Adderley streets in the heart of Cape Town, can be a confusing muddle, but this is where all rail and most bus transport (both intercity and from elsewhere in the city) and most minibus taxis converge. Everything you need for your next move is within two or three blocks of here, including tourist information (see p.39).

Buses

Cape Town has two public bus services: the well-established and slow **Golden Arrow** service, and the newly launched **MyCiTi rapid bus system**.

MyCiTi buses

MyCiTi **buses** are part of the government's initiative to improve public transport in South Africa's major centres. In Cape Town the bus rapid transport network emulates a rail system, with stations along dedicated trunk roads served by express buses. The initial phase was launched in 2011, at the time of this edition's research period, with three main routes running from the **Civic Centre bus station** on the Foreshore. These go to **Table View** (northern suburbs), **the airport** and around the **city centre**, including the **Waterfront**. The city authorities have said that this service will be incorporated into a comprehensive network of nine routes in mid-2012, expanding over the city centre, the Waterfront, the City Bowl suburbs and the Atlantic seaboard as far as Hout Bay (see box below). **Tickets** are sold at bus

---

GO TOPLESS

The open-top, hop-on, hop-off red **Cape Town Sightseeing Bus** (☎021 511 6000, ⊛www .citysightseeing.co.za; 1-day ticket R120, children R60) is an extremely convenient and, on a fine day, fun way of getting to the major sights. It's also a great way to get around with kids – the headphone commentary runs one channel for adults and another for children, which features the voices of Blatjan Baboon and Madisa Mongoose among others. They operate two tours (below); buses leave from the Two Oceans Aquarium at the Waterfront.

The Mini Peninsula Tour (daily May to mid-Sept every 45 min, mid-Sept to April every 35 min; 9am–3.25pm) stops at Cape Town Tourism in Burg Street, *The Mount Nelson Hotel*, Kirstenbosch, World of Birds, Imizamo Yethu Township, Mariner's Wharf in Hout Bay, Camps Bay and Sea Point.

The City Centre Tour (daily May to mid-Sept every 20 min, mid-Sept to April every 15 min; 9.10am–4.30pm) stops at Cape Town Tourism, St George's Cathedral, SA Museum, Jewish Museum, District Six Museum, Castle of Good Hope, Gold Museum, Cableway, Camps Bay, Sea Point.

ENGLISH/AFRIKAANS STREET NAMES

Many towns along the Garden Route have **bilingual street names** with English and Afrikaans alternatives sometimes appearing along the same road. Often the Afrikaans name will bear little resemblance to the English one, something it's worth being aware of when trying to map read. In Cape Town you'll also find Afrikaans direction signs; for example signs for the airport will sometimes use the Afrikaans word "Lughawe".

We have included a list of Afrikaans terms you may encounter on signage in "Language" (see p.272).

stops or on buses. Fares hadn't been finalized at the time of writing, but are expected to be competitive with minibus taxis. For further details and up-to-date information contact the Cape Town Transport **information line** ☎0800 65 64 63 or visit the **MyCiTi website** ⓦwww.capetown.gov.za/en/myciti.

Golden Arrow buses

Golden Arrow buses ply Cape Town's main roads and tend to be slow, often getting snarled up in congested traffic. The only frequent and reliable Golden Arrow services are those from the centre to the Waterfront, Sea Point and down the Atlantic seaboard to Hout Bay. The **Waterfront bus** (Mon–Fri every 10min, Sat & Sun every 15min) leaves from the station with stops en route in Riebeeck and Buitengragt streets; and the one to **Sea Point** (Mon–Sat 20 daily) leaves from the Golden Acre terminal and runs along Main Road through **Mouille Point** and **Green Point**. The bus service down the Atlantic seaboard goes about twice an hour during the day via Camps Bay as far as Hout Bay. Buses to the southern suburbs are best avoided: the train is much quicker and more efficient. **Tickets** are sold by the driver: state your destination to them, and pay when you get on. **Fares** are cheap: a ticket for the station to the Waterfront is R6. For timetables, enquire at the Golden Arrow **information booth** (toll-free ☎0800 65 64 63, ⓦwww.gabs.co.za) at the Golden Acre bus terminal.

Taxis

The term "**taxi**" refers, somewhat confusingly, to conventional metered cars, jam-packed minibuses and *rikkis*. Regulated **metered taxis** don't cruise up and down looking for fares; you'll need to go to the

MYCITI CENTRAL ROUTES

INNER CITY INTERIM CIRCULAR ROUTE

Buses operate Mon–Fri 6am–8pm; Sat 7am–8pm; Sun 8am–8pm; every 20 minutes, except during rush hour when they run every ten minutes; Mon–Fri 6.30–9am & 3.30–6pm.

Loop 1: Civic Centre–Cape Town International Convention Centre–Cape Town Stadium–Watefront–Civic Centre.

Loop 2: Civic Centre–train station–Strand St–Long St–Orange St–Gardens Centre– Loop St–Adderley St–Civic Centre.

ROUTES EXPECTED FROM MID-2012

A new network for the city centre, City Bowl, Sea Point, Waterfront and the Atlantic seaboard to Hout Bay is planned for mid-2012. Buses are expected to be pretty frequent with at least one every 20 minutes during the day:

F01 Hout Bay to Cape Town via Camps Bay and Sea Point taking in Clifton and Camps Bay as well as a number of stops within Hout Bay including Imizamo Yethu township.

F02 Waterfront via the city centre and Kloof Nek to Camps Bay.

F03 Sea Point via the city centre to Gardens and Vredehoek.

F04 Sea Point to Fresnaye and Cape Town.

F05 Bo-Kaap via city centre and Zonnebloem to Salt River.

F06 Civic Centre to City Bowl via Long St, Kloof St, Gardens and Oranjezicht.

F07 Civic Centre to Gardens Centre via Zonnebloem and Vredehoek.

F08 Highlands Estate via Vredehoek, Gardens and the city centre.

F65 Tamboerskloof via Gardens and the city centre.

RELIABLE TAXI SERVICES

The three companies listed below run a prompt, 24-hour service, seven days a week, unless otherwise stated.

Excite Taxis (☎ 021 448 4444, ⓦ excitetaxis.co.za). Fares are R9 a kilometre within their normal operating area (city centre to southern suburbs), but there may be an additional charge if your pick-up or drop-off point is further flung than this.
Marine Taxis (☎ 021 434 0434, ⓦ marinetaxis.co.za). The largest and one of the oldest taxi outfits in the Mother City with seven-seater cabs. Fares are R11 a kilometre; they have card payment facilities in the car.

Rikkis (☎ 0861 745 547, ⓦ rikkis.co.za). Rikkis has one of the lowest fare-structures in town and operates in Hout Bay and the southern suburbs (Mon–Thurs 6.30am–2am, Fri–Sun 24 hours) as well as the city centre (24-hour, seven days). Fares are calculated at R10 a zone: so a ride from the Waterfront to the City Bowl, for example, would set you back about R60; they also offer a cheaper option for shared rides.

taxi ranks around town, including the Waterfront, the train station and Greenmarket Square, or phone to be picked up (see box above). Taxis must have the driver's name and identification clearly on display and the meter clearly visible. **Fares** work out at around R10–12 per kilometre.

Minibus taxis

Minibus taxis are cheap, frequent and bomb up and down the main routes at tearaway speeds. They can be hailed from the street – you'll recognize them from the hooting and booming music – or boarded at the central taxi rank, adjacent to the train station. Once you've boarded, pay the assistant, who sits near the driver, and tell him when you want to get off. **Fares** should be under R10 for most trips. As well as risky driving, be prepared for **pickpockets** working the taxi ranks.

Rikkis and shuttle buses

Rikkis are ex-London taxi cabs, operating all hours and aimed principally at tourists; you need to book them by telephone (☎ 086 174 5547, ⓦ www.rikkis .co.za). They offer private or cheaper shared rides and operate within three distinct areas: central (City Bowl and the Atlantic seaboard as far as Hout Bay; private R35–50, shared R25–35); the southern suburbs (Claremont and Constantia; R65–75); plus in and around Hout Bay (R60). They also offer airport shuttles (R200 one way for the first passenger, with discounts after that).

In the same vein but a little cheaper, the **Backpacker Bus** (pre-booking recommended; ☎ 021 439 7600, ☎ 082 809 9185, ⓦ www .backpackerbus.co.za) offers transport from backpacker lodges to Kistenbosch and Stellenbosch. They have a well-priced airport shuttle service with two buses plying the route to and from Cape Town International (8am–5pm; R160 for the first person with discounts after that).

Cyclecabs

Cyclecabs – two-passenger vehicles drawn by pedal power – are a great, relaxed way of getting around the city centre when the weather is fine. The distinctive tricycles operate in the vicinity of the Company's Gardens, the Castle, the Foreshore and the V&A Waterfront. Cyclecabs cruise around and also rank outside the Slave Lodge in Adderley Street as well as the South African Museum. You can call one on ☎ 086 196 7537 or ☎ 072 907 7333 or hail one in the street. Fares are negotiated with the cabbie, but you can expect to pay from R5 for a short hop from the station to the Company's Gardens.

Trains

Cape Town's suburban **train** service is run by **Metrorail** (timetable information ☎ 0800 656 463, ⓦ www.metrorail.co.za). The only route likely to be useful to visitors is the relatively reliable if slightly run-down line that sets off from Cape Town station down through the southern suburbs and all the way down the False Bay seaboard as far as Simon's Town. Three other lines run east from Cape Town to Strand (through Bellville), to the Cape Flats, and to the outlying towns of Stellenbosch and Paarl; however, the journeys aren't recommended, as they run through some of the less safe areas of the Flats. Even on a False Bay train, never board an empty carriage.

The service to the False Bay seaboard must be one of the world's greatest urban train journeys. It reaches the coast at Muizenberg and continues south to Simon's Town, sometimes so spectacularly close to the ocean that you can feel the spray and peer into rock pools. The stretch of the line to Fish Hoek is well served, with several trains an hour. Services to Simon's Town run every forty to sixty minutes.

There are no signposts to the stations on the streets., so if you're staying in the southern suburbs, ask for directions at your accommodation. Tickets must be bought at the station before boarding – you're best off in the first-class carriages, which are reasonably priced (for example, Cape Town–Muizenberg is about R12 one-way). Third class (curiously, there's no second class) tends to be more crowded, and in the mornings is often filled with the harmonies of domestic workers singing on their way to work.

Intercity buses

Baz Bus (☎021 439 2323, ⓦbazbus.com) operates an extremely useful hop-on/hop-off service daily between Cape Town and Port Elizabeth in both directions, via Mossel Bay, George, Knysna, Plettenberg Bay, Storms River and Jeffrey's Bay, with other stops possible along the N2. The service is aimed squarely at backpackers, with buses stopping off at hostels en route. The Cape Town–Port Elizabeth fare is R1320 one-way, though there are also better-value seven-, fourteen- and 21-day passes costing R1470, R2470 and R2970. Bookings can be made directly or through hostels or the Baz office within the central tourist offices in Cape Town.

South Africa's three established **intercity bus** companies are Greyhound (☎083 915 9000, ⓦwww.greyhound.co.za), Intercape (☎086 128 7287, ⓦwww.intercape.co.za) and Translux (☎086 158 9282, ⓦwww.translux.co.za); between them, they reach most towns in the country. Travel on these buses is safe, good value and very comfortable, the vehicles invariably equipped with air conditioning and toilets. Fares vary according to distances covered and the time of year, with peak fares corresponding approximately to school holidays; at other times you can expect about thirty percent off. As a rough indication you can expect to pay the following fares for single journeys from Cape Town: to Paarl, R185; Mossel Bay, R225; Port Elizabeth, R315.

Greyhound, Intercape and Translux intercity buses leave from around the interlinked complex in Cape Town's centre that includes the train station and **Golden Acre** shopping mall (see p.49). Note that Intercape and Translux arrive on the northeast side of the station, off Adderley Street, while Greyhound arrives on the northwest side in Adderley itself.

Translux, Greyhound and Intercape also operate the no-frills budget bus lines **City to City**, **Cityliner** and **Budgetliner** respectively, whose schedules and prices are listed on their main websites. There is also a host of small private companies about which

information is thin on the ground; your best bet is to enquire at the bus station the day before you travel.

Domestic flights

Driving the Garden Route in one direction – say out from Cape Town – and flying back from Port Elizabeth is a good (and popular) option, especially if time is short. The flight takes just over an hour and fares compare favourably with the money you'll spend covering the distance in a rental car, stopping over at places en route. You can pick up a ticket for as little as R600 one-way if you book about a month ahead, or about 50 percent more at shorter notice.

By far the biggest domestic airline is **South African Airways** (SAA), with its associates **SA Airlink** and **SA Express** (reservations for the three are through SAA) with flights to **George** and **Port Elizabeth**, among other further flung destinations. There are a number of smaller airlines that fly to **George** and **Port Elizabeth**, of which the most significant are **1Time** (☎011 086 8000, ⓦwww.1time.aero), **British Airways Comair** (☎086 043 5922, ⓦba.com) and its budget subsidiary **kulula.com** (☎086 158 5852, ⓦkulula.com).

None of the airlines offers discounts for students or pensioners.

Driving and cycling

Cape Town has good roads and several fast freeways that, outside peak hours (7–9am & 4–6pm), can whisk you across town in next to no time. The obvious landmarks of Table Mountain and the two seaboards make orientation straightforward, particularly south of the centre, and some wonderful journeys are possible. The most notable are the drives along the Atlantic seaboard to Hout Bay and **Chapman's Peak Drive**, a narrow, winding, cliff-edge road with the Atlantic breaking hundreds of metres below; and around the **Cape Point** section of the Table Mountain National Park, via the False Bay seaboard.

National roads (with an "N" prefix) and **provincial roads** (with an "R" prefix) in the rest of the Western Cape are of a generally high standard. The only time you're likely to encounter adverse conditions is during school holidays, particularly the Easter and December breaks, when the N1 and N2 become fairly congested, nerves fray, alcohol is copiously consumed and drivers' behaviour deteriorates accordingly.

Petrol stations are frequent on the major routes of the country, and usually open 24 hours a day. Off the major routes, though, stations are less frequent, so fill up whenever you get the chance. Stations are rarely self-service; instead, attendants fill up your car, check oil, water and tyre pressure if you ask them to, and often clean your windscreen even if you don't. A tip of at least R5 is always appreciated.

Regulations

You drive on the **left-hand side**, with **speed limits** ranging from 60kph in built-up areas to 100kph on rural roads and 120kph on highways and major arteries. In addition to roundabouts, which follow the British rule of giving way to the right, there are four-way stops, where the rule is that the person who got there first leaves first, and you are not expected to give way to the right. Note that traffic lights are often called **robots** in South Africa.

Foreign **driving licences** are valid in South Africa for up to six months, provided they are printed in English. If you don't have such a licence, you'll need to get an International Driving Permit before arriving in South Africa (available from national motoring organizations). When driving, make sure you have your driving licence and passport on you at all times.

Car and bike rental

Given Cape Town's scant public transport, **renting** a vehicle is the only convenient way of exploring the Cape Peninsula, and needn't break the bank. There are dozens of competing car rental companies to choose from (see below). To get the best deal, either pick up one of the brochures at the Cape Town Tourism office or book beforehand (often cheaper) with an international company which might offer particular deals tied in with your airline or credit card company. Many backpacker hostels have cheaper deals with agencies too.

For **motorbike rental**, Le Cap Motorcycle Hire, B9 Edgemead Business Park, on the corner of Link Way & Southdale Road, Edgemead (☎072 259 0009, ⓦ www.lecap.co.za), provides all the necessary gear and rents out serious bikes (from R470 daily, plus R1/km; weekly rental available). They also do motorbiking tours with pre-arranged accommodation.

For **cyclists**, one of the most popular – and hair-raising – road routes is along the narrow hairpins of Chapman's Peak Drive, which offer stupendous views of the Atlantic. There are also a number of dedicated mountain-biking routes in the peninsula's nature reserves. Mountain bikes are available from Downhill Adventures, Shop 10 Overbeek Building, corner of Kloof and Orange streets (☎021 422 0388, ⓦwww.downhilladventures.co.za), for R160 a day. They also offer organized cycle outings that include trips to Cape Point, the Winelands and Tokai Forest.

CAR RENTAL AGENCIES

Alamo ⓦ alamo.com
Auto Europe ⓦ www.autoeurope.com
Avis ⓦ avis.com
Budget ⓦ budget.com
Cheap Motorhome Rental ⓦ www.cheapmotorhomes.co.za
Dollar ⓦ www.dollar.com
Drive Africa ☎ 021 447 1144, ⓦ www.driveafrica.co.za
Europcar ⓦ europcar.com

DRIVING TIPS

The only real challenge you'll face on the roads is **other drivers**. South Africa has among the world's worst road accident statistics – the result of reckless driving, drunken drivers (see p.34) or defective, overloaded vehicles. Keep your distance from cars in front, as domino-style pile-ups are common. Watch out also for **overtaking** traffic coming towards you. Overtakers often assume that you will head for the **hard shoulder** to avoid an accident (it is legal to drive on the hard shoulder, but be careful as people frequently walk on it). If you do pull into the hard shoulder to let a car overtake, the other driver will probably thank you by flashing the hazard lights. If oncoming cars **flash their headlights** at you, it probably means that there is a **speed trap** up ahead.

Driving in and around Cape Town presents a few peculiarities all of its own. An unwritten rule of the road on the peninsula is that **minibus taxis** have the right of way – and will push in front of you without compunction and will routinely run through amber lights as they change to red – as will many Capetonians.

Take care approaching a **freeway** in Cape Town: the slip roads frequently feed directly into the fast lane, and Capetonians routinely exceed the 100kph freeway and 120kph highway speed limits. Furthermore, there's often little warning of branches off to the suburbs, only the final destination of the freeway being signed. Your best bet is to plan your journey, and make sure you know exactly where you're going.

Hertz Ⓦ hertz.com
Holiday Autos Ⓦ www.holidayautos.co.uk
Kea Rentals Ⓦ www.kea.co.za
Maui Ⓦ www.maui.co.za
National Ⓦ nationalcar.com
SIXT Ⓦ sixt.com
Tempest Ⓣ 086 003 1666, Ⓦ www.tempestcarhire.co.za
Thrifty Ⓦ thrifty.com
Vineyard Car Hire Ⓦ www.vineyardcarhire.co.za

Tours

Cape Town is awash with tour packages, from standard, through-the-window outings that take you from one sight to the other, to really excellent specialist packages. For some depth, opt for one of the cultural tours, which cover all aspects of Cape Town life, or feel the exhilaration of the peninsula's environment on foot or from the saddle of a bike. If you want to cover a lot of ground in a day, then the personalized Cape Peninsula trips offered by Cape Convoy are a great alternative to the tour buses. Almost all these companies will pick you up from your accommodation and drop you off again at the end of the day.

WALKING TOURS

One of the best Cape Town orientations at the start of a visit is on a walking tour through central Cape Town. Tours run by these two companies depart mid-morning daily, except Sundays, from the Visitor Information Centre in Burg Street, lasting roughly three hours. You need to book in advance.

Footsteps to Freedom Ⓣ 083 452 1112, Ⓦ www
.footstepstofreedom.co.za; R150. Offers a tour that takes in historical sights and buildings with a conscious politico/socio slant.

Cape Town on Foot Ⓣ 021 462 4252, Ⓦ www.wanderlust.co.za; R150. Run by an ex-teacher and writer, takes in the city centre as well as the Bo-Kaap, and can be taken in English or German.

CULTURAL TOURS

A number of smaller companies offer niche cultural tours; the most popular of these are townships tours, the safest way to see the African and coloured areas that were created under apartheid. Almost all companies will pick you up from your accommodation and drop you off again at the end of the day, and tours generally start from R600, less for classic township tours.

Andulela Tours Ⓣ 021 790 2592, Ⓦ www.andulela.com. Fabulous selection of under-the-skin tours which could get you drumming, bead-making or cooking in the African townships, visiting homes to hear music of well-known Cape Jazz musicians, cooking Cape Malay food in the Bo-Kaap, doing a soccer tour, visiting the Winelands, or learning more about baboons with a conservationist at Cape Point. They can also take you further afield to the Cederberg to look at rock art.

Bonani Our Pride Ⓣ 021 531 4291 or Ⓣ 082 446 7974, Ⓦ www
.bonanitours.co.za. Recommended tours to meet people as well as to visit sights of political significance in the townships. They do township evening tours, gospel tours where you visit Xhosa churches on a Sunday morning, and Xhosa folklore tours.

Coffee Beans Routes Ⓣ 021 424 3572, Ⓦ www
.coffeebeansroutes.com. Music and cultural specialists who are the people to go with for a Cape Town Jazz Safari, soccer route tour or to find out what's happening in the poetry/performance scene in the townships.

Off Beat Tours Ⓣ 021 788 788 6613, Ⓔ simric1@gmail.com.
Teacher, storyteller and musician, Simric Yarrow puts an eco slant on his entertaining Cape Town tours, whether walking at Cape Point, weaving quirky historical yarns in central Cape Town, visiting township projects, taking in poetry or gigs or tippling at organic wine farms.

GENERAL TOURS

If you want a trip that covers more distance – the major peninsula sights and beyond – there are a couple of excellent operators.

Cape Convoy Ⓣ 021 531 1928, Ⓦ capeconvoy.com. Tours in a canopied Land Rover, just like being on a safari vehicle in the Kruger National Park, with a passionate and fun Brit, Rob Salmon. He'll do a reduced price (R1000) if you book the two most popular tours, full-day Cape Point and the Table Mountain and Robben Island tour. Trips can also be arranged to the Winelands and to the nearest safari park to see some wildlife, a couple of hours out of Cape Town.

Day Trippers Ⓣ 021 511 4766, Ⓦ daytrippers.co.za. An excellent company if you want an active Peninsula and Cape Point day tour that includes cycling and hiking. They also go further afield to hike and cycle in the Cederberg, Little Karoo and Winelands.

Health

You can put aside most of the health fears that may be justified in some parts of Africa; run-down hospitals and bizarre tropical diseases aren't typical of Cape Town and the Garden Route, and malaria isn't an issue here at all. All tourist areas enjoy generally high standards of hygiene and safe drinking water. The only hazard you're likely to encounter, and the one the majority of visitors are most blasé about, is the sun.

Public **hospitals** are fairly well equipped but are facing huge pressures, under which their attempts to maintain standards are unfortunately buckling. Expect long waits and frequently indifferent treatment. **Private hospitals** or clinics are usually a better option for travellers and are well up to British or North American standards. You'll get to see a doctor quickly and costs are not excessive, unless you require major surgery, in which case health insurance is a must.

INOCULATIONS

No specific inoculations are compulsory if you arrive in South Africa from the West. A yellow fever vaccination certificate is necessary if you've come from a country or region where the disease is endemic, such as Kenya, Tanzania or tropical South America.

The Hospital for Tropical Diseases in London advises that you ensure your polio and tetanus vaccinations are up to date. In addition, it recommends a course of shots against **typhoid** and an injection against **hepatitis A**, both of which can be caught from contaminated food or water – though this is extremely unlikely in the region covered by this guide.

If you decide to have an armful of jabs, start organizing them **six weeks** before departure. If you're going to another African country first and need the yellow fever jab, note that a yellow fever certificate only becomes valid ten days after you've had the shot.

Dental care in South Africa is well up to British and North American standards, and is generally no more expensive. You'll find dentists in Cape Town and most smaller towns, listed under "Dentists" and doctors under "Medical" at the back of the White Pages telephone directory.

MEDICAL RESOURCES FOR TRAVELLERS

Canadian Society for International Health ☎ 613 241 5785, ⓦ csih.org. Extensive list of travel health centres.
CDC ☎ 1 800 232 4636, ⓦ cdc.gov/travel. Official US government travel health site.
International Society for Travel Medicine ☎ 1 404 373 8282, ⓦ istm.org. Has a full list of travel health clinics.
Hospital for Tropical Diseases Travel Clinic ⓦ www.thehtd .org. Online destination health advice for travellers, inoculations, and an online shop selling goods such as first-aid kits, mosquito nets and suncream.
MASTA (Medical Advisory Service for Travellers Abroad) ⓦ masta.org The website gives details of your nearest clinic.
The Travel Doctor ☎ 1300 658 844, ⓦ tmvc.com.au. Lists travel clinics in Australia and New Zealand
Travel Doctor ☎ 0861 300 911, ⓦ www.traveldoctor.co.za. Lists travel clinics in South Africa.
Tropical Medical Bureau ⓦ tmb.ie. Website offers extensive advice for travellers, with a number of clinics based in Ireland.

STATE HOSPITALS AND CLINICS IN CAPE TOWN

Groote Schuur Hospital Drive, Observatory ☎ 021 404 9111. Just off the M3, this is the largest state hospital in Cape Town.
Somerset Hospital Beach Road, Mouille Point ☎ 021 402 6911. A state hospital with outpatient and emergency departments, although it's generally overcrowded, understaffed and under-equipped.

PRIVATE HOSPITALS, DOCTORS AND CLINICS

The two largest **private hospital groups** are **Netcare** (emergency response ☎ 082 911, ⓦ www.netcare.co.za) and **Medi-Clinic** (emergency response operated by ER24 ☎ 084 124, ⓦ www.mediclinic.co.za) chains, with hospitals all over the Cape

Peninsula; in addition to the hospitals listed below Netcare runs over two dozen **Medicross Medical Centres** (ⓦ medicross .co.za) across the Western Cape, which are not open 24 hours, but do operate extended hours.
Cape Town Medi-Clinic 21 Hof St, Oranjezicht ☎ 021 464 5500; emergency ☎ 021 464 5555. Close to the city centre in the middle of the City Bowl.
Christiaan Barnard Memorial Hospital 181 Longmarket St ☎ 021 480 6111. Most central of the Netcare private hospitals is convenient for the city centre, the V&A Waterfront, De Waterkant and the Atlantic seaboard.
Constantiaberg Medi-Clinic Burnham Road, Plumstead ☎ 021 799 2911; emergency ☎ 021 799 2196. In the southern suburbs, this is the closest private hospital to the False Bay seaboard.
UCT Private Academic Hospital Anzio Road, Observatory ☎ 021 442 1800. Netcare hospital adjacent to Groote Schuur in the heart of the southern suburbs.

Stomach upsets

Stomach upsets from food are rare. Salad and ice – the danger items in many other developing countries – are both perfectly safe. As with anywhere, though, don't keep food for too long, and be sure to wash fruit and vegetables as thoroughly as possible.

If you do get a **stomach bug**, the best cure is lots of water and rest. Papayas – the flesh as well as the pips – are a good tonic to offset the runs. Otherwise, most chemists should have non-prescription anti-diarrhoea remedies.

Avoid jumping for **antibiotics** at the first sign of illness. Instead keep them as a last resort – they don't work on viruses and they annihilate your gut flora (most of which you want to keep), making you more susceptible next time round. Most tummy upsets will resolve themselves if you adopt a sensible fat-free diet for a couple of days, but if they do persist without improvement (or are accompanied by other unusual symptoms), then see a doctor as soon as possible.

The sun

The **sun** is likely to be the worst hazard you'll encounter in South Africa, particularly if you're fair-skinned.

Short-term effects of **overexposure** to the sun include burning, nausea and headaches. This usually comes from overeager tanning, which can leave you looking like a lobster. The fairer your skin, the slower you should take tanning. Start with short periods of exposure and **high protection sunscreen** (at least SPF 15), gradually increasing your time in the sun and decreasing the factor of the sunscreen. Many people with fair skins, especially those who freckle easily, should take extra care, starting with a very high factor screen (SPF 25–30) and continue using at least SPF 15 for the rest of their stay.

Overexposure to the sun can cause sunburn to the surface of the eye, inflammation of the cornea and can result in serious short- and long-term damage. Good **sunglasses** can reduce ultraviolet (UV) light exposure to the eye by fifty percent. A **broad-brimmed hat** is also recommended.

The last few measures are especially necessary for **children**, who should ideally be kept well covered at the seaside. Don't be lulled into complacency on **cloudy days**, when UV levels can still be high. UV-protective clothing is available locally, but it's best to buy before you arrive. If you don't come with this gear, make sure children wear T-shirts at the beach, and use SPF 30 sunscreen liberally and often.

Bites and stings

Bites and stings in South Africa are comparatively rare. **Snakes** are present, but hardly ever seen as they move out of the way quickly. The sluggish puff and berg adders are the most dangerous, because they often lie in paths and don't move when humans approach. The best advice if you get bitten is to note what the snake looked like and get yourself to a clinic or hospital. Most bites are not fatal and the worst thing you can do is to panic: desperate measures with razor blades and tourniquets risk doing more harm than good.

Tick-bite fever is occasionally contracted from walking in the bush, particularly in long wet grass. The offending ticks can be minute and you may not spot them. Symptoms appear a week later – swollen glands and severe aching of the joints, backache and fever. The disease will run its course in three or four days. Ticks you may find on yourself are not dangerous, just repulsive at first. Make sure you pull out the head as well as the body (it's not painful). A good way of removing small ones is to smear Vaseline or grease over them, making them release their hold.

Scorpion stings and **spider bites** are painful but almost never fatal, contrary to popular myth. Scorpions and spiders abound, but they're hardly ever seen unless you turn over logs and stones. If you're collecting wood for a campfire, knock or shake it before picking it up. Another simple precaution when camping is to shake out your shoes and clothes in the morning before you get dressed.

Rabies is present throughout southern Africa with dogs posing the greatest risk, although the disease can be carried by other animals. If you are bitten, you should go immediately to a clinic or hospital. Rabies can be treated effectively with a course of injections.

Sexually transmitted diseases

HIV/AIDS and venereal diseases are widespread in southern Africa among both men and women, and the danger of catching the virus through sexual contact is very real. Follow the usual precautions regarding safer sex; international brand condoms are widely available from pharmacies and supermarkets. There's no special risk from medical treatment in the country, but if you're travelling overland and you want to play it safe, take your own needle and transfusion kit.

The media

With two rather parochial daily English-language newspapers, plus a few magazines devoted mainly to entertainment and tourism, Cape Town's media are unlikely to blow anyone away. Radio and TV are dominated by South Africa's national broadcasters, with a few local radio offerings that include a talk station, a pioneering black community station and several others that play sounds from classical to pop.

Newspapers and magazines

Cape Town has two fairly uninspiring daily English **newspapers**, owned by the same company: the **Cape Times** comes out on weekday mornings, while the afternoon **Cape Argus** also comes out during the week, but has Saturday and Sunday morning editions. Both are dominated by local news, with a smattering of national and international coverage. In addition there's the national **Business Day**, which is the best daily source of hard countrywide and international news.

Unquestionably the country's intellectual heavyweight ("heavy" being the operative word) is the **Mail & Guardian**, which comes out on Friday; it benefits enormously from its association with the London *Guardian* (from which it draws most of its international coverage). South Africa's **Sunday Times** can attribute the biggest circulation in the country – roughly half a million copies – to its well-calculated mix of solid investigative reporting, gossip, material from the British press and salacious rewrites of stories lifted from foreign tabloids. The **Sunday Independent**, part of the same stable as Britain's *Independent* newspapers and their Irish counterparts (as are the *Cape Times* and *Cape Argus*), projects a more thoughtful image than the *Sunday Times*, but is ultimately thin on substance. The **Sowetan**, targeted at a mainly black Jo'burg audience, is widely available across the country and provides a less exclusively white perspective on South African issues.

For **events listings** in Cape Town you could check out the rather tepid supplements that appear in the mainstream press at the weekend. The *Top of the Times* supplement comes with Friday's *Cape Times*, and the *Good Weekend* pullout with the Saturday *Cape Argus*, but hands down best of the bunch is the *Mail & Guardian*'s Friday supplement, which injects some attitude into its reviews and listings.

Both local papers and international publications such as *Time*, *Newsweek*, *The Economist* and the weekly overseas editions of the British *Daily Mail*, the *Telegraph* and the *Express* are available from corner stores and newsagents.

Of the local news **websites**, the one run by the *Mail & Guardian* (Ⓦ mg.co.za) stands out for its daily news coverage, its extensive blogs and opinion pieces as well as coverage of arts, entertainment and, in fact, every aspect of South African life. The online version of Independent Newspapers, which publishes the *Cape Argus* and *Cape Times*, is also worth a look (Ⓦ iol.co.za).

Television

The South Africa Broadcasting Corporation's three TV channels churn out a mixed bag of domestic dramas, game shows, sport, soaps and documentaries, filled out with lashings of familiar imports. **SABC 1, 2** and **3** share the unenviable task of trying to deliver an integrated service, while having to split their time between the eleven official languages. English turns out to be most widely used, with SABC 3 broadcasting almost exclusively in the language, while SABC 2 and SABC 1 spread themselves thinly across the remaining ten languages, with a fair amount of English creeping in even here.

A selection of sports, movies, news and specialist channels are available to subscribers to the **M-Net** satellite service, which is piped into many hotels. South Africa's first and only free-to-air independent commercial channel **e.tv** won its franchise in 1998 on the promise of providing a showcase for local productions, a pledge it has signally failed to meet – its output has substantially consisted of uninspired and uninspiring imports.

There is no cable TV in South Africa, but **DSTV** (Ⓦ www.dstv.co.za) offers a **satellite television** subscription service with a selection of sports, movies, news (including BBC, CNN and Al Jazeera) and specialist channels, some of which are piped into hotels.

Radio

Given South Africa's low literacy rate and widespread poverty, it's no surprise that **radio** is a highly popular medium. The SABC operates a national radio station for each of the eleven official language groups. The English-language national service, **SAfm** (104–107FM, Ⓦ www.safm.co.za), is heavily laden with dull phone-in shows, but has two passable news programmes, one in the morning (5.30–8am) and the other in the evening (4–6pm).

Cape Town stations include **Cape Talk** (567AM, Ⓦ www.capetalk.co.za), which puts out wall-to-wall chatter consisting of news, reviews, discussions and phone-ins varying from first rate to pedestrian, as well as wall-to-wall musical golden oldies during the daytime at weekends; and **Bush Radio** (89.5FM, Ⓦ www.bushradio.co.za), one of South Africa's first community stations, which attempts to actively involve members of Cape Town's black community, who were denied a voice under apartheid. Apart from hosting debates about significant issues to the community and broadcasting informative social documentaries, Bush Radio also pumps out great local music. A number of other local stations are devoted to 24-hour music, the most successful being **Heart Radio** (109.4FM, ⓦ www.1049.fm), which targets high-income black and coloured listeners in the Mother City with its mix of jazz fusion, funk, soul and R&B. Somewhat staid by comparison is **Fine Music Radio** (101 FM, ⓦ www. fmr.co.za), which politely delivers the classics and a smattering of respectable jazz.

Festivals

Many of the Western Cape's events take place outdoors in summer, and make full use of the city's wonderful setting. They include the **Cape Town Minstrel Carnival** a unique event rooted in the city's coloured community, while the **Kirstenbosch Summer Sunset Concerts**, which run from late December to early April, are a must. Winter tends to be quiet, but it does herald the arrival of calving whales, and in their wake the **Hermanus Whale Festival** in September, which packs out this small southern Cape settlement.

Tickets for many of the events listed below are available from Computicket (☎083 915 8000, ⓦ www.computicket.co.za).

JANUARY

Cape Town Minstrels Carnival Jan 2 and the following three Saturdays. South Africa's longest and most raucous annual party, the carnival brings over ten thousand spectators to watch the parade through the city centre. It starts on Jan 2 for the Tweede Nuwe Jaar or "Second New Year" celebrations – an extension of New Year's Day unique to the Western Cape. Central to the festivities are the brightly decked-out coloured minstrel troupes that vie in singing and dancing contests. Tickets are best reserved through Computicket – you won't get such a good view if you buy tickets at the gate on the day.

Maynardville Shakespeare Festival Mid-Jan to mid-Feb; ⓦ maynardville.co.za. A usually imaginative production of one of the Bard's plays is staged each year in the beautiful setting of the Maynardville Open Air Theatre in Wynberg.

FEBRUARY

Cape Town Pride Pageant ⓦ capetownpride.co.za. Series of gay-themed events over two weeks, kicking off with a pageant at which Mr and Mrs Gay Pride are crowned and taking in a bunch of parties and a street parade.

MARCH

Cape Argus Pick'n Pay Cycle Tour First half of the month; ⓦ cycletour.org.za. The largest and arguably most spectacular, individually timed bike race in the world, with 30,000 participants on the 105km course – much of it along the ocean's edge – draws many thousands of spectators along the route. You can pick up entry forms from Pick'n Pay supermarkets, cycle shops or enter online. Book early as it is heavily subscribed.

Cape Town International Jazz Festival Last weekend of the month; ⓦ capetownjazzfest.com. Initiated in 2000 as the Cape Town counterpart of the world-famous North Sea Jazz Festival, this event has now come of age and acquired a local identity. Notable past performers have included Courtney Pine, Herbie Hancock, and African greats such as Jimmy Dludlu, Moses Molelekwa, Youssou N'Dour, Miriam Makeba and Hugh Masakela.

Cape Town Carnival Middle of the month; ⓦ capetowncarnival .com. Rio-style street extravaganza that kicked off in 2010, the carnival is centred on Long Street with floats, parades and general euphoria intended to celebrate Cape Town's cultural diversity and richness. In 2011 expert float-builders were flown in from Rio to inject some pizzazz into the whole enterprise.

Out of the Box Festival ⓦ www2.outtheboxfestival.com. Extraordinary week-long event that brings together exciting puppetry from all over the subcontinent and beyond with family, adult and film programmes. Held every eighteen months alternating between March and September.

APRIL

Klein Karoo Nasionale Kunstefees First week of the month; ⓦ kknk.co.za. South Africa's largest Afrikaans arts and culture festival packs out the Karoo *dorp* of Oudtshoorn with festival goers, turning the otherwise dozy town into one big jumping, jiving party. If you don't understand Afrikaans, you'll still find enough English offerings as well as dance, music and other performance to keep you busy.

Two Oceans Marathon Second half of the month; ⓦ twooceansmarathon.org.za. Another of the Cape's big sports events, this is in fact an ultra-marathon (56km), with huge crowds lining the route to cheer on the participants. A less scenic half-marathon is held at the same time.

Pink Loerie Mardi Gras End of the month; ⓦ www.pinkloerie .com. Five-day gay pride celebration of parties, contests, cabaret, drag shows and performance in Knysna, South Africa's oyster capital.

MAY

Franschhoek Literary Festival Middle of the month; ⓦ www .flf.co.za. Three-day celebration of books, writers and wine in the Winelands food capital, Franschhoek, featuring leading local and international writers, editors and cartoonists.

Good Food & Wine Show End of the month; ⓦ www .gourmetsa.com. Celebrity chefs from around the world performing is just one of the compelling attractions that make this Cape Town's foodie event of the year. There are also hands-on workshops, delicious nibbles and wine as well as kitchen implements and books for sale.

JUNE

Encounters South African International Documentary Film Festival Middle of the month; ⓦ encounters.co.za. Fortnight-long showcase of documentary film-making from South Africa and the world.

JULY

Knysna Oyster Festival First ten days of the month;
Ⓦ oysterfestival.co.za. Just over a week of carousing and oyster-eating in all its forms along the Garden Route, kicked off with a road-bike race and closed with the Knysna Marathon.

AUGUST

Cape Town Comedy Festival First half of the month; Ⓦ www .comedyfestival.co.za. Africa's biggest comedy festival brings the world's hottest acts to the Mother City for a week.

SEPTEMBER

Hermanus Whale Festival Towards the end of the month;
Ⓦ whalefestival.co.za. To coincide with peak whale-watching season, the southern Cape town of Hermanus (see p.167) stages a week-long annual festival of arts and the environment. Activities include plays, a craft market, a children's festival and live music.

Out of the Box Festival Ⓦ www2.outtheboxfestival.com.
See March.

Out in Africa South African Gay & Lesbian Film Festival
End of the month; Ⓦ oia.co.za. Purportedly the most popular movie festival in the country, screening gay- and lesbian-themed international and local productions.

NOVEMBER (TO MARCH)

Kirstenbosch Summer Sunset Concerts Every Sun from end of the month to early April; ☎ 021 799 8783. Among the musical highlights of the Cape Town calendar are the popular concerts held on the magnificent lawns of the botanical gardens at the foot of Table Mountain. Performances begin at 5.30pm and cover a range of genres, from local jazz to classical music. Come early to find a parking place, bring a picnic and some Cape fizz – and enjoy. Tickets available at the gate.

DECEMBER

Mother City Queer Projects Early in the month (see p.143).
A hugely popular party attracting thousands of gay revellers, for which a vast venue is chartered. Outlandish get-ups, multiple dancefloors and a mood of sustained delirium make this event a real draw.

Carols by Candlelight Thurs–Sun before
Christmas; ☎ 021 799 8783. The botanical gardens' annual carol singing and Nativity tableau is a Cape Town institution, drawing crowds of families with their picnic baskets. The gates open at 7pm and the singing kicks off at 8pm.

Franschhoek Cap Classique and Champagne
Festival Beginning of the month; Ⓦ webtickets.co.za. Popular three-day bacchanalia of bubbly sampling – a vast selection of local and French sparkling wine is on hand – and gourmandizing in the Cape Winelands.

Spier Summer Festival December till March; Ⓦ spier.co.za. Four months of major arts events, at the Spier wine estate, near Stellenbosch, which are increasingly taking on an African flavour, featuring music, opera, dance, stand-up comedy and theatre.

Parks, reserves and wilderness areas

The region covered by this guide is bookended by two major national parks: at the western extreme is the Table Mountain National Park, a patchwork of wilderness that covers the full extent of the Cape Peninsula; and at the eastern end is Addo Elephant National Park which, apart from the pachyderms, is also home to lions, buffalos, leopards and rhinos – the only such major game reserve in the southern half of the country.

Between the two lie a series of provincial reserves and national parks, many of which are worth incorporating into any journey across the Southern Cape. In addition to the aforementioned, among the top wilderness areas in the country are **De Hoop Nature Reserve**, with its massive dunes and its status as one of the best places in the world for land-based whale watching; and the **Tsitsikamma section of the Garden Route National Park**, which attracts large numbers of visitors for its ancient forests, cliff-faced oceans and the dramatic Storms River Mouth.

All the national parks covered in this guide fall under the aegis of **South African National Parks** (☎ 012 428 9111, Ⓦ www.sanparks.org). A few reserves mentioned, including De Hoop and Goukamma, are run by **CapeNature** (Ⓦ www .capenature.org.za).

Entry fees and accommodation

National parks charge a **conservation fee,** which is usually **payable daily**. At most of the national parks covered by this book this comes to between R80 and R140 per day for foreign visitors (half-price for children), though citizens of the Southern Africa Development Community (SADC: includes Angola, Botswana; Congo, Lesotho, Malawi, Mauritius, Mozambique, Namibia, South Africa, Swaziland, Tanzania, Zambia and Zimbabwe) pay half the adult foreigner's rate. South African residents pay a quarter of the adult foreigner's rate.

In the case of Table Mountain National Park there is a daily conservation fee of R80 (children

TOP PARKS AND WILDLIFE AREAS

PARK	PRINCIPAL FOCUS	DESCRIPTION & HIGHLIGHTS	DETAILS
Addo Elephant National Park	Endangered species	The only Big Five national park in the southern half of the country, known for its three-hundred-strong elephant herd	p.248
Agulhas National Park	Marine and coastal ecology	Rugged southernmost tip of Africa with rich plant biodiversity and significant archeological sites	p.175
De Hoop Nature Reserve	Marine mammals and coastal *fynbos*	A combination of whales, massive dunes, *fynbos* and spectacular coastline.	p.180
Garden Route National Park	Marine and coastal, and endangered species	Focused on three sections: • Wilderness and its lakes, rivers, lagoons, forest, *fynbos*, beaches and sea. • Knysna, a marine area that covers the lagoon and its dramatic headlands. The lagoon area protects the endangered Knysna sea horse. • Tsitsikamma, featuring cliffs, tidal pools, deep gorges and evergreen forests; offers snorkelling, scuba diving and forest trails.	Chapter 17
Goukamma Nature Reserve	Marine and coastal ecology	Comprises a river and estuary with some of the highest vegetated dunes in South Africa.	p.201
Robberg Marine and Nature Reserve	Rocky headland ecology	The promontory is a fine example of the interaction of plant and animal life on southern coastal headlands and a good place to spot seals at work; good hiking.	p.219
Table Mountain National Park (formerly Cape Peninsula National Park)	The natural areas of the peninsula	Famed for the extraordinary diversity of flora and fauna living in the wild areas within and around Cape Town. The area spans Table Mountain, the Boulders Beach penguin colony and the Cape of Good Hope reserve.	Chapters 3 & 6

R20), which applies to all visitors. Entry into CapeNature reserves generally costs around R30 (children R15) a day per person, irrespective of nationality.

Most national parks and some of the CapeNature Conservation reserves have **accommodation**, which generally has a pleasantly rustic atmosphere in keeping with the wilderness surrounds. Units vary from rondavels at De Hoop Nature Reserve that start at R300 per person a night, to pretty comfortable, fully equipped en-suite cottages and chalets at the Garden Route and Addo Elephant national parks that start at around R750 a night for a couple. Some reserves have family units that sleep four or more, and you'll find **camping facilities** at virtually all the reserves.

You can **book** park accommodation in advance (to stay in high season, do so several months in advance) through SANParks if the park in question is managed by them or, in the case of a CapeNature site, through the park itself (details in the guide and on its website). Note that if you try booking for South African National Parks over the phone you could well be in for a long wait; contacting them online is recommended.

Crime and personal safety

Despite horror stories of sky-high crime rates, most people visit South Africa without incident; be careful, but don't be paranoid. This is not to underestimate the issue – crime is probably the most serious problem facing the country. But some perspective is in order: crime is disproportionately concentrated in the townships rather than areas frequented by most visitors.

Protecting property and "security" are major national obsessions, and it's difficult to imagine what many South Africans would discuss at their dinner parties if the problem disappeared. A substantial percentage of middle-class homes subscribe to the services of armed private security firms. The other obvious manifestation of this obsession is the huge number of alarms, high walls and electronically controlled gates you'll find, not just in the suburbs, but even in less deprived areas of some townships.

Guns are openly carried by police – and often citizens. In many high streets you'll spot firearms shops rubbing shoulders with places selling clothes or books, and you'll come across notices asking you to deposit your weapon before entering the premises.

If you fall victim to a **mugging**, you should take very seriously the usual advice not to resist, and do as you're told. The chances of being mugged can be greatly minimized by using common sense and following a few simple rules (see box below).

SAFETY TIPS

IN GENERAL:
- don't openly display expensive watches, jewellery, cameras or videos in cities.
- if you are accosted, remain calm and cooperative.

WHEN ON FOOT:
- grasp bags firmly under your arm.
- don't carry excessive sums of money on you.
- always know where your valuables are.
- don't leave valuables exposed (on a seat or the ground) while having a meal or drink.
- don't let strangers get too close to you – especially people in groups.

ON THE ROAD:
- lock all your car doors, especially in cities.
- keep rear windows sufficiently rolled up to keep out opportunistic hands.
- never leave anything worth stealing in view when your car is unattended.

ON THE BEACH:
- take only the bare essentials.
- don't leave valuables, especially cameras, unattended.
- safeguard car keys by pinning them to your swimming gear, or putting them in a waterproof wallet or splash box and taking them into the water with you.

AT ATMS:
Cash machines are favourite hunting grounds for sophisticated con men, who use cunning rather than force to steal money. Never underestimate their ability and don't get drawn into any interaction at an ATM, no matter how well-spoken, friendly or distressed the other person appears. If they claim to have a problem with the machine, tell them to contact the bank. Don't let people crowd you or see your personal identification number (PIN) when you withdraw money; if in doubt, go to another machine. Finally, if your card gets swallowed, report it without delay.

WHEN PAYING WITH A CARD:
- never let your plastic out of your sight.
- at a restaurant, ask for a portable card reader to be brought to your table.
- at the till, keep an eye on your card.

Drugs

Alcohol is unquestionably the most widely used and abused drug in South Africa, followed by dagga (pronounced like "dugger" with the "gg" guttural, as in the Scottish pronunciation of "loch") or cannabis in dried leaf form. Locally grown and produced, it is fairly easily available and the quality is generally good – but this doesn't alter the fact that it is illegal.

Alcohol and drink-driving

Strangely, for a country that sometimes seems to be on one massive binge, South Africa has laws that prohibit drinking in public – not that anyone pays any attention to them. The **drink-drive laws** are routinely and brazenly flouted, making the country's roads the one real danger you should be concerned about. People routinely stock up their cars with booze for long journeys and even at petrol stations you'll find places selling liquor. Levels of alcohol consumption go some way to explaining why, during the Christmas holidays, over a thousand people die in an annual period of carnage on the roads. However, concerted attempts are being made to deal with the problem, including the widely publicized Arrive Alive campaign and the confiscation of the vehicles of drunk drivers and drivers travelling well over the speed limit.

Sexual harassment

South Africa's extremely high incidence of **rape** doesn't as a rule affect tourists. However, at heart the majority of the country's males, regardless of race, hold onto fairly sexist attitudes. Sometimes your eagerness to be friendly may be taken as a sexual overture – be sensitive to potential crossed wires and unintended signals.

Women should take care while travelling on their own, and should avoid hitchhiking or walking alone in deserted areas. This applies equally to Cape Town, the countryside or anywhere after dark. Minibus taxis should be ruled out as a means of transport after dark, especially if you're not exactly sure of local geography.

The police

For many black South Africans, the **South African National Police** (SANP) still carry strong associations of collaboration with apartheid and a lot of public relations work has still to be done to turn the police into a genuine people's law enforcement agency. Dismally paid, poorly trained, shot at (and frequently hit), underfunded, badly equipped, barely respected and demoralized, the police keep a low profile. If you ever get stopped, at a roadblock for example (one of the likeliest encounters), always be courteous. And if you're driving, note that under South African law you are required to carry your **driving licence** at all times.

If you are robbed, you will need to report the incident to the police, who should give you a case reference for insurance purposes – though don't expect too much crime-cracking enthusiasm, or to get your property back.

Travel essentials

Climate

As a winter rainfall area, Cape Town typically is at its coldest, wettest and stormiest from May to August. Having said that, it's not uncommon to have days or weeks of gloriously sunny days at this time of year. During the peak of the summer (November to February) you can expect long sunny days (and the blast of the seasonal southeasterly wind) with average temperatures peaking at 27ºC in February.

Costs

The most expensive thing about visiting South Africa is getting there. Once you've arrived, you're likely to find it a relatively inexpensive destination. How cheap you find South Africa will depend partly on exchange rates at the time of your visit – since becoming fully convertible (after the advent of democracy in South Africa) the rand has seen some massive fluctuations against sterling, the dollar and the euro.

When it comes to **daily budgets**, your biggest expense is likely to be **accommodation**. If you're willing to stay in backpacker dorms and self-cater, you should be able to sleep and eat for under £22/\$36/€25 per person per day. If you stay in B&Bs and guesthouses, eat out once a day, and have a snack or two you should budget for at least double that. In luxury hotels expect to pay upwards of £150/US\$250/€175 a day, while luxury safari lodges in Addo and the private game reserves will set you back from £200/US\$325/€230 a day to way beyond. **Extras** such as car rental,

AVERAGE MONTHLY TEMPERATURES AND RAINFALL

	Jan	Feb	Mar	Apr	May	Jun	Jul	Aug	Sep	Oct	Nov	Dec
Cape Town												
max/min (°C)	26/16	27/16	25/14	23/12	20/9	18/8	18/7	18/8	19/9	21/11	24/13	25/15
max/min (°F)	79/60	80/60	78/58	73/53	69 48	65/46	65/45	65/46	67/48	70/51	74/56	77/59
Rainfall (mm/inches)	15/0.6	17/0.7	20/0.8	41/1.6	69/2.7	93/3.7	82/3.2	77/3.0	40/1.6	30/1.2	14/0.6	17/0.7
Tsitsikamma National Park												
max/min (°C)	23/17	22/17	21/16	20/14	19/12	18/10	17/10	17/10	17/11	19/13	20/14	22/16
max/min (°F)	73/63	72/63	70/61	68/57	66/54	64/50	63/50	63/50	63/52	66/55	68/57	72/61
Rainfall (mm/inches)	77/3.0	70/2.8	81/3.2	80/3.1	86/3.4	75/3.0	78/3.1	111/4.4	66/2.6	83/3.3	78/3.1	60/2.4

outdoor activities, horseriding and safaris will add to these figures substantially. While most museums and art galleries impose an **entry fee**, it's usually quite low: only the most sophisticated attractions charge more than £1/$1.50/€1.

Electricity

South Africa's **electricity** supply runs at 220/230V, 50Hz AC. Sockets take unique round-pinned plugs; see ⓦ www.kropla.com for details. Most hotel rooms have sockets that will take 110V electric shavers, but for other appliances US visitors will need an adaptor to make their appliances compatible with South Africa's 220V system.

Emergencies

Police ☎ 1011, state ambulance ☎ 10177, ER24 private ambulance and paramedic assistance ☎ 084 124.

Entry requirements

Nationals of the EU, the US, Canada, Australia and New Zealand don't require a **visa** to enter South Africa. As long as you carry a passport that is valid for at least six months and with at least two empty pages you will be granted a temporary visitor's permit, which allows you to stay in South Africa for up to ninety days. All visitors should have a valid return ticket; without one, you may be required to pay the authorities the equivalent of your fare home (the money will be refunded after you have left the country). Visitors may also need to prove that they have sufficient funds to cover their stay.

Applications for visa extensions must be made at one of the main offices of the Department of Home Affairs, where you will be quizzed about your intentions and your funds. Their address in Cape Town is 56 Barrack St (☎ 021 462 4970). The

Department also has offices in a number of towns – check in the telephone directory or on its website (ⓦ www.home-affairs.gov.za), and make sure that the office you're intending to visit is able to grant extensions.

SOUTH AFRICAN DIPLOMATIC MISSIONS ABROAD

Australia corner State Circle and Rhodes Place, Yarralumla, Canberra, ACT 2600 ☎ 02 6272 7300, ⓦ www.sahc.org.au.
Canada 15 Sussex Drive, Ottawa, Ontario K1M 1M8 ☎ 613 744 0330, ⓦ www.southafrica-canada.ca.
Netherlands Wassenaarseweg 40, 2596 CJ, The Hague ☎ 070 392 4501, ⓦ www.zuidafrika.nl.
New Zealand c/o the High Commission in Australia, see above.
UK Consular Section 15 Whitehall, London SW1A 2DD ☎ 020 7925 8900, ⓦ www.southafricahouseuk.com.
US 4301 Connecticut Ave, NW, Van Ness Building Suite 220 Washington, DC 20008 ☎ 202 232 4400, ⓦ www.southafrica -newyork.net/homeaffairs/index.htm. Consulates: 333 E 38th St, 9th floor, New York, NY 10016 ☎ 212 213 4880; 6300 Wilshire Blvd, Suite 600, Los Angeles, CA 90048 ☎ 323 651 0902.

FOREIGN DIPLOMATIC MISSIONS IN CAPE TOWN

The embassies for most countries are in Pretoria, but the following have consulates in Cape Town:
Canada 19th Floor, South African Reserve Bank building, 60 St George's Mall ☎ 021 423 5240.
Netherlands 100 Strand St ☎ 021 421 5660.
UK 15th Floor, Southern Life Centre, 8 Riebeek St ☎ 021 405 2400.
US 2 Reddam Ave, Westlake ☎ 021 702 7300.

Insurance

It's wise to take out an **insurance policy** to cover against theft, loss and illness or injury prior to visiting South Africa. A typical travel insurance policy usually provides cover for the loss of baggage, tickets and – up to a certain limit – cash or cheques, as well as cancellation or curtailment of

ROUGH GUIDES TRAVEL INSURANCE

Rough Guides has teamed up with WorldNomads.com to offer great travel insurance deals. Policies are available to residents of over 150 countries, with cover for a wide range of adventure sports, 24hr emergency assistance, high levels of medical and evacuation cover and a stream of travel safety information. Roughguides.com users can take advantage of their policies online 24/7, from anywhere in the world – even if you're already travelling. And since plans often change when you're on the road, you can extend your policy and even claim online. Roughguides.com users who buy travel insurance with WorldNomads.com can also leave a positive footprint and donate to a community development project. For more information go to Ⓦ roughguides.com/shop.

your journey. Most of them exclude so-called **dangerous sports** unless an extra premium is paid: in South Africa this can mean scuba diving, white-water rafting, windsurfing, horseriding, bungee jumping and paragliding. In addition to these it's well worth checking whether you are covered by your policy if you're hiking, kayaking, pony trekking or game viewing on safari, all activities people commonly take part in when visiting South Africa. Many policies can be chopped and changed to exclude coverage you don't need – for example, sickness and accident benefits can often be excluded or included at will. If you do take **medical coverage**, ascertain whether benefits will be paid as treatment proceeds or only after you return home, and if there is a 24-hour medical emergency number. When securing **baggage cover**, make sure that the per-article limit will cover your most valuable possession. If you need to make a claim, you should keep receipts for medicines and medical treatment, and in the event you have anything stolen, you must obtain an official statement from the police.

Internet

Finding somewhere to access the **internet** will seldom be a problem in Cape Town and the Garden Route: cybercafés are found even in relatively small towns, and most backpacker hostels and hotels have internet and email facilities. Expect to pay R10–25 an hour for online access. If you are carrying your own device you'll also be able to take advantage of the wireless hotspots at a small (but growing) number of airports, cafés, malls and accommodation.

Mail

The deceptively familiar feel of South African post offices can lull you into expecting an efficient British- or US-style service. In fact, post within the country is slow and unreliable, and money and valuables frequently disappear en route. Expect domestic delivery times from one city to another of about a week – longer if a rural town is involved at either end. **International airmail** deliveries are often quicker, thanks to the city's direct flights to London. A letter or package sent by surface mail can take up to six weeks to get from South Africa to London.

Most towns of any size have a **post office**, generally open Monday to Friday 8.30am to 4.30pm and Saturday 8 to 11.30am (closing earlier in some places). The ubiquitous private **PostNet** outlets (Ⓦ www.postnet.co.za) offer many of the same postal services as the post office and more, including **courier services**. Courier companies like FedEx (☎ 0800 033 339, Ⓦ www.fedex.com/za) and DHL (☎ 086 034 5000, Ⓦ www.dhl.co.za) are more expensive and available only in the larger towns, but they are far more reliable than the mail.

Stamps are available at post offices and also from newsagents, such as the CNA chain, as well as supermarkets. Postage is relatively inexpensive – it costs about R4 to send a postcard by airmail to anywhere in the world, while a small letter costs about R5 to send. You'll find **poste restante** facilities at the main post office in most larger centres, and in many backpackers hostels.

Maps

You'll find up-to-date maps of Cape Town, its suburbs, the Winelands and the Garden Route in the guide, but if you're looking for more substantial maps, make sure they're up to date as many **place names** in South Africa were changed after the 1994 elections – and changes are still being made. Bartholomew produces an excellent map of South Africa, including Lesotho and Swaziland (1:2,000,000), as part of its World Travel Map series.

South Africa's motoring organization, the **Automobile Association**, sells a wide selection of good regional maps (free to members) from its offices.

For travel around the **Western Cape** (including the Cape Peninsula and the Garden Route), the most accurate, up-to-date and attractive touring and hiking maps – the best bar none – are those produced by Cape Town cartographers Slingsby Maps (Ⓦ www.slingsbymaps.com).

Money

South Africa's currency is the **rand** (R), often called the "buck", divided into 100 **cents**. Notes come in R10, R20, R50, R100 and R200 denominations and there are coins of 5, 10, 20 and 50 cents, as well as R1, R2 and R5. At the time of writing, the **exchange rate** was hovering at around R11 to the pound sterling, R7 to the US dollar, R10 to the euro and R7 to the Australian dollar.

All but the tiniest settlement will have a **bank** where you can **change money** swiftly and easily. **Banking hours** are Monday to Friday 9am to 3.30pm, and Saturday 9am to 11am; the banks in smaller towns usually close for lunch. In major cities, some banks operate **bureaux de change** that stay open until 7pm. Outside banking hours, some hotels will change money, although this entails a fairly hefty **commission**. You can also change money at branches of American Express and Rennies Travel.

Cards and travellers' cheques

Credit and debit cards are the most convenient way to access your funds in South Africa. Most international cards can be used to withdraw money at **ATMs**, open 24 hours a day in the cities and elsewhere. Plastic can come in very handy for hotel bookings and for paying for more mainstream and upmarket tourist facilities, and is essential for car rental. **Visa** and **Mastercard** are the cards most widely accepted in major cities.

Travellers' cheques make a useful backup as they can be replaced if lost or stolen. American Express, Visa and Thomas Cook are all widely recognized brands; both US dollar and sterling cheques are accepted in South Africa.

Travellers' cheques and plastic are useless if you're heading into remote areas, where you'll need to carry **cash**, preferably in a safe place, such as a leather pouch or waist-level money belt that you can keep under your clothes.

Opening hours and holidays

The **working day** starts and finishes early in South Africa: shops and businesses generally open on **weekdays** at 8.30am or 9am and close at 4.30pm or 5pm. In small towns, many places close for an hour over **lunch**. Many **shops** and businesses close around noon on Saturdays, and most shops are closed on Sundays. However, in every neighbourhood, you'll find small shops and supermarkets where you can buy groceries and essentials after hours.

Some establishments have summer and winter opening times. In such situations, you can take **winter** to mean April to August or September, while **summer** constitutes the rest of the year.

School holidays in South Africa can disrupt your plans, especially if you want to camp, or stay in the national parks and the cheaper end of accommodation (self-catering, cheaper B&Bs, etc), all of which are likely to be booked solid during those periods. If you do travel to South Africa over the school holidays, book your accommodation well in advance, especially for the national parks.

The longest and busiest holiday period is **Christmas (summer)**, which for schools stretches

SOUTH AFRICAN PUBLIC HOLIDAYS

Many shops and tourist-related businesses remain open over public holidays, although often with shorter opening hours. Christmas Day and Good Friday, when most of the country shuts down, are the only exceptions. The main holidays are:

New Year's Day (Jan 1)
Human Rights Day (March 21)
Good Friday, Easter Monday (variable)
Freedom Day (April 27)
Workers' Day (May 1)

Youth Day (June 16)
National Women's Day (Aug 9)
Heritage Day (Sept 24)
Day of Reconciliation (Dec 16)
Christmas Day (Dec 25)
Day of Goodwill (Dec 26)

over most of December and January. Flights and train berths can be hard to get from December 16 to January 2, when many businesses and offices close for their annual break. You should book your **flights** – long-haul and domestic – as early as six months in advance for the Christmas period. The inland and coastal provinces stagger their school holidays, but as a general rule the remaining school holidays roughly cover the following periods: **Easter**, mid-March to mid-April; **winter**, mid-June to mid-July; and spring, late September to early October. Exact **dates** for each year are given on the government's information website: ⓦ www.info.gov.za/aboutsa/schoolcal.htm.

Phones

South Africa's **telephone** system, dominated by **Telkom**, generally works well. Public phone booths are found in every city and town, and are either coin- or card-operated. While **international calls** can be made from virtually any phone, it helps to have a **phonecard**, as you'll be lucky to stay on the line for more than a minute or two for R20. Phonecards come in R20, R50, R100 and R200 denominations, available at Telkom offices, post offices and newsagents.

Mobile phones (referred to locally as cell phones or simply cells) are extremely widely used in South Africa, with more mobile than land-line handsets in use. The competing networks – Vodacom, MTN, Cell C and VirginMobile – cover all the main areas and the national roads connecting them.

You can use a GSM/tri-band phone from outside the country in South Africa, but you will need to arrange a **roaming agreement** with your provider at home; be warned that this is likely to be expensive. A far cheaper alternative is to buy a **local SIM card** while you're in South Africa. (For this to work, you'll need to make sure your phone has been "unblocked" to accept another network.) The local SIM card contains your South African phone number, and you pay for airtime. Very inexpensive starter packs (R100 or less) containing a **SIM card** and some airtime can be bought from the ubiquitous mobile phone shops and a number of other outlets, including supermarkets and the CNA chain of newsagents and supermarkets.

Another option is to **rent** just a South African SIM card or a phone and SIM card when you arrive. Cards start at R5 a day and phones at R7. Phone (and GPS) rental can also be arranged when you arrange car rental. Among the companies that offer

this are Avis, Budget, Hertz and National (see p.25) as does the Baz Bus (see p.24). There are rental outlets at the major airports: Cape Town, Port Elizabeth and George.

PHONE RENTAL COMPANIES

Rent a Mobile ⓦ www.rentamobile.co.za. Rental arm of MTN.
Vodashop Renta Fone ⓦ www.rentafone.net. Vodacom's phone rental wing.

CALLING HOME FROM SOUTH AFRICA

To dial out of South Africa, the **international access code** is ☎ 00. Remember to omit any initial zero in the number of the place you're phoning.
Australia international access code + 61
Ireland international access code + 353
New Zealand international access code + 64
UK international access code + 44
US and Canada international access code + 1

Taxes

Value-added tax (VAT) of fourteen percent is levied on most goods and services, though it's usually already included in any quoted price. Foreign visitors older than seven can claim back VAT on goods over R250. To do this, you must present an official tax receipt with your name on it for the goods, a non-South African passport and the purchased goods themselves, at the **airport** just before you fly out. You need to complete a VAT refund control sheet (VAT 255), which can be obtained at international airports. For further information contact the VAT Refund Administrator (☎ 011 394 1117, ⓦ www.taxrefunds.co.za).

Time

There is only one **time zone** throughout South Africa, two hours ahead of GMT year-round. If you're flying from anywhere in Europe, you shouldn't experience any jet lag.

Tipping

Ten to fifteen percent of the tab is the normal **tip** at restaurants and for taxis – but don't feel obliged to tip if service has been shoddy. Keep in mind that many of the people who'll be serving you rely on tips to supplement a meagre wage on which they support huge extended families. **Porters** at hotels normally get about R5–10 per bag. At South African garages and filling stations, someone will always be on hand to fill your vehicle and clean your windscreen, for which you should tip around R5. It is also usual at **hotels** to leave some money for the person who services your room. Many establishments, especially private game lodges, take (voluntary) communal tips when you check out – by far the fairest system, which ensures that all the low-profile staff behind the scenes get their share.

Tourist information

There are several official **tourist information bureaus** in Cape Town and most towns have some sort of information office, but in this fast-changing country, the best way of finding out what's happening is often by word of mouth, and for this **backpacker hostels** are invaluable. If you're seeing South Africa on a budget, the useful notice boards, constant traveller traffic and largely helpful and friendly staff you'll encounter in backpacker hostels will greatly smooth your travels.·

There are countless **guidebooks** on walks around Cape Town, hikes up Table Mountain, dive sites, fishing locations, surfing breaks and windsurfing spots. For the best-stocked shelves and nicest atmosphere, head to one of the Exclusive Books stores (see p.134). You'll also find useful books on all aspects of South Africa at the secondhand bookshops down Long Street.

To find out **what's on**, check out the entertainment pages of the daily newspapers or better still buy the *Mail & Guardian*, which comes out every Friday and lists the coming week's offerings in a comprehensive pullout supplement.

TOURIST INFORMATION BUREAUS

Cape Town Tourism The Pinnacle, Burg & Castle streets (☎ 021 426 4260) Oct–March Mon–Fri 8am–6pm, Sat 8am–2pm & Sun 8.30am–1pm; April–Sept Mon–Fri 8.30am–5pm, Sat & Sun 8.30am–1pm; Cape Town Tourism also has a bureau at the airport; Ⓦ capetown.travel.

GOVERNMENT SITES

Australian Department of Foreign Affairs Ⓦ dfat.gov.au.
British Foreign & Commonwealth Office Ⓦ fco.gov.uk.
Canadian Department of Foreign Affairs Ⓦ international.gc.ca.
Irish Department of Foreign Affairs Ⓦ foreignaffairs.gov.ie.
New Zealand Ministry of Foreign Affairs Ⓦ mfat.govt.nz.
US State Department Ⓦ state.gov/.

Travellers with Disabilities

Facilities for **disabled travellers** in South Africa are not as sophisticated as those found in the developed world, but they're sufficient to ensure you have a satisfactory visit. By accident, often, rather than design, you'll find pretty good accessibility to many buildings, as South Africans tend to build low (single-storey bungalows are the norm), with the result that you'll have to deal with fewer stairs than you may be accustomed to. As the car is king, you'll frequently find that you can drive to, and park right outside, your destination.

There are **organized tours** and holidays specifically for people with disabilities, and **activity-based packages** are increasingly available. These offer the possibility for wheelchair-bound visitors to take part in safaris, sport and a vast range of adventure activities, including whitewater rafting, horseriding, parasailing and zip-lining. Tours can either be taken as self-drive trips or as packages for large groups. The contacts below will be able to put you in touch with South Africa travel specialists.

If you want to be more independent on your travels, it's important to know where you can expect help and where you must be self-reliant, especially regarding transport and accommodation. It's also vital to know your limitations, and to make sure others know them. If you do not use a wheelchair all the time but your walking capabilities are limited, remember that you are likely to need to cover greater distances while travelling (often over rougher terrain and in hotter temperatures) than you are used to. If you use a wheelchair, have it serviced before you go and take a repair kit with you.

USEFUL CONTACTS

Ⓦ **disabledtravel.co.za** Website of occupational therapist Karin Coetzee aimed at disabled travellers, with listings of accommodation, restaurants and attractions personally evaluated for accessibility as well as hugely useful links to everything from car rental and tours to orthopaedic equipment.
Ⓦ **access-able.com** US-based website for travellers with disabilities that includes some useful information about South Africa.

LONG STREET

The city centre

Cape Town's city centre is spectacularly situated, dominated by Table Mountain to the southwest and the pounding Atlantic to the northeast. It is the most historically intense district in the country and the oldest urban area in South Africa, boasting some interesting museums, and it pulses with the cultural fusion that has been Cape Town's hallmark since its founding in 1652. Strand Street marks the edge of Cape Town's original beachfront (though you'd never guess it today), with the Lower City Centre to the northeast and the Upper City Centre to the southwest. The obvious orientation axis, however, is Adderley Street, which connects the main train station in the north with St George's Cathedral. Southwest of here is the symbolic heart of the city, with the Houses of Parliament, museums, historic buildings, archives and De Tuynhuys, the office of the president, arranged around the Company's Gardens.

Northwest of Adderley Street is the closest South Africa gets to a European quarter – a tight network of streets with cafés, buskers, bookstores, street stalls and antique shops congregating around the pedestrianized **St George's Mall** and **Greenmarket Square**.

Parallel to St George's Mall, **Long Street**, the quintessential Cape Town thoroughfare, is lined with colonial Victorian buildings that house pubs, bistros, nightclubs, backpacker lodges, bookshops and antique dealers, from whose wrought-iron balconies you can catch glimpses of Table Mountain and the sea. The **Bo-Kaap**, or Muslim quarter, three blocks further northwest across Buitengragt, exudes a piquant contrast to this, with its minarets, spice shops and cafés selling curried snacks.

Southeast of Adderley Street and close to one another lie three historically loaded sites. The **Castle of Good Hope** – the oldest building in South Africa – is an indelible symbol of Europe's colonization of South Africa, a process whose death knell was struck from nearby **City Hall**, the attractive Edwardian building from which Nelson Mandela made his first speech after being released. In front of the hall is an open area called the Grand Parade, the site of the 2010 Football World Cup Fan Park. South of the castle lie the poignantly desolate remains of **District Six**, the coloured inner-city suburb that was razed in the name of apartheid.

GETTING AROUND CITY CENTRE

BY BUS

MyCiTi ☎0800 65 64 63, ⓦwww.capetown.gov.za/myciti. Buses currently run from the Gardens at the edge of the City Bowl through the city centre to the Civic Centre and then on to the Waterfront. From mid-2012, nine new routes are expected to be in service, several of which will run through the city centre, bringing you within a short walk of most of the central attractions. Buses #F02, #F03 and #F06 will go through the city centre up Long St returning along Loop St; while several routes cross the centre at right angles to this: #F04 along Strand St, #F05 along Darling and Wale sts, and #F07 along Darling St. MyCiTi services run every 10 to 20min during the day.

City Sightseeing ☎021 511 6000, ⓦcitysightseeing .co.za. Buses also stop at all the major attractions in the city centre.

The Upper City Centre

Once *the* place to shop in Cape Town, **Adderley Street**, lined with handsome buildings from several centuries, is still worth a stroll today. Its attractive streetscape has been blemished by a series of large 1960s shopping centres, but just minutes away from crowded malls, among the streets and alleys around Greenmarket Square, you can still find some human scale and historic texture.

Low-walled channels, ditches, bridges and sluices once ran through Cape Town, earning it the name Little Amsterdam. During the nineteenth century, the canals were buried underground, and in 1850 Heerengracht (Gentlemen's Canal), formerly a waterway that ran from the Company's Gardens down to the sea, was renamed Adderley Street (see box, p.44). There's little evidence of the canals today, except in name – one section of the street is still called Heerengracht and a parallel street to its west is called Buitengragt (sometimes spelled Buitengracht after the Dutch style, and meaning the Outer Canal).

The destruction of old Cape Town continued well into the twentieth century, with the razing of many of the older buildings. One of the ugliest newcomers is the **Golden Acre shopping complex**, dominating the northeastern (harbour) end of Adderley Street. Built in the 1970s, it's Cape Town's public transport hub today, connected to the bus and train stations by a not-too-friendly network of subways and walkways, but nevertheless giving an authentic taste of ordinary Capetonians doing their shopping, something you won't find at the sanitized Victoria and Alfred Waterfront. On Saturday mornings, if you exit onto Adderley Street, you'll often encounter the sounds of busking brass bands or choirs. Among the pavements and pedestrianized sections outside, which run down to the station, there's a closely packed **flea market** offering curios, crafts and electronic goods (but watch your

1

THE LANGUAGE OF COLOUR

It's striking just how un-African Cape Town looks and sounds. Halfway between East and West, Cape Town drew its population from Africa, Asia and Europe, and traces of all three continents are found in the genes, language, culture, religion and cuisine of South Africa's coloured population. Afrikaans (a close relative of Dutch) is the mother tongue of over half the city's population. Having said that, a very substantial number of Capetonians are born English-speakers and English punches well above its weight as the local lingua franca, which, in this multilingual society, virtually everyone can speak and understand.

Afrikaans is the mother tongue of a large proportion of the city's coloured residents, as well as many whites. The term "coloured" is contentious, but in South Africa it doesn't have the same tainted connotations as in Britain and the US; it refers to South Africans of mixed race. Most brown-skinned people in Cape Town (over fifty percent of Capetonians) are coloureds, with Asian, African and Khoikhoi ancestry.

In the late **nineteenth century**, Afrikaans-speaking whites, fighting for an identity, sought to create a "racially pure" culture by driving a wedge between themselves and coloured Afrikaans-speakers. They reinvented Afrikaans as a "white man's language", eradicating the supposed stigma of its coloured ties by substituting Dutch words for those with Asian or African roots. In 1925, the white dialect of Afrikaans became an official language alongside English, and the dialects spoken by coloureds were treated as inferior deviations from correct usage.

For Afrikaner nationalists this wasn't enough, and after the introduction of apartheid in 1948, they attempted to codify perceived racial differences. Under the **Population Registration Act**, all South Africans were classified as white, coloured or African. These classifications became fundamental to what kind of life you could expect. There are numerous cases of families in which one sibling was classified coloured with limited rights and another white with the right to live in comfortable white areas, enjoy superior job opportunities and be able to send their children to better schools and universities.

With the demise of **apartheid**, the make-up of residential areas is shifting – and so is the thinking on ethnic terminology. Some people now reject the term "coloured" because of its apartheid associations, and refuse any racial definitions; others, however, proudly embrace the term, as a means of acknowledging their distinct culture, with its slave and Khoikhoi roots.

wallet). A little further south lies a **flower market**, run by members of the **Bo-Kaap** Muslim community.

Standard and First National banks
Adderley St

Two grandiose bank buildings stand on opposite sides of Adderley Street; the fussier of the two is the former **Standard Bank**, fronted by Corinthian columns and covered with a tall dome – a temple to the partnership of empire and finance. Renovated, it is now an upmarket 220-seater **restaurant**, complete with palm trees to the ceiling, and named *Riboville* after a famous racehorse. The **First National Bank**, completed in 1913, was the last South African building designed by Sir Herbert Baker (see box, p.96). If you pop in for a quick look, still in place inside the banking hall you'll find a solid timber circular writing desk with the original inkwells, resembling an altar.

The Groote Kerk
Daily 9.30am–4.30pm • Free

Sometimes described as "Cape Gothic" in style, the **Groote Kerk** (Great Church) diagonally opposite the First National Bank, is essentially a Classical building with Gothic and Egyptian elements. Designed and built between 1836 and 1841 by Hermann Schutte, a German who became one of the Cape's leading early nineteenth-century architects, the church replaced an earlier Baroque one that had become too small for the swelling ranks of the Dutch Reformed congregation at the Cape. The

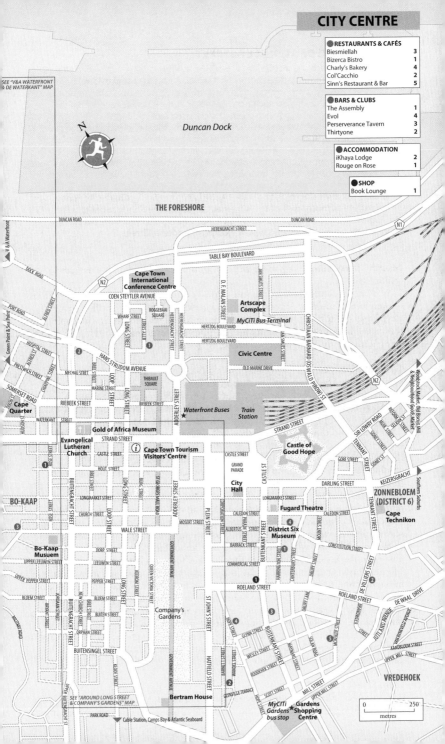

CITY CENTRE

● RESTAURANTS & CAFÉS
Biesmiellah	3
Bizerca Bistro	1
Charly's Bakery	4
Col'Cacchio	2
Sinn's Restaurant & Bar	5

● BARS & CLUBS
The Assembly	1
Evol	4
Perserverance Tavern	3
Thirtyone	2

● ACCOMMODATION
iKhaya Lodge	2
Rouge on Rose	1

● SHOP
Book Lounge	1

SEE "V&A WATERFRONT & DE WATERKANT" MAP

Duncan Dock

N

THE FORESHORE

DUNCAN ROAD
DUNCAN ROAD
N1
HERENGRACHT STREET

TABLE BAY BOULEVARD

DOCK ROAD
V & A Waterfront
N2
Green Point & Sea Point
PORT ROAD
ALFRED ROAD

Cape Town International Conference Centre
COEN STEYTLER AVENUE
N2

D. F. MALAN STREET
JAN SMUTS STREET
Artscape Complex
MyCiTi Bus Terminal

HOSPITAL STREET
PRESTWICH STREET
DARLING STREET
PREMIER STREET
WHARF STREET
ROGGEBAAI SQUARE
HERENGRACHT STREET
HERTZOG BOULEVARD
HERTZOG BOULEVARD
CHRISTIAAN BARNARD (OSWALD PIROW) ST
JAN SMUTS STREET

MECHAU STREET
HANS STRIJDOM AVENUE
LOOP STREET
LONG STREET
BREE STREET
Civic Centre
OLD MARINE DRIVE
N2

MARINE STREET
THIBAULT SQUARE

SOMERSET ROAD
RIEBEEK STREET
BREE STREET
LONG STREET
RIEBEEK STREET
BUITENGRACHT STREET
SIR LOWRY ROAD
Woodstock Market, Old Biscuit Mill & Neighbourhood Goods Market
RESERVOIR ST
SELKIRK ST

Cape Quarter
WATERKANT STREET
HUDSON STREET

Waterfront Buses
Train Station
ADDERLEY STREET

STRAND STREET
SIR LOWRY ROAD
TENNANT STREET
LONG STREET
SIDNEY ST

Gold of Africa Museum
STRAND STREET
Cape Town Tourism Visitors' Centre
Castle of Good Hope
GORE STREET

Evangelical Lutheran Church
CASTLE STREET
CASTLE ST
CASTLE STREET
DARLING STREET
KEIZERSGRACHT

BO-KAAP
BREE STREET
HOUT STREET
ST GEORGE'S MALL ROAD
ADDERLEY STREET
GRAND PARADE
City Hall
ZONNEBLOEM (DISTRICT 6)
TENNANT STREET
Cape Technikon

LONGMARKET STREET
CHURCH STREET
BUITENGRACHT STREET
LOOP STREET
BREE STREET
BURG STREET
LONGMARKET STREET
CALEDON STREET
Fugard Theatre
CALEDON STREET
DE VILLIERS STREET

Bo-Kaap Museum
ROSE STREET
WALE STREET
CORPORATION STREET
MOSERT STREET
ALBERTUS STREET
PARADE STREET
District Six Museum
CONSTITUTION STREET

DORP STREET
LEEUWEN STREET
KEEROM STREET
LONG STREET
BARRACK STREET
HARRINGTON STREET
CANTERBURY STREET
MOUNT STREET
DRURY LANE

UPPER LEEUWEN STREET
PEPPER STREET
QUEEN VICTORIA STREET
COMMERCIAL STREET
ROELAND STREET
ROELAND STREET
DE WAAL DRIVE

UPPER PEPPER STREET
BLOEM STREET
NEW CHURCH STREET
BREE STREET
BUITEN STREET
ST JOHN'S STREET
GOVERNMENT AVENUE
HOPE STREET
GLYNN STREET
BUITENKANT STREET
MAYNARD STREET
SOLAN ROAD
DEVONPORT ROAD
JUTLAND AVENUE
AANDBLOEM STREET
UPPER MILL STREET

BLOEM STREET
JORDAAN STREET
ORPHAN STREET
Company's Gardens
WESLEY STREET
ROODEHEK STREET
SCOTT STREET
MILL STREET
VREDEHOEK

BUITENSINGEL STREET
UPPER BUITENGRACHT ST
HATFIELD STREET
GLYNVILLE TERRACE
HOPE STREET
MyCiTi Gardens bus stop
Gardens Shopping Centre
UPPER MILL STREET

SEE "AROUND LONG STREET & COMPANY'S GARDENS" MAP
PARK ROAD
Cable Station, Camps Bay & Atlantic Seaboard
Bertram House
0   250
metres

1

THE NAMING OF ADDERLEY STREET

Although the Dutch used Robben Island (see p.64) as a political prison, the South African mainland only narrowly escaped becoming a second Australia, a **penal colony** where British felons and enemies of the state could be dumped. By the 1840s, "respectable Australians" were lobbying for a ban on the transportation of criminals to the Antipodes, and the British authorities responded by trying to divert convicts to the Cape.

In 1848, the British ship *Neptune* set sail from Bermuda for Cape Town with a cargo of 282 prisoners. There was outrage when news of its departure reached Cape Town; five thousand citizens gathered on the Grand Parade the following year to hear prominent liberals denounce the British government, an event depicted in *The Great Meeting of the People at the Commercial Exchange* by Johan Marthinus Carstens Schonegevel, which hangs in the Rust-en-Vreugd Museum (see p.54). When the ship docked in September 1849, governor Sir Harry Smith forbade any criminal from landing while, back in London, politician **Charles Adderley** successfully addressed the House of Commons in support of the Cape colonists. In February 1850, the *Neptune* set off for Tasmania with its full complement of convicts, and grateful Capetonians renamed the city's main thoroughfare **Adderley Street**.

beautiful freestanding clock tower adjacent to the newer building is a remnant of the original church.

The soaring space created by the vast vaulted ceiling and the magnificent pulpit, a masterpiece by sculptor Anton Anreith and carpenter Jan Jacob Graaff, are worth stepping inside for. The pulpit, supported on a pair of sculpted lions with gaping jaws, was carved by Anton Anreith after his first proposal, featuring Faith, Hope and Charity, was rejected by the church council for being "too Popish".

The Slave Lodge

Adderley and Wale sts • Mon–Sat 10am–5pm • R20 • ⓦ iziko.org.za/slavelodge

At the top corner of Adderley Street, just as it veers sharply northwest into Wale Street, **The Slave Lodge** was built in 1679 to house the human chattels of the Dutch East India Company (VOC) – the largest single slaveholder at the Cape.

For nearly two centuries – more than half the city's existence as an urban settlement – Cape Town's economic and social structures rested on slavery (see box opposite). By the 1770s, almost a thousand slaves were held at the lodge. Under VOC administration, the lodge also became the Cape Colony's main brothel, its doors thrown open to all comers for an hour each night. Following the British takeover and the auctioning of the slaves, the lodge became the Supreme Court in 1810, and remained so until 1914, after which the building was used as government offices.

The Slave Lodge has redefined itself as a museum of slavery as well as human rights, with exhibits showing the family roots, ancestry and peopling of South Africa, and changing exhibitions which have covered the likes of Steve Biko and slavery in Brazil. Taking an audio headset allows you to follow the footsteps of German salt trader Otto Menzl as he is taken on a tour of the lodge in the 1700s, it gives you a good idea of the miserable conditions at the time. One stop is an installation of the *Meermin*, one of several ships sent to Madagascar in the eighteenth century to bring men, women and children into slavery in the Cape. Another is an alcove with a column of light listing the names of slaves in rings; the rings elicit the markings on a tree trunk, as it was under the Slave Tree that slaves were bought and sold. Though the actual **Old Slave Tree** is long gone, the spot is marked by a simple and inconspicuous plinth behind Slave Lodge, on the traffic island in Spin Street.

Long Street

Parallel to Adderley Street, buzzing one-way **Long Street** is one of Cape Town's most diverse thoroughfares, and best known as the city's main nightlife strip. When it was first settled by Muslims some three hundred years ago, Long Street marked Cape Town's boundary; by the 1960s, it had become a sleazy alley of drinking holes and whorehouses. Miraculously, it's all still here, but with a whiff of gentrification and a tedious section of discount furniture shops and fast-food joints. It deserves exploration from the Wale Street intersection onwards. Mosques still coexist alongside bars, while antique dealers, craft shops, bookshops and cafés do a good trade. The street is packed with backpacker hostels and a couple of upmarket hotels, though the proliferation of nightclubs here means it can be very noisy into the early hours. At night it's perfectly safe to pub or club crawl, and you'll always find taxis and some street food.

Long Street Baths

Long and Orange sts • **Pool** daily 7am–7pm • R12 • **Turkish baths** Men Tues 1–7pm, Wed & Fri 8am–7pm, Sun 8am–noon; women Mon, Thurs & Sat 9am–6pm • R40 an hour • ☎ 021 400 3302

The **Long Street Baths** is an unpretentious and relaxing historic Cape Town institution, established in 1908 in an Edwardian building that occupies the top of the road, where it hits Buitensingel. For a quiet swim and steam avoid lunchtime, when local office workers pile in for a quick dip. The Turkish baths are open separately to men and women and you can have a massage as well.

Palm Tree Mosque

185 Long St • Closed to the public

Further north, an unmistakable landmark, the **Palm Tree Mosque** is fronted by a lone palm tree, its fronds caressing the upper storey. Significant as the only surviving eighteenth-century house in the street, it was erected in 1780 by Carel Lodewijk Schot as a private dwelling. The house was bought in 1807 by Frans van Bengal, a member of the local Muslim community, and a freed slave, Jan van Boughies, who became its imam, turning the upper floor into a mosque and the lower into his living quarters.

Pan African Market

76 Long St • Oct–April Mon–Fri 8.30am–5.30pm, Sat 9am–3.30pm; May–Sept Mon–Fri 9am–5pm, Sat 9am–3pm • Ⓦ panafrican.co.za

Across Wale Street is one of Cape Town's most intriguing places for African crafts, and

---

SLAVERY AT THE CAPE

Slavery was officially **abolished** at the Cape in 1838, but its legacy lives on in South Africa. The country's **coloured inhabitants**, who make up fifty percent of Cape Town's population, are largely descendants of slaves, political pisoners from the East Indies and indigenous Khoisan people, and some historians argue that apartheid was a natural successor to slavery. Certainly, domestic service, still widespread throughout South Africa, and certain labour practices such as the "dop system", in which workers on some wine farms are partially paid in rations of cheap plonk, can be traced directly back to slavery.

By the end of the eighteenth century, the almost 26,000-strong slave population of the Cape exceeded that of the free burghers. Despite the profound impact this had on the development of social relations in South Africa, it remained one of the most neglected topics of the country's history, until the publication in the 1980s of a number of studies on slavery. There's still a reluctance on the part of most coloureds to acknowledge their slave origins.

Few if any slaves were captured at the Cape for export, making the colony unique in the African trade. Paradoxically, while people were being captured elsewhere on the continent for export to the Americas, the Cape administration, forbidden by the VOC (see p.265) from enslaving the local indigenous population, had to look further afield. Of the 63,000 slaves imported to the Cape before 1808, most came from East Africa, Madagascar, India and Indonesia, representing one of the broadest cultural mixes of any slave society. This diversity initially worked against the establishment of a unified group identity, but eventually a **Creolized culture** emerged which, among other things, played a major role in the development of the **Afrikaans** language.

1

one of the easiest to miss. The inconspicuous frontage of the **Pan African Market** belies the three-floor warren of passageways and rooms, which burst at the hinges with traders selling vast quantities of art and artefacts from all over the continent. Hidden among less inspiring offerings you'll find terrific masks from West Africa, brass leopards from Benin as well as contemporary South African art textiles, and vendors selling CDs and musical instruments. This is also the place to get kitted out in African garb with in-house seamstresses at the ready.

The South African Missionary Meeting-House Museum

40 Long St • Mon–Fri 9am–4pm • Free

Further towards the harbour end of Long Street, the **South African Missionary Meeting-House Museum** was the first missionary church in the country, where slaves were taught literacy and instructed in Christianity. This exceptional building, completed in 1804 by the South African Missionary Society, boasts one of the most beautiful frontages in Cape Town. Dominated by large windows, the facade is broken into three bays by four slender Corinthian pilasters surmounted by a gabled pediment. Inside, an impressive Neoclassical timber **pulpit** perches high above the congregation on a pair of columns, framing an inlaid image of an angel in flight.

Cape Heritage Square

From Long Street head northwest down Shortmarket Street to **Cape Heritage Square**, the largest restoration project ever undertaken in Cape Town. The keystone of the 1771 complex, the *Cape Heritage Hotel*, is one of the most stylish places to stay in the city (see p.107). It opens onto a cluster of restaurants and wine bars set around a tranquil courtyard, in which the oldest known (and still fruit-bearing) vine in South Africa continues to flourish. The square is worth visiting for the architecture and the general sense of tranquillity, best absorbed with a good glass of Cape wine under shady umbrellas.

The Bo-Kaap

Minutes from Parliament, on the slopes of Signal Hill, is the **Bo-Kaap**, one of Cape Town's oldest and most fascinating residential areas. Its streets are characterized by brightly coloured nineteenth-century Dutch and Georgian terraces – an image that has become a bit of a tour-brochure cliché – which conceal a network of alleyways that are the arteries of its **Muslim community**. The Bo-Kaap harbours its own strong identity, made all the more unique by the destruction of District Six, with which it had much in common. A particular dialect of Afrikaans is spoken here, although it is steadily being eroded by English.

Bo-Kaap residents descend from slaves brought over by the Dutch in the sixteenth and seventeenth centuries. They were known collectively as "**Cape Malays**", still heard today, even though it's a misnomer: most originated from Africa, India, Madagascar and Sri Lanka, with fewer than one percent actually from what's now Malaysia.

SLAVERY AND SALVATION

The **South African Missionary Society** was founded in 1799 by the Reverend Vos, who was alarmed that many slaveholders neglected the religious education of their property. The owners believed that once their slaves were baptized, their emancipation became obligatory – a misunderstanding of the law, which merely stated that Christian slaves couldn't be sold. Vos, himself a slaveholder, saw proselytization to those in bondage as a Christian duty, and even successfully campaigned to end the prohibition against selling Christian slaves, which he believed was "a great obstacle in this country to the progress of Christianity", because it encouraged owners to avoid baptizing their human possessions.

1

EXPLORING THE BO-KAAP

The easiest way to get to the Bo-Kaap is by foot along Wale Street, which trails up from the south end of Adderley Street and across Buitengragt, to become the main drag of the Bo-Kaap. There's a deceptively quaint feel to the area: apart from Wale and Rose streets, this is not really a place to explore alone.

Joining one of the **tours** that take in the museum and walk you around the district is the best way to explore. The most reliable (and cheapest, at R150 including the museum entrance fee) is run by Bo-Kaap Guided Tours (☎ 021 422 1554 or ☎ 082 423 6932, ✉ shireen.narkedien @gmail.com). It lasts two hours and is operated by residents of the area, whose knowledge goes beyond the standard tour-guide script. The same outfit also offers a similar tour for R300 that culminates at the house of a Bo-Kaap resident for lunch, and where you get to watch the Cape Muslim meal being prepared and cooked. For this, you need to book at least two days in advance.

Bo-Kaap Museum

71 Wale St • Mon–Sat 10am–5pm • R10 • ⓦ iziko.org.za/bokaap

If you're exploring the Bo-Kaap on your own, a good place to head is the **Bo-Kaap Museum**, near the Buitengragt end. It consists mainly of the family house and possessions of Abu Bakr Effendi, a nineteenth-century religious leader brought out from Turkey by the British in 1862 as a mediator between feuding Muslim factions. He became an important member of the community, founded an Arabic school and wrote a book in the local vernacular – now regarded as possibly the first book to be published in what can be recognized as Afrikaans. The museum also has exhibits exploring the local brand of Islam, which has its own unique traditions and nearly two dozen *kramats* (shrines) dotted about the peninsula.

Auwal

Dorp St

The **Auwal** was South Africa's first official mosque, founded in 1797 by the highly influential Imam Abdullah ibn Qadi Abd al-Salam (commonly known as Tuan Guru or Master Teacher), a Moluccan prince and Muslim activist who was exiled to Robben Island in 1780 for opposing Dutch rule in the Indies. While on the island he transcribed the Koran from memory and wrote several important Islamic commentaries, which provided a basis for the religion at the Cape for almost a century. On being released in 1792, he began offering religious instruction from his house in Dorp Street, before founding the Auwal nearby. Ten more mosques, whose minarets spice up the quarter's skyline, now serve the Bo-Kaap's ten thousand residents.

Greenmarket Square

Turning east from Long Street into Shortmarket Street, you'll skim the edge of **Greenmarket Square**, which is worth a little exploration to take in the cobbled streets, coffee shops and grand buildings. As its name implies, the square started as a vegetable market, though it spent many ignominious years as a car park. Human life has returned, and it's now home to a flea market, selling crafts, jewellery and hippie clobber. This is also one of the best places in Cape Town to buy from Congolese and Zimbabwean traders, selling masks and malachite carvings, and you'll find plenty of souvenirs and presents to take home.

Michaelis Collection

Old Town House, Greenmarket Square • Mon–Fri 10am–5pm, Sat 10am–4pm • Free • ☎ 021 481 3933, ⓦ iziko.org.za/michaelis

On the western side are the solid limewashed walls and small shuttered windows of the **Old Town House,** entered from Longmarket Street. Built in the mid-1700s, this beautiful example of Cape Dutch architecture, with a fine interior, has seen duty as a

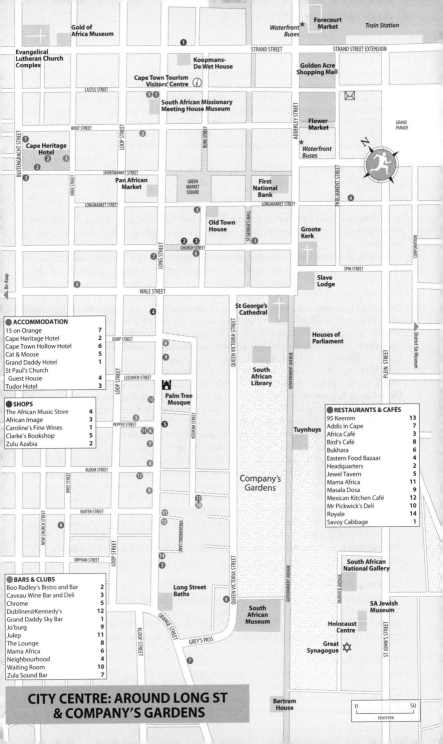

Gold of Africa Museum

Evangelical Lutheran Church Complex

Koopmans-De Wet House

Cape Town Tourism Visitors' Centre (i)

South African Missionary Meeting House Museum

Waterfront Buses

Forecourt Market

Train Station

STRAND STREET

STRAND STREET EXTENSION

Golden Acre Shopping Mall

CASTLE STREET

HOUT STREET

Cape Heritage Hotel

BUITENGRACHT STREET

LOOP STREET

BREE STREET

BURG STREET

ADDERLEY STREET

Flower Market

GRAND PARADE

Waterfront Buses

N

SHORTMARKET STREET

Pan African Market

GREEN MARKET SQUARE

First National Bank

PARLIAMENT STREET

CORPORATION

LONGMARKET STREET

LONGMARKET STREET

Old Town House

Groote Kerk

LONG STREET

CHURCH STREET

ST GEORGE'S MALL

SPIN STREET

Slave Lodge

Bo-Kaap

WALE STREET

St George's Cathedral

District Six Museum

● **ACCOMMODATION**
15 on Orange	7
Cape Heritage Hotel	2
Cape Town Hollow Hotel	6
Cat & Moose	5
Grand Daddy Hotel	1
St Paul's Church Guest House	4
Tudor Hotel	3

Houses of Parliament

QUEEN VICTORIA STREET

DORP STREET

LEEUWEN STREET

GOVERNMENT AVENUE

South African Library

PLEIN STREET

● **SHOPS**
The African Music Store	4
African Image	3
Caroline's Fine Wines	1
Clarke's Bookshop	5
Zulu Azabia	2

Palm Tree Mosque

PEPPER STREET

KEEROM STREET

Tuynhuys

BLOEM STREET

BUITEN STREET

BREE STREET

NEW CHURCH STREET

Company's Gardens

● **RESTAURANTS & CAFÉS**
95 Keerom	13
Addis in Cape	7
Africa Café	3
Bird's Café	8
Bukhara	6
Eastern Food Bazaar	4
Headquarters	2
Jewel Tavern	5
Mama Africa	11
Masala Dosa	9
Mexican Kitchen Café	12
Mr Pickwick's Deli	10
Royale	14
Savoy Cabbage	1

ORPHAN STREET

LOOP STREET

South African National Gallery

PADDOCK AVENUE

SA Jewish Museum

ST JOHN'S STREET

● **BARS & CLUBS**
Boo Radley's Bistro and Bar	2
Caveau Wine Bar and Deli	3
Chrome	5
Dubliner@Kennedy's	12
Grand Daddy Sky Bar	1
Jo'burg	9
Julep	11
The Lounge	8
Mama Africa	6
Neighbourhood	4
Waiting Room	10
Zula Sound Bar	7

Long Street Baths

KLOOF STREET

ORANGE STREET

GREY'S PASS

South African Museum

QUEEN VICTORIA STREET

Holocaust Centre

Great Synagogue

Bertram House

CITY CENTRE: AROUND LONG ST & COMPANY'S GARDENS

0   50
metres

1

CHANGING TIMES

A small Muslim shantytown, tucked away next to the old quarry below the cemetery, brings the immediacy of South Africa's housing crisis right to the edge of the city centre. Modern, low-cost developments, looking down from the heights of **Signal Hill** onto the photogenic Bo-Kaap townscape, have helped alleviate the community's **housing shortage**, but have added nothing to the architectural charm of the protected historic core bounded by Dorp and Strand streets, and Buitengragt and Pentz streets. Furthermore, many Bo-Kaap residents, tempted by the high prices their cottages can fetch, have sold them to outsiders who value the central location and picturesque quality of the area, a process which is seen to be diluting the Muslim lifestyle in the area. The closing of a landmark **Halal butchery** is another clear sign, as are the establishment of several guesthouses and a couple of cafés in Rose Street.

---

guardhouse, a police station and Cape Town's city hall. Today it houses the **Michaelis Collection** of minor but interesting seventeenth-century Dutch and Flemish landscape paintings.

The seventeenth century was one of great prosperity for the Netherlands and has been referred to as the Dutch "Golden Age", during which the Netherlands threw off the yoke of its Spanish colonizers and sailed forth to establish colonies of its own in the East Indies and, of course, at the Cape. The wealth that trade brought to the Netherlands stimulated the development of the arts, with paintings reflecting the values and experience of Dutch Calvinists. A notable example is **Frans Hals**' *Portrait of a Woman*, hanging in the upstairs gallery. Executed in shades of brown, relieved only by the merest hint of red, it reflects the Calvinist aversion to ostentation. The sitter for the picture, completed in 1644, would have been a contemporary of the settlers who arrived at the Cape some eight years later. Less dour and showing off the wealth of a middle-class family is the beautiful *Couple with Two Children in a Park*, painted by **Dirck Dirckz Santvoort** in the late 1630s, in which the artist displays a remarkable facility for portraying sensuous fabrics, which glow with reflected light; you can almost feel the texture of the lace trimming.

Other paintings, most of them quite sombre, depict mythological scenes, church interiors, still lifes, landscapes and seascapes, the latter being very close to the seventeenth-century Dutch heart, often illustrating vessels belonging to the Dutch East India Company or the drama of rough seas encountered by trade ships. A tiny **print room** on the ground floor has a small selection of works by Daumier, Gillray and Cruikshank, as well as one of **Goya**'s most famous works, *El Sueño de la Razón Produce Monstruos* (The Sleep of Reason Produces Monsters).

Small visiting exhibitions also find space here, and there are regular evening classical concerts in the Frans Hals room; the web lists forthcoming events. **Alfresco lunches** in the courtyard *Ivy Garden Restaurant* are a recommended antidote to the bustle of the square.

St George's Mall

Heading east from the square, you come to **St George's Mall**, a pedestrianized road that runs northeast from Wale Street to Thibault Square, near the train station. Coffee shops, snack bars and lots of street traders and buskers make this a more pleasant route between the station and the Company's Gardens than Adderley Street.

St George's Cathedral

5 Wale St

At the southern end of the mall, at Queen Victoria and Wale streets, **St George's Cathedral** is as interesting for its history as for its Herbert Baker Victorian Gothic design; on September 7, 1986, **Desmond Tutu** hammered on its doors symbolically

1

demanding to be enthroned as South Africa's first black archbishop. Three years later, he heralded the last days of apartheid by leading thirty thousand people from the cathedral to the City Hall, where he coined his now famous slogan for the new order: "We are the rainbow people!" he told the crowd, "We are the new people of South Africa!"

Church Street

Church Street (which crosses the mall towards its southern end) and its surrounding area abound with antique dealers, and on the pedestrianized section (where it is crossed by Burg St), you'll find an informal antiques market. Prices are competitive and you may pick up unusual pieces of jewellery, bric-a-brac, Africana and even old sheet music.

Government Avenue

A stroll down **Government Avenue**, the southwest extension of Adderley Street, makes for one of the most serene walks in central Cape Town. This oak-lined, pedestrianized boulevard runs past the rear of Parliament through the Gardens, and its benches are frequently occupied by snoring *bergies* (tramps).

The South African Library

5 Queen Victoria St • Mon, Tues, Thurs & Fri 9am–6pm, Wed 10am–5pm • Free

Looming on your right as you enter the northeastern end of Government Avenue, the **South African Library** houses one of the country's best collections of antiquarian historical and natural history books, covering southern Africa. Built with the revenue from a tax on wine, it opened in 1822 as one of the first free libraries in the world.

Company's Gardens

Stretching from here to the South African Museum, the **Company's Gardens** were the *raison d'être* for the Dutch settlement at the Cape. Established in 1652 to supply fresh greens to Dutch East India Company ships travelling between the Netherlands and the East, the gardens were initially worked by imported slave labour. This proved too expensive, as the slaves had to be shipped in, fed and housed, so the Company opted for outsourcing: it phased out its farming and granted land to free burghers, from whom it bought fresh produce. At the end of the seventeenth century, the gardens were turned over to botanical horticulture for Cape Town's growing colonial elite. Ponds, lawns, landscaping and a crisscross web of oak-shaded walkways were introduced. It was during a stroll in these gardens that **Cecil Rhodes** (a statue of whom you'll find here) first plotted the invasion of Matabeleland and Mashonaland (which together became Rhodesia and subsequently Zimbabwe). He also introduced an army of small, furry colonizers to the gardens – North American grey squirrels. Today the gardens are full of local plants, the result of long-standing European interest in Cape botany; experts have been sailing out since the seventeenth century to classify and name specimens. The gardens are still a pleasant place to meander, and feature a delightful outdoor café, that serves burgers, toasted sandwiches and the like, under massive trees.

De Tuynhuys

Continuing along Government Avenue from the South African Library, past the rear of Parliament, you can peer through an iron gate to see the grand buildings and tended flowerbeds of **De Tuynhuys**, the office (but not residence) of the president.

Under the governorship of **Lord Charles Somerset** (1814–26), an official process of Anglicization at the Cape included the enforcement of English as the sole language in the courts, but equally important was his private obsession with architecture, which saw the demolition of the two Dutch wings of **De Tuynhuys** in Government Avenue. Imposing contemporary English taste, Somerset reinvented the entire garden frontage with a Colonial Regency facade, characterized by a veranda sheltering under an elegantly curving canopy, supported on slender iron columns.

1

The South African National Gallery

Government Ave, Company's Gardens • Tues–Sun 10am–5pm • R15 • ⓦ iziko.org.za/sang

At the point where tiny Gallery Lane joins Government Avenue, the **South African National Gallery** is an essential port of call for anyone interested in the local art scene, and includes a small but excellent permanent collection of contemporary South African art. Displays change every three months as the number of items far exceeds the capacity of the exhibition space, but one of the pieces that regularly makes an appearance is **Jane Alexander**'s powerfully ghoulish plaster, bone and horn sculpture, *The Butcher Boys* (1985–86), created at the height of apartheid repression. It features three life-size figures with distorted faces that exude a chilling passivity, expressing the artist's interest in the way violence is conveyed through the human figure. Alexander's work is representative of "**resistance art**", which exploded in the 1980s, broadly as a response to the growing repression of apartheid. Resistance art was inspired by the idea that artists had a responsibility to engage politically; it spanned a wide range of subject matter, styles and media. **Paul Stopforth**'s powerful graphite-and-wax triptych, *The Interrogators* (1979), featuring larger-than-life-size portraits of three notorious security policemen, is a work of monumental hyperrealism.

Many other artists, unsurprisingly for a culturally diverse country, aren't easily categorized; while works have tended to borrow from Western traditions, their themes and execution are uniquely South African. The late **John Muafangejo** employed biblical imagery in works such as *The Pregnant Maria* (undated), producing highly stylized, almost naive black-and-white linocuts, while in *Challenges Facing the New South Africa* (1990), **Willie Bester** used paint and found shantytown objects to depict the melting pot of the Cape Town squatter camps.

Since the 1990s, and especially in the post-apartheid period, the gallery has engaged in a process of redefining what constitutes contemporary **indigenous art** and has embarked on an acquisitions policy that "acknowledges and celebrates the expressive cultures of the African continent, particularly its southern regions". Material that would previously have been treated as ethnographic, such as a major **bead collection** as well as carvings and **craft objects**, is now finding a place alongside oil paintings and sculptures.

The only permanent collection consists of minor works by British artists, including George Romney, Thomas Gainsborough, Joshua Reynolds and some Pre-Raphaelites. The gallery has a **café** serving light lunches, snacks, coffees and cakes, as well as an excellent shop.

The South African Jewish Museum

Next to the National Gallery but accessed from 88 Hatfield St • Sun–Thurs 10am–5pm, Fri 10am–2pm • R50 • ⓦ sajewishmuseum.co.za

The **South African Jewish Museum** is partially housed in South Africa's first synagogue, built in 1863. One of Cape Town's most ambitious permanent exhibitions, it tells the story of South African Jewry from its beginnings over 150 years ago to the present – a narrative which starts in the Old Synagogue from which visitors cross, via a gangplank, to the upper level of a two-storey building, symbolically re-enacting the arrival by boat of the first Jewish immigrants at Table Bay harbour in the 1840s. Multimedia interactive displays, models and Judaica artefacts explore Judaism in South Africa, drawing parallels between Judaism and the ritual practices and beliefs of South Africa's other communities. The **basement** level houses a walk-through reconstruction of a Lithuanian *shtetl* or village (most South African Jews have their nineteenth-century roots in Lithuania). A restaurant, shop and auditorium are also housed in the museum complex.

Cape Town Holocaust Centre

88 Hatfield St • Daily 10am–5pm, Fri till 1pm • Free • ⓦ cbolocaust.co.za

Opened in 1999, the **Holocaust Exhibition** is one of the most moving and brilliantly executed museums in Cape Town. Housed upstairs in the Holocaust Centre (in the same complex as the Jewish Museum), it resonates sharply in a country that only recently emerged from an era of racial oppression – a connection that the exhibition makes explicitly.

Exhibits trace the history of anti-Semitism in Europe, culminating with the Nazis' Final Solution; they also look at South Africa's Greyshirts, who were motivated by Nazi propaganda during the 1930s and were later absorbed into the National Party. To conclude, a 20-minute video tells the story of survivors who eventually settled in Cape Town.

The Great Synagogue

The **Great Synagogue** next door is one of Cape Town's outstanding religious buildings. Designed by the Scottish architects Parker & Forsyth and completed in 1905, it features an impressive dome and two soaring towers after the style of central European Baroque churches. To see the arched interior and the alcove decorated with gilt mosaics, you need to ask at the Holocaust Centre, and may be asked to provide some form of identification.

The South African Museum

25 Queen Victoria St • Daily 10am–5pm • R15 • ⓦ iziko.org.za/sam

The nation's premier museum of natural history and human sciences, the **South African Museum and Planetarium**, west of Government Avenue, is notable for its **ethnographic galleries** which contain some good displays on the traditional arts and crafts of several African groups, some exceptional examples of rock art (entire chunks of caves in the display cases), and casts of the stone birds found at the archeological site of Great Zimbabwe, in southeastern Zimbabwe. Upstairs, the **natural history galleries** display mounted mammals, dioramas of prehistoric Karoo reptiles and Table Mountain flora and fauna. The highlight is the four-storey "whale well", in which a collection of beautiful whale skeletons hang like massive mobiles, accompanied by the eerie strains of their song.

Planetarium

25 Queen Victoria St • Shows daily 11am–3pm, Tues till 8pm • Closed first Mon of month outside school holidays • R20 • ⓦ iziko.org.za/planetarium

The attached **planetarium** is recommended if you want to see the constellations of the southern hemisphere, with an informed commentary. There's also a changing programme of shows covering topics such as San sky myths, with some programmes geared specially for kids. Leaflets at the museum provide a list of forthcoming attractions, and you can buy a monthly chart of the current night sky.

Bertram House

Mon & Fri 10am–5pm • Donation • ⓦ iziko.org.za/bertram

At the southernmost end of Government Avenue you'll come upon **Bertram House**, whose beautiful two-storey brick facade looks out across a fragrant herb garden. Built in the 1840s, the museum is significant as the only surviving brick Georgian-style house in Cape Town, and displays typical furniture and objects of a well-to-do colonial British family in the first half of the nineteenth century.

The site was bought in 1839 by John Barker, a Yorkshire attorney who came to the Cape in 1823. His wife, Ann Bertram Findlay, who died in 1838, was responsible for building it, and Barker bestowed her middle name on the house. Declared a National Monument in 1962, Bertram House was extensively restored in the 1980s (and again in 2010): imported face brick and Welsh slate were used to re-create the original facade, while the interior walls were redecorated in their earlier dark green and ochre, based on the evidence of paint scrapings. The reception rooms are decorated in the Regency style, while the porcelain is predominantly nineteenth-century English, although there are also some very fine Chinese pieces.

1

Houses of Parliament
Parliament St

South Africa's **Houses of Parliament**, east of Government Avenue, are a complex of interlinking buildings, with labyrinthine corridors connecting hundreds of offices, debating chambers and miscellaneous other rooms. Many of these are relics of the 1980s reformist phase of apartheid when, in the interests of racial segregation, there were three distinct legislative complexes sited here to cater to different "races".

The original wing, completed in 1885, is an imposing Victorian Neoclassical building which first served as the legislative assembly of the Cape Colony. After the Boer republics and British colonies amalgamated in 1910, it became the parliament of the Union of South Africa. This is the old parliament, where over seven decades of repressive legislation, including apartheid laws, were passed. It's also where **Hendrik Verwoerd**, the arch-theorist of apartheid, met his bloody end at the hand of Dimitri Tsafendas, a parliamentary messenger who inexplicably went off the rails, committing the act because, as he told police, "a tapeworm ordered me to do it". Due to his mental state, the assassin escaped the gallows to outlive apartheid – albeit in an institution. Verwoerd's portrait, depicting him as a man of vision and *gravitas*, used to hang over the main entrance to the dining room. In 1996 it was removed "for cleaning", along with paintings of generations of white parliamentarians.

The National Assembly
Tours Mon–Fri hourly 9am–noon • Free, book one week in advance • ☎ 021 403 2001, ⓦ parliament.gov.za

The new chamber was built in 1983 as part of the **tricameral parliament**, P.W. Botha's attempt to avert majority rule by trying to co-opt Indians and coloureds – but in their own separate debating chambers. The "tricameral" chamber, where the three non-African "races" on occasions met together, is now the **National Assembly**, where you can watch sessions of parliament. One-hour **tours** take in the old and new debating chambers, the library and museum. Take some kind of identification with you to the Plein Street entrance, opposite the Receiver of Revenue. This is also the place to get day tickets to the **debating sessions** – the most interesting of which is question time (Wed from 3pm), when you can hear ministers being quizzed by MPs.

Rust en Vreugd
78 Buitenkant St • Mon–Fri 10am–5pm • Donation • ⓦ iziko.org.za/rustvreugd

The most beautiful of Cape Town's house museums, **Rust en Vreugd**, a couple of blocks east of the Gardens, was built in 1778 for Willem Cornelis Boers, the colony's Fiscal (a powerful position akin to the police chief, public prosecutor and collector of taxes rolled into one), who was forced to resign in the 1780s following allegations of wheeler-dealing and extortion. Under the British occupation, it was the residence of Lord Charles Somerset during his governorship (1814–26).

The house was once surrounded by countryside, but now stands along a congested route that brushes past the edge of the central business district. Designed by architect Louis Michel Thibault and sculptor Anton Anreith, the two-storey facade features a pair of stacked balconies, the lower one forming a stunning portico fronted by four Corinthian columns carved from teak. The front door, framed by teak pilasters, is a real work of art, rated by architectural historian de Bosdari as "certainly the finest door at the Cape". Above the door, the fanlight is executed in elaborate Baroque style.

Inside, the William Fehr Collection of artworks on paper occupies two ground-floor rooms and includes illustrations by important documentarists such as **Thomas Baines**, who is represented by hand-coloured lithographs and a series of watercolours recording a nineteenth-century expedition up Table Mountain. **Thomas Bowler**, another prolific recorder of Cape scenes, painted his striking landscape of Cape Point from the sea in 1864, showing dolphins frolicking in the foreground.

The property is defined by a boundary of bay trees. A tranquil escape from the busy street, the **garden** is a reconstruction of the original eighteenth-century semi-formal one, laid out with herbaceous hedges and gravel walkways, and features a lawn with a gazebo.

Castle of Good Hope

Buitenkant and Darling sts • Daily 9am–4pm • Free tours daily 11am, noon & 2pm • R28 • ⓦ castleofgoodhope.co.za

From the outside, South Africa's oldest official building looks somewhat miserable, and its position behind the train station and city-bus terminal, does nothing to dispel this. Nevertheless the **Castle of Good Hope** is well worth the entrance fee; inside, a meticulous ten-year restoration has returned the decor to the British Regency style introduced in 1798. It also has some fine contemporary cultural/political **exhibitions** – check the website for details.

Tours of the rest of the castle cover the main features, including the prison cells and dungeons, with their centuries-old graffiti painstakingly carved by prisoners. In the elegant courtyard there is a very pleasant **tea shop**, with Table Mountain looming over the west wall. The Castle is also home to the Defence Force's Western Province Command; you may see armed soldiers marching through the courtyard.

The William Fehr Collection

Elaborately carved double doors at the rear of the *kat* balcony open onto four interlocking rooms that were the heart of VOC government at the Cape and which now house the bulk of the **William Fehr Collection**, one of the country's most important exhibits of decorative arts. The contents, acquired by businessman William Fehr from the 1920s, were sold and donated to the government in the 1950s and 1960s and continue to be displayed informally as Fehr preferred. The galleries are filled with items found in middle-class Cape households from the seventeenth to nineteenth centuries, with some fine examples of elegantly simple Cape furniture from the eighteenth century. Early colonial views of Table Bay appear in a number of paintings, including one by Aernot Smit that shows the Castle in the seventeenth century, right on the shoreline. Among the fascinating items of antique oriental ceramics are a blue-and-white Japanese porcelain plate from around 1660, displaying the VOC monogram, and a beautiful polychrome plate from China dating to about

---

EUROPE'S TOEHOLD AT AFRICA'S FOOT

Finished in 1679, complete with the essentials of a moat and torture chamber, the Castle replaced Van Riebeeck's earlier mud and timber fort, which stood on the site of the Grand Parade. The Castle was built along seventeenth-century European principles of fortification, comprising strong bastions from which the outside walls could be protected by crossfire. For 150 years, the Castle remained the symbolic heart of the Cape administration, and the centre of social and economic life, but in the late nineteenth century – when the colony had expanded far beyond its walls – there were at least three attempts by the authorities to demolish it, as it was regarded as a white elephant.

The original, seaward entrance had to be moved to its present position facing landward, because the spring tide sometimes came crashing in – a remarkable thought given how far aground it is now thanks to land reclamation. The **entrance gate** displays the coat of arms of the United Netherlands and those of the six Dutch cities in which the VOC chambers were situated. Still hanging from its original wooden beams in the tower above the entrance is the **bell**, cast in 1697 by Claude Fremy in Amsterdam; it was used variously as an alarm signal and as a summons to residents to receive pronouncements.

Inside the walls, the courtyard is sliced in half by a defensive twelve-metre-high structure, or *kat*, from which cannons could be fired. The exquisite ceremonial **kat balcony** provides entry to the *kat* and was where ordinances were pronounced; it's flanked by two shallow curving staircases, and has a portico supported on six fluted Ionic columns carved from solid teak.

1750, which depicts a fleet of Company ships in Table Bay against the backdrop of a very oriental-looking Table Mountain.

The Grand Parade to The City Hall

To the northwest of the Castle, the **Grand Parade** is a large open area where the residents of District Six used to come to trade. On Wednesdays and Saturdays it still transforms itself into a **market**, where you can buy a whole array of bargains ranging from used clothes to spicy food.

The Grand Parade appeared on TV screens throughout the world on February 11, 1990, when 100,000 people gathered to hear **Nelson Mandela** make his first speech after being released from prison, from the balcony of the **City Hall**. A slightly fussy Edwardian building dressed in Bath stone, the City Hall manages, despite its drab surroundings, to look impressive against Table Mountain. For the 2010 FIFA World Cup, the Grand Parade came into prominence again as the site of the **Fan Park** with 64 football matches broadcast live from a number of screens.

District Six

South of the Castle, in the shadow of Devil's Peak, is a vacant lot shown on maps as the suburb of **Zonnebloem**. Before being demolished by the apartheid authorities, it was an inner-city slum known as **District Six**, an impoverished but lively community of 55,000 predominantly coloured people. Once regarded as the soul of Cape Town, the district harboured a rich – and much mythologized – cultural life in its narrow alleys and crowded tenements: along the cobbled streets, hawkers rubbed shoulders with prostitutes, gangsters, drunks and gamblers, while craftsmen plied their trade in small workshops. This was a fertile place of the South African imagination, inspiring novels, poems, jazz and the blockbuster *District Six: The Musical*, by David Kramer, which in the late 1980s played to packed houses and spawned a series of hits.

In 1966, apartheid ideologues declared District Six a **White Group Area** and the bulldozers moved in, taking fifteen years to drive its presence from the skyline, leaving only the mosques and churches. But, in the wake of the demolition gangs, international and domestic outcry was so great that the area was never developed apart from a few luxury townhouses on its fringes and the hefty **Cape Technikon**, a college that now occupies nearly a quarter of the former suburb. After years of negotiation, the original residents are moving back under a scheme to develop low-cost housing in the district.

The District Six Museum

25a Buitenkant St • Mon 9am–2pm, Tues–Sat 9am–4pm • R20 • Ⓦ districtsix.co.za

Few places in Cape Town speak more eloquently of the effect of apartheid on the day-to-day lives of ordinary people than the compelling **District Six Museum**. On the northern boundary of District Six, on the corner of Buitenkant and Albertus streets, the museum occupies the former **Central Methodist Mission Church**, which offered solidarity and ministry to the victims of forced removals right up to the 1980s, and became a venue for anti-apartheid gatherings. Today, it houses a series of fascinating displays that include everyday household items and tools of trades, such as hairdressing implements, as well as documentary photographs, which evoke the lives of the individuals who once lived here. Occupying most of the floor is a huge map of District Six as it was, annotated by former residents, who describe their memories, reflections and incidents associated with places and buildings that no longer exist. There's also an almost complete collection of original street signs, secretly retrieved at the time of demolition by the man entrusted with dumping them into Table Bay. Their **coffee shop** does snacks, including traditional, syrupy *koeksisters*.

1

Strand Street

A major artery from the N2 freeway to the central business district, **Strand Street** neatly separates the Upper from the Lower city centre. Between the mid-eighteenth and mid-nineteenth centuries, Strand Street was one of the most fashionable streets in Cape Town because of its proximity to the shore – it used to run along the beachfront. Its former cachet is now only discernible from the handful of quietly elegant National Monuments left standing amid the roar of traffic.

Gold of Africa Museum

96 Strand St, just off Buitengragt • Mon–Sat 9.30am–5pm • R30 • ⓦ goldofafrica.com

Since the discovery of gold near Johannesburg in the late nineteenth century, South Africa has been closely associated in the Western mind with the precious metal and the riches it represents. However, the outstanding **Gold of Africa Museum** focuses on a completely different side to gold – the exquisite artworks crafted by nineteenth- and twentieth-century African goldsmiths from Mali, Senegal, Ghana and the Côte d'Ivoire. Arguably the most important such collection in the world, acquired in 2001 from the Barbier-Mueller Museum in Geneva, it traces Africa's ancient gold routes, and includes several hundred beautiful items – precious masks, crocodiles, birds, a gold crown and human figures; the highlight is the sculpted **Golden Lion** from Ghana that is the symbol of the museum. There's also a small auditorium with a continuous film show; a **restaurant** that serves pan-African cuisine with Malian puppets performing between courses; a **studio** where goldsmiths practise their art and where you can learn smithing; and a **shop** selling postcards, gold leaf and beautiful little souvenirs.

Evangelical Lutheran Church

Corner of Buitengragt and Strand sts • Mon, Wed & Fri 9am–noon • Free

Next door to the Gold of Africa Museum stands the **Evangelical Lutheran Church**, converted by Anton Anreith in 1785 from a barn. The establishment of a Lutheran church in Cape Town struck a significant blow against the extreme **religious intolerance** that pervaded under VOC rule. Before 1771, when permission was granted to Lutherans to establish their own congregation, Protestantism was the only form of worship allowed and the Dutch Reformed Church held an absolute monopoly over saving people's souls. The Lutheran Church's congregation was dominated by Germans, who at the time constituted 28 percent of the colony's free burgher population.

The facade of the Evangelical Lutheran Church includes Classical details such as a broken pediment perforated by the clock tower, as well as Gothic features such as arched windows. Inside, the magnificent **pulpit**, supported on two life-size Herculean figures, is one of Anreith's masterpieces; the white swan perched on the canopy is a symbol of Lutheranism.

Koopmans-De Wet House

35 Strand St • Mon–Fri 10am–5pm • R15 • ⓦ iziko.org.za/koopmans

Sandwiched between two office blocks close to Cape Town Tourism, **Koopmans-De Wet House** is an outstanding eighteenth-century pedimented Neoclassical townhouse and museum, accommodating a very fine collection of antique furniture and rare porcelain. An inexpensive guide booklet gives interesting contextual background to the house and its history, while a separate brochure describes items in the collection: both are available at the entrance.

The earliest sections of the house were built in 1701 by **Reyner Smedinga**, a well-to-do goldsmith who imported the building materials from Holland. The house changed hands more than a dozen times over the following two centuries, with minor additions made in the 1760s and a second storey added between 1774 and 1790. In 1806, it came into the hands of the De Wet family, eventually becoming the home of **Marie Koopmans-De Wet** (1834–1906), a prominent figure on the Cape social and political circuit.

The house represents a fine synthesis of Dutch elements (sash windows and large entrance doors) with the demands of local conditions; the huge rooms, lofty ceilings and shuttered windows reflect the high summer temperatures, while the front *stoep* has plastered masonry seats at each end. The **lantern** in the fanlight of the entrance to the house was a feature of all Cape Town houses in the eighteenth and early nineteenth centuries, its purpose to shine light onto the street and thus hinder slaves from gathering at night to plot.

The Lower City Centre

In the mid-nineteenth century, the city's middle classes viewed the **Lower City Centre** and its low-life activities with a mixture of alarm and excitement – a tension that remains today. **Lower Long Street** divides the area just inland from the docklands into two. To the east is the **Foreshore**, an ugly post-World War II wasteland of grey corporate architecture, among which is the **Artscape Centre**, Cape Town's premier arts complex. The Foreshore is at last being redeveloped, its centrepiece being the successful **Cape Town International Convention Centre**, linked by a canal and pedestrian routes with the Waterfront.

The Foreshore

The Foreshore, an area of reclaimed land northeast of Strand Street, stretching to the docks, and east of Lower Long Street, was developed in the late 1940s in a spirit of modernism – large highly planned urban spaces – that was sweeping the world. It was intended to turn Cape Town's harbour into a symbolic gateway to Africa; instead, it turned out as a series of large concrete boxes surrounded by acres of windswept tarmac car parks. The opening in 2004 of the prestigious International Convention Centre (and its proximity to some high-rise hotels and parking garages) has opened up the area, but there is no street life at all, and no reason to explore.

Heerengracht

Heerengracht, a truncated two-lane carriageway running from Adderley Street to the harbour, has massive roundabouts at each end solemnly guarded by statues of Jan van Riebeeck and Bartholomeu Dias. It was meant to be the ceremonial axis through this grand scheme, joining the city to the sea, but it never quite makes it to the water, coming to a disappointing standstill at the dock perimeter fence, before bearing east under the dismal shadow of the N1 and N2 flyovers.

Artscape Complex

D.F. Malan St just east of Heerengracht • Ⓦ artscape.co.za

The only building worth visiting here – but only when there's something on – is the **Artscape Complex**, Cape Town's monumental performance venue with its huge theatre, an opera house and the compact Arena Theatre. Artscape is the home of Cape Town Opera, which features the best of South Africa's singers, and Jazzart, the Western Cape's longest-established contemporary dance company.

Duncan Dock

North of the Foreshore, **Duncan Dock** is Cape Town's working harbour. Work started on the dock in 1938, swallowing the city beachfronts at Woodstock and Paarden Island to cater for the growing supertanker traffic that was outstripping the capacity of the Victoria and Alfred Docks. The dock today is a forbidding industrial landscape of large ships and towering cranes cut off from the city by an enormous perimeter fence.

THE V&A WATERFRONT

V&A Waterfront, Robben Island and De Waterkant

The Victoria and Alfred Waterfront, known simply as the Waterfront, is Cape Town's original Victorian harbour, incorporating nineteenth-century buildings, shopping malls, waterside piers and a functioning harbour that all share a magnificent Table Mountain backdrop. Redeveloped in the 1990s, it the city's most fashionable area for shopping, eating and drinking, and incorporates the Nelson Mandela Gateway – the embarkation point for unmissable trips to Robben Island. West of the Foreshore, with the Waterfront to its north, is De Waterkant, a once down-at-heel district that has gentrified at a cracking pace to become Cape Town's self-styled gay quarter and a significant draw for tourists with plentiful accommodation, bars and shops.

GETTING AROUND

V&A WATERFRONT

The Waterfront is one of the easiest points in Cape Town to reach **by public transport**. Arriving by **car**, you'll find yourself well catered for, with several car parks and garages. If you want to leave by **taxi**, there are several ranks dotted about, such as the one on Breakwater Boulevard.

BY BUS

Golden Arrow ⓦ gabs.co.za. Municipal buses leave for the Waterfront from Adderley Street, from outside the train station and from Beach Road in Sea Point.

MyCiTi ☎ 0800 65 64 63, ⓦ www.capetown.gov .za/myciti. Buses currently run from the Gardens at the edge of the City Bowl through the city centre to the Civic Centre and then on to the Waterfront. From mid-2012 nine

are expected to be launched, two of which will serve the Waterfront: #F02 from the Waterfront to Camps Bay via the city centre and Kloof Nek; and #F03 from Sea Point to the City Bowl via the Waterfront and the city centre. Both are expected to run every 10 to 20min during the day.

City Sightseeing ☎ 021 511 6000, ⓦ citysightseeing .co.za. Buses link the Waterfront with a number of major sights in the city centre and on the peninsula.

2

The V&A Waterfront

Throughout the first half of the nineteenth century, arguments raged in Cape Town over the need for a proper dock. The Cape was often known as the **Cape of Storms** because of its vicious weather, which left Table Bay littered with wrecks. Many makeshift attempts were made to improve this including the construction of a lighthouse in 1823, and work was begun on a jetty at the bottom of Bree Street in 1832. Clamour for a harbour grew in the 1850s, with the increase in sea traffic arriving at the Cape, reaching its peak in 1860, when the Lloyds insurance company refused the risk of covering ships dropping anchor in Table Bay.

The British colonial government dragged its heels due to the costs involved, but eventually conceded; on a suitably stormy September day in 1860, at a huge ceremony, the teenage Prince Alfred tipped the first batch of stones into Table Bay to begin the **breakwater**, the westernmost arm of the harbour. Convicts were enlisted to complete the job and in 1869, the dock – consisting of two main basins – was completed, and the sea was allowed to pour in.

Victoria Wharf

Red Shed • Mon–Sat 9am–9pm, Sun 10am–9pm

The shopping focus of the Waterfront is **Victoria Wharf**, an enormous flashy mall on two levels, extending along Quays Five and Six. It's here that most visitors to the Waterfront arrive. The restaurants and cafés on the mall's east side, with their outdoor seating, have fabulous views of Table Mountain across the busy harbour. On the west side of Victoria Wharf and physically linked to it, the rather contrived **Red Shed Craft Workshop** brings together craft workers such as glass-blowers, leatherworkers, township artists and jewellery-makers under one huge roof. Outdoor action centres around **Market Square** and the **Agfa Amphitheatre**, where you can occasionally catch some musical performances (see p.128). Beyond Victoria Wharf is the Pierhead and, further on, the Marina.

Two Oceans Aquarium

Dock Rd • Daily 9.30am–6pm • R96 • ⓦ aquarium.co.za

At the Marina's North Wharf, the **Two Oceans Aquarium** showcases the Cape's unique marine environment, where the warm Indian Ocean mingles with the cold Atlantic. A designated route (which you're not obliged to follow) takes in the nine major galleries in sequence.

The ground floor

The route begins with the **Indian Ocean**, where you'll see tank after tank of psychedelic fish. One of the most beautiful displays features scores of small gossamer jellyfish

V&A WATERFRONT & DE WATERKANT

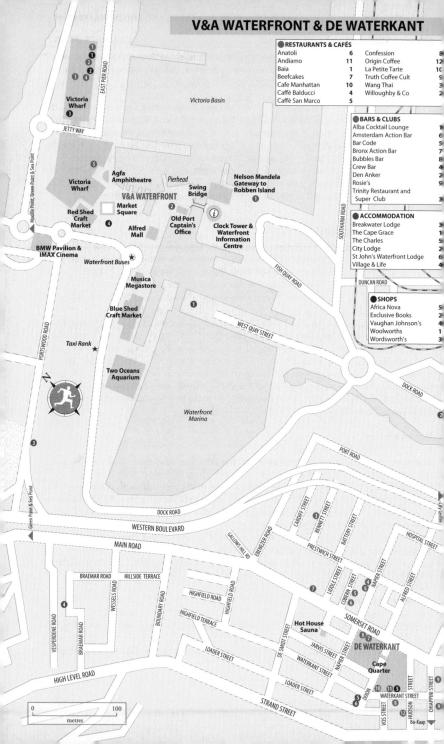

RESTAURANTS & CAFÉS

Anatoli	6	Confession	8
Andiamo	11	Origin Coffee	12
Baia	1	La Petite Tarte	10
Beefcakes	7	Truth Coffee Cult	9
Cafe Manhattan	10	Wang Thai	3
Caffè Balducci	4	Willoughby & Co	2
Caffè San Marco	5		

BARS & CLUBS

Alba Cocktail Lounge	1
Amsterdam Action Bar	6
Bar Code	5
Bronx Action Bar	7
Bubbles Bar	8
Crew Bar	4
Den Anker	2
Rosie's	9
Trinity Restaurant and Super Club	3

ACCOMMODATION

Breakwater Lodge	3
The Cape Grace	1
The Charles	5
City Lodge	2
St John's Waterfront Lodge	6
Village & Life	4

SHOPS

Africa Nova	5
Exclusive Books	2
Vaughan Johnson's	4
Woolworths	1
Wordsworth's	3

Victoria Basin

Victoria Wharf

EAST PIER ROAD

JETTY WAY

Agfa Amphitheatre

Pierhead

Swing Bridge

Nelson Mandela Gateway to Robben Island

Victoria Wharf

V&A WATERFRONT

Market Square

Old Port Captain's Office

Clock Tower & Waterfront Information Centre

SOUTHARM ROAD

Red Shed Craft Market

Alfred Mall

BMW Pavilion & IMAX Cinema

Waterfront Buses

FISH QUAY ROAD

DUNCAN ROAD

Musica Megastore

Blue Shed Craft Market

WEST QUAY STREET

PORTSWOOD ROAD

Taxi Rank

Two Oceans Aquarium

Waterfront Marina

DOCK ROAD

Green Point & Sea Point

Mouille Point, Green Point & Sea Point

PORT ROAD

LILY CENTRE

DOCK ROAD

WESTERN BOULEVARD

CARDIFF STREET

BENNETT STREET

BATTERY STREET

HOSPITAL STREET

MAIN ROAD

PRESTWICH STREET

NAPIER STREET

ALFRED STREET

BRAEMAR ROAD

HILLSIDE TERRACE

EBENEZER ROAD

GALLOWS HILL RD

LIDDLE STREET

COBERN STREET

WESSELS ROAD

BOUNDARY ROAD

HIGHFIELD ROAD

HIGHFIELD ROAD

VESPERDENE ROAD

BRAEMAR ROAD

HIGHFIELD TERRACE

LOADER STREET

DE SMIDT STREET

Hot House Sauna

JARVIS STREET

NAPIER STREET

SOMERSET ROAD

DE WATERKANT

Cape Quarter

HIGH LEVEL ROAD

LOADER STREET

WATERKANT STREET

LOADER STREET

DIXON

VOS STREET

WATERKANT STREET

HUDSON

STRAND STREET

STREET

CHAPPINI STREET

Bo-Kaap

0   100
metres

floating gently in their ultraviolet-lit cylindrical tank like parachutists. To the rear of the ground floor, the **Diversity Hall**, as its name implies, contains an astonishing variety of strange marine creatures, including giant spider crabs, octopuses, sea horses and the deadly devil firefish, whose lacy beauty disguises lethal spines.

The basement

The **basement** houses the **Alpha Activity Centre**, a good place to keep kids occupied, with free organized activities such as puppet shows and face painting, and computers that allow youngsters to explore marine ecology. The centre is combined with the **Diving Animals** display, where you can watch a group of resident Cape fur seals frolicking underwater.

The top floor

The **top floor**, reached via a ramp, accommodates the **Story of Water**, which, in glorious reconstruction, traces the course of a river from its mouth to its source, via a salt marsh and lagoon. Not to everyone's taste, it features a small colony of African penguins (which you can see in their natural habitat at Boulders Beach; see p.102), while captive sea birds fly about the rafters. In the **Kelp Forest** in an adjacent gallery, a dense jungle of giant seaweed sways hypnotically with the rhythmic surge of the water; you can sit in the small amphitheatre and gaze at beautiful shoals of silvery fish shimmering through sunlit sea. From here, a ramp takes you in a gentle downward spiral through the **Predators** exhibit, for many visitors the most compelling attraction of all. A massive tank, open to the ocean, houses some large resident ragged-tooth sharks, which glide past as you walk through a glass underwater tunnel; other species confined here include rays and giant turtles.

Shark feeding

Sun 3pm • Dive R570, gear included • book a day in advance on ☎ 021 418 3823

Among the highlights of the aquarium is the **shark feeding**, when you can watch *raggies* – ragged-tooth sharks – being hand-fed by divers. If you have an Open Water 1 diving qualification, you can actually **dive** in the predators tank.

The Clock Tower

Visitor centre daily 9am–9pm • ☎ 021 405 4500, Ⓦ www.tourismcapetown.co.za

From the Pierhead you can use the **swing bridge** to cross to the Clock Tower Precinct, named after the **Clock Tower**, which houses the small Waterfront Information Centre. Cape Town's finest architectural folly, this odd-looking octagonal structure with Gothic windows, was built as the original Port Captain's office in 1882 and consists of three stacked rooms with a stairwell running through its core. The mirror room on the second floor enabled the Port Captain to survey all the activities of the harbour without leaving his office. Next door to the Clock Tower, the **Clock Tower Centre** is a compact two-storey shopping mall, with the very substantial **Cape Tourism visitor centre**.

Nelson Mandela Gateway

Clock Tower Precinct • Daily 7.30am–5.30pm • Free

The **Nelson Mandela Gateway**, adjacent to the Clock Tower, is the embarkation point for ferries to Robben Island. The two-storey building incorporates a **restaurant** with a great view and a small museum with hi-tech **interactive displays**, featuring the history of Robben Island, the voices of prisoners and resistance songs.

Robben Island

Lying only a few kilometres from the commerce of the Waterfront, flat and windswept **Robben Island** is suffused by a meditative, otherworldly silence. This key site of South Africa's liberation struggle was intended to silence apartheid's domestic critics, but instead became an international focus for opposition to the regime. Measuring six square kilometres and sparsely vegetated by low scrub, it was Nelson Mandela's "home" for nearly two decades.

ESSENTIALS   **ROBBEN ISLAND**

Visiting The catamaran from the Waterfront (daily 9am, 1pm & 3pm) takes 30 to 45min to reach Robben Island, where ex-prisoners and ex-warders work as guides, sharing their experiences. After arrival at the tiny Murray's Bay harbour, you are taken on a bus tour around the island and a tour of the prison.

Tickets Although a number of vendors sell tickets for cruises that may go close to Robben Island, the only ones

that will get you onto it (R200, including voyage, entry and 3hr 30min tour) must be bought from the Nelson Mandela Gateway. Bookings must be made well in advance with a credit card, as the boats are often full, especially around December and January (☎021 413 4233, ⍵robben-island .org.za). Be sure to present your booking reference number and arrive half an hour before departure to collect your ticket.

The bus tour

The bus tour stops off at several historical landmarks, the first of which is the **kramat**, a beautiful shrine built in memory of Tuan Guru, a Muslim cleric from present-day Indonesia who was imprisoned here by the Dutch in the eighteenth century. On his release, he helped to establish Islam among slaves in Cape Town, where it has flourished ever since. The tour also passes a leper graveyard, and male leper church completed to a Sir Herbert Baker design in 1895. Both are quiet reminders that the island was a place of exile for leprosy sufferers up till 1931, when they relocated to Pretoria, leaving the lighthouse keeper and his family the island's only inhabitants.

Robert Sobukwe's house

Robert Sobukwe's house seems to echo with loneliness, and is perhaps the most affecting relic of incarceration on the island. It was here that Sobukwe, leader of the Pan Africanist Congress (a radical offshoot of the ANC), was held in solitary confinement for nine years. He was initially sentenced to three years, but was regarded as so dangerous by the authorities that they passed a special law – the "Sobukwe Clause" – to keep him on Robben Island for a further six years. No other political prisoners were allowed to speak to him, but he would sometimes gesture his solidarity with other sons of the African soil by letting sand trickle through his fingers as they walked past. After his release in 1969, Sobukwe was restricted to Kimberley under house arrest, until his death from cancer in 1978.

The lime quarry

Another stopoff is the **lime quarry** where Nelson Mandela and his fellow inmates spent countless hours of hard labour. The soft, pale stone is extremely bright under the summer sun, as a result of which Mandela and others have in later years suffered eye disorders. As the years passed, the lime quarry became a place of furtive study among the prisoners, with the help of sympathetic warders.

Wildlife spotting

The bus tour also takes in a stretch of coast dotted with shipwrecks and abundant sea birds and waterfowl, including the elegant **sacred ibis**. You may also spot some of a recently expanded population of **antelope**: springbok, eland and bontebok.

The Maximum Security Prison

The **Maximum Security Prison**, a forbidding complex of unadorned H-blocks on the edge of the island, is introduced with a tour through the famous **B-Section**; you'll be guided by a former inmate, after which you're free to wander. B-Section is a small

2

"WE SERVE WITH PRIDE": THE HISTORY OF ROBBEN ISLAND

Nelson Mandela may have been the most famous Robben Island prisoner, but he wasn't the first. In the seventeenth century the island became a place of banishment for those who offended the political order (initially the Dutch, later the British and the Afrikaner Nationalists). The island's first prisoner was the indigenous Khoikhoi leader **Autshumato**, who learnt English in the early seventeenth century and became an emissary of the British. After the Dutch settlement was established, he was jailed on the island by Jan van Riebeeck in 1658. The rest of the seventeenth century saw a succession of East Indies political prisoners and Muslim holy men exiled here for opposing Dutch colonial rule.

During the nineteenth century, the **British** used Robben Island as a dumping ground for deserters, criminals and political prisoners, in much the same way as they used Australia. Captured **Xhosa leaders** who defied the British Empire during the Frontier Wars of the early to mid-nineteenth century were transported by sea from the Eastern to the Western Cape to be imprisoned, and many ended up on Robben Island. In 1846, the island's brief was extended to include a whole range of the **socially marginalized**: criminals and political detainees were now joined by vagrants, prostitutes, lunatics and the chronically ill. All were victim to a regime of brutality and maltreatment, even in hospitals. In the 1890s, a leper colony existed alongside the social outcasts. Lunatics were removed in 1921 and the lepers in 1930. During World War II, the **Defence Force** took over the island to set up defensive guns against a feared Axis invasion, which never came.

Robben Island's greatest era of notoriety began in 1961, when it was taken over by the **Prisons Department**. Prisoners arriving at the island prison were greeted by a slogan on the gate that read: "Welcome to Robben Island: We Serve with Pride." By 1963, when Nelson Mandela arrived, it had become a maximum-security prison. All the warders – but none of the prisoners – were white. Prisoners were only allowed to send and receive one letter every six months, and common-law criminals and political prisoners were housed together until 1971, when they were separated in an attempt to further isolate the politicals. Harsh conditions, including routine beatings and forced hard labour, were exacerbated by geographical location. There's nothing but sea between the island and the South Pole, so icy winds routinely blow in from across the Atlantic – and inmates were made to wear shorts and flimsy jerseys. Like every other prisoner, Mandela slept on a thin mat on the floor (until 1973, when he was given a bed because he was ill) and was kept in a solitary confinement cell, measuring two metres square, for sixteen hours a day.

Amazingly, the prisoners found ways of **protesting**, through hunger strikes, publicizing conditions when possible (by using visits from the International Committee of the Red Cross, for example) and, remarkably, by taking legal action against the prison authority to stop arbitrary punishments. They won improved conditions over the years, and the island also became a university behind bars, where people of different political views and generations met; it was not unknown for prisoners to give academic help to their warders.

The last political prisoners were released from Robben Island in 1991 and the remaining common-law prisoners were transferred to the mainland in 1996. On January 1, 1997, control of Robben Island was transferred from the Department of Correctional Services to the Department of the Arts, Culture, Science and Technology, which established it as a museum. In December 1999 the entire island was declared a **UN World Heritage Site**.

compound full of tiny rooms that has become legendary in South African history; initially a place of defeat for the resistance movement, it ironically came to incubate and concentrate the energies of liberation. **Mandela's cell** has been left exactly as it was, without embellishments or display, but the rest have been left locked and empty.

In the nearby **A-Section**, the "Cell Stories" exhibition skilfully suggests the sparseness of prison life. The tiny isolation cells feature personal artefacts loaned by former prisoners (including a functional saxophone made of found objects), plus boards bearing quotations, recordings and photographs.

Towards the end of the 1980s, cameras were sneaked onto the island, and inmates took snapshots of each other, which have been enlarged to almost life size and mounted as the **Smuggled Camera Exhibition** in the **D-Section** communal cells. The jovial demeanour of the prisoners indicates their realization that the end was within sight; moreover, the warm camaraderie that evidently connects them suggests how people endured so many years of captivity. Another good section of the prison visit is the **Living Legacy** tour in **F-Section**, in which ex-political prisoner guides describe their lives here and answer your questions.

De Waterkant

2

As an atmospheric central neighbourhood in easy striking distance of the city centre, the Waterfront and the Atlantic seaboard, De Waterkant has a lot going for it and is a colourful place to base yourself. Its terraces, which date back to the mid-eighteenth century, line cobbled streets that trawl up the mountainside. The district plays up its assets for all they're worth, with a high number of its houses turned over to guesthouses and self-catering flats. Within easy wandering distance of everything are restaurants, delis, clubs, art dealers, interior design boutiques and a couple of very upmarket shopping malls – one of them the sizeable **Cape Quarter**. With a clutch of **gay-friendly nightclubs and pubs** (see p.143), the area officially just outside De Waterkant, on the east side of **Somerset Road**, which heads from the city centre into Green Point, is known as the **Pink Village** – Cape Town's gay district.

Private Collections
Corner of Waterkant and Hudson sts • Mon–Sat 9am–5.30pm & Sat 8am–1pm

Among De Waterkant's dozens of upmarket arty shops, Private Collections is easy to miss yet is possibly the most extraordinary. A massive warehouse on two levels, it's packed to the rafters with truly amazing wooden architectural pieces, furniture and interior items from all over India, many of them antiques. Even if you're not planning on buying anything, just pop in and prepare to be awed.

Prestwich Memorial
Corner of Buitengragt and Somerset rds • Mon–Fri 7am–6pm, Sat &Sun 8am–2pm • Free

The **Prestwich Memorial**, housed in an elegant modernist structure, accommodates **2500 sets of human bones**, excavated in 2003, of forgotten and marginalized Capetonians – many of them slaves buried in the vicinity in the seventeenth and eighteenth centuries. A collection of interesting interpretation boards provides accounts of burial practices, historic hospitals in the vicinity and, across one wall, a reproduction of a beautiful panorama of Cape Town from the sea painted by Robert Gordon in 1778.

TABLE MOUNTAIN

Table Mountain and the City Bowl Suburbs

The icon that for hundreds of years and from hundreds of kilometres announced Cape Town to seafarers, Table Mountain, dominates the northern end of the peninsula. For visitors today, the 1087-metre flat-topped massif, with dramatic cliffs and eroded gorges rising out of two oceans, is one of the world's great physical symbols, an icon for the Mother City itself. Between the mountain and the CBD lie the City Bowl Suburbs – very desirable residential districts. Given its proximity to the city centre and the Atlantic seaboard, as well as to restaurants and entertainment, and the great views across the centre to the harbour, the City Bowl is understandably popular with visitors and home to numerous B&Bs, guesthouses and backpacker lodges from which to choose.

GETTING AROUND

BY BUS

MyCiTi ☎ 0800 65 64 63, ⓦ www.capetown.gov.za /myciti. From mid-2012 several new routes will serve the City Bowl: #F02 Sea Point to Gardens and Vredehoek via the city centre; #F06 Civic Centre to Gardens and Oranjezicht; #F07 Civic Centre to Gardens and Vredehoek via Zonnebloem; #F65 Civic Centre to Gardens and Tamboerskloof via the city centre.

An interim MyCiTi inner circle service will operate until these new services come on stream. This goes from Gardens

TABLE MOUNTAIN AND THE CITY BOWL

at the edge of the City Bowl through the city centre to the Civic Centre and then on to the Waterfront. All the MyCiTi services will run every 10–20 minutes during the day. For getting to the Table Mountain lower cable station you will be able to take the #F02 Waterfront to Camps Bay bus and get off at Kloof Nek, from where it's a 1km walk.

City Sightseeing ☎ 021 511 6000, ⓦ citysightseeing .co.za. The open-topped City Sightseeing bus stops at the lower cable station.

Table Mountain

The north face of **Table Mountain** overlooks the city centre, flanked by the distinct formations of **Lion's Head** and **Signal Hill** to the west and **Devil's Peak** to the east. A series of gable-like formations known as the **Twelve Apostles** makes up the mountain's drier west face and the southwest face towers over Hout Bay. The forested east, looming over the southern suburbs, gets the most rain.

The mountain is a wilderness where you'll find wildlife and 1400 species of flora. Indigenous mammals include baboons, dassies (see box below) and porcupines. Getting up and down the mountain can be a doddle via the highly popular **cable car** at the western table, though **climbing** up will give you a greater sense of achievement; if you're up to the challenge it's best to go on a **guided hike** (see p.71).

The cable car

Daily every 10–15 min: Jan & Dec 8am–9pm; Feb & March 8.30am–7.30pm; April 8.30am–5.30pm; May–Oct 8am–6pm; Nov 8am–7pm • R180 • Operations can be disrupted by bad weather or maintenance work; for information on current schedules call ☎ 021 424 8181, or check ⓦ tablemountain.net

The highly popular **cable car** offers dizzying views across Table Bay and the Atlantic. The state-of-the-art Swiss system is designed to complete a 360-degree rotation on the way, giving passengers a full panorama. Cars leave from the **lower cableway station** on Tafelberg Road. You can make a real outing of it by going up for breakfast or a sunset drink and meal at the vamped-up eco-restaurant; the upper station is an incomparable spot from which to watch the sun go down.

ARRIVAL AND DEPARTURE

TABLE MOUNTAIN

Cable cars leave from the **lower cableway station** on Tafelberg Road, clearly signposted at Kloof Nek.

By car If you're driving, you'll find parking along Tafelberg Road, but you may be in for a bit of a walk in peak season – the stretch of parked cars can extend several hundred metres.

DASSIES

The outsized fluffy guinea pigs you'll encounter at the top of Table Mountain are **dassies** or hyraxes (*Procavia capensis*) which, despite their appearance, aren't rodents at all, but the closest living relatives of elephants. Their name (pronounced like "dusty" without the "t") is the Afrikaans version of *dasje*, meaning "little badger", given to them by the first Dutch settlers. Dassies have poor body temperature control and, like reptiles, rely on shelter against both hot sunlight and the cold. They wake up sluggish and seek out rocks where they can catch the sun in the early morning – this is one of the best times to look out for them. One adult stands sentry against predators and issues a low-pitched warning cry in response to a threat.

Dassies are very widely distributed, having thrived in South Africa with the elimination of predators, and can be found in suitably rocky habitats all over the country. They live in colonies consisting of a dominant male and eight or more related females and their offspring.

By bus or taxi You can get to the lower cableway station by *rikki*, metered taxi, or in one of the minibus taxis that ply the route here from Adderley Street. The open-topped City Sightseeing bus also serves the cableway.

Climbs and walks

Reckoned the most-climbed massif in the world, Table Mountain offers gorgeous hikes. There are hundreds of possible walks and climbs on its slopes, but unless you're going with a knowledgeable guide, it's recommended that you attempt one of the **routes** outlined here, which are the simplest. Every year the mountain strikes back, taking its toll of lives; it may look sunny and clear when you leave, but conditions at the top could be very different – strong sun and violent winds can be brutal. The most common issues are people losing the track (often because of mist suddenly descending) and becoming trapped; if you plan on tackling one of the walks without a guide, go properly prepared (see box opposite).

TOURS   **TABLE MOUNTAIN**

There are half-day or full-day **guided hikes** which are thoroughly recommended, the hikes tailored to your level of fitness and with some rock climbing possible; prices include transport and packed lunches. You may choose to come back the easy way by cable car, or partially abseil. Both operators listed below **charge** from R450 per person for a hike, but this excludes the cost of the cable car for your return trip.

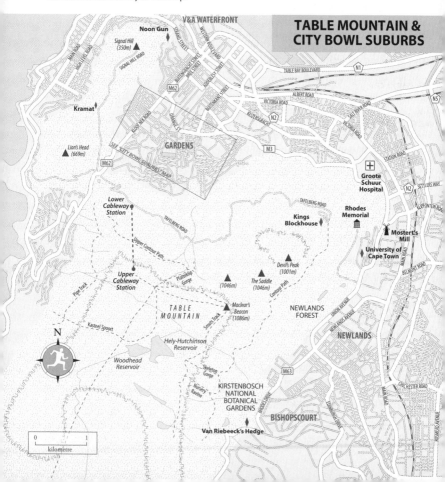

TABLE MOUNTAIN SAFETY

- Don't climb alone. As well as general mountain-safety issues, there have been a number of tourist muggings over the past decade, so it's recommended you walk with a guide.
- Inform someone that you're going up the mountain; tell them your route, when you're leaving and when you expect to be back.
- Leave early enough to give yourself time to complete your route during daylight.
- Don't try to descend via an unknown route. If you get lost in poor weather, seek shelter, keep warm and wait for help.
- Never leave even the tiniest scrap of litter on the mountain.
- Never make fires. No cooking is allowed, even on portable stoves – mountain fires are a serious hazard in Cape Town, especially during the dry, hot summer months.

WEAR:

- Good footwear. Boots or running shoes are recommended.
- A broad-rimmed hat.

TAKE:

- A backpack.
- A water bottle; allow two litres per person.
- Enough food for the trip.
- A warm top.
- A windbreaker.
- Sunglasses.
- High-factor sunscreen.
- Plasters for blisters.
- A map (available from Cape Union Mart at the Waterfront, or Cavendish Square Shopping Centre in Claremont).

Margie ☎ 021 715 6136, ⓦ tablemountainwalks.co.za. A registered Table Mountain Guide leads the classic Table Mountain ascents, as well as other stunning routes on the peninsula. She will pick you up for free from your accommodation, and provide refreshments and lunch.

High Adventure ☎ 021 689 1234, ⓦ highadventure. co.za. Runs guided hikes up Table Mountain, geared to your level of fitness and with experienced guides.

Signal Hill and Lion's Head

From the roundabout at the top of **Kloof Nek** – the saddle between Table Mountain and Lion's Head, over which Kloof Nek Road runs to reach the Atlantic seaboard – the fairly steep 3.5km Signal Hill Road runs the length of **Signal Hill** to a car park and lookout at the northern end, with good views over Table Bay, the docks and the city. A cannon was formerly used for sending signals to ships at anchor in the bay, and the **Noon Gun**, still fired from its slopes daily, sends a thunderous rumble through the Bo-Kaap and city centre below. Halfway along the road you'll see a sacred Islamic *kramat* (shrine), one of several dotted around the peninsula, which "protect" the city (see box, p.72).

You can also walk up **Lion's Head**, a hike that seems to bring out half the population of Cape Town every full moon. One of the attractions of the two-kilometre Lion's Head ascent is that as you spiral up around the mountain, there are constantly changing views of the city and the ocean. Two routes start along Signal Hill Road: one at the Kloof Nek end and the other halfway along the road at the *kramat*. The relatively easy hike takes sixty to ninety minutes, mostly along a track, then a path with minor rock scrambling and a ladder at one point, as well as chains to assist hikers up a short vertical ascent (a longer diversion bypasses the chains).

Platteklip Gorge

The first recorded ascent to the summit of Table Mountain was by the Portuguese captain Antonio de Saldanha, in 1503. He wisely chose **Platteklip Gorge**, the gap visible from the front table (the north side), which, as it turned out, is the most accessible way up. A short and easy extension will get you to Maclear's Beacon; at 1086m, it is the **highest point** on the mountain. The Platteklip route starts out at the lower cableway station and has the added advantage of ending at the upper station, so you can descend in a car.

From the lower station, walk east along Tafelberg Road until you see a high embankment built from stone and maintained with wire netting. Just beyond and to the left of a small dam is a sign pointing to Platteklip Gorge. A steep fifteen-minute climb brings you onto the **Upper Contour Path**. About 25m east along this, take the path indicated by a sign reading "Contour Path/Platteklip Gorge". The path zigzags from here onwards and is very clear. The gorge is the biggest cleavage on the whole mountain, leading directly and safely to the top, but it's a very steep, three-hour slog, even if you're reasonably fit. Once on top, turn right and ascend the last short section onto the **front table** for a breathtaking view of the city. A sign points the way to the upper cableway station – a fifteen-minute walk along a concrete path thronging with visitors.

Maclear's Beacon

Maclear's Beacon is about 35 minutes from the top of the Platteklip Gorge on a path leading eastward, with white squares on little yellow footsteps guiding you all the way. The path crosses the front table with Maclear's Beacon visible at all times. From the top you'll get views of False Bay and the Hottentots Holland Mountains to the east.

Skeleton Gorge

This route allows you to combine a visit to the gardens at Kirstenbosch (see p.79) with an ascent up Table Mountain via one route and a descent down another, starting and ending at the gardens' **restaurant**. This entire walk lasts four to five hours. From the restaurant, follow the **Skeleton Gorge** signs that will lead you onto the **Contour Path**. At the Contour Path, a plaque indicates that this is **Smuts' Track**, the route favoured by Jan Smuts, the Boer leader and South African prime minister. The plaque marks the start of a broad-stepped climb up Skeleton Gorge, involving wooden steps, stone steps, wooden ladders and loose boulders. Be prepared for steep ravines and difficult rock climbs – and under no circumstances stray off the path. It requires reasonable fitness, and can take two hours. Skeleton Gorge can be an unpleasant way down, especially in the wet season when it gets slippery.

Nursery Ravine is recommended for the descent. At the top of Skeleton Gorge, walk a few metres to your right to a sign indicating **Kasteelspoort**. It's just 35 minutes from the top of Skeleton along the Kasteelsport path to the head of Nursery Ravine. The descent returns you to the 310m Contour Path, which leads back to Kirstenbosch.

SACRED CIRCLE

A number of Muslim holy men and princes were exiled from the East Indies by the Dutch during the late seventeenth and early eighteenth centuries and brought to the Cape, where some became revered as *auliyah* or muslim saints. The *kramats*, of which there are nearly two dozen in the province, are their burial sites, shrines and places of pilgrimage. The Signal Hill *kramat* is a shrine to Mohamed Gasan Galbie Shah, a follower of Sheik Yusuf, a Sufi scholar, who was deported to the Cape in 1694 with a 49-strong retinue. According to tradition, he conducted Muslim prayer meetings in private homes and slave quarters, becoming the founder of Islam in South Africa. Sheik Yusuf's *kramat* on the Cape Flats is said to be one of a sacred circle of six *kramats*, including one on Robben Island, that protect Cape Town from natural disasters.

CITY BOWL SUBURBS

RESTAURANTS & CAFÉS

Aubergine	4
Bombay Bicycle Club	12
Carlyle's on Derry	1
Daily Deli	7
Lazari	10
Limoncello	9
Melissa's	11
Miller's Thumb	8
Mount Nelson Hotel	5
Raith Gourmet	6
Sawaddee	2
Societi Bistro	3

ACCOMMODATION

African Sun	12
Ashanti Lodge and Guest House	13
The Backpack	1
Belmont House	15
Bergzicht	8
Blencathra	16
Cape Milner Hotel	3
Cape Town Backpackers	5
Hippo Boutique Hotel	4
Leeuwenvoet House	11
Lezard Bleu	17
Mount Nelson Hotel	6
Nine Flowers Guest House	7
Saasveld Lodge	10
Underberg Guest House	9
Welgelegen Guest House	14
Zebra Crossing	2

BARS

Planet Bar	1
Rafiki's	2

SHOPS

Mabu Vinyl	1
Wine Concepts	2

The City Bowl suburbs

The City Bowl suburbs, the residential area south of Orange Street and the Company's Gardens, gently climbing the lower slopes of Table Mountain, is not so much a district to explore as one in which to consume. That there are so many good restaurants, pubs and coffee bars along the throbbing artery of **Kloof Street** – the continuation of Long Street – is indicative of the affluence of the area. Along Kloof you'll also find the **Labia**, an art-house **cinema** complex that attracts movie buffs from all over the peninsula.

The most obvious landmark of the district is the **Mount Nelson Hotel** (see p.109), on the south side of Orange Street in the suburb of **Gardens**, an area that takes its name from the historic gardens on the opposite side of the road. Harking back to the heyday of British colonialism, the grand hotel is announced by a gigantic white pedimented gateway supported on nearly two dozen Corinthian columns.

Behind the hotel, the suburbs on either side of Kloof Street have a strong urban vibe found in few other parts of Cape Town, where sleazy but rapidly gentrifying flatland rubs up against airy Victorian villas, modern cottages and stylish pieds-à-terre. The most elevated residential areas, close to Kloof Nek, including **Higgovale**, **Oranjezicht** and **Tamboerskloof**, are packed with properties that carry suitably elevated price tags.

3

CAPE SUGARBIRD, KIRSTENBOSCH GARDENS

The southern suburbs

Away from Table Mountain and the city centre, the southern suburbs, the formerly whites-only residential areas, stretch out down the east side of Table Mountain, ending just before Muizenberg on the False Bay coast. Greener and more forested than the drier, hotter Atlantic Coast, this side of the peninsula is home to the sublime Kirstenbosch National Botanical Gardens. Further afield, in the Constantia Winelands, lie South Africa's oldest wineries, at Klein Constantia, Groot Constantia, Buitenverwachting and Steenberg, each centred on its own historic eighteenth-century Cape Dutch homestead; and in the same vicinity is the dappled Tokai Forest, a relaxing refuge from the midsummer sun – and the howling southeaster.

East of the **M5 highway**, which skirts through the margins of the southern suburbs as far as Muizenberg, lie the **Cape Flats** – the windswept flatlands that splay out towards the airport, which became the apartheid dumping ground for Africans and coloureds.

GETTING AROUND	SOUTHERN SUBURBS

By car The quickest way of reaching the southern suburbs from the city centre, Waterfront or City Bowl suburbs is the M3 highway; outside rush hour, it takes about thirty minutes to get from the centre to Tokai, where the highway ends.

By train The Metrorail train line from the central station to Fish Hoek and Simon's Town runs through the southern suburbs and provides a handy means of getting to most of them, however stops are too far from Rhodes Memorial, Kirstenbosch, Constantia (and its winelands) and Tokai to be practical, and in these cases you'll have to rely on your own wheels, taxis or the Sightseeing bus.

By bus ☎ 021 511 6000, ⓦ citysightseeing.co.za. The hop-on-hop-off City Sightseeing bus goes to Kirstenbosch and Groot Constantia.

Woodstock

First and oldest of the suburbs, as you take an easterly exit from town, is **Woodstock**, windblown and not particularly leafy, but redeemed by some nice Victorian buildings that were originally occupied by working-class coloureds and have now been gentrified. The focus of the revival is the **Old Biscuit Mill** in Albert Road with its terrific Saturday morning organic and artisanal food market, where you can eat yourself silly, wander about craft shops and visit art galleries.

Salt River and Observatory

To the east of Woodstock, **Salt River** is a harsh, industrial, mainly coloured area, while **Observatory**, abutting its southern end, is generally regarded as Cape Town's bohemian hub, a reputation fuelled by its proximity to the University of Cape Town in Rondebosch and its large student population. Many of the houses here are student digs, but the narrow Victorian streets are also home to young professionals, hippies and arty types. The refreshingly dilapidated and peeling arcades on Observatory's Lower Main Road, and the streets off it, have some nice cafés and lively bars, as well as a wholefood shop, organic café, African fabrics shop and a couple of antiques emporiums. The huge **Groote Schuur Hospital**, which overlooks the freeway that sweeps through Observatory, was the site of the world's first heart transplant in 1967.

Mowbray

Along Station Road, away from the mountain and south of Observatory, is **Mowbray**, originally called Drie Koppen – Three Heads – after the heads of three murderers impaled there in 1724, but its name was changed in the 1840s. In the nineteenth century, this was the home of philologist Willem Bleek, who lived with a group of San convicts given up by the colonial authorities so that he could study their languages and attitudes. Bleek's pioneering work still forms the basis of much of what we know about traditional Khoisan life. There isn't much to see here, just a small row of shops and some attractive Victorian buildings.

Rosebank

Rosebank, to Mowbray's south, has a substantial student community, some staying in the so-called Tampax Towers, the unmistakable circular residential blocks on Main Road. Just beyond them is the brown-brick **Baxter Theatre**, one of Cape Town's premier arts complexes (see p.129).

Irma Stern Museum

Cecil Rd, Rosebank • Tues–Sat 10am–5pm • R10 • ⓦ irmastern.co.za

Irma Stern is acknowledged as one of South Africa's pioneering artists, more for the fact that she brought modern European ideas to the colonies in the twentieth century than for any huge contribution she made to world art. The **Irma Stern Museum** was the artist's home for 38 years until her death in 1966, and is definitely worth visiting for a look at Stern's collection of Iberian, African, Oriental and ancient artefacts. The whole house, in fact, reflects the artist's fascination with exoticism, starting with her own Gauguinesque paintings of stereotyped African figures as well as the fantastic carved doors she brought back from Zanzibar, and the very untypical garden that brings a touch of the tropics to Cape Town, with its exuberant bamboo thickets and palm trees. Three of the rooms in the house have been left as Stern furnished them and there is also a display of her art materials and tools.

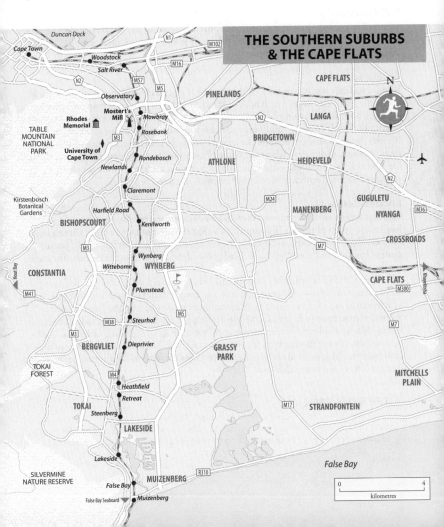

THE SOUTHERN SUBURBS & THE CAPE FLATS

THE LIFE AND WORKS OF IRMA STERN

Born in a backwater town in South Africa in 1894 to German-Jewish parents, Stern studied at Germany's Weimar Academy. In reaction to the academy's conservatism, she adopted **expressionist distortion** in her paintings, some of which were included in the Neue Sezession Exhibition in Berlin in 1918. Stern went on several expeditions into Zanzibar and the Congo in the 1940s and 1950s, where she found the source for her intensely sensuous paintings that shocked South Africa at the time.

Although Stern's work was appreciated in Europe, when she returned to South Africa after World War II, critics claimed that her style was simply a cover for technical incompetence. South African art historians now regard her as the towering figure of her generation. One of her most famous works is the much reproduced *The Eternal Child* (1916), a simple but vibrant portrait of a young girl, while *The Wood Carriers* (1951) uses raw ochres, browns and oranges to create an exoticized portrayal of a pair of African women.

Rondebosch

South of Rosebank, neighbouring **Rondebosch** is home to the **University of Cape Town** (UCT), whose nineteenth-century buildings sit grandly on the mountainside, each handsomely festooned with creepers.

Groote Schuur

Rhodes features big in this neck of the woods: if you head south from the Woolsack down the M3 (here known as Rhodes Drive), you'll pass **Groote Schuur**, another house built for him. Bordering on Main Road, Groote Schuur is one of Herbert Baker's most celebrated South African buildings, exemplifying the Cape Dutch Revival style. Rhodes' large estate here became the official prime ministerial residence of the Cape, then of South Africa, and when the country switched to a presidential system it became the home of the president – though Nelson Mandela preferred to use a nearby residence named Genadendal. Neither house is open to the public.

Rhodes Memorial

Reached via a signposted road that spurs northwest off the M3, just as Rhodes Drive becomes the Princess Anne Interchange

Just to the north of the UCT campus is the **Rhodes Memorial**. On a site chosen by Herbert Baker and Rudyard Kipling, the monument sits grandiosely conspicuous against the slopes of Devil's Peak as herds of wildebeest and zebra nonchalantly graze on the slopes nearby.

Built in 1912 to resemble a Greek temple, the memorial celebrates Rhodes' energy with a sculpture of a wildly rearing horse. The empire-builder's bust is planted at the top of a towering set of stairs, lined with reclining lions inspired by the Avenue of the Sphinxes at Karnak in Egypt. Carved in stone beneath the bust is a ponderous inscription by Kipling: "The immense and brooding spirit still shall order and control." Also on site is a **tea garden** with terrific views of Cape Town. Below the memorial, alongside the M3, is the incongruous **Mostert's Mill**, a windmill built two centuries ago when there were wheat fields here.

THE WOOLSACK

Of passing interest on the campus is the **Woolsack**. This "cottage in the woods for poets and artists", just off Woolsack Road, was designed in 1900 by Sir Herbert Baker for **Cecil John Rhodes**. Rhodes invited **Rudyard Kipling** to "hang up his hat there" whenever he visited the Cape. Taking his friend at his word, Kipling fled the English winter every year from 1900 to 1907, bringing his family to Cape Town and spending five to six months at the Woolsack, where he is said to have written his famous poem *If*. The house is now occupied by the university's architecture faculty.

From the memorial you can walk to the **King's Blockhouse**, formerly a signalling station to Muizenberg, and onto the Contour Path that follows the eastern side of the mountain, way above the southern suburbs to Constantia Nek.

Newlands

Continuing south from Rondebosch along either the Van der Stel Freeway (the M3) or the more congested Main Road, you pass some of Cape Town's most prestigious suburbs. **Newlands**, almost merging with Rondebosch, is home to the city's famous rugby and cricket stadiums. Worth a stopoff here is the **Montebello Craft and Design Centre** (see p.134).

Claremont

The well-heeled suburb of **Claremont**, south of Newlands, is an alternative focus to the city centre for shopping and entertainment, with two cinema complexes and plenty of shops at **Cavendish Square Mall** (see p.136). Alongside the high-quality shops, hawkers sell clothes, vegetables and herbs; closer to Claremont station, you can buy tasty *boerewors* from women cooking them outdoors.

Bishopscourt

A little further south, beyond the signpost to Kirstenbosch Gardens, is **Bishopscourt**. As the name suggests, it's home to the Anglican bishop of Cape Town, and it was in a mansion here that Archbishop Desmond Tutu lived even in the years when blacks weren't supposed to live in whites-only suburbs. Partly because of its prime siting – some plots have views of both Newlands Forest and the sea – this is one of the poshest areas in Cape Town; a number of consuls live here in huge properties behind high walls, which are about all you see as you pass through the area.

4

Wynberg

Further down the line, **Wynberg** is known for its Maynardville Shakespearean **open-air theatre** (see p.129) and its quaint row of shops and restaurants in Wolfe Street. By contrast, Wynberg's Main Road offers a distinctly less genteel shopping experience. It's an interesting stroll past street vendors and fabric shops, as well as food outlets catering to the large number of workers travelling between Wynberg and Khayelitsha in the Cape Flats.

Kirstenbosch National Botanical Gardens

Rhodes Ave · Daily April–Aug 8am–6pm; Sept–March 8am–7pm · R37 · **Open air concerts** ☏ 021 799 8783, ⓦ sanbi.org · Dec–March 5.30–7pm; see box below · The City Sightseeing Bus stops at the gardens several times a day

Five kilometres south of Rondebosch, the **Kirstenbosch National Botanical Gardens** are one of the planet's great natural treasure houses, a status acknowledged in 2004 when they became part of South Africa's sixth UNESCO World Heritage Site – the first

---

KIRSTENBOSCH CONCERTS

If you're visiting the gardens in **summer**, one of the undoubted delights is to bring a picnic for a Sunday evening **open-air concert**, where you can lie back on the lawn, sip Cape wine and savour the mountain air and sunsets. Otherwise, there's an outdoor **coffee shop**, open daily for breakfast, lunch and teas, plus a restaurant with a fire going for winter days, though eating out in the gardens is more about the fabulous location than the food or service.

4

VERGELEGEN HOMESTEAD

CAPE DUTCH ARCHITECTURE

Cape Dutch style, which developed in the Western Cape countryside from the seventeenth to the early nineteenth century, is so distinctively rooted in the Winelands that it has become an integral element of the landscape. The dazzling limewashed walls glisten in the midst of glowing green vineyards, while the thatched roofs and elaborate curvilinear gables mirror the undulations of the surrounding mountains. Although there were important developments in the internal organization of Cape houses during this period, their most obvious element is the **gable**. Central gables set into the long side of roofs were unusual in Europe, but became the quintessential feature of the Cape Dutch style.

In central Cape Town, the gable only survived until the 1830s, to be replaced by buildings with flush facades and flat roofs. **Arson** appears to be a major reason for this – fires, purportedly started by slaves, including one that razed Stellenbosch in 1710, and Cape Town's **great fires** of 1736 and 1798 led officials to ban thatched roofs and any protrusions on building exteriors, which resulted in the flush facades that typify early nineteenth-century Cape Town houses. With the disappearance of pitched roofs, the urban gable withered away, surviving symbolically in some instances as minimal roof decoration; an example of this is the wavy parapet on the **Bo-Kaap Museum** (1763–68) in Wale Street.

But the threat of fire spreading from one building to another was a less serious consideration in the countryside. Consequently, VOC building regulations carried little weight and the pitched roof survived, as did gables, becoming the hallmark of country manors. From functional origins, gables evolved into **symbols of wealth**, with landowners vying to erect the biggest, most elaborate and most fashionable examples. Some fine ones can be found on the historic estates of the Winelands, as well as at Tokai Manor, Groot Constantia, Klein Constantia and Buitenverwachting.

botanical garden in the world to achieve this. The listing recognizes the international significance of the *fynbos* plant kingdom that predominates here.

Kirstenbosch is the oldest and largest botanical garden in South Africa, created in 1895 by Cecil Rhodes, whose camphor and fig trees are still here. Today, over 22,000 indigenous plants – and a research unit and library – attract researchers and botanists from all over the world. There's a nursery selling local plants, while characteristic Cape plants, found nowhere else in the world, are cultivated on the slopes

The gardens are magnificent, glorying in lush shrubs and exuberant blooms. Little signboards and paved paths guide you through the highlights of the gardens, with trees and plants identified to enhance the rambling. The most interesting route is the one created for blind visitors, with labels in Braille and an abundance of aromatic and textured plants.

The gardens trail off into wild vegetation, covering a huge expanse of the rugged eastern slopes and wooded ravines of Table Mountain. The setting is quite breathtaking – this is a great place to have tea and stroll around gazing up the mountain, or to wander onto the paths, which meander steeply to the top of Table Mountain with no fences cutting off the way. Two popular paths, starting from the Contour Path above Kirstenbosch, are **Nursery Ravine** and **Skeleton Gorge** (see p.72).

Note that **women** should not walk alone in the isolated upper reaches of Kirstenbosch, where there have been some attacks on lone hikers.

Constantia and its winelands

There is no public transport to this area, although several tours run from central Cape Town every day • All estates listed below are clearly marked off the M3

South of Kirstenbosch lie the elegant suburbs of **Constantia** and the Cape's oldest **winelands**. Luxuriating on the lower slopes of Table Mountain and the Constantiaberg, with tantalizing views of False Bay, the winelands are an easy drive from town, not more than ten minutes off the Van der Stel Freeway (the M3), which runs between the centre and Muizenberg.

The winelands began cultivated life in 1685 as the farm of **Simon van der Stel**, the governor charged with opening up the fledgling Dutch colony to the interior. Thrusting himself wholeheartedly into the task, he selected for his own use an enormous tract of the choicest land set against the Constantiaberg. He named the estate after his daughter Constancia, and this is now (with a minor change of spelling) the name of Cape Town's oldest and most prestigious residential area. Exuding the easy ambience of landed wealth, Constantia is a green and pleasant place, shaded by oak forests and punctuated with farm stalls, stables, the Constantia Shopping Mall and, of course, the vineyards.

Constantia grapes have been making wine since Van der Stel's first output in 1705. After his death in 1712, the estate was divided up and sold off as the modern **Groot Constantia**, **Klein Constantia** and **Buitenverwachting**. In 1990, the nearby Steenberg Estate was bought up by a large Johannesburg mining conglomerate. All four estates are open to the public and offer tastings; they're definitely worth visiting if you aren't heading further afield to the Winelands proper.

Groot Constantia

Cellar tours daily on the hour 10am–4pm • R35 including five wines to taste and a souvenir glass; booking essential • **Wine tasting** daily: May–Sept 10am–4.30pm; Oct–April 9am–5.30pm • R30 • ☎ 021 794 5128, ⓦ grootconstantia.co.za

The largest estate and the one most geared to tourists is Groot Constantia, a terrific example of Cape Dutch grandeur reached along an oak-lined axis that passes through vineyards with the hazy blue Constantiaberg as its backdrop. Its big pull is that it retains the rump of Van der Stel's original estate, as well as the original buildings, though its portrayal of life in a seventeenth-century colonial chateau makes scant reference to the slave labour that underpinned its operations.

The manor house

The **manor house**, a quintessential Cape Dutch building, was Van der Stel's original home, modified at the end of the eighteenth century by the French architect Thibault. It's thought that the magnificent gables were added in the eighteenth or early nineteenth centuries, with an allegorical figure representing Abundance recessed into a niche in the central gable. The interior forms part of the **museum** and is decorated in a style typical of eighteenth- and nineteenth-century Cape landowners, containing interesting Neoclassical as well as Louis XV and XVI furniture and Delft and Chinese ceramics.

The cellar

If you walk straight through the house and down the ceremonial axis, you'll come to the so-called **cellar** (actually a two-storey building above ground), fronted by a brilliant relief pediment. Attributed to the sculptor Anton Anreith, it depicts a riotous bacchanalia, featuring Ganymede, a young man so handsome that Zeus, in the form of an eagle, carried him off to be the cup-bearer of the gods. Inside, you can see a collection of wine-related objects dating from antiquity – such as amphoras – to the present.

Klein Constantia

Klein Constantia Rd • Mon–Fri 9am–5pm, Sat 9am–3pm • ⓦ kleinconstantia.com

Smaller in scale than Groot Constantia, **Klein Constantia** offers free wine tasting in less regimented conditions than at the bigger estate, and although the buildings are far humbler, the settings are equally beautiful. **Klein Constantia** has a friendly atmosphere and produces some fine wines, such as its **Cabernet Sauvignon Reserve** and a number of excellent whites, among which its **Semillon** really stands out. Something of a

4

THE HISTORY OF THE TOWNSHIPS

The African townships were historically set up as dormitories to provide labour for white Cape Town, not as places to build a life, which is why they had no facilities and no real hub. The **men-only hostels**, another apartheid relic, are at the root of many of the area's social problems. During the 1950s, the government set out a blueprint to turn the tide of Africans flooding into Cape Town. No African was permitted to settle permanently in the Cape west of a line near the Fish River, the old frontier over 1000km from Cape Town; women were entirely banned from seeking work in Cape Town and men prohibited from bringing their wives to join them. By 1970 there were ten men for every woman in Langa (see opposite).

In the end, apartheid failed to prevent the influx of work-seekers desperate to come to Cape Town. Where people couldn't find legal accommodation they set up **squatter camps** of makeshift iron, cardboard and plastic sheeting. During the 1970s and 1980s, the government attempted to demolish these and destroy anything left inside – but no sooner had the police left than the camps reappeared, and they are now a permanent feature of the Cape Flats. One of the best known of all South Africa's squatter camps is **Crossroads**, whose inhabitants suffered campaigns of harassment that included killings by apartheid collaborators and police, and continuous attempts to bulldoze it out of existence. Through sheer determination and desperation its residents hung on, eventually winning the right to stay.

Today, the government is making attempts to improve conditions in the shantytowns by introducing electricity, running water and sanitation, as well as building tiny brick houses to replace the shacks.

TOURS AND HOMESTAYS

If you want to really get under the skin of the townships, there's no better way than staying in one of the **township B&Bs** which offer pleasant, friendly and safe accommodation (see box, p.113). A couple of specialist tours (see p.26) will take you to musicians' homes and clubs in the Cape Flats or township areas to hear some authentic Capetonian sounds. In addition, Our Pride Tours (❶021 531 4291) does Sunday-morning gospel excursions to the townships, calling at various churches.

curiosity is its **Vin de Constance**, the re-creation of an eighteenth-century Constantia wine that was a favourite of Napoleon, Frederick the Great and Bismarck. It's a delicious dessert wine, packaged in a replica of the original bottle, and makes an original souvenir. Look out for the **wildlife** here, notably the guinea fowls that roam the estate munching on beetles that attack young vine leaves; in summer, migrant steppe buzzards prey on unsuspecting starlings, which eat the grapes.

Buitenverwachting

On Klein Constantia Rd • **Buildings** Mon–Fri 9am–5pm, Sat 9am–1pm • Free • **Picnic lunches** Nov–April Mon–Sat noon–4pm • R110; booking essential – contact Adrienne for picnics • ☏ 021 794 1012 or ☏ 083 257 6083, ⓦ buitenverwachting.co.za

Buitenverwachting (roughly pronounced "bay-tin-fur-vuch-ting", with the "ch" as in the Scottish rendition of loch), is a bucolic place in the middle of the suburbs, with sheep and cattle grazing in the fields as you approach the main buildings. Despite deep historic roots, the estate now treats its employees much better than most.

The architecture and setting at the foot of the Constantiaberg are good reasons to come here, as are the top-ranking wines. Overlooking the vineyards and backing onto the garden, the **homestead** was built in 1794 (the 1769 on the gable appears to be wrong) by Arend Brink, and features an unusual gabled pediment broken with an urn motif. There is a fantastic restaurant here (see p.120) and, for a day out on the farm (they have cattle and horses, too), they also do luxury picnic lunches, which you can enjoy under the oaks.

The Cape Flats and the townships

4

East of the northern and southern suburbs, among the industrial smokestacks and the windswept **Cape Flats**, reaching well beyond the airport, is Cape Town's largest residential quarter, taking in the **coloured districts**, **African townships** and shantytown **squatter camps**. The Cape Flats are exactly that: flat, barren and populous, exclusively inhabited by Africans and coloureds in separate areas, with the M5 acting as a dividing line between it and the southern suburbs.

Several projects are under way to encourage **tourists** into the townships but, as a high proportion of Cape Town's nearly two thousand annual murders take place here, the recommended way to visit is on one of the **tours** listed in Basics p.26, which safely navigate visitors through the townships. It's also possible to stay overnight (see box, p.13).

Langa

Langa is the oldest and most central township, lying just east of the white suburb of Pinelands and north of the N2. In this relentlessly grey place, without the tiniest patch of green relief, you'll find women selling sheep and goats' heads, alongside state-of-the-art public phone bureaus run by enterprising township businessmen from inside recycled cargo containers. Families live in smart suburban houses within the townships (many Africans who can afford to move out say they find the white suburbs sterile and unfriendly) while, not far away, there are former men-only hostels where as many as three families share one room.

Mitchell's Plain

South of the African ghettoes is **Mitchell's Plain**, a coloured area stretching down to the False Bay coast (you'll skirt Mitchell's Plain if you take the M5 to Muizenberg). More salubrious than any of the African townships, Mitchell's Plain reflects how, under apartheid, lighter skins meant better conditions, even if you weren't quite white. But for coloureds the forced removals were no less tragic, many being summarily forced to vacate family homes because their suburb had been declared a White Group Area. Many families were relocated here when District Six was razed (see p.56), and their

---

HIKING IN THE ARBORETUM

Several tracks and trails crisscross the arboretum and plantation, providing easy walks and mountain-biking trails (bring your own bike). Longer hikes include the walk from the entrance gate to **Elephant's Eye Cave** (6km there and back), which can easily be completed in well under three hours. The route passes through pine forests before opening into montane *fynbos* that covers the slopes of the Constantiaberg, eventually leading to the cave, which offers terrific panoramas. Ask for a **map** and directions at the entrance gate or at the adjacent café.

---

communities never fully recovered – one of the symptoms of dislocation and poverty is the violent gangs that have become an everyday part of Mitchell's Plain youth culture.

Tokai

Effectively the southern extension of Constantia, forested **Tokai** is an excellent area for leafy recreation away from the centre, with some relaxed and child-friendly places for eating and drinking, and sheltered from the southeaster.

To drive to Tokai from the centre of Cape Town, head south along the M3 and exit north onto Ladies Mile Road; continue for 100m before turning south into Spaanschemat River Road (M42), signposted Tokai, which runs through the suburb. You can easily combine Tokai with a trip to the seaside, as the suburb is fifteen minutes' drive from the False Bay seaboard.

Tokai Forest

Most people come out to Tokai for the well-marked hiking paths and mountain-biking trails in the pine plantations of the **Tokai Forest**. You can get here from Spaanschemat River Road, turning west into Tokai Road, which heads straight to the forest. About 500m from Spaanschemat River Road, the road passes through pine forests equipped with picnic tables, though you'd do well to carry on to the arboretum for the best picnic spots. A little further along the road from the picnic sites, you can't fail to see the imposing **Tokai Manor House** (not open to the public). Designed by Louis Michel Thibault and built around 1795, this National Monument is an elegant gem of Cape Dutch architecture combined with the understated elegance of French Neoclassicism.

Tokai Arboretum

Daily dawn to dusk • R10 donation • Café closed Mon

The historic tree plantation that constitutes the **Tokai Arboretum** is a National Monument. It's the work of Joseph Storr Lister, who was a nineteenth-century Conservator of Forests for the Cape Colony. In 1885 he experimented with planting 150 species of trees from temperate countries, with oaks and eucalyptus featuring extensively as well as some beautiful California redwoods. Storr discovered that conifers were best suited to the Cape; hence the plantation to the west of the arboretum, owned by the Safcol timber company, consists mainly of pines. The arboretum is the best place to begin rambling and an ideal place to bring **children**, with outdoor seating, plenty of shade and logs to jump on and over. There's also a car park and a **café** close to the entrance gate for tea and scones.

HOUT BAY

The Atlantic seaboard

The suburbs along the Atlantic seaboard cling in a dramatic ribbon to the slopes of Table Mountain. Although the waters on their western flank can be very chilly, the Atlantic seaboard offers mind-blowing views from some of the most incredible coastal roads in the world, particularly beyond Sea Point. The coast itself consists of a series of bays and white-sand beaches edged with smoothly sculpted bleached rocks; inland, the Twelve Apostles, a series of rocky buttresses, gaze down onto the surf. The beaches are ideal for sunbathing, and it's from this side of the peninsula that you can watch the sun create fiery reflections on the sea and mountains behind as it sinks into the ocean. Making the most of the views, and beautiful-people-watching, are some of the city's trendiest outdoor cafés and bars.

5

Llandudno, Sandy Bay, Noordhoek, Kommetjie and Scarborough are not served by public transport.

BY BUS

Golden Arrow ☎ 0800 65 64 63, ⊕ gabs.co.za. run frequent services along the Atlantic seaboard from the Golden Acre shopping centre in town. Most of which go to Sea Point, while a significant number continue on to Hout Bay. There are also regular buses to Mouille Point.

MyCiTi ☎ 0800 65 64 63, ⊕ www.capetown.gov.za/myciti. From mid-2012, several buses are expected to serve the Atlantic seaboard: #F01 Civic Centre to Hout Bay via Adderley St, Somerset Rd, Clifton and Camps Bay (serving a number of points in Hout Bay including Imizamo Yethu); #F02 Waterfront to Camps Bay via the Civic Centre, Long St, Kloof St and over Kloof Nek; #F03 Sea Point to the City Bowl via Mouille Point, Civic Centre, Long St, Gardens and Vredehoek; and #F04 Sea Point to the Civic Centre via High Level Rd and Strand. All the MyCiTi services will run every 10–20 minutes during the day.

City Sightseeing ☎ 021 511 6000, ⊕ citysightseeing.co.za. A service runs from the Clock Tower at the Waterfront via Kirstenbosch and Constantia Nek to: World of Birds (1hr 15min), ImiZamo Yethu (1hr 20min), Hout Bay Harbour (1hr 30min), Camps Bay (1hr 50min) returning via Sea Point (mid-Sept to April every 35 min, May to mid-Sept every 45 min).

Mouille Point

Just to the west of the V&A Waterfront, Mouille Point and its close neighbour, Green Point, are among the suburbs closest to the city centre. **Mouille** ("moo-lee") **Point** is known principally for its squat rectangular Victorian lighthouse, commissioned in the 1820s and famous for its red-and-white-striped exterior.

Green Point

Mouille Point merges with the larger suburb of **Green Point**, which continues both inland from it and west along the ragged Atlantic shore. Green Point's proximity to the Waterfront – an easy ten-minute amble – and its position along the coast has turned this once sleazy district into a humming area with good accommodation and cafés.

Sea Point

Nudging up to the western edge of Green Point, **Sea Point** is a cosmopolitan area crammed with apartment blocks, tourist accommodation and restaurants. The Sea Point promenade is the best way to appreciate the rocky coastline and salty air, along with pram-pushing mothers, old ladies, power walkers and joggers. People picnic and play ball games on the grassy parkland beside the coastal walkway, while busy Main Road, a block nearer Lion's Head, is frequented by drunks, hookers and middle-class shoppers, creating an edgy mix of sleaze and respectability.

Sea Point Pavilion Swimming Pool

Lower Beach Rd · May–Nov 9am–5pm; Dec–April 7am–7pm · R15

At the westernmost end of the promenade is a set of four unheated **saltwater/chlorine pools**, alongside the crashing surf, which its fans breathlessly claim is the most beautifully located pool in the world. The largest of the four is Olympic-sized, making it a popular training tank for many of Cape Town's long-distance swimmers. There are also two kids' splash pools and a fully equipped diving pool for the brave. Gloriously unmodernized since it was built in the 1960s – a large part of its attraction – the complex was slated by its owners, the city council, for demolition with permission for an upmarket hotel to go up on the prime site. Happily, after a three-year battle that culminated in the Supreme Court of Appeal in 2011, lobby group Seafront for All stayed the developer's hand and saved the much-adored institution for the community.

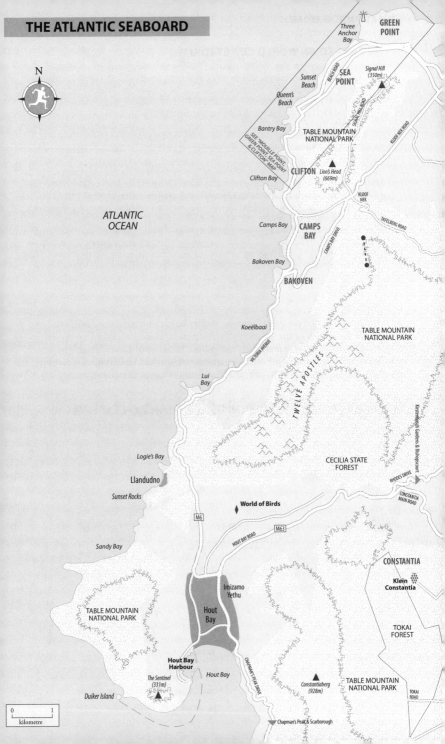

THE CAPE TOWN WORLD CUP STADIUM

Described by British architecture critic Jonathan Glancey as "a stunning white apparition … in a sublime setting", **Cape Town Stadium** was arguably the jewel in South Africa's 2010 World Cup crown, and the sight of the Netherlands spectacular 3–2 win over Argentina in the semi-final. The towering, 68,000-seater stadium relies on natural light, and at night the open-meshed roof can blaze up to resemble an ethereal UFO.

In 2011, once the final World Cup whistle had been blown, the **Ajax Cape Town** football team used it as their home ground and, in the same year, it was packed to the rafters when Irish rockers U2 came to town. In a less sublime outing for Neil Diamond, they actually removed some of the seats.

But it isn't all rock and roll: with the FIFA World Cup party over, Capetonians woke up to a nasty hangover in November 2010 when it was revealed that it will cost nearly R50 million a year to run the stadium, and that **taxpayers** will most likely be footing the bill. On top of that, in February 2011 it was revealed that there had been **corruption** in the tender process for the project, which was initially quoted at R2.9 billion (US$400 million) but had ballooned to R4.4 billion (US$600 million) by completion. It's alleged that the six major construction companies involved in building the World Cup stadiums and infrastructure around the country had colluded in **bid rigging** to share out bloated contracts among themselves. At the time of writing, tours of the stadium had come to an end, and the website brought down.

Bantry Bay

At the westernmost edge of Sea Point lies **Bantry Bay**, combining the density of Sea Point with the wealth of the Atlantic suburbs; here mansions are raked up on steep slopes above the Atlantic, guarded by the granite boulders of Lion's Head. The upmarket resort hotels and self-catering apartments are just far enough for comfort from the hubbub of Sea Point, but within walking distance of restaurants.

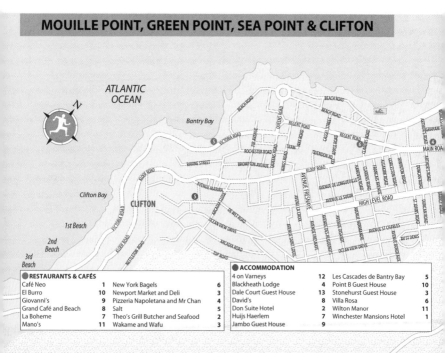

MOUILLE POINT, GREEN POINT, SEA POINT & CLIFTON

● RESTAURANTS & CAFÉS			
Café Neo	1	New York Bagels	6
El Burro	10	Newport Market and Deli	3
Giovanni's	9	Pizzeria Napoletana and Mr Chan	4
Grand Café and Beach	8	Salt	5
La Boheme	7	Theo's Grill Butcher and Seafood	2
Mano's	11	Wakame and Wafu	3

● ACCOMMODATION			
4 on Varneys	12	Les Cascades de Bantry Bay	5
Blackheath Lodge	4	Point B Guest House	10
Dale Court Guest House	13	Stonehurst Guest House	3
David's	8	Villa Rosa	6
Don Suite Hotel	2	Wilton Manor	11
Huijs Haerlem	7	Winchester Mansions Hotel	1
Jambo Guest House	9		

5

Clifton

Fashionable **Clifton** sits on the most expensive real estate in Africa. It is studded with fabulous seaside apartments and boasts four sandy, interlinked **beaches** that you can reach via steep stairways. The sea here is good for surfing and safe for swimming, but bone-chillingly cold, though Clifton is notably sheltered from the southeaster in summer. First Beach (they're all numbered) is frequented by muscular frisbee-players, surfers and their female counterparts, but is usually the least crowded of the four. Second and Third beaches are split between the teenies and thirtysomethings, with beautiful men sun worshipping and sometimes cruising on Third; if in doubt, head for Fourth, which is favoured by families with small kids by day because it has the fewest steps, while on still summer evenings, mellow groups of young people with candles hang out from sunset onwards.

Bring your own **refreshments**, as there's only one overpriced café on Fourth Beach, and parking can be tricky along Victoria Road in summer.

Camps Bay

The suburb of **Camps Bay** climbs the slopes of Table Mountain and is scooped into a small amphitheatre, bounded by the Lion's Head and the Twelve Apostles. This, and the airborne views across the Atlantic, make Camps Bay one of the most desirable places to live in Cape Town. The main drag, Victoria Road, skirts the coast and is packed with trendy restaurants, frequented by beautiful people, while the wide sandy beach is enjoyed by families of all shapes and colours. Lined by a row of palms and some grassy verges with welcome shade for picnics, Camps Bay beach is very busy around the Christmas and Easter breaks. However, it's exposed to the southeaster, and there's the usual Atlantic chill and an occasional dangerous backwash.

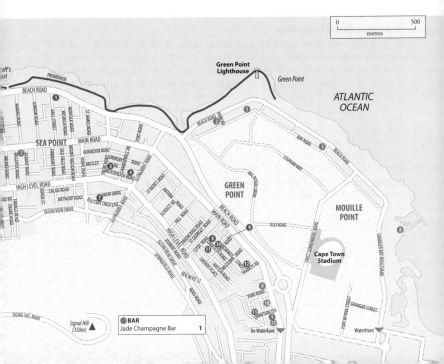

5

Llandudno

There's little development between Camps Bay and the wonderful little cove of **Llandudno**, 20km from Cape Town along Victoria Road. Here a steep and narrow road winds down past smart homes to the shore, where the sandy beach is punctuated at either end by magnificent granite boulders and rock formations. This is a good sunbathing spot and a choice one for bring-your-own sundowners.

Sandy Bay

Isolated **Sandy Bay**, Cape Town's main nudist beach and a popular gay and lesbian hangout, can only be reached via a twenty-minute walk from Llandudno. In the apartheid days, the South African police went to ingenious lengths to trap nudists, but nowadays the beach is relaxed, so feel free to come as undressed – or dressed – as feels comfortable. A path leads from the south end of the Llandudno car park, through *fynbos* vegetation and across some rocks, to the beach; it's a fairly easy walk, but watch out for broken glass if you're barefoot. There are no facilities whatsoever, so come prepared with supplies.

Hout Bay

Although no longer the quaint fishing village it once was, **Hout Bay** still has a functioning fishing harbour and is the centre of the local crayfish industry. Some 20km from the centre, it's a favourite day-trip, and despite ugly modern development and a growing shantytown, the natural setting is quite awesome, with the Sentinel and Chapman's Peak defining the entry to the bay. Highly unusual for Cape Town with its legacy of apartheid town planning, poor black areas nose right up to wealthy white ones here. Away from the harbour, the village is just managing to hang onto a shred of its historic ambience.

ImiZamo Yethu township

As you approach from Constantia Nek, you come to the township of ImiZamo Yethu, a tightly packed shackland settlement crawling up the hillside more or less in the middle of Hout Bay. ImiZamo Yethu was first settled during the late 1980s, the dying days of apartheid, by Xhosa job seekers from Willowvale in the rural Eastern Cape. Its population is now estimated at between twelve and thirty thousand. Although conditions are pretty dire (the highest levels of E. Coli ever recorded in South Africa were found in the Disa River which flows through the settlement), there's a surprising amount of optimism about. One of the most positive recent developments has been the building of 450 brick houses with the help of Irish millionaire Niall Mellon, who was so appalled by the conditions he saw in ImiZamo Yethu during a visit in 2002, that he set up the Niall Mellon Township Trust dedicated to providing subsidized housing in townships across South Africa and which has now become the biggest housing charity in the country.

TOURS OF IMIZAMO YETHU

Although it is unsafe to wander in by yourself, you can take a fun, two-hour **walking tour** (daily at 10.30am, 1pm & 4pm; R75; ☎083 719 4870, ⊕www.suedafrika.net/imizamoyethu) with enthusiastic and accomplished guide **Afrika Moni**, who knows the place and its history inside out. He walks you through his home township, stopping to chat to proprietors of informal "spaza" shops, sipping traditional beer at a *shebeen*, as well as popping into shacks and brick houses. Tours go and start from the **police station** at the entrance to the township, where there are reserved parking places for visitors driving there; the City Sightseeing bus comes out here too.

5

DUIKER ISLAND CRUISES

The best way to take in the landscape is on one of the short cruises just out of Hout Bay, from the harbour to **Duiker Island**, sometimes called "seal island" because it's home to a massive **seal colony**. It makes for a great trip, and the seals are delightful clowns, even if their fishy smell that emanates from the colony will make you wish you'd packed your nose plugs.

South African, or Cape, fur seals are the largest of the fur seals, which accounts for their popularity among hunters, who began harvesting them in the seventeenth century, severely depleting the population by 1893 when restrictions were introduced. Controlled hunting in South Africa continued till 1990 when it was finally suspended, with the exception of two culls on Malgas Island in 1999 and 2000 to protect gannet populations.

Of the operators that run tours (10 daily departures all year round; 45 min; R65) **Nauticat** (☎021 790 7278, ⓦwww.nauticatcharters.co.za) and **Circe Launches** (☎021 790 1040, ⓦcircelaunches.co.za) have glass-bottomed boats which allow you to see the seals and other marine denizens in action under water, as well as kelp forests when conditions are clear. Apart from the seals, the outings also provide fabulous views from the water of the Sentinel, the distinctive formation on the promontory that guards one side of the bay.

World of Birds

Valley Rd • Daily 9am–5pm • R70 • **Monkey jungle** daily 11.30am–1pm & 2–3.30pm • ⓦworldofbirds.org.za • **Feeding times**: penguins 11.30am and 3.30pm; pelicans 12.30pm; birds of prey 4.15pm

If you like birds, you'll love **World of Birds**, Hout Bay's biggest institutional attraction, which accommodates more than three thousand birds in surprisingly pleasant and peaceful walk-through aviaries and four hundred small mammals.

The birds include indigenous species such as cranes, vultures, ostriches and pelicans, as well as a number of feathered exotics. A large walk-in monkey jungle counts cute squirrel monkeys among its inhabitants, which visitors are allowed to pet.

There's a café serving light lunches, or you can picnic at the Flamingo Terrace. Children are well catered for with a couple of playground areas, and feeding time for the penguins, pelicans and birds of prey are a likely winner. The setting with lush gardens and a mountainous backdrop makes for a very tranquil outing; you'll need about two hours to get the most out of your visit.

Chapman's Peak Drive

Toll charge R30 • ☎021 791 8222, ⓦchapmanspeakdrive.co.za

The thrilling **Chapman's Peak Drive** is one of the world's great ocean drives, winding along a cliff-edge east of Hout Bay to Noordhoek. There are a number of safe viewpoints along the route, some of which have picnic sites, so bring a snack and refreshments and stop to enjoy the spectacular view. The road is occasionally closed due to rockfalls, so it's advisable to phone or visit their website to check out the current situation.

Noordhoek

Noordhoek, a fast-developing settlement at the southern end of the descent from Chapman's Peak Drive, consists of smallholdings and riding stables in a gentle valley planted with oaks. When Chapman's Peak is closed, Noordhoek is accessible via the M3 south over Oukaapseweg.

Signposted on the left, if you're heading south through town, is the *Red Herring* restaurant and pub (see p.127), which has views of the beach; it's set back from the sea, about ten minutes' walk from the car park. Also signposted in the vicinity is *Monkey Valley Resort* (see p.113), which welcomes non-guests for reasonably priced meals with great views.

5

Noordhoek Farm Village

Daily Sept–April 9am–5pm & May–Aug 10am–4pm • Free • ☎ 021 789 2812, ⓦ noordhoekvillage.co.za

The Noordhoek Farm Village close to the signposted entrance to Chapman's Peak drive, is essentially a rural mall, but it's one of the pleasantest shopping venues on the Cape Peninsula and caters incredibly well for kids, which accounts for its popularity with families. A regular weekend outing for many Cape Town families, it's laid out like a Cape Dutch farm complex, the manor houses a hotel and the outbuildings, arranged around a yard, house a restaurant, café alongside the children's playground as well as a pub, deli and several craft shops.

The beach

A long, wide untamed white-sand beach stretches 6km across Chapman's Bay to Kommetjie. The sands are fantastic for walking and **horseriding**, but can resemble a sandblaster when the southeaster blows. Swimming is cold, though **surfers** relish the rough waters around the rocks to the north.

Kommetjie

Although only a few kilometres south of Noordhoek along the beach, getting to **Kommetjie** by road involves a fifteen-kilometre detour inland, but is also great for walking, either around the rocky parts near Slangkop lighthouse, or on the sands towards Noordhoek. Kommetjie is another favourite surfing spot, though surfing in these parts is only for the very experienced; if you want to learn, Muizenberg is the place (see p.94).

Scarborough

The developing and idyllic village of **Scarborough**, almost 10km by road from Kommetjie, is the most far-flung settlement along the peninsula with cold, turquoise water and white sands. It's a lovely, easy drive to Scarborough from Simon's Town, winding over the spine of the peninsula, and onto Cape Point. The only reasonable food in town can be found at the *Camel Rock* restaurant (see p.121).

BEACH HUTS, ST JAMES

The False Bay seaboard to Cape Point

In summer, the waters of False Bay are several degrees warmer than those on the Atlantic seaboard, which is why Cape Town's oldest and most popular seaside developments are along this flank of the peninsula. A series of village-like suburbs, backing onto the mountains, each served by a Metrorail station, is dotted all the way south from Muizenberg, through St James, Kalk Bay, Fish Hoek and down to Simon's Town. Each has its own character and places to eat, drink and sleep, while Simon's Town, one of South Africa's oldest settlements, makes either a pleasant day-trip or useful base for visiting the African penguins at Boulders, just south of town, and Cape Point itself. It's the less fashionable, less glamorous and less-moneyed side of the peninsula, but no less beautiful.

6

By car Driving here from central Cape Town, the best route is along the M3 south to Muizenberg. Boyes Drive, a high-level alternative to Main Road, runs for about 5km between the suburbs of Lakeside at the southern end of the M3 and Kalk Bay, and offers spectacular views across to the Hottentots Holland Mountains on the east side of False Bay. The road is also one of several spots on the Cape Peninsula where, at the right time of year, you might spot whales (see box, p.97).

By train The train ride to Simon's Town is reason enough to visit, and from Muizenberg most stations are situated close

to the surf. From Cape Town there are roughly two trains an hour Mon–Fri (5am–7pm) to Simon's Town (1hr 15min; R13) and more frequently to Fish Hoek (58 min; R10), both services via Muizenberg (48 min; R10), St James (51 min; R10) and Kalk Bay (53 min; R10); on Sat & Sun services are reduced to roughly one an hour from Cape Town to Simon's Town. Metrorail (☎ 021 449 6478, ⓦ www.metrorail .co.za) provides telephonic timetable information or you can get downloadable pdfs from their website.

Muizenberg

Once boasting South Africa's most fashionable beachfront, **Muizenberg** (pronounced "mew-zin-burg"), 27km from the city centre, is now rather run-down, but is attempting to re-create itself with a new beachfront housing development and a splurge of good coffee shops – and nothing can detract from its long, safe and fabulous **beach** where brightly coloured beach huts are cheerful reminders of a more elegant heyday. During the 1920s, it was visited by the likes of Agatha Christie, who enjoyed riding its waves while holidaying here: "Whenever we could steal time off", she wrote, "we got out our surf boards and went surfing."

The beach

Muizenberg's gently shelving, sandy beach is the most popular along the peninsula for swimming, especially on Sundays in summer, though it can be very windy. There's good surfing in its breakers, where grown-ups and children can take **surfing lessons** (see p.140).

A **waterslide** and **minigolf** at the northern end of the beach also help keep kids well occupied. Away from the shoreline, Muizenberg's shabby-chic village high street is worth a wander, frequented by the artistic fraternity in Muizenberg as well as a Congolese community.

The Historical Mile

A short stretch of the shore, starting at Muizenberg station, is known as the **Historical Mile**, dotted with a run of notable buildings and easily explored on foot. **Muizenberg station**, an Edwardian-style edifice completed in 1913, is now a National Monument, while the **Posthuys** is a rugged whitewashed and thatched building dating from 1673 and a fine example of the Cape vernacular style.

Rhodes' Cottage Museum

246 Main Rd • Summer daily 10am–3pm, winter 11am–2pm • Free

Controversial millionaire mining magnate, politician and empire builder Cecil John Rhodes bought this modest cottage in Muizenberg in 1899, as his country retreat. His intention was to spend time here while his more monumental pile Rust en Vrede (closed to the public), designed by Sir Herbert Baker, was being built next door at no.

BEACH SAFETY TIPS

Don't take anything valuable onto the beach, and don't leave anything unguarded when you're on it, since opportunist theft is rife. Guards are present at the beachfront car park, so preferably leave valuables in your car boot. Some of the beachfront establishments will look after car keys while you head for the water; a good bet is *Knead* coffee shop, which keeps them for their customers at the cash till.

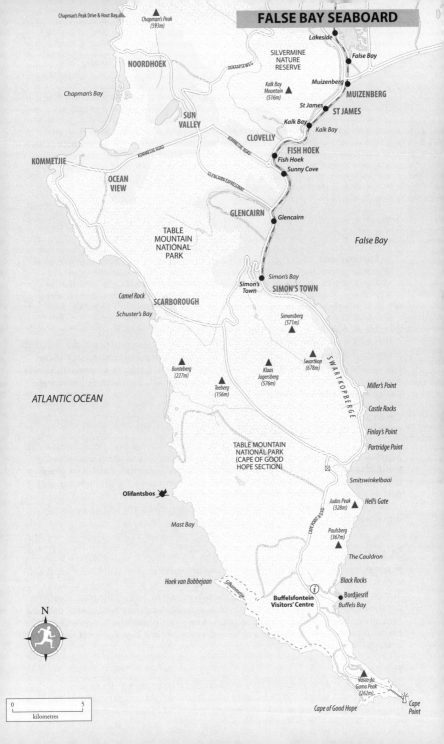

6

THE CAPE DUTCH REVIVAL

During the 1890s, millionaire tycoons like British expatriate **Cecil John Rhodes** found themselves at the top of the South African pecking order. These men saw themselves as an Anglo-African aristocracy lording it over the country much as the landed gentry did back in Britain. The so-called **Randlords** (Johannesburg mining magnates) and people like Rhodes in the Cape were among the biggest patrons of architecture, and they sought a language to express their new power and status.

Rhodes commissioned **Herbert Baker**, a young English architect schooled in the British Arts and Crafts Movement and who worked with Sir Edward Lutyens, to build **Groote Schuur** (1898), his home on Klipper Road in Rondebosch, which is now South Africa's official presidential residence. In looking for precedents, Baker identified Cape Dutch architecture as a suitable model – it was old and it represented wealth, making it the closest equivalent in South Africa to the stately homes of England.

Baker used recognizable **Cape elements** such as gables, curving multi-paned windows and steeply pitched roofs, at the same time drawing on English traditions, for example barley-sugar chimneys that hark back to Tudor architecture, while bird figures removed by Rhodes from Great Zimbabwe were used to suggest the gargoyles of Gothic architecture.

This style came to be known as **Cape Dutch Revival**, and was again used by the architect at **Rust en Vrede** (1902), Rhodes' seaside residence, adjacent to Rhodes' Cottage Museum in Muizenberg. The Cape Dutch Revival has become well established in South African architectural parlance: the twentieth century saw the appearance of Cape Dutch features, particularly gables, in suburban houses, no matter how inappropriate the scale or context.

---

244. He died at the cottage in 1902 before the house was completed.

The cottage contains memorabilia painting a distinctly rosy portrait of the man, with photographs, a model of the Big Hole in Kimberley in the Northern Cape (where Rhodes made his fortune at the diamond diggings), and a curious diorama of World's View in Zimbabwe's Matopos Hills, where he was buried. The cottage's lovely *fynbos* garden straggles up the hillside.

Casa Labia

192 Main Rd • Tues–Sun 10am–4pm • Free • ☎ 021 788 6068, ⓦ casalabia.co.za

The most idiosyncratic of the buildings along the historical mile, and closest to St James, **Casa Labia** was completed in 1930 as the residence of the Italian consul, Count Natale Labia. Built in the eighteenth-century Venetian style, it's a glorious piece of architectural bling on Main Road and worth popping into just for the palazzo's film-set **interiors**. It also houses a **cultural centre** that puts on concerts and talks, a **gallery** that features contemporary South African art, and an opulently furnished café.

St James

St James, 2km south of Muizenberg, is more upmarket than its neighbour, peppered with mountainside homes that are accessible for the most part up long stairways between Main Road and Boyes Drive. The best reason to hop off the train here is for the **sheltered tidal pool** and the twenty-minute walk along the **paved coastal path** that runs along the rocky shore to Muizenberg – one of the peninsula's easiest and most rewarding walks, with panoramas of the full sweep of False Bay. Look out for seals, and in season, whales.

The beach

The compact St James beach draws considerable character from its much-photographed Victorian-style bathing huts, whose bright, primary colours catch your eye as you pass by road or rail. The beach tends to be overcrowded at weekends and during school holidays; far fewer visitors take the trouble to stroll along the short footpath that leads south along the lawned shore from St James to the adjacent sandy stretch of **Danger Beach**, an excellent spot for sunbathing and building sand castles. As the name suggests, its surf should be treated with respect as there is a powerful undertow here.

Kalk Bay

One of the most southerly and smallest of Cape Town's suburbs, **Kalk Bay** centres around a lively working harbour with wooden fishing vessels, mountain views and a strip of shops brimming with collectables, antiques dealers and plenty of places to eat and drink. Kalk Bay somehow managed to slip through the net of the Group Areas Act, making it one of the few places on the peninsula with an intact coloured community, and Kalk Bay and the larger Hout Bay (see p.90) are the only harbour settlements still worked by coloured fishermen. Kalk Bay is also home to numerous artists and creative types who thrive on the village atmosphere and the natural beauty of the place.

The settlement is arranged around the small docks, where you can watch the boats come in; you can also buy fresh fish, which are flung onto the quayside and sold in spirited and noisy auctions. The harbour is busiest on Saturdays and Sundays when Capetonians descend to pick up something for a weekend braai or to have lunch at one of the several terrifically located **restaurants** in the area (see p.122), some within spitting distance of the breakers.

WHALE SPOTTING ON THE FALSE BAY SEABOARD

The most common whales you'll see off the Cape are **southern rights**, and the warmer **False Bay** side of the peninsula has the best **whale-watching spots** in season (roughly August to November). There is some chance of spotting them on the **Atlantic seaboard** too (see p.85); whichever seaboard you're visiting, you should have **binoculars** handy. The months when you are more or less guaranteed sightings are **September and October.**

Boyes Drive, running along the mountainside behind Muizenberg and Kalk Bay, provides an outstanding vantage point. To get there by car, head out on the M3 from the city centre to Muizenberg, taking a sharp, signposted right into Boyes Drive, at Lakeside, from where the road begins to climb, descending finally to join Main Road between Kalk Bay and Fish Hoek.

Alternatively, sticking close to the shore along Main Road, the stretch between **Fish Hoek** and **Simon's Town** is recommended, with a particularly nice spot above the rocks at the south end of Fish Hoek Beach, as you walk south towards Glencairn. **Boulders Beach** at the southern end of Simon's Town has a whale signboard, and smooth rocky outcrops above the sea to sit on and gaze out over the water.

Even better vantage points are further down the coast between Simon's Town and **Smitswinkelbaai**, where the road goes higher along the mountainside. Without a car, you can get the train to Fish Hoek or Simon's Town and whale-spot from the Jager's Walk beach path that runs along the coast from Fish Hoek to Sunny Cove, just below the train line.

It's worth noting that there are more spectacular spotting opportunities further east, especially around Hermanus and De Hoop (see p.180).

Although False Bay is great for land-based whale watching, on a boat you get a different perspective: you're in the mammal's own element and you may just get a closer look. It also offers the chance of spotting other marine mammals, including humpbacks, killer whales and dolphins. Simon's Town Boat Company (☎083 257 7760, ⊕boatcompany.co.za), based at the Simon's Town pier, is the only outfit licensed to do False Bay boat-based **whale-watching trips** (R750); they also do cruises around Cape Point (R350), to Seal Island (R250) and historic guided tours that include a visit to the Naval Dockyard and a **tour of a submarine** (R80).

6

Fish Hoek

Fish Hoek, south of Kalk Bay, boasts one of the peninsula's finest family **beaches** along the False Bay coast. The best and safest swimming is at its southern end, where the surf is moderately warm, tame and much enjoyed by boogie boarders. Thanks to the beach, there's a fair amount of accommodation (see p.114), but this is otherwise one of the dreariest suburbs along the False Bay coast. An obscure by-law banning the sale of alcohol in supermarkets or bottle stores boosts the town's image as the Mother Grundy capital of the peninsula.

Facilities include a playground, changing rooms, toilets, fresh water and the *Fish Hoek Galley Seafood Restaurant* (see p.122) right on the beach. From behind the restaurant, a picturesque concrete pathway called **Jager's Walk** provides a good vantage point for seeing whales. It skirts the rocky shoreline above the sea for 1km to Sunny Cove, from where it continues for 6km as an unpaved track to Simon's Town.

Simon's Town

Just 40km from Cape Town, roughly halfway down the coast to Cape Point, **Simon's Town** makes the perfect base for a mellow break along the peninsula, offering easy day-trips by train to Cape Town. Despite being South Africa's principal naval base, and incidentally the country's third-oldest European settlement, **Simon's Town** isn't the hard-drinking, raucous place you might expect. It's exceptionally pretty, with a preserved streetscape, slightly marred on the ocean side by the domineering **naval dockyard**, but this, and glimpses of naval squaddies square-bashing behind the high walls or strolling to the station in their crisp white uniforms, are what give the place its distinct character. A few kilometres to the south is the rock-strewn **Boulders Beach**, with its colony of nonchalant **African penguins** – reason in themselves to venture here.

Brief history

Founded in 1687 as the winter anchorage of the Dutch East India Company, Simon's Town was one of several places in and around Cape Town modestly named by **Governor Simon van der Stel** after himself. Its most celebrated visitor was Lord Nelson, who convalesced here as a midshipman while returning home from the East in 1776.

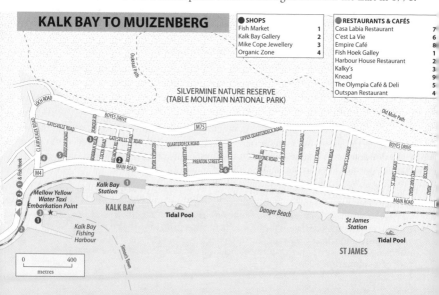

Nineteen years later, the British sailed into Simon's Town and occupied it as a bridgehead for their first invasion and occupation of the Cape. After just seven years they left, only to return in 1806. Simon's Town remained a British base until 1957, when it was handed over to South Africa.

There are fleeting hints, such as the occasional mosque, that the town's predominantly white appearance isn't the whole story. In fact, the first **Muslims** arrived from the East Indies in the early eighteenth century, imported as slaves to build the Dutch naval base. After the British banning of the slave trade in 1807, ships were compelled to disgorge their human cargo at Simon's Town, where one district became known as Black Town. In 1967, when Simon's Town was declared a White Group Area, there were 1200 well-established coloured families descended from these slaves. By the early 1970s, the majority had been forcibly removed under the Group Areas Act to the township of Ocean View, whose inspiring name belies its desolation.

6

ARRIVAL AND DEPARTURE   SIMON'S TOWN

By train If you're travelling by train to Simon's Town you can arrange to be collected by a *rikki* (☎ 072 387 4366); they charge R10/km for up to four people: a one-way trip to Boulders will set you back R40; an excursion to Cape Point returning you to the station R500.

Kalk Bay–Simon's Town Water taxi Mellow Yellow Water Taxi runs an hourly service (enquiries and bookings

☎ 073 473 7684, ⓦ watertaxi.co.za; 9am–4pm; R100 one way, R150 return per person) between Kalk Bay Harbour (leaving on the half-hour) and Simon's Town public jetty at the marina (leaving on the hour). Although tickets can be bought on the boat, it's best to book ahead as the vessel takes a maximum of ten passengers and services are subject to the weather and whales crossing.

Simon's Town Museum
Court Rd • Mon–Fri 10am–4pm, Sat 10am–1pm • R10

The building now housing the **Simon's Town Museum** was once the Old Residency, built in 1772 for the Governor of the Dutch East India Company, and has also served as the slave quarters (the dungeons are in the basement) and town brothel. The museum's motley collection includes maritime material and an inordinate amount of information and exhibits on Able Seaman Just Nuisance, a

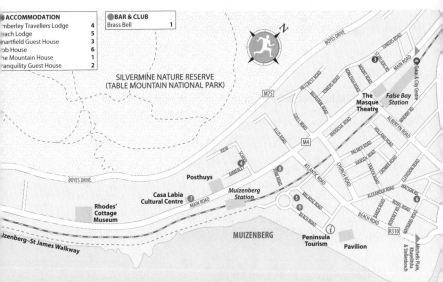

ACCOMMODATION
mberley Travellers Lodge 4
each Lodge 5
nartfield Guest House 3
ob House 6
he Mountain House 1
ranquility Guest House 2

BAR & CLUB
Brass Bell 1

6

much-celebrated seafaring **Great Dane**. He enjoyed drinking beer with the sailors he accompanied into Cape Town, and was adopted as a mascot by the South African Royal Navy in World War II.

The building also reputedly still houses the **ghost** of Eleanor, the 14-year-old daughter of Earl McCartney, who lived here in the closing years of the eighteenth century. Forbidden by her parents from playing on the sands with the children of coloured fishermen, Eleanor would escape to the beach through a secret tunnel she had discovered. The dankness of the tunnel supposedly gave her pneumonia, from which she tragically died.

South African Naval Museum
West Dockyard, accessed from St George's St • Daily 10am–4pm • Free

At the **South African Naval Museum**, lively displays include the inside of a submarine, a ship's bridge that simulates rocking, and a lot of official portraits of South African naval commanders from 1922 to the present. Although much altered now, the museum is housed in the original Dutch East India Company magazine and storehouse, which was taken over by the Royal Navy when it installed its headquarters in Simon's Town in 1810.

Jubilee Square and the Marina

In the centre of Simon's Town, a little over 1km south of the station, lies **Jubilee Square**, a palm-shaded car park just off St George's Street. Flanked by some cafés and shops, the street has on its harbour-facing side a broad walkway with a statue of the ubiquitous Able Seaman Just Nuisance and a few stalls selling curios. A couple of sets of stairs lead down to the **Marina**, a modest development of shops and restaurants set right on the waterfront. The best **fish and chips** is to be had at the *Salty Seadog* (see p.123).

Seaforth beach

Seaforth is the closest access point to a large viewing platform where the greatest numbers of penguins in Simon's Town congregate. It also has one of the best beaches for swimming, where clear, deep waters lap around rocks. It's calm, protected and safe, but not pretty (it's bounded on one side by the looming grey mass of the naval base), though it does have plenty of lawn shaded by palm trees, and a **restaurant** with outdoor seating and fresh fish on the menu.

You can access the Boulders penguin reserve (see p.102) via a pathway leading from Seaforth, 2km east of Jubilee Square, as well as from the signposted car park at Boulders itself.

SILVERMINE NATURE RESERVE

Rising up behind Boyes Drive is the **Silvermine Nature Reserve** (dawn–dusk; R30) which runs across the peninsula's spine, almost stretching to the west side at Chapman's Peak. Comprising part of the Table Mountain chain of peaks, it offers **walks** with fabulous views of False Bay, the mountains and montane *fynbos*, or picnics next to an idyllic **lake**.

By car, it's most easily reached via the **Oukaapseweg** (Old Cape Road, the M64), signposted at the southern end of the M3. It's also possible to get into the eastern half of the reserve (entrance free) via paths that strike up from Boyes Drive, including a set of stairs in Kalk Bay that heads up from Boyes Drive just as it makes a sharp turn down to the harbour. The climb is well worth the effort for the superb **aerial views** of the Indian Ocean.

The excellent Slingsby **map** of Silvermine is widely available at outdoor shops such as Cape Union Mart, with the hiking trails marked on; otherwise there is a sketchy one handed out as you enter the gate.

Boulders Beach and the penguin reserve

Penguin reserve Feb–March 8am–6.30pm; April–Sept 8am–5pm; Oct–Nov 8am–6.30pm; Dec–Jan 7am–7.30pm • R40

The most popular local beach, **Boulders** takes its name from the huge rounded rocks that create a cluster of little coves with sandy beaches and clear, cold sea pools that make for wonderful swimming. However, the main reason people come to Boulders is for the **African penguins** in the Boulders section of the Table Mountain National Park, a fenced **reserve** on Boulders Beach. African penguins usually live on islands off the west side of the South African coast, the Boulders birds forming one of only two mainland colonies in the world. This is also the only place where the endangered species are actually increasing in numbers, and provides a rare opportunity to get a close look at them.

Miller's Point

Almost 5km to the south of Simon's Town is the popular **Miller's Point** resort, which has a number of small sandy beaches and a tidal pool protected from the southeaster. Along Main Road, the notable *Black Marlin* **restaurant** (see p.122) attracts busloads of tourists, while the boulders around the point attract rock agama, black zonure lizards and dassies.

Smitswinkelbaai

The last place before you get to the Cape of Good Hope Section of the Table Mountain National Park is **Smitswinkelbaai** (pronounced "smits-vin-cull-buy"). This little cove has a small beach safe for swimming, but feels the full blast of the southeaster. It's not accessible **by car**, as local property-owners fiercely guard their privacy; to get there, you must park next to the road and walk down a seemingly endless succession of stairs.

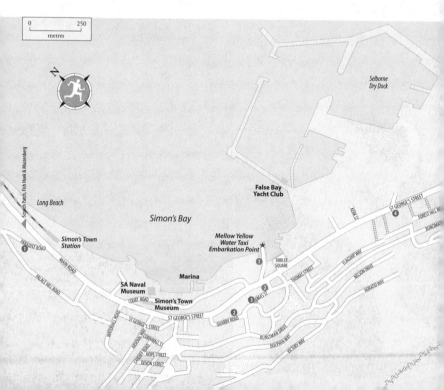

SHARK COUNTRY

False Bay is one of the best places in the country to encounter Great White sharks. For one thing, the False Bay sharks are on average about a third bigger than their Gansbaai counterparts.

Apex Shark Expeditions (Quayside Building, Shop no. 3, Main Road, Simon's Town ☎021 786 5717, ⓦapexpredators.com) is operated by naturalists Chris and Monique Fallows, who have worked with National Geographic and the BBC. They operate a range of marine trips in False Bay, among them shark-cage diving. Their emphasis is on observing shark behaviour – and that of other marine creatures that you'll encounter on the trip out to Seal Island – rather than the adrenaline rush. Trips are in groups of a maximum twelve people, which means you have a pretty personalized experience and get twenty to thirty minutes in the cage. Trips leave from the Simon's Town pier and prices vary according to season (and the corresponding likelihood of encountering a shark): Feb–March R1350, April–May R1700, June–Aug R2400.

6

Cape of Good Hope Nature Reserve

Daily April–Sept 7am–5pm; Oct–March 6am–6pm • R80 • ☎021 780 9526, ⓦwww.tmnp.co.za, ⓦwww.capepoint.co.za

Most people who visit the **Cape of Good Hope section** of Table Mountain National Park are here to see the southernmost tip of Africa and the place where the Indian and Atlantic oceans meet at **Cape Point**. In fact, this is the site of neither: the continent's real tip is at Cape Agulhas, some 300km southeast of here (see p.175), but Cape Point is a lot easier to get to and an awesomely dramatic spot nonetheless – and one not to miss. The reserve sits atop massive sea cliffs with huge views, strong seas, and an even wilder wind, which whips off caps and sunglasses as visitors gaze southwards from the old lighthouse buttress.

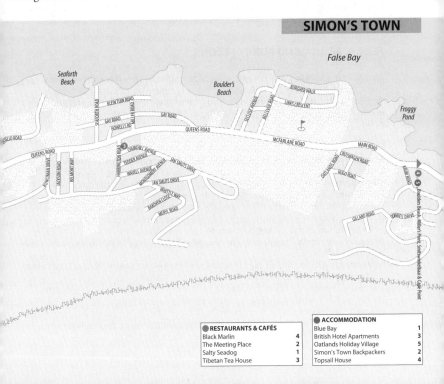

SIMON'S TOWN

● RESTAURANTS & CAFÉS	
Black Marlin	4
The Meeting Place	2
Salty Seadog	1
Tibetan Tea House	3

● ACCOMMODATION	
Blue Bay	1
British Hotel Apartments	3
Oatlands Holiday Village	5
Simon's Town Backpackers	2
Topsail House	4

6

The funicular

R45 return

From the car park, it's a short, steep walk – one crawling with tourists – up to the famous viewpoint, the original lighthouse. A **funicular** runs the less energetic to the top of the first lighthouse, where there's a shop selling knick-knacks. Built in 1860, the **lighthouse** was too often dangerously shrouded in cloud, and failed to keep ships off the rocks, so in 1914 another was built lower down and closer to the Point. This second lighthouse isn't always successful in averting disasters, but is still the most powerful light beaming onto the sea from South Africa.

The beaches

You'll find the **beaches** along signposted side roads branching out from the Cape Point road through the reserve. The sea here is too dangerous for swimming, but there are safe tidal pools at the adjacent **Buffels Bay** and **Bordjiesrif**, midway along the east shore. Both have braai stands, but more southerly Buffels Bay is the nicer, with big lawned areas and some sheltered spots to have a picnic, but don't produce any food if there are baboons in the vicinity.

Walks

There are several marked **walks** in the Cape of Good Hope section. If you're planning a big hike it's best to set out early, as shade is rare and the wind can be foul, especially during summer, often increasing in intensity as the day goes on. One of the most straightforward **hiking routes** is the signposted forty-minute trek from the car park at Cape Point to the more westerly **Cape of Good Hope**. For exploring the shoreline, a clear path runs down the Atlantic side, which you can join at **Gifkommetjie**, signposted off Cape Point Road. From the car park, several sandy tracks drop quite steeply down the slope across rocks, and through bushes and milkwood trees to the shore, along

---

FLORA, FAUNA AND FURRY FELONS

Most visitors make a beeline for Cape Point, seeing the rest of the reserve through a vehicle window, but walking is the best way to appreciate indigenous Cape **flora**. At first glance the landscape appears rocky and bleak, with short, wind-cropped plants, but the vegetation is surprisingly rich. Amazingly, many bright blooms in Britain and the US, including varieties of geraniums, freesias, gladioli, daisies, lilies and irises, are hybrids grown from indigenous Cape plants.

Along with indigenous plants and flowers, you may well spot some of the animals living in the reserve's **fynbos** habitat. **Ostriches** stride through the low *fynbos*, and occasionally **African penguins** come ashore. A distinctive bird on the rocky shores is the **black oystercatcher** with a bright red beak, jabbing limpets off the rocks. You'll also see **Cape cormorants** in large flocks on the beach or rocks, often drying their outstretched wings. Running up and down the water's edge (where, as on any other beach walk in the Cape, you'll see piles of shiny brown *Ecklonia* kelp) are **white-fronted plovers** and **sanderlings**, probing for food left by the receding waves. As for mammals, **baboons** lope along the rocky shoreline, while **bontebok**, **eland** and **red hartebeest** graze along the heathery slopes, as do **Cape rhebok** and **grysbok**. If you're very lucky, you may even see some of the extremely rare **Cape mountain zebras**.

Baboons may look amusing, but be warned: they can be a menace. Keep your car windows closed, as it's not uncommon for them to invade vehicles, and they're adept at swiping picnics. You should lock your car doors even if you only plan to get out for a few minutes to admire the view as there are growing reports of baboons opening unlocked car doors while the vehicle owner's back is turned. Do not ever unwrap food or eat or drink anything if baboons are in the vicinity. Feeding them is illegal and provocative and can incur a fine. Authorized baboon-chasers are in evidence in several places, warding them off.

VISITING THE CAPE OF GOOD HOPE

Most visitors see the Point as part of a circular trip, returning via Kommetjie and the especially scenic Chapman's Peak Drive (see p.91).

Numerous **tours** spend a day stopping off at the peninsula highlights; Day Trippers (☎021 511 4766) runs fun tours for R545 (including a picnic lunch), some of which give you the option of **cycling** part of the way.

However you get there, go as early as you can in the day to avoid tour buses and the likelihood of the wind gusting more strongly as the day progresses.

The **Buffelsfontein Visitors' Centre** (daily 7.30am–5pm), 8km from the entrance gate, is worth a look, boasting attractive displays about the local fauna and flora as well as video screenings on the ecology of the area.

There's also a rather good restaurant here called the *Two Oceans* (see p.123).

6

which you can walk in either direction. Take **water** on any walk in the reserve, as there are no reliable fresh sources.

Navigators have been braving the rocks, winds and swells of Cape Point since the Portuguese first "rounded the Cape" in the fifteenth century. Plenty of wrecks lie submerged off its coast, and at **Olifantsbos** on the west side you can walk to a US ship sunk in 1942, and a South African coaster that ran aground in 1965.

KWANDAWE PRIVATE GAME RESERVE

Accommodation

Standards of accommodation are very high in Cape Town, and cover an impressive range of options. In the city centre, you'll find outstanding boutique hotels, luxury guesthouses and welcoming hostels, often boasting spectacular views of Table Mountain or the ocean. Stretch further along the Garden Route and discover country retreats in beautiful settings, eco-lodges built within forests and sumptuous beds in grand Victorian townhouses – at prices that would only get you a good B&B back home. Other than in the cheapest rooms, you'll always get a private bath or shower, and you'll often have use of a garden and pool, or your own private patio. One unusual prospect – and one of very few ways to experience black South Africa – is to stay in one of the African townships in Cape Town.

Although there's not much in the way of budget hotels, modest budgets are catered for by two main options. **Backpacker lodges** offer basic hostel accommodation in a dormitory, usually from around R120 per person, and most have double rooms too, with prices according to the level of luxury or en-suite facilities. There's been a rise in "**boutique**" backpackers, which, as well as dorms, offer almost luxurious doubles, percale cotton sheets and feather duvets. Some backpacker places have family accommodation, some are quiet, but most, as is to be expected, are about socializing. They are independently run, and listed in the free *Coast to Coast* booklet, which covers the whole country and is widely available in tourist information offices and hostels countrywide.

    Self-catering apartments and cottages are a worthy alternative to a hotel. You can expect the kitchen to come with crockery and cutlery, and for linen and towels to be provided. One of the best things about self-catering is the wide choice of location: you'll find them on farms, near beaches and in forests and wilderness areas and they're especially popular in Kalk Bay. ⓦsafarinow.com or Peninsula Tourism, Beach Road Pavilion, Muizenberg (ⓦcapetown.travel) have a great range of villas and apartments.

    Family accommodation is plentiful, and hotels often have rooms with extra beds or interconnecting rooms; kids usually stay for half-price. Note, however, that some of the posher B&Bs do not accept children as guests.

ESSENTIALS

Rates In this guide (including the Beyond the city chapters), accommodation prices are, unless stated otherwise, quoted as the lowest price per double room in high season, though for backpacker hostels the rate for dorms is per person. Note, however, that on the ground many rates are quoted per person rather than per room – make sure which it is when you phone to book. An English breakfast is almost always included in the rate – if not, it should be available to order.

Seasons High season basically refers to the South African summer – though note that prices rise again within this period, over Christmas and New Year and also over Easter – when it's strongly recommended that you book ahead. There's a lull in the midwinter low season (June–Aug), during which time you should have no problem finding plenty of good-value places to stay, often with hefty discounts. You can also try negotiating a cheaper price for a room on the day.

Booking If you find everything booked up or want greater choice Cape Town Tourism has an efficient accommodation booking desk if you are stuck in high season.

CITY CENTRE

Cape Town's liveliest street for clubs and restaurants is **Long Street**. There are a number of **backpacker lodges** and a couple of hotels on Long Street itself, and several places east of Long Street around the museum complex and the Company's Gardens. From here you can walk to all the museums, trawl Cape Town's best bars and clubs, and find transport easily out of the centre or to the Waterfront. Expect rooms fronting Long Street to be noisy.

★ **Cape Heritage Hotel** 90 Bree St ☎021 424 4646, ⓦcapeheritage.co.za; map p.49. An exceptionally stylish, elegant and tastefully restored boutique hotel located in a row of houses dating back to 1771, in Cape Heritage Square, just below the Bo-Kaap. The rooms are spacious and decorated with contemporary hand-crafted objects and original paintings; the service is charming. R2520

Cape Town Hollow Hotel 88 Queen Victoria St ☎021 423 1260, ⓦcapetownhollow.co.za; map p.49. A multistorey hotel with all mod cons, including a/c and cable TV, in every room. It's two minutes from the South African Museum and National Gallery, an easy and pleasant walk away via the Company's Gardens. It's worth paying a bit more for a mountain-facing room. R2400

Cat & Moose 305 Long St ☎021 423 7638, ⓦcatandmoose.co.za; map p.49. The most stylish of the Long St lodges, housed in an eighteenth-century building a couple of doors from the steam baths at the south end of the city centre. Timber floors, rugs, earthy reds and ochres as well as some African masks imbue it with a warm ethnic feel. The dorms, triples and double rooms are arranged around a small leafy courtyard, with a plunge pool. Dorms R120, doubles R340

Grand Daddy Hotel 38 Long St ☎021 424 7247, ⓦdaddylonglegs.co.za; map p.49. A feature of the *Grand Daddy* are the seven retro-cool American Airstream trailers, decorated by local artists, that sit on the roof, linked by wooden walkways. Besides staying in a snug trailer on the

7

rooftop, the hotel does have double rooms, also imaginative, colourful and funky with queen-sized beds. **R1500**

iKhaya Lodge Wandel St, Dunkley Square ☎ 021 461 8880, ⊕ ikhayalodge.co.za; map p.43. A guesthouse on a pretty square, right by the Gardens and museums and close to trendy places to eat. En-suite rooms in the main lodge building have balconies over looking the square, and a few luxury lofts boast ethnically-inspired decor. Offers 24hr reception, satellite TV and wi-fi throughout. **R650**

Rouge on Rose 25 Rose St, at the corner of Hout St ☎ 021 426 0298, ⊕ rougeonrose.co.za; map p.43. Nine, new, comfortable suites in a Bo-Kaap guesthouse, on an increasingly gentrified street, with great views across to

Signal Hill or the city. Convenient microwave and catering basics if you fancy a night in, and free internet. **R1200**

St Paul's Church Guest House 182 Bree St ☎ 021 423 4420, ⊕ stpaulschurch.co.za; map p.49. A charming, well-managed and inexpensive guesthouse in a Georgian building (formerly a maternity hospital) on a calm street on the city-centre fringes, within easy striking distance of the sights. The rooms are large, comfortable and light with huge windows and shared bathrooms. **R650**

Tudor Hotel 153 Longmarket St ☎ 021 424 1335, ⊕ tudorhotel.co.za; map p.49. En-suite B&B rooms in a quiet, very central and reasonably priced hotel, overlooking cobbled Greenmarket Square. **R1100**

7 V&A WATERFRONT AND DE WATERKANT

In keeping with the gentrified ambience of the **V&A Waterfront** (usually referred to simply as the Waterfront), accommodation here tends to be expensive; there are, however, a couple of more modestly priced places to stay. It's a good choice if you like shopping in a self-contained safe area, and want to be able to walk to restaurants and cafés, and it boasts a pleasing harbour atmosphere. Nearby, **De Waterkant** is an area of pretty, cobbled streets and terraced houses, with some excellent, upmarket self-catering accommodation and good local restaurants within easy reach of the city's best nightlife.

Breakwater Lodge Portswood Rd, Waterfront ☎ 021 406 1911 (ask for Lodge Reservations), ⊕ breakwaterlodge.co.za; map p.62. The most affordable place to stay in the Waterfront, this hotel is linked to Cape Town University's Graduate School of Business. It's pretty characterless; choose it only if the location is what matters most. **R1215**

The Cape Grace West Quay, Waterfront ☎ 021 410 7100, ⊕ capegrace.com; map p.62. One of South Africa's most expensive and exclusive hotels, in a perfect location, and deserving of every accolade. Each room opens onto harbour or Table Mountain views. **R5000**

City Lodge Corner of Alfred and Dock rds, Waterfront ☎ 021 419 9450, ⊕ citylodge.co.za; map p.62. A perfectly adequate, if rather austere hotel chain, less than 1km from both the Waterfront and the city centre. The rooms have TV and there's a small swimming pool. Rates are cheaper Fri–Sun nights, and you can also pick up discounts using the hotel's room-auction site ⊕ bid2stay.co.za. **R1500**

St John's Waterfront Lodge 6 Braemar Rd ☎ 021 439 1404, ⊕ stjohns.co.za; map p.62. The closest hostel to the Waterfront (a 15min walk away), well run by friendly and helpful staff. Accommodation comes in dorms and doubles, with communal facilities including two swimming pools, a great garden and a bar, internet access, a coin-operated washing machine and a travel centre. Dorms **R120**, doubles **R400**

★ **Village and Life** Reception at 1 Loader St, De Waterkant ☎ 021 409 2500, ⊕ villageandlife.com; map p.62. Attractively restored historic cottages adjacent to the Bo-Kaap and less than 1km from the Waterfront, Green Point and city centre. The luxury cottages in Waterkant, Loader, Dixon and Napier sts have up to three bedrooms; some have garages, swimming pools and roof gardens with harbour or mountain views. Also part of the district are two B&B establishments. The company also has self-catering apartments for rent in the Waterfront itself. **R1000**

CITY BOWL SUBURBS

The **City Bowl suburbs** are popular for accommodation, and the most northerly sections are just five to ten minutes' walk from the Company's Gardens and the museums. A few backpacker lodges can be found along **Kloof Street**, the continuation of trendy Long Street, with some great cafés and restaurants. It's quieter and leafier than the city centre, especially the further up the mountainside you go, with gardens, good views and swimming pools at the more comfortable guesthouses. **New Church Street** is quieter traffic-wise than Long Street for backpacker accommodation, and several hostels have comfortable en-suite doubles.

African Sun 3 Florida Rd, Vredehoek ☎ 021 461 1601, ⊕ afpress@iafrica.com; map p.73. A small self-catering apartment, attached to a family house a little over 1km

from the city centre. Furnished with pared-back ethnic decor, it's run by friendly, well-informed owners, both well-known published writers who also offer literary evenings and tours as an extra. Good value. R590

Ashanti Lodge and Guest House 11 Hof St, Gardens ☎ 021 423 8721, ☻ashanti.co.za; map p.73. This massive, refurbished two-storey Victorian mansion has marbling and ethnic decor, soaring ceilings, a nicely kept front garden and a swimming pool with sun terrace. The private rooms (with twin or double beds, and shared bath) and dorms (sleeping 6–8) are furnished with custom-made wrought-iron bunks and beds. The bar is very lively, so if you are not a party animal, head for their guesthouse nearby in Union St, which has en-suite rooms (R600). Dorms R140, doubles R600

The Backpack 74 New Church St, Tamboerskloof ☎ 021 423 4530, ☻backpackers.co.za; map p.73. An excellent lodge in three interconnected houses, on the cusp of the City Bowl suburbs and the city centre, and easily walkable to both. It is furnished with bold colours and ethnic fabrics, with plenty of outdoor space, including a pool terrace in its own garden. Accommodation is in dorms (sleeping 4–8) and private rooms; some rooms are suitable for families. Dorms R145, doubles R550

Belmont House 10 Belmont Ave, Oranjezicht ☎ 021 461 5417, ☻capeguest.com; map p.73. A tastefully restored 1920s house with seven, fresh rooms, each with its own shower or bath. Rooms are on a B&B basis, and you can self-cater during the day in the communal kitchen. R700

Bergzicht 5 Devonport Rd, Tamboerskloof ☎ 021 423 8513, ☻bergzicht@kingsley.co.za; map p.73. Friendly and informal guesthouse with attentive hosts, good views and a pool. Rooms are simply furnished without pretension. R995

★ **Blencathra** Corner of De Hoop and Cambridge aves, Tamboerskloof ☎ 021 424 9571, ☻www.blencathra.co.za; map p.73. A large relaxed family house with stunning views on the slopes of Lion's Head 2km from the city centre and 4km from the Atlantic. They offer peaceful, spacious self-catering rooms, four of which are en suite, attracting a young crowd who want to avoid the backpacker scene. The garden has seating and a swimming pool. Dorms R150, doubles R800

Cape Milner Hotel 2a Milner Rd, Tamboerskloof ☎ 021 426 1101, ☻www.capemilner.com; map p.73. A smart, reasonably priced hotel, partly incorporating an early eighteenth-century building, at the foot of Signal Hill. The airy rooms all boast views of Table Mountain and minimalist decor, and the service is good. There's also a swimming pool, restaurant and bar on the premises. R1300

Cape Town Backpackers 81 New Church St ☎ 021 426 0200, ☻capetownbackpackers.com; map p.73. Just off Kloof St, an excellent hostel with the usual hostel facilities, including a travel desk and a great range of rooms, from deluxe en suites with their own balconies to standard dorms. The roof terrace boasts views of Table Mountain. Dorms R130, doubles R650

Hippo Boutique Hotel 5–9 Park Rd, Gardens ☎ 021 423 2500, ☻hippotique.co.za; map p.73. Trendy hotel in a good location. Each spacious room has its own kitchenette and coffee maker, a PC and free wi-fi. With convenience and modernity being at the heart of the style here, you don't have to walk further than downstairs for a Mexican or Thai meal, which can also be delivered to your room. R1290

Leeuwenvoet House 93 New Church St, Tamboerskloof ☎ 021 424 1133, ☻leeuwenvoet.co.za; map p.73. A tranquil restored Victorian guesthouse, with twelve en-suite rooms kitted out with pine and wicker furniture, and equipped with TV, phone and fan. Situated on a major thoroughfare with secure parking, it's just a 15min walk from the city centre. R1290

Lezard Bleu 30 Upper Orange St, Oranjezicht ☎ 021 461 4601, ☻lezardbleu.co.za; map p.73. Seven luxurious en-suite rooms, furnished with maple beds and cupboards in a spacious open-plan 1960s house. Each room has sliding doors opening onto a garden and swimming pool. It also boasts one of the best rooms in central Cape Town – a tree house in the garden. R1220

Mount Nelson Hotel 76 Orange St, Gardens ☎ 021 483 1000, ☻mountnelson.co.za; map p.73. Cape Town's *grande dame*: a fine and famous high colonial Victorian hotel, built in 1899 (and extended in the late 1990s). Perfectly located, and set in extensive established gardens, with arrival along a palm-lined colonnade, it takes itself terribly seriously and charges accordingly. Rooms are not that large, but its location makes it a highly popular choice for internationals in the movie industry, parliamentarians or anyone whose work trip is being sponsored. R6000

Nine Flowers Guest House 133 Hatfield St, Gardens ☎ 021 462 1430, ☻nineflowers.com; map p.73. Very conveniently located right by the museums and pleasant Dunkley Square, this nine-roomed restored Victorian guesthouse is minimally and immaculately furnished and kept. Off-street parking. R1050

Saasveld Lodge 73 Kloof St, Tamboerskloof ☎ 021 424 6169, ☻saasveldlodge.co.za; map p.73. A rather impersonal 1950s-style, four-storey guesthouse on a buzzing thoroughfare lined with good restaurants, less than 1km from the centre. The rooms are en suite and have TV and phone. R850

TOP 5 B&BS

Blackheath Lodge Sea Point, see p.112.
Chartfield Guesthouse Kalk Bay, see p.114.
Cob House Muizenberg, see p.114.
Stonehurst Guesthouse Sea Point, see p.112.
Welgelegen Boutique Guesthouse City Bowl Suburbs, see p.110.

7

Underberg Guest House 6 Tamboerskloof Rd, Tamboerskloof ☎021 426 2262, ⊚underberg guesthouse.co.za; map p.73. Located on the doorstep of the city centre, this Victorian guesthouse offers excellent value. Its high ceilings and compact size – there are only eleven rooms – create an atmosphere that is both intimate and airy. R1200

★ **Welgelegen Boutique Guest House** 6 Stephen St, Gardens ☎021 426 2373, ⊚welgelegen.co.za; map p.73. A Victorian guesthouse with mountain views, styled with a luxurious mix of old classic and African chic, and with a spa treatment room and massages for guests, and a DVD library The owners are green and socially aware,

involved in everything from recycling initiatives to poverty alleviation projects. R1850

Zebra Crossing 82 New Church St ☎021 422 1265, ⊚zebra-crossing.co.za; map p.73. Cape Town's only backpacker lodge that actually boasts about being quiet, with a child-friendly attitude and off-street parking. On the northern edge of the City Bowl suburbs, it's an easy walk to the Kloof St restaurants and pubs as well as those in the city centre. The café-bar serves full meals and decent coffee, and there are two pleasant terraces under vines. Accommodation is in spacious dorms, doubles and a few singles, with the best rooms taking in views of the mountain. Dorms R120, doubles R420

SOUTHERN SUBURBS

Cape Town's gracious **southern suburbs – Rosebank**, **Claremont**, **Newlands** and **Rondebosch**, on the forested side of the mountain – are home to Kirstenbosch Gardens as well as the fine Newlands cricket and rugby grounds. **Observatory** is the closest suburb to the city centre, with buzzing cafés, a couple of backpacker lodges and reasonable nightlife.

33 South Boutique Backpackers 48 Trill Rd, Observatory ☎021 447 2423, ⊚33southbackpackers .com. This spacious Victorian house caters to backpackers who are looking for a few creature comforts. It boasts an excellent location in a quiet street, a couple of minutes from both the train station and Lower Main Rd, with its nightlife and cafés. They offer rooms of a similar standard in other parts of Cape Town – for example in Kalk Bay, Bo-Kaap and Khayelitsha (see website for details). Dorms R120

Carmichael House 11 Wolmunster Rd, Rosebank ☎021 689 8350, ⊚carmichaelhouse.co.za. A two-storey guesthouse, close to the University of Cape Town, in a building dating from the turn of the last century, with six big rooms equipped with phone, safe and hairdryer. There's a peaceful garden, a swimming pool and secure parking, plus wi-fi or the use of a laptop at reception to check your email. R820

The Courtyard Liesbeek Ave, Mowbray ☎021 448 3929, ⊚citylodge.co.za. A beautiful early nineteenth-century Cape Dutch homestead under thatch, with terracotta floors, brass chandeliers and large lawns in a semi-rural setting, though not in an area you would want to explore. Exceptional value, considering the level of luxury. R1200

Elephant's Eye Lodge 9 Sunwood Drive, Tokai

☎021 715 2432, ⊚elephantseyelodge.co.za. Half a dozen rooms at a friendly B&B family home in a converted Cape Dutch farmhouse, in its own large grounds with a pool, minutes from Tokai Forest, a golf course and the wine estates of Constantia. R750

Gloucester House Bed & Breakfast 54 Weltevreden Ave, Rondebosch ☎021 689 3894, ⊚gloucesterhouse .co.za. A private house with two bedrooms, and a lounge/dining room for self-catering. Guests may use the large garden, swimming pool and barbecue area. R500

Ivydene Off Glebe Rd, Rondebosch ☎021 685 1747, ⊖ivydene@mweb.co.za. Five flats in a delightful old Cape farmhouse near the university, with a garden, swimming pool and a friendly atmosphere. There are discounts for stays over a week or more. R450

★ **The Vineyard** Corner of Colinton and Protea rds, Newlands ☎021 657 4500, ⊚vineyard.co.za. One of the city's top stays, in luxurious rooms, and better value than the *Mount Nelson* or *Cape Grace*, being out of the city centre, in a restored 1799 country villa, decorated in a contemporary style. The extensive gardens are like a peaceful country estate's, with an outstanding panorama of the forested slopes of Table Mountain. Great choice for a pampered stay with a spa and large heated swimming pool. R1900

ATLANTIC SEABOARD

Historically Cape Town's hotel and high-rise land, this is now packed with a range of accommodation, making it a good alternative to the City Bowl if you want to be close to both the city centre and the ocean. The well-heeled mountainside suburb of **Camps Bay** has soaring views over the Atlantic, with the advantage of being near the city centre and an upmarket Californian feel in its laidback restaurants and bars. Though nearby **Llandudno** lacks shops or restaurants, it can boast similar vistas and a supremely beautiful beach. **Hout Bay** is the main urban concentration along the lower half of the peninsula, with a harbour, pleasant waterfront development and the only public transport beyond Camps Bay.

FROM TOP CAPE HERITAGE HOTEL (P.107); GRAND DADDY HOTEL (P.107); SHAMWARI PRIVATE GAME RESERVE (P.253) >

7

GREEN POINT

Dale Court Guest House 1 Exhibition Terrace Rd ☎021 439 8774, ⓦdalecourt.co.za; map p.88. Conveniently located, reasonable if unremarkable B&B that accommodates children. The guesthouse manages the eight-storey block opposite, comprising functional self-catering apartments for families. **R950**

David's 12 Croxteth Rd ☎021 439 4649, ⓦdavids.co.za; map p.88. An elegant and airy B&B in a quiet residential street just off the main road, popular with men. Separate from the guesthouse are a selection of self-catering apartments, which it manages. **R770**

Jambo Guest House 1 Grove Rd ☎021 439 4219, ⓦjambo.co.za; map p.88. Small, atmospheric establishment with four luxury en-suite rooms and one garden suite, in a quiet cul-de-sac off Main Rd. The lush, leafy exterior and enclosed garden with a pond are delightfully relaxing and the service is excellent. **R1300**

Point B Guest House 14 Pine Rd ☎021 434 0902 or ☎083 627 5583, ⓦpointb.co.za; map p.88. Four rooms inside, and another in the garden of a 1900s house all brightly decorated, with wicker furniture. Great personal service, and there's poolside seating on a bricked terrace. **R1000**

Wilton Manor 15 Croxteth Rd ☎021 434 7869, ⓦwiltonmanor.co.za; map p.88. A quiet and friendly guesthouse with a homely atmosphere in a Victorian house close to the city centre. The service is good, and there's also a small garden. **R1200**

SEA POINT AND BANTRY BAY

★ **Blackheath Lodge** 6 Blackheath Rd ☎021 439 2541, ⓦblackheathlodge.co.za; map p.88. Superb owner-run guesthouse in a Victorian home that just gets everything right. Down a quiet backstreet, it's close to the Sea Point action. The ten rooms are large and airy (some with views of Lion's Head), and the king-sized beds are the most comfortable you'll find in Cape Town. Breakfast is served on a courtyard-garden deck overlooking the pool. **R1550**

Don Suite Hotel 249 Beach Rd, Sea Point ☎021 434 1083, ⓦwww.don.co.za; map p.88. A five-storey block of 27 self-catering apartments across the road from the beachfront promenade and 300m from the lively Main Rd restaurant strip. All the flats are modern and well equipped; rates vary depending on whether or not you get a view. **R1500**

Huijs Haerlem 25 Main Drive ☎021 434 6434, ⓦhuijshaerlem.co.za; map p.88. Elegant and friendly guesthouse in two adjacent houses furnished with Dutch antiques. Each of its eight rooms has a sea view, a vista of Signal Hill or overlooks the lovely garden. **R1450**

★ **Les Cascades de Bantry Bay** 48 De Wet Rd, Bantry Bay ☎021 434 5209, ⓦlescascades.co.za; map p.88. One of the most beautiful guesthouses in the country, in a prime position perched above the Atlantic. Every room has a full sea view and deck or balcony and there are lounges, verandas and swimming pools and a spa to complement the excellent service. Unusually for such an upmarket, honeymoon destination, it does take children. **R2150**

★ **Stonehurst Guest House** 3 Frere Rd, Sea Point ☎021 434 9670, ⓦstonehurst.co.za; map p.88. An airy tin-roofed Victorian residence with original fittings and furnished with an attractive melange of antiques and collectables by the friendly antique-dealer owner, Jan. There's a pleasant front garden, a kitchen for self-catering and a guest lounge. Most rooms are en suite, and some have balconies. Great value and location, a couple of roads back from busy Main Rd. **R650**

Villa Rosa 277 High Level Rd, Sea Point ☎021 434 2768, ⓦvilla-rosa.com; map p.88. A friendly eight-room guesthouse in a brick-red two-storey Victorian house on the lower slopes of Signal Hill, two blocks from the beachfront promenade. Decorated with simplicity and style, all rooms have TVs, phones and safes, but only some, on the upper floor, have sea views. **R975**

★ **Winchester Mansions Hotel** 221 Beach Rd, Sea Point ☎021 434 2351, ⓦwinchester.co.za; map p.88. A 1920s hotel, in a prime spot across the road from the seashore, with an atmosphere straight from the pages of Agatha Christie, though the best rooms are thoroughly fresh and contemporary. A cool Italianate courtyard restaurant is overlooked by balconies draped in luxuriant creepers. There's a good restaurant, too. **R2400**

CAMPS BAY AND BAKOVEN

Atlantic Guest House 3 Berkeley Rd, Camps Bay ☎021 438 4341, ⓦthebayatlantic.com. Supremely laidback and rather wonderful double-storey family home-turned-guesthouse. Rooms range from a small room with no view (probably the cheapest room in Camps Bay if it's the area you are after) to more luxurious ones with decks and superb views of the Atlantic (R1500). **R700**

Bateleur Rontree 12 Rontree St, Camps Bay ☎021 438 4783, ⓦbateleurshouse.co.za. Straightforward guesthouse notable for its friendly service and spectacular sea views from the pool deck and some rooms. Simply furnished ensuite rooms with tiled floors flow out onto a wooden deck. The guesthouse makes the most of outdoor living. **R990**

Bay Hotel Victoria Rd, Camps Bay ☎021 438 4444, ⓦthebay.co.za. Luxurious, glitzy five-star hotel on the fashionable beachfront strip. Its late-1980s construction blends neo-Cape Dutch with Mediterranean styles and cane furniture, to conjure up a laidback colonial fantasy. Rooms start from small, but well-appointed "Traveller's Rooms". **R2800**

Leeukop 25 Sedgemoor Rd, Camps Bay ☎021 438 1361, ⓦleeukop.co.za. Near the beach and cafés, this is a comfortable and stylishly decorated apartment adjoining the cheerful proprietor's home, boasting mountain views

AFRICAN TOWNSHIP HOMESTAYS

One of the best ways of getting a taste of the African townships is spending a night there, which is made possible by the growing number of township residents offering **B&B accommodation**. You'll have a chance to experience the warmth of *ubuntu* – traditional African hospitality – by staying with a family with whom you'll eat breakfast and dinner; they will often take you around their area to *shebeens*, music venues, church or just to meet the neighbours. **Prices** go from R500–600 per double, considerably cheaper than being in the centre of Cape Town, and this is probably your best chance of meeting black South Africans socially.

Some B&Bs will send someone to **meet you** at the airport; if you're driving they'll give you detailed directions or meet you at a convenient and obvious landmark. If you book through **Cape Tourism Centre** in Guguletu (☎ 021 637 8449, ⓦ capetowntravel.co.za) they will drop you off.

and a small patio garden. The flat is fully equipped but for a little extra the owner will fix you up breakfast. R1000
Ocean View House 22 Victoria Rd, Bakoven ☎ 021 438 1982, ⓦ oceanview-house.com. A river runs through the grounds of this family-run, eccentrically blue-and-yellow boutique hotel, set in a gorgeous garden that borders a *fynbos* reserve. The fourteen spacious rooms are comfortably furnished in a contemporary style and have either mountain or sea views. R1950

HOUT BAY, LLANDUDNO AND NOORDHOEK

★ **Ekogaia Farm Cottages** 2 Nthombeni Way, Noordhoek ☎ 021 789 1751 or ☎ 083 403 2623, ⓦ ekogaia.co.za. Two thatched, self-catering cottages on an attractive, organic smallholding with plenty of privacy. Both are built to a "low eco-footprint" model, and have outdoor patios, mountain and sea views, plus play areas for children. R650
★ **Hout Bay Hideaway** 37 Skaife St, Hout Bay ☎ 021 790 8040, ⓦ houtbay-hideaway.com. Outstanding guesthouse with genuine verve – Persian rugs, Art Deco armchairs, huge beds – and generally bursting with luxurious touches. Each of the four rooms has a mountain or sea view, and outdoor decks where your private breakfast is served. At the back there's a saltwater infinity pool in a *fynbos* garden that disappears onto the mountain side. R1500
★ **Houtkapperspoort** Hout Bay Main Rd, around 5km from Hout Bay and 15km from the city centre ☎ 021 794 5216, ⓦ houtkapperspoort.co.za. Rustic one- and two-bedroom, stone-and-brick self-catering cottages set up against the Table Mountain Nature Reserve, close to Constantia Nek. You can take paths straight from the estate up the mountain slopes, play tennis or take a dip in the solar-heated pool. R1300
Kopanong Khayelitsha ☎ 021 361 2084 or ☎ 082 476 1278, ⓦ kopanong-township.co.za. One of the most dynamic B&B operations in the township, run by the tireless Thope Lekau, who is on a mission to replace gawping tourists in their buses with guests who engage

with township life. This former NGO worker will treat you to a history of the township, introduce you to local music and dish up a traditional family breakfast. A traditional dinner is available on request, as is a guided tour.
Monkey Valley Resort Mountain Rd, Noordhoek ☎ 021 789 8000, ⓦ monkeyvalleyresort.com. An attractive group of mainly wooden and thatched chalets spread over several acres of Chapman's Peak, some 40km south of the city centre. Overlooking Noordhoek Beach, the site is surrounded by indigenous vegetation, though the only monkeys you'll find are in the name. You can eat in the restaurant, self-cater or stay on a B&B basis, in a variety of accommodation options, depending on the size of the group. Doubles R1500, self-catering cottages R2700
Majoro's Khayelitsha ☎ 021 361 3412 or ☎ 082 537 6882, ⓦ majoros-bed-and-breakfast.com. Hosted by the charming Maria Maile in her family home, which has two rooms that share a bath and toilet. Dinner includes traditional fare such as *mielie pap*, after which you can watch TV with the family, and next day you'll be treated to an English breakfast of sorts, which may include bacon and egg alongside fish cakes, sausage and home-made steamed bread.
Malebo's Khayelitsha ☎ 021 361 2391. Three rooms sharing bath and toilet facilities in the welcoming home of Lydea Masoleng and her husband. In the morning you'll be served a continental breakfast; dinners, which combine Western fare with traditional African food, are available on request. You're welcome to join your hosts on outings to a *shebeen* or, on Sunday, to church.
Maneo Langa ☎ 021 694 2504. Friendly hostess Thandiwe Peter offers accommodation in two rooms outside the house and one inside the family home, in Cape Town's oldest township, and the closest to the city centre, so most guests drive here. She will take guests to some of the township highlights, including a local *shebeen*.
Sunbird Mountain Retreat & Lodge Boskykloof Rd, Hout Bay ☎ 021 790 7758, ⓦ sunbirdlodge.co.za. Four pleasant, spacious self-catering apartments, and a guesthouse that includes a family unit, all nestling in a forest high up on the mountainside. All the rooms have

7

great views and there's a secluded swimming pool. Apartment R600 , double R900

★ **Sunset on the Rocks** 11 Sunset Ave, Llandudno ☎ 021 790 2103, ⊛ sunsetontherocks.co.za. This is a magical hideaway on one of the loveliest coves on the peninsula; three compact, self-contained flats sit in the midst of a wonderful *fynbos* garden belonging to charming proprietors Brian and Helen Alcock. Llandudno itself is shy of any shops and restaurants, but Hout Bay is only 10min away by car. R600

FALSE BAY SEABOARD

This is the area to look in if you want to swim every day, surf or walk on beaches, as well as enjoy excellent restaurants. Once hugely popular because of its stunning beach and bay views, it is now a bit run-down and its peeling beachfront hotels have been replaced by surfing schools and a couple of cafés. To its south is salubrious **St James**, while the jewel of the crown is **Kalk Bay** with its working harbour, antique shops and arty cafés. **Fish Hoek**, further south, is recommended for its beach but not much else, while **Simon's Town** is still regarded by many as a separate village, although it's now technically part of the metropolis.

MUIZENBERG TO FISH HOEK

Amberley Travellers Lodge 15 Amberley Rd, Muizenberg ☎ 021 788 7032 or ☎ 082 686 1864; map p.98. A restored two-storey house, off Main Rd and a hop across the railway line to the beach, with gleaming wooden floors and spacious rooms and kitchen. R280

Beach Lodge Surfers Corner, Muizenberg ☎ 021 788 1771, ⊛ thebeachlodge.co.za; map p.98. At the beach above a surfing shop, the *Beach Lodge* offers clean, bright budget rooms, the best of which have balconies fronting the promenade, though you'll hear the surf pounding wherever you are. Suitable for families. R360

★ **Chartfield Guest House** 30 Gatesville Rd, Kalk Bay ☎ 021 788 3793, ⊛ chartfield.co.za; map p.98. Unpretentious accommodation, 100m from Kalk Bay station, restaurants and shops. The well-kept, rambling house sits halfway up the hill overlooking the harbour, with terrific sea views from some rooms. R900

★ **Cob House** 13 Watson Rd, Muizenberg ☎ 021 788 6613, ⊛ cobhouse.co.za; map p.98. The greenest B&B in Cape Town, run by an exceptionally friendly family and set just 200m from the beach. There is only one, comfy guest room but it can sleep up to four and the reasonable rate includes a room service organic breakfast. The owner, Simric Yarrow (teacher, storyteller and musician) also runs excellent tours around the city. R700

The Mountain House 7 Mountain Rd, Clovelly ☎ 083 455 5664, ⊛ themountainhouse.co.za; map p.98. Beautiful self-catering accommodation equidistant between Fish Hoek and Kalk Bay. Built in the garden of local architect Carin Hartford, the two-bedroom cottage has windows on all sides to capitalize on the incredible mountain setting, with the living space flowing out to a timber deck. R900

Tranquility Guest House 25 Peak Rd, Fish Hoek ☎ 021 782 2060, ⊛ www.tranquil.co.za; map p.98. Warm and welcoming, on Fish Hoek mountainside with ocean views (the beach is within walking distance). There are four cosy B&B en-suite rooms, plus a self-catering apartment with its own entrance for the same price. Guests can soak in the outdoor jacuzzi. R1200

SIMON'S TOWN AND AROUND

Blue Bay 48 Palace Hill Rd ☎ 021 786 1700, ⊛ bbay .co.za; map p.102. Luxurious self-catering home with stupendous ocean views and tranquil ambience, 1km from the centre of Simon's Town. There are four double rooms, two of which you can have extra beds in. You can take the entire place as a whole, or just rent a room. R1000

British Hotel Apartments 90 St George's St ☎ 021 786 2214, ⊛ britishhotel.co.za; map p.102. Three-bedroom self-catering apartments in a grand 1898 Victorian hotel, that once had Cecil Rhodes and the nineteenth-century explorer, Mary Kingsley, as guests; there are also more modest doubles with baths. Part of a picturesque main street, this is an experience rather than just somewhere to stay, with Victorian colonial decor, high ceilings and huge balconies overlooking the street and the docks. A tiny double room is available for R500. R1400

Oatlands Holiday Village Froggy Pond, 3km from Simon's Town ☎ 021 786 1410, ⊛ oatlands.co.za; map p.102. Across the road from the beach and near a golf course, this family resort is set in large grounds with its own pool and playground. There are over twenty self-catering chalets of various sizes, sleeping two to six people; there's also a pub and restaurant on the premises. R550

Simon's Town Backpackers 66 St George's St ☎ 021 786 1964, ⊛ www.capepax.co.za; map p.102. Conveniently located in the heart of Simon's Town, within walking distance of the station. The double rooms are fairly spacious and there's a large balcony with a view of the waterfront. You can rent one of the bicycles and ride to Cape Point or paddle in a kayak past the penguin colony. Dorms R140, doubles R380

Topsail House 176 St George's St ☎ 021 786 5537, ⊛ topsailhouse.co.za; map p.102. An old convent converted into a backpacker lodge, with more space than average, though a tad staid. There are various accommodation options including an extraordinary bedroom in a chapel, though the en-suite doubles upstairs are the nicest. R420

LUNCHTIME AT KALKY'S

Eating

Eating out is one of the highlights of visiting Cape Town. The city has a large number of relaxed and convivial restaurants and cafés that generally serve imaginative food of a high standard. Prices are inexpensive compared with much of the developed world, and you can eat innovative food by outstanding chefs in upmarket restaurants, for the kind of money you'd spend on a pizza back home. One element that seems to unite the country is a love of meat, making it an ideal place to try out all kinds of interesting varieties, from ostrich to springbok, while good-quality steaks are inexpensive and freely available. As for seafood, you can expect fresh fish at every good restaurant. Cape Town itself is a good source of cold-water fish such as hake, often served as English-style fish and chips, and snoek, a delicious but bony fish.

ETHICAL EATING

It's a sad fact, but fish stocks are declining worldwide. If you want to do your bit and be ecologically responsible, go for a tasty Cape fish like **yellow tail**, which is not endangered and has a low carbon footprint, coming straight from the seas around the city. Although Kingklip and Cape salmon are on many menus, these are ones to avoid ethically. The **Southern African Sustainable Seafood Initiative (SASSI)** can inform you about the conservation status of different kinds of seafood; text the name of the fish you're buying, or are about to order, to ☏079 499 8795 to check its status.

As a visitor, you might struggle to keep in check the locals' assumption that meat – and lots of it – is the ideal choice for your meals, but **vegetarians** need not despair, as there's always at least one concession to meatless food on menus. Even steakhouses will have a meat-free option and generally feature reasonable salad bars.

Cape cuisine (see box below) must be sampled at least once. It's the exclusive focus of some restaurants in the city, though many of the dishes considered as Cape cuisine have actually crept into the staple South African diet and can be found on menus throughout Cape Town, and indeed the country.

The obvious accompaniment to your meals is locally produced **Cape wine**, costing R60 and up for a bottle of something quaffable, though **beer** is definitely the national drink (see p.127). Note that Muslim establishments Cape cuisine don't allow alcohol at all.

Although there are some fantastic culinary highlights in Cape Town, choosing a place to eat may sometimes be more about the venue than the food; there are several places boasting fabulous views or swinging atmosphere, which cover up the less fabulous cuisine. Several restaurants have live music and are as much about the food as the wine.

ESSENTIALS

Dining is generally rather early, don't expect to walk into a restaurant at 10pm and get a full or decent meal.

Prices given in brackets are for an average main course.

CITY CENTRE

AROUND LONG STREET

95 Keerom 95 Keerom St ☏021 422 0765; map p.49. Flash, fabulous and expensive, with fresh and light Italian nouvelle cuisine, with offerings such as grilled beef, butternut ravioli or seared tuna, though the decor is a little stark (R150). Mon–Sat 7–9.30pm, Thurs & Fri noon–2.30pm.

Addis in Cape 41 Church St ☏021 424 5722; map p.49. This friendly restaurant has a lovely laidback atmosphere. You'll find delicious traditional Ethiopian dishes on the menu and yummy *injera* (flat bread) to soak up the flavours and eat with your fingers (R100). Mon–Sat noon–3pm & 6–10.30pm.

Africa Café 108 Shortmarket St, Cape Heritage Square ☏021 422 0221; map p.49. Probably the best tourist restaurant in Cape Town for African cuisine, with a fantastic selection of dishes from across the continent. Given that you're served a communal feast of sixteen dishes, and that you can have as many extra helpings as you like, the R250-per-head price tag is

CAPE CUISINE

Styles of cooking brought by Asian and Madagascan slaves have evolved into **Cape cuisine** (sometimes known as **Cape Malay** food – a misnomer given that few slaves came from Malaysia). Associated with Cape Town's Muslim community, the food is characterized by mild, semi-sweet curries with a strong Indonesian influence, and though it doesn't offer that much variety, it can be delicious. Dishes include **bredie** (stew), of which **waterblommetjiebredie**, made using water hyacinths, is a speciality; **bobotie**, a spicy minced dish served under a savoury custard; and **sosaties**, a local version of kebab using minced meat. For dessert, dates stuffed with almonds make a light and delicious end to a meal, while **malva** pudding is a rich combination of milk, sugar, cream and apricot jam.

pretty reasonable. Booking essential. Mon–Sat 6.30–10pm.

★ **Birds Café** 127 Bree St ☎021 426 2534; map p.49. Trestle tables are laid out on upturned crates in this airy, central venue, where you can happily check your emails over a cappuccino. They use organic ingredients where possible in their highly recommended conical chicken pies, generous salads, home-made lemonade and fresh bakes. Portions can be big enough for two. The price is reasonable but the service sluggish (R60). Mon–Fri 7am–5pm, Sat 8am–2pm.

Bukhara 33 Church St ☎021 424 0000; map p.49. An upmarket and popular North Indian restaurant with green marble floors and a show kitchen where you can watch chefs at work. The food is superb though expensive, though portions are large and there is creative use of local meat cooked with traditional Indian spices such as ostrich tikka. Booking is essential (R110). Daily noon–3pm, 6–11pm.

Eastern Food Bazaar The Wellington, Darling St ☎021 461 2458; map p.49. Good, cheap, canteen-style restaurant with an Indian and Cape Malay menu. You queue up to order, often with long waits at lunchtime. Faloodas and Lassis made fresh to drink; no alcohol or smoking permitted (R35). Daily 11am–10pm.

Headquarters Heritage Square, 100 Shortmarket St ☎021 424 6373; map p.49. There is only one thing on the menu – prime free-range Namibian sirloin steak and butter sauce with perfect matchstick chips and salad. On Friday nights they have a DJ with relaxing beats, hotting up around 10pm when the tables are pushed back for dancing. Monday nights you get two meals for the price of one. Booking always essential (R165). Mon–Sat 11.30am–10.30pm.

Jewel Tavern 101 St George's Mall ☎021 422 4041; map p.49. Once an unpretentious Taiwanese sailors' eating house, it still serves superb food, though it has lost its charming harbour atmosphere in a central, though far more convenient, venue. Try the great hot and sour soup and spring rolls, sometimes made while you watch (R95). Daily 11am–3pm & 5–10pm.

Mama Africa 178 Long St ☎021 424 8634; map p.49. Food from around the continent, including a mixed grill of springbok, impala, kudu, ostrich and even crocodile. You can also sit at the 12m bar – in the form of a green mamba – and listen to live African music (R90). Tues–Fri 11am–4pm, Mon–Sat 6.30–11pm.

Masala Dosa 167 Long St ☎021 424 6772; map p.49. Inexpensive and fast South Indian cuisine with a taste of Bollywood decor. Worth visiting just for the ginger and apple lassis (R70). Daily 11.30am–10.30pm.

Mexican Kitchen Café 13 Bloem St ☎021 423 1541; map p.49. A casual restaurant serving good-value burritos, enchiladas, nachos and calamari fajitas, with some fine vegetarian options and deli-style takeaways, and the best

---

> **TOP 5 DELIS**
> **Giovanni's Deli World** Green Point, see p.120.
> **The Kitchen** Woodstock, see p.120.
> **Newport Market and Deli** Mouille Point, see p.121.
> **The Olympic Café and Deli** Kalk Bay, see p.122.
> **Raith Gourmet** Gardens, see p.119.

frozen margaritas in town. Fun atmosphere, with sombreros to wear and pictures of Frida Kahlo outside (R70). Daily 11am–11pm & until midnight on Fri and Sat.

Mr Pickwick's Deli 158 Long St; map p.49. This is the number one place to come for midnight munchies. Hearty and cheap "tin-plate" meals, including a challenging range of hot and cold "foot-long" sandwiches are dished out even after the pubs close (R50). Daily 8am–2am.

Royale 273 Long St ☎021 422 4536; map p.49. A hip hangout serving inexpensive gourmet burgers that pack a surprise with unusual combinations, such as brie or roasted vegetables, in the bun. Choose from lamb, beef, chicken and seven vegetarian patties including tofu. Normally packed, so book ahead, especially if you would like a balcony seat with street views (R75). Mon–Sat noon–10.30pm.

★ **Savoy Cabbage Restaurant and Champagne Bar** 101 Hout St ☎021 424 2626; map p.49. Sophisticated and innovative European-style peasant food, madly expensive but worthwhile for one of the best gourmet meals in town. The seasonally influenced menu changes all the time, but their tomato tart with goat's milk cheese and caramelized onion is a hit and you will find it difficult to choose between all the delectable meat offerings (R140). Mon–Fri noon–2pm, Mon–Sat 7–10pm.

ELSEWHERE IN THE CENTRE

Biesmiellah On the corner of Upper Wales and Pentz sts, Bo-Kaap ☎021 423 0850; map p.43. One of the oldest restaurants for traditional Cape cuisine; rather than a sit-down meal, join local residents in the queue for their takeaway samosas and delicious savoury wraps called salomes (R35). Mon–Sat 7am–10pm.

★ **Bizerca Bisttro** 15 Jetty St, Foreshore ☎021 418 0001; map p.43. You are unlikely to eat better in Cape Town, than at this inner-city gourmet bistro with a modern, funky feel. The food, from French chef Laurent Deslandes is light, elegant and creative, using local ingredients and arrayed on the blackboard, with impossible meat or fish choices and incredible desserts. Not cheap, but you never feel ripped off and service is excellent. Booking

8

AFRICAN FOOD

Around the centre of Cape Town you will find a couple of restaurants offering African food, but these are geared towards tourists – you would never find a full-blooded Xhosa worker eating in Long Street. The best way to experience the African food in the **townships** is by staying over in one of the B&Bs (see box p.113), or by taking a tour that incorporates an organized township meal or a drink in a *shebeen* (see p.26).

You are not going to find authentic places to eat and drink if you just drive about in the townships, which would be unwise and unsafe in any event, but there is one notable exception: *Mzoli's*, in the closest township to the centre and in easy driving distance, has even caught the attention of Jamie Oliver, who adored the **barbecued meat**.

essential (R110). Mon–Fri noon–2.30pm, Mon–Sat 6–10pm.

Charly's Bakery 38 Canterbury St; map p.43. Do not be fooled by the plain decor here: these are the most spectacular and decorative cakes in Cape Town in a modest location. Try the Death by Chocolate – a very rich, moist cake – or the double chocolate cheesecake. Also does breakfasts and light lunches (R50). Mon–Fri 8am–5pm, Sat 8.30am–3pm.

Col'Cacchio Seeff House, 42 Hans Strijdom Ave ☎021 419 4848; map p.43. An offbeat pizza restaurant, and one of a chain, which also serves pasta and salads and also has a range of low-fat and heart-friendly pizzas if you are feeling guilty. There are over forty different designer pizza toppings, such as smoked salmon, sour cream and rocket (R95). Mon–Fri 9am–10.30pm, Sat & Sun 6–10.30pm.

Sinn's Restaurant and Bar Wembley Square, McKenzie Rd ☎021 465 0967; map p.43. Busy, all-day spot, in a trendy complex, with a decidedly continental air

and good food, from rye bread and salad to bouillabaisse, served (promptly) to a hip, young crowd. It is family friendly too, with a menu for under-12 diners and it's also known for excellent cocktails and snacks (R90). Daily 9am–11pm.

Truth Coffee Cult Prestwich Memorial, Somerset Rd ☎021 419 2945; map p.43. Coffee as good as it gets in this tranquil café with white umbrellas and plenty of shade on the terrace. A great spot for breakfast or lunch (R60). Mon–Fri 7am–5pm, Sat 7am–3pm, Sun 9am–2pm.

Mzoli's NY 115, Gugulethu, N2 Modderdam Rd off ramp, close to the airport ☎021 638 1355. Best at lunchtime (you need to book a table and phone for directions), when you can join a local crowd and devour tasty meat barbecued (*tshisanyama* – "chi-san-knee-yama") for you out the back. Serves meat and more meat, ranging from chops, *boerewors* sausage, cuts of beef and lamb served with dumplings *pap* (thick maize porridge), meat sauce and *chakalaka*, a tomato salad. Not suitable for vegetarians and those with small appetites.

V&A WATERFRONT AND DE WATERKANT

The **Waterfront** offers a variety of food, from chain eateries and unimpressive quick eats after a bout of shopping or before you take in a movie, to outdoor people-watching cafés and smart fish restaurants. You'll also find some of the best sushi in town here. **De Waterkant** has some nice places to eat; head for the Cape Quarter building with its array of restaurants, delis and cafés.

THE WATERFRONT

Baia Upper Level, Quay 6 ☎021 421 0935; map p.62. Sit on the terraced balcony and take in the views of Table Mountain while dining on masterfully cooked fresh fish and seafood; the spicy bouillabaisse is worth trying. Booking essential, especially for dinner (R140). Daily noon–11pm.

Caffè Balducci Quay 6 ☎021 421 6002; map p.62. An upmarket café-restaurant with a fresh feel, lovely views, and interesting Californian/Italian food with South African overtones. Try the biltong salad with blue cheese and caramelized nuts. Expensive, but worth it, with a popular sushi bar just outside the front door (R110). Daily 9am–midnight.

Caffè San Marco Piazza level, Victoria Wharf ☎021 418 5434; map p.62. A coffee shop and bar with outdoor seating, offering an all-day breakfast menu, good sandwiches on Italian breads and fresh salads. The grilled calamari with garlic and chilli is delicious, and they sell eighteen flavours of ice cream and sorbet (R90). Daily 8.30am–11.30pm.

Grand Café and Beach Haul Rd off Beach Rd Granger Bay ☎021 425 0551; map p.62. There is a French Riviera atmosphere at this waterside venue, where a beach has been artificially created. Not as kitsch as it sounds, it is a jolly place, popular with the young and beautiful set. The fusion-style food has an Asian and Portuguese influence, and a fun option for a group is to order a huge pizza to feed the whole table (R150). Wed–Sat noon–midnight, Sun noon–11pm.

Wang Thai Shop 2, 61 Victoria Wharf ☎021 421 8702; map p.62. Possibly Cape Town's best Thai restaurant, serving such delights as hot and spicy prawn soup, steamed fish with lemon juice and chilli, and its special – thinly sliced, seared sirloin (R85). Daily 11am–10.30pm.

★ **Willoughby & Co** Shop 6182, Lower Level, Victoria Wharf ☎021 418 6115; map p.62. Despite a shortage of sea views, this is hands down the best fish restaurant at the Waterfront, serving fantastic sushi and seafood in a lively atmosphere (R100). Daily noon–11pm.

DE WATERKANT

★ **Anatoli** 24 Napier St ☎021 419 2501; map p.62. A Turkish restaurant bursting with personality and set in an early twentieth-century warehouse. This place is great for vegetarians, and the excellent meze includes exceptionally delicious Greek vine-wrapped *dolmades*, and there are at least twenty others to choose from on a starters platter. It also serves superb desserts, such as pressed dates topped with cream (R90). Mon–Sat 7–10.30pm.

Andiamo Cape Quarter piazza, Dixon St ☎021 421 3688; map p.62. Busy Italian deli with a courtyard restaurant serving salads, pastas and sandwiches. The deli itself does a great selection of meats, cheeses, salads, dips and fresh breads – phone ahead and they'll put a picnic or platter together for you (R70). Daily 9am–11pm.

Origin Coffee 28 Hudson St ☎021 421 1000; map p.62. Home-roasted coffees from across Africa and beyond to Asia and Latin America, and their range of teas is equally appealing. Although you can complement your drink with a little something to eat, food is secondary to the quality of the beans (R70). Mon–Fri 7am–5pm, Sat 9am–2pm.

CITY BOWL SUBURBS

Aubergine 39 Barnet St ☎021 465 4909; map p.73. Unbeatable choice for a 5-star dinner, with a garden to sit in to enjoy the top-quality Afro-Asian cooking of chef Harald Bresselschmidt. Expensive, but memorable. If you aren't up for a full-on dinner (which starts at 7pm), they also do fabulous tapas and sundowners from 5pm (R160). Mon, Tues & Sat 5–10pm, Wed–Fri noon–2pm & 5–10pm.

★ **Bombay Bicycle Club** 158 Kloof St ☎021 423 6805; map p.73. Don't expect Indian cuisine, but a totally fun place for a great evening out, with things to play with in every area, whether it's sitting at a table with swings, or wearing silly hats. Food includes grills, soups, pastas and carpaccios. Booking essential as it's always full (R100). Mon–Sat 6–11pm, though the bar is open from 4pm.

Carlyle's on Derry 17 Derry St, Gardens ☎021 461 8787; map p.73. A friendly place where you'll need to book in advance for a table. From 6pm they serve a great selection of thin-based, gourmet pizzas such as fig and blue cheese, Thai chicken and coriander, or lemon-infused ham and rocket (R70). Daily 4.30– 10.30pm.

Daily Deli 110 Kloof St, Gardens; map p.73. Pavement café with mountain views, in a row of attractive Victorian houses, popular with the local creative set. Great for coffee and cake, croissants, sandwiches and breakfast that they serve throughout the evening. Always chock-a-block (R60). Daily 10am–10pm.

Lazari Corner of Upper Maynard St and Vredehoek Ave ☎021 461 9865; map p.73. A meeting place for City Bowl locals with a sister branch in De Waterkant. Fresh, interesting breakfasts (served all day) and lunches including bangers and mash, salads, pasta, falafels, home-made cakes and biscuits (R70). Mon–Fri 7.30am–4pm, Sat 8am–3pm, Sun 8.30am–2.30pm.

Limoncello 8 Breda St, Gardens ☎021 461 5100; map p.73. A small and reliable Italian trattoria serving excellent pastas and pizzas with an emphasis on fresh ingredients. Serves possibly the best calamari in Cape Town and a great risotto of the day (R90). Mon–Fri noon– 3.30pm, 6.30–11pm, Sat & Sun 6.30–11pm.

Melissa's 94 Kloof St, Gardens; map p.73. Interesting breakfasts, first-rate sandwiches and salads and fine desserts in the small café, while the food emporium sells freshly made Mediterranean fare (R60). Mon–Fri 7.30am–9pm, Sat & Sun 8am–9pm.

Miller's Thumb 10b Kloof Nek Rd ☎021 424 3838; map p.73. Consistently good seafood dishes, with a selection of line fish done in a variety of ways served in a cheerful environment – the restaurant is in a house in a residential area. If you're not into fish, they also do juicy steaks (R120). Mon & Sat 6.30–10.30pm, Tues–Fri 12.30–2pm & 6.30–10pm.

Mount Nelson Hotel 76 Orange St, Gardens; map p.73. Colonial-style afternoon tea in Cape Town's oldest and most gracious hotel is a definite culinary highlight of the city, the large tea table piled with hot and cold pastries, classic savouries like smoked salmon sandwiches, and scrumptious cakes. You can skip lunch and dinner after the R170 feast you get here. Daily 2.30–5.30pm.

★ **Raith Gourmet** Gardens Shopping Centre, Mill St Gardens; map p.73. Meat-focused, German deli and café, inside a mall, with an exceptional selection of foods and some marvellous sandwiches; specialities include sauerkraut fried with strips of bacon (R60). Mon–Fri 8.30am–6pm, Sat 8.30am–1pm.

Sawaddee 12 Rheede St ☎021 422 1633; map p.73. An informal Thai restaurant close to the Labia cinema. It's not much to look at, but the calamari with pepper and garlic sauce is recommended, and it's a good, reasonably priced spot to grab a bite before or after watching a movie (R75). Mon–Sat 6–10.30pm.

Societi Bistro 50 Orange St ☎ 021 424 2100; map p.73. Friendly bistro with a great atmosphere and good Italian-style food, in a lovely restored building and garden virtually opposite the *Mount Nelson* hotel and Labia cinema. Sometimes they do special deals if you are going to the Labia, and there is a fireplace for winter evenings. Their risotto is always a hit, and starters include ox tongue, roasted bone marrow and lamb's liver (R110). Mon–Sat noon–11pm.

SOUTHERN SUBURBS

Buitenverwachting Buitenverwachting Estate, Constantia ☎ 021 794 3522. The expensive restaurant on this idyllic wine estate is ideal for an elegant, special (though not stiflingly formal) occasion with beautifully plated food. Seafood and venison feature regularly or you can opt for a variety of titillating tastes from their four- or seven-course degustation menu (R275). Tues–Sat noon–3pm & 7–9.30pm.

Chandani 85 Roodebloem Rd, Woodstock ☎ 021 447 7887. Great North Indian food – besides the more expensive and centrally located *Bukhara*, you are unlikely to do better in Cape Town for Indian dining. Vegetarians can breathe a sigh of relief at the array. Set in a tastefully restored Victorian house, in a gritty neighbourhood (R80). Mon–Sat noon–3pm, 6–10.30pm.

Common Ground Café 23 Milner Rd, Rondebosch ☎ 021 686 0154. Attached to a church, this is an unlikely contender for the best coffee in town, but the baristas are true artists who take their business seriously, going beyond the normal to decorate the foam of your cappuccino to order. They also offer among the most reasonably priced breakfasts in town, and have a small sandwich menu and pay-by-weight lunchtime buffet. The atmosphere is relaxed – there are sofas on recline on – and the views of Table Mountain across Rondebosch Common are sublime (R35). Mon–Fri 7am–4pm, Sat 8am–2pm, Sun 8.30am–2pm & 5.30am–8.30pm.

Gardener's Cottage 31 Newlands Ave, Montebello Estate, Newlands. Browse outstanding arts and crafts and enjoy croissant and egg breakfasts, baked potatoes, line fish or pasta, within a complex of old farm buildings under shady pines and oaks. It is recommended for tea and cake, and while the food is fine, it's a place to choose for the craft shopping, shady trees and mountain outlook (R70). Tues–Fri 8am–4.30pm, Sat & Sun 8.30am–4.30pm.

★ **Kirstenbosch Tea Rooms** Rhodes Drive, Newlands ☎ 021 797 4883. The gorgeous park setting as well as pleasing, fresh and creative Cape country food – particularly the pickled fish or home-made burgers – is the draw here. Though the large self-service place by the main entrance is ideal for kids to roam around as you drink tea by the river, avoid it if you want a meal and head instead for the tearoom by the upper entrance to the Gardens. They have some good options for vegetarians and you can order a gourmet picnic (R80). Daily 8.30am–5pm.

★ **The Kitchen** 111 Sir Lowry Rd, Woodstock ☎ 021 462 2201. Run by one of the stallholders at the Neighbourhood Goods market nearby, only the freshest ingredients are used to create fabulous, inventive sandwiches and a range of lentil, chickpea and couscous salads. This is one of the best and cheapest places in town, especially if you are vegetarian, for a casual, good-value lunch (R45). Mon–Fri 8am–4pm.

Olive Station Levantine Restaurant & Deli Rondebosch Village Shopping Centre, Main Rd, Rondebosch ☎ 021 686 8224. Fabulous Middle Eastern breakfasts, wood-fired pitta pockets, breads, pastries and meze, as well as a nice range of olives, Cape olive oils and deli products on sale (R60). Mon–Fri 8am–6pm, Sat 8am–2pm.

River Café Constantia Uitsig Wine Estate, Spaanschemat River Rd ☎ 021 794 3010. An outstanding lunch – or breakfast stop (their Eggs Benedict has a reputation up and down the peninsula) – at the Uitsig Wine Estate. The ambience among the vineyards is tranquil and, in keeping with the rural setting, the food is fresh and imaginative country bistro style. Sit indoors or eat alfresco with views of the mountains (R110). Daily 8.30–11am, 12.30–3pm & 6.30–9pm.

ATLANTIC SEABOARD

GREEN POINT

El Burro 81 Main Rd, Green Point ☎ 021 433 2364; map p.88. Mexican food served without too much cheese and grease, plus a good view from the balcony of Green Point Stadium, this spot is casual, young and fun (R80). Mon–Sat noon–11.30pm.

★ **Giovanni's Deliworld** 103 Main Rd; map p.88. With both indoor and pavement seating for interesting people-watching, this lively Italian deli and coffee shop, right across from the Stadium with its own screen for sport-watching, offers delicious coffee, excellent made-to-order sandwiches, salads and dips, and good pre-packaged meals (R60). Daily 8am–9pm.

Mano's 39 Main Rd ☎ 021 434 1090. Popular with model-types and generally beautiful people, this place serves Italian staples and exciting salads, and one of the best *crème brûlées* in town. After dinner, the party continues in champagne bar *Jade*, upstairs (see p.126) (R90). Mon–Sat noon–10.30pm.

Theo's Grill Butcher and Seafood 163 Beach Rd ☎ 021 439 3494; map p.88. Right on the beachfront, *Theo's* offers superb Greek-style meat and seafood dishes. Good family venue too with its outside seating and casual feel (R95). Mon–Sun 11.30am–10pm.

MOUILLE POINT

Café Neo 129 Beach Rd; map p.88. Deli-style food with a Greek influence including meze platters, salads, greek yogurt for breakfast with nuts and honey, sandwiches, plus the big draw of an outdoor seating area with umbrellas, offering views of either Green Point stadium or the lighthouse. Vegetarians can do well here (R60). Daily 7am–7pm.

★ **Newport Market and Deli** 47 Beach Rd; map p.88. A light, airy deli with views onto Table Bay, and serving coffee, excellent gourmet sandwiches, salads and some hot dishes such as Thai green curry and noodles, or burgers. Their smoothies and power pack blends make a welcome change from breakfast fry-ups and toasted sandwiches – just right if you are walking or jogging along the Sea Point promenade. Mon–Sun 7am–10pm.

Wakame and Wafu 47 Beach Rd ☎ 021 433 2377; map p.88. Trendy Asian-fusion food with killer desserts – try the chocolate and banana spring rolls. Every table has a view of the ocean and upstairs is *Wafu*, a popular contender for the drinking spot with the best sea views in Cape Town. *Wafu* offers a tapas and dim sum menu with no starters or main course (R90), while *Wakame* does more formal meals (R110). Each place has its own sushi bar too. Booking essential. Daily noon–3pm, 6–10pm.

SEA POINT

★ **La Boheme Wine Bar & Bistro** 341 Main Rd ☎ 021 434 6539; map p.88. Interesting, well-presented French country-style food and lovely wines by the glass at least 60 to choose from. Dishes include ostrich meatballs with tagliatelli, potato gnocchi and roasted pork belly. There's pavement seating for people-watching. An enjoyable and inexpensive night out. Next door is their sister espresso and tapas bar, if you want just a sandwich with brilliant coffee (R80). Mon–Sat 12–2.30pm, 7.30–10.15pm.

Mr Chan 178a Main Rd ☎ 021 439 2239; map p.88. Worthwhile Chinese restaurant, serving happy customers for the last twenty years with excellent Hong Kong-style beef, prawns, roast duck and, for vegetarians, braised bean curd and mixed vegetable (R80). Mon–Sun noon–2.30pm, 6–10.30pm.

New York Bagels 51 Regent Rd; map p.88. Deli with a mix of Eastern European and Mediterranean Jewish food.

Choose from an array of bagels and home-made fillings, from chopped liver to herring, and salads to take away. Outstanding choice for filling a sunset picnic basket, or to munch on at the Sea Point Pool lawns, a block away (R30). Daily 7am–8pm.

Pizzeria Napoletana 178 Main Rd ☎ 021 434 5386; map p.88. Family-styled, real Italian restaurant with hearty, good-value cooking. Somewhat dry atmosphere at times, but the food is delicious and reasonable (R70). Mon–Sat 6.30–10pm.

CAMPS BAY AND POINTS SOUTH

Café Caprice 37 Victoria Rd, Camps Bay ☎ 021 438 8315. Directly opposite Camps Bay beach, this lively, albeit pretentious, Mediterranean-style restaurant is a great place to soak up streetlife and sunshine (R90). Daily 9am till midnight.

Café Roux Noordhoek Farm Village ☎ 021 789 2538. Wholesome and healthy food with a contemporary feel, offering breakfasts, gourmet sandwiches, fish and chips and other simple fare, with a menu (and garden) that caters to children. Sit under umbrellas, gaze at the mountains and have tea after doing Chapman's Peak (R60). Tues–Sun 8.30am–5pm.

Camel Rock Main Rd, Scarborough ☎ 021 780 1122. A local hangout that makes scant effort to cater to tourists, this homely joint is notable more for the fact that it's the only place for a beer and bite in these far-flung parts, than for its unexceptional seafood dishes and curries. Wed–Mon 11am–9pm.

★ **Food Barn** Noordhoek Farm Village ☎ 021 789 1390. Gourmet French food from an acclaimed chef, Franck Dangereux, served at reasonable prices compared to the other top restaurants in the city centre. The food is great, and worth suffering the slow service, kids are welcome and you can sit on a sunny veranda in beautiful rural Noordhoek surrounds. Booking essential (R120). Tues–Sat noon–2.30pm, Wed–Sat 7–9.30pm.

La Cuccina Food Store Victoria Mall, Victoria Rd, Hout Bay. High-quality deli and café food in pleasant surrounds, the delicious food compensating for the lack of sea views. At lunchtime it has a buffet of quiches, salads and lasagne (R70). Daily 8am–7pm.

Mariners Wharf Bistro The Harbour, Hout Bay. A relaxed, well-run and very popular seafood restaurant with terrace seating overlooking the harbour. The views outshine the food, which you can eat in or take away from the downstairs outlet (R80). Daily 10am–9pm.

Paranga's Shop 1, The Promenade, Victoria Rd, Camps Bay ☎ 021 438 0404. Popular hangout at the beach, a place to see and be seen while you pick at salads, seafood, pasta or sushi. There's a variety of champagne on offer while you watch the sun sinking into the ocean (R155). Daily 9.30am–10.30pm.

8

Salt *Ambassador Hotel*, 34 Victoria Rd, Bantry Bay ☎ 021 439 7258; map p.88. Top chef at work to create food with a French influence, their braised lamb in a herb crust is recommended or orange-glazed line fish. The views couldn't be better, the plush hotel is built on a rocky cliffside, fronting the Atlantic ocean. Expensive, but if you don't want to eat you can always just sink a beer and watch the sunset, or alternatively eat at their street-level deli across the road, which lacks the same position, but is far cheaper and less pretentious (R160). Daily 12.30–2.30pm, 6.30–10pm.

FALSE BAY SEABOARD

MUIZENBERG

Casa Labia Restaurant 192 Main Rd, Muizenberg ☎ 021 788 6068; map p.98. Contemporary Italian food and English-style teas in *palazzo* surroundings, with oil paintings, antiques and beautiful table linen. Courtyard dining comes with mountain views (R60). Tues–Sun 10am–4pm.

Empire Café 11 York Rd ☎ 021 788 1250; map p.98. Coffee, including organic, and pastries while you sit upstairs and gaze at passing trains and the blue ocean beyond, or work at your computer, use free wi-fi and wait for the surf to come up. Their tasty pastas make a wholesome lunch and your waiter may slide down the banisters to despatch your order, though it's a rather slower process bringing the goods up (R50). Mon–Sun 8am–4pm.

Knead Muizenberg Beachfront ☎ 021 788 2909; map p.98. People come here in droves to sample the first-rate breads, crusty sandwich platters and cakes at this vibrant venue right at Surfer's Corner. Gusty outdoor seating as well as an indoor counter from which you can still admire the ocean, but service is consistently chaotic and slow (R60). Daily 7.30am–5pm.

KALK BAY

★ **C'est La Vie** Rosmead Ave, Kalk Bay ☎ 083 676 7430; map p.98. Unassuming and charming French-styled bakery up a cobbled street, offering pavement breakfasts, real baguettes and orange juice, croissants and excellent coffee. Wed–Sun 7am–3pm.

Fish Hoek Galley Fish Hoek Beach ☎ 021 782 3354, ⊕ fishhoekgalley.com; map p.98. Friendly family restaurant right on the beach that makes a good lunch stop, with outdoor seating and a large interior that lives up to its name by packing in the seating. Although they do meat and poultry, seafood's what you eat here (and the menu is extensive): line fish, or if you don't have a conscience about depleting fish stocks you can go the whole hog and gorge on their Royal Flush Seafood Extravaganza that includes prawns, lobster, mussels, oysters, fish and calamari (R100). Daily noon–3pm & 5–10pm.

Harbour House Restaurant On the harbour ☎ 021 788 4133; map p.98. Seafood and Mediterranean food, at a memorable venue with a spectacular setting on the breakwater of Kalk Bay harbour; book a table with bay views or enjoy sundowners on the deck. There's a fireplace and comfortable sofas for winter (R130). Mon–Sun noon–10pm for drinks, lunch noon–4pm, 6–10pm.

Kalky's On the harbour; map p.98. For years, this totally unpretentious eatery has been serving the fishing community the best traditional fish and chips on the peninsula and great-value seafood platters. Fish is hauled off the boats and straight into the frying pan; wait a bit longer and you can have your catch grilled. You sit at benches to eat, though takeaway is available (R40). Daily 10am–8pm.

★ **The Olympia Café & Deli** Main Rd; map p.98. One of the few places that draws parochial uptown Capetonians down to the False Bay seaboard. Always buzzing, a tad scruffy and with views of the harbour, *Olympia* offers great coffee accompanied by their own freshly baked goods. Gourmet lunch menus are chalked up on a board, with local fish and mussels often featured. They don't take bookings, so arrive early for dinner, otherwise join the queue (R80). Daily 7am–9pm.

Outspan Restaurant On the corner of Main Rd and Boyes Drive; map p.98. A humble setting with a few umbrellas and outdoor seating, close to the harbour and railway line, this is an excellent spot to eat barbecued fish with an appetizing smell of fish cooking on open fires wafting about the tables (R70). Daily noon–9pm.

SIMON'S TOWN

The small Waterfront area is always worth a wander, with several restaurants and gift shops fronting the boats

Black Marlin Main Rd, south of Simon's Town ☎ 021 786 1621, ⊕ blackmarlin.co.za; map p.102. Every kind of sea denizen, apart from its namesake, is on the menu at this hugely popular restaurant on the road to Cape Point. (Tour buses pull in here for lunch, but their passengers are coralled off into a separate section.) While there's nothing wrong with the food, don't expect pyrotechnics, although the clifftop views from the outdoor tables, make up for any lack of culinary fireworks – especially when there are whale sightings (R200). Mon–Fri noon–10pm, Sat & Sun 8am–10pm.

The Meeting Place 98 St George's St ☎ 021 786 5678; map p.102. At street level, sofas and newspapers are perfect props for a lazy deli-style breakfast or toasted sarnies lunch. Upstairs, with a harbour-view

8

balcony, is a more upmarket restaurant and bar, serving more expensive fare, such as fresh line fish and steaks (R50 downstairs, R90 upstairs). Tues & Sun 9am–4pm, Wed–Sat 9am–9pm.

Salty Sea Dog Waterfront ☎021 7861918; map p.102. There's nothing fancy about this small restaurant on the wharf, but they do plain old fish and chips extremely well. With indoors and alfresco seating it makes a great lunch stop on an outing to Cape Point (R75). Mon–Sat 8.30am–9pm & Sun 8.30am–4.30pm.

Tibetan Teahouse 2 Harrington Rd, Seaforth Beach ☎021 786 1544; map p.102. Traditional Tibetan recipes, with a yak-free lentil stew, as the menu's completely vegetarian. You'll find the venue signalled by its prayer flags (R55). Tues–Sun 10am–5pm.

CAPE POINT

Two Oceans Cape Point ☎021 702 0703, ⓦtwo -oceans.co.za. The real star of the show at this primarily seafood-focused restaurant is the sublime view from its alfresco deck that seems to float out a million miles above the ocean, taking in the whole of False Bay and its mountains – it's a great place to see whales in season. As well as fish and chips, calamari, lobster and seafood platters, they also have tapas and kids' menus, and fried breakfasts till 11am (R150). Daily 9am–5pm.

8

Drinking and nightlife

Being a hedonistic city – especially in the summer – Cape Town has plenty of great places to drink and party, especially on Long Street where it's safe and busy, and there are taxis to get you home. In the summer, the Atlantic Seaboard, notably Camps Bay, is a great option, where the party starts with the first sundowners. When it comes to live music, the best-known South African musicians are sadly better appreciated, and better remunerated, abroad than in their own country. Live music generally happens at a few restaurants and bars, where you may expect a small cover charge when it's on. If anyone good is in town, you will pick that up on posters or a listings magazine.

ESSENTIALS

Opening hours Most liquor licences stipulate that the last round is served at 2am, but this is far from strictly followed; bars often stay open until the last customer leaves. Clubs get going after 10pm and are pretty international in flavour, with DJs mixing house hits you're bound to recognize.

Prices How much a drink costs obviously depends on the venue – a local beer in a sports bar might set you back R15, with international brews costing upwards of R20. A smart bar will charge up to R40 for a cocktail, while glasses of delicious Cape wine begin around R25. Some clubs may have a cover charge, but this is usually only when they have live music on and it's never more than R100.

Food You'll find that many drinking places are also restaurants, and may be better known as the latter; in a city where wine is produced, food and wine definitely go together. Many bars and clubs offer food as well, for those hungry moments before or after dancing.

Safety It's really not a good idea to walk around late at night, so take a taxi number out with you (see box below for a list).

LONG STREET AND THE CITY BOWL SUBURBS

Boo Radley's Bistro and Bar 62 Hout St ☎021 424 3040, ⓦbooradleys.co.za; map p.49. Classic cocktails are the signature of this slick and sociable New York-style bistro with a long, polished bar counter, and black and white chequerboard floor. Great for lunch too or after a show meal, with salads, creative sandwiches and heavier meals on offer at reasonable prices (R100). Mon–Sat 10am–late.

Caveau Wine Bar and Deli Heritage Square, 92 Bree St ☎021 422 1367; map p.49. Appealing and tranquil courtyard setting in a listed building, off a busy road. The wide variety of Cape wines sold by the glass, in addition to sushi on offer, is a good enough reason to stop off for lunch or dinner, though it's a popular breakfast spot too. Mon–Sat 7am–10pm.

Dubliner@Kennedy's 251 Long St ☎021 424 1212 ⓦthedubliner.co.za; map p.49. Crammed, wildly popular traditional Irish pub with Guinness and pilsner on tap, pub meals from lunch until midnight daily, and live music from 10pm every night. Upstairs you can relax with a pint and sing along to a honky-tonk piano. Other features include flat screens for sporting events and a pool table. Daily noon–late.

Grand Daddy Sky Bar Grand Daddy Hotel, 38 Long St ⓦgranddaddy.co.za; map p.49. Rooftop Bedouin tent-style bar with sofas and deck chairs amid seven trailer home hotel rooms. Recommended for the views and the amazing cocktails, which include fresh juices and herbal infusions, and artisanal beers. During happy hour go wild and try a few champagne or pomegranate cocktails. Daily noon–8.30pm.

Jo'burg 218 Long St ☎021 422 0142; map p.49. A good, if crowded, place to hang out, grooving to a fresh soundtrack or playing pool against one of the hip, local patrons. Most people end up here at some point during a night out on Long St, and it's one of the few places open on Sunday nights. Cool off on the open-air patio outside. Mon–Sat noon–4am, Sun 6pm–4am.

★ **Julep** 2 Vredenburg Lane, off Long St ☎021 423 4276; map p.49. You'll find the best cocktails and snacks in town in this small, but lively two-roomed bar, discreetly tucked away down an alley. You'll be forgiven for thinking you're in a friend's living room, with comfy couches and intimate table lamps. Tues–Sat 5.30pm–2am.

Mama Africa 178 Long St ☎021 424 8634, ⓦafrica-adventure.org; map p.49. A relaxed and spacious restaurant-bar, popular with tourists, *Mama Africa* boasts a 12m bar in the form of a long pink snake. This is your

GETTING HOME SAFELY

Most Capetonians you meet will tell you that walking around after dark, alone and inebriated is to be avoided at all costs. Heed their words; even if you are in a group, it's a good idea to take the number of a taxi company out with you as few taxis cruise for fares. The three companies listed below run a 24-hour service, seven days a week unless otherwise stated, and are prompt and reliable.

Excite Taxis – ☎021 448 4444. Fares are R9 a kilometre within their normal operating area (city centre to southern suburbs), but there may be an additional charge if your pick-up or drop-off point is further flung than this.

Marine Taxis – ☎021 434 0434. The largest and one of the oldest taxi outfits in the Mother City with seven-seater cabs. Fares are R11 a kilometre; they have card payment facilities in the car.

Rikkis – ☎0861 745 547. Rikkis has one of the lowest fare-structures in town and operates in Hout Bay and the southern suburbs (Mon–Thurs 6.30am–2am, Fri–Sun 24 hours) as well as the city centre (24-hour, seven days). Fares are calculated at R10 a zone: so a ride from the Waterfront to the City Bowl, for example, would set you back about R60; they also offer a cheaper option for shared rides.

9

chance to try ostrich, crocodile or a Malagasy fish dish with your drink, while an African marimba band plays every night of the week except Sunday. Daily 7–10pm; Summer lunch Tues–Fri noon–4pm.

Neighbourhood 163 Long St ☎021 424 7260; map p.49. Lively sports bar, perfect for guzzling beers and watching sports on the giant screen in the lounge. The balcony is great from sundowner time onwards, and the bar serves a good selection of local and imported beers, as well as reasonably priced bar food. Mon–Sun noon–2am.

Planet Bar Mount Nelson Hotel, 76 Orange St Ⓦmountnelson.co.za; map p.49. A smart sundowner bar, popular with well-heeled Capetonians, particularly on Friday nights after work. Emerge through an old-fashioned lobby into a modern salon with couches in elegant surroundings, with gardens and views of Table Mountain. No shorts dress code. Daily noon–11pm.

Rafiki's 13b Kloof Nek ☎021 426 4731; map p.49.

A laidback bar with a wraparound veranda where you can hang out all day slowly getting sozzled, cheering on sports teams on the big screen or making use of the wi-fi hotspot. There are roaring fires during the winter months, and it's always popular with backpackers and locals alike. Try their chilli-poppers and everything-on-it pizzas. Daily noon–2am.

Waiting Room 273 Long St ☎021 422 4536, Ⓦroyaleeatery.co.za; map p.49. Upstairs from the *Royale* is this popular, retro-chic bar and dancefloor with a roof deck to cool down on. While music is mostly courtesy of DJs, there is usually a live band once a week. Mon–Sat 6pm–2am.

Zula Sound Bar 194 Long St Ⓦzulabar.co.za; map p.49. Live, local talent of variable quality, showcased every night (music, comedy, odd poetry reading), and a well-priced restaurant with nachos, salads, chicken wings and burgers. Also a balcony to relax on, with Cape wines, as well as a games room. Fri noon–4am, Sat–Thurs 4pm–4am.

ELSEWHERE IN THE CENTRE

The Assembly 61 Harrington St, Zonnebloem ☎021 465 7286, Ⓦtheassembly.co.za; map p.42. One of the most popular places in town to party away the night, this spacious warehouse, formally a factory, has plenty of tequila and DJs who rock the crowd with indie, rock, pop and electronica, as well as live bands. Sat 9pm–4am.

Evol 69 Hope St ☎083 562 2583; map p.42. Named after a Sonic Youth album, this is the best place in town to hear DJs mix alternative, electro, punk and particularly indie music for a committed crowd. Good dancing though it's a bit of a grungy venue. Fri 10pm till late.

Perserverance Tavern 83 Buitenkant St, Gardens

☎021 461 2440; map p.42. The oldest pub in Cape Town, dating back to 1836 when sailors and soldiers frequented it, is now worth a visit if nothing else than to look at the restoration work, wooden floors and original fittings, then to sink some cheap beers and fries, before moving on to *The Assembly* or the like. Mon–Sat noon–late.

Thirtyone 31st Floor, Absa Centre, 2 Riebeeck St ☎021 421 0581, Ⓦthirtyone.co.za; map p.42. One of the city's most stylish clubs set at the top of one of the city's tallest buildings, providing albatross views of the metropolis below. It's smart and rather exclusive, providing a blend of funky house from the decks. Fri & Sat 10pm–4am.

V&A WATERFRONT AND DE WATERKANT

The **Waterfront** is good for a quiet drink, boasting a couple of good bars in a triangle close to each other. The party heats up in Somerset Road and up into **De Waterkant**, and there are a couple of good spots in Green Point, near the Stadium. Most of the places in De Waterkant are listed in the Gay Cape Town chapter (see p.143).

Alba Cocktail Lounge Pierhead, above the Hilderbrand Restaurant ☎021 425 3385; map p.62. Cocktails and snacks in the stunning setting equipped with sofas and fireplace for winter, looking out over the Waterfront. In summer, enjoy an Albatizer (jellytots & gin) on the outdoor deck. Daily 11am–midnight.

Den Anker Pierhead. A quayside pub and Continental-style bistro, patronized by tourists and well-heeled locals. *Den Anker* specializes in imported Belgian beers, both on tap and bottled, and Cape wines by the glass. Not cheap, but good value for money. Daily 11am–midnight.

Jade Champagne Bar 39 Main Rd above Manos Restaurant, Green Point ☎021 439 4108; see map p.62. Classy lounge-bar with plush sofas, chandeliers, two bars and a semi-enclosed balcony to relax. DJs play on Wednesdays. Wed–Sat 8pm–2am.

Trinity Restaurant and Super Club 15 Bennett St, Green Point ☎021 421 1367; map p.62. Sophisticated and contemporary brick warehouse with several levels of places to eat, drink, watch sport or dance. Mondays are jazz evenings, while Tuesdays promise comedy. Mon–Sat 12pm–4am.

> ### TOP 5 DRINKS WITH A VIEW
> **Alba Cocktail Lounge** V&A Waterfront, see p.126.
> **Brass Bell** Kalk Bay, see p.127.
> **Grand Daddy Sky Bar** City Centre, see p.125.
> **La Med** Clifton, see p.127.
> **Thirtyone** City Centre, see p.126.

9

ALL ABOUT THE BEER

South Africans tend to be fiercely loyal to their brand of **beer**, though they all taste pretty much the same, given that virtually all beer in the country is produced by the huge South African Breweries (SAB) monopoly, one of the world's largest beer makers. It's given a good run for its money by Namibian Breweries, whose Windhoek Lager is rated by cognoscenti as better than SAB's offerings, such as Castle. **Lager** is the predominant style, likely to taste a bit thin and bland to a British palate, though it can be wonderfully refreshing drunk ice-cold on a sweltering day. One or two **microbreweries** have sprung up, best known of which are Mitchell's in Knysna, which produces some distinctive **ales**, and Birkenhead in Stanford; their beers can be found at some bottle stores and bars between Cape Town and Port Elizabeth. Imported beers are expensive compared with the local product, with the exception of the great Czech Pilsner Urquell, which has been bought by SAB as part of its global expansion.

SOUTHERN SUBURBS

Brass Bell Kalk Bay station, Main Rd, Kalk Bay ☎ 021 788 5455, ⓦ brassbell.co.za; map p.73. The *Brass Bell* has arguably the best location on the peninsula, with False Bay's waves breaking against the wall of its outdoor terrace. It's a fantastic watering hole, serving decent fish and chips if liquid nourishment is not enough. Daily 11am–2am.

Caveau at the Mill 13 Boundary Rd, off Main Rd, Newlands ☎ 021 685 5140. A great place if you want to try quality Cape wines by the glass – there are over seventy to choose from – and match them with some good cheese, meat or a more substantial meal. Sit at tables under trees by the river at the historical Josephine Mill. Tues–Sat 7am–10pm, Sun 10am–3pm.

Dizzy Jazz Café 41 Camps Bay Drive, Camps Bay ☎ 021 438 2686. A crowded and lively pub, ideal for beer drinkers with its selection of draughts, and for getting a last one in when everywhere else is closed. It has a big veranda, pub meals, a tiny dancefloor and features a variety of live music nightly, with a R30 cover charge. Daily noon–4am.

Foresters' Arms 52 Newlands Ave, Newlands ☎ 021 689 5949. Preppie students and professionals gather to quaff draught beer at the very popular and busy *Forries* in the heart of leafy Newlands. A big wood-panelled pub, it boasts a beautiful hedged-in courtyard where you can grab a bench for a lazy afternoon pint. Mon–Sat 10am–11pm, Sun 10am–6pm.

Obz Café Lower Main Rd, Observatory. A great place to start an exploration of the different spots along Lower Main Rd, this has been a meeting point forever in Obs, with a good bar, big windows for people-watching. Mon–Sun 7am–1am.

Tiger Tiger Stadium 103 Main Rd, Claremont ⓦ tigertiger.co.za. Reliable for parties, Saturday nights are especially good, with six luxurious bars and a spacious dancefloor with commercial music pumped out of a state-of-the-art sound system. Tues, Thurs–Sat 8pm–4am.

ATLANTIC SEABOARD

Café Caprice 37 Victoria Rd, Camps Bay ☎ 021 438 8315. A beach-facing hangout for the tanned and gorgeous celebs and wannabes, just right for cocktails. Families are welcome during the day for breakfast and lunch but the pace increases at sunset and pavement tables are like gold dust. They show major sporting events on big screens and DJs feature nightly during the summer, winding down to weekend nights only during the rest of the year. Tues–Sun 8am till late.

Dunes 1 Beach Rd, Hout Bay ☎ 021 790 1876. Right on Hout Bay beach, this is a popular hangout for families, especially on sunny weekend afternoons when kids roar about. Mon–Sun 9am–10pm for dining, winter from 10am.

La Med Bar and Restaurant Glen Country Club, Victoria Rd, Clifton ☎ 021 438 5600. A great sundowner venue overlooking the rocks at Clifton. This is a favourite spot for hang-gliders from Lion's Head, after they've landed in the adjacent field. Big screens are great for matches plus they have live music at the weekend. Mon–Fri noon–late, Sat & Sun 9.30am–late.

Red Herring On the corner of Pine and Beach rds, Noordhoek ☎ 021 789 1783. An informal, friendly pub and restaurant, with an outdoor deck overlooking the panoramic Noordhoek Valley, popular with families, surfers, beachgoers and their dogs. Particularly busy on warm weekend afternoons, and live music gets going on Sunday evenings. Daily 11am–11pm.

West End and Club Galaxy College Rd, Rylands ☎ 021 637 9132, ⓦ superclubs.co.za. Definitely the most happening place on the Flats with a massive sound system, these two long-established nightclubs, with four dance-floors, featuring pumping mainstream house at the *Galaxy* and contemporary fusion at *West End*, draw a smart young crowd. Galaxy Thurs–Sat 9pm–4am; West End Fri & Sat 5pm–4am.

THE ARTSCAPE THEATRE, CAPE TOWN

The Arts and film

You'll find a satisfying and easily accessible range of dramatic and musical performances on offer in Cape Town. Theatres are scarcely full, and tickets are a bargain compared to the prices you'd pay in London or New York, and, despite the lack of arts funding from the government, there is a creative and lively arts scene. The best strategy in finding out what's on in Cape Town is to check out the offerings at the two major arts venues, the Baxter and Artscape, where you are likely to find something appealing, be it a play, a classical concert, some opera, contemporary dance or comedy. Cape Town is known for its brand of Cape Jazz, but there is nowhere regular to pick that up, though the best jazz event of the year happens in late March at the annual Cape Town International Jazz Festival (see p.30).

ESSENTIALS

Listings Posters tied onto street lights are often the way people discover what is on, the daily *Cape Times* and *Argus* carry listings and reviews, and the *021* listings magazine (ⓦ021cape.com) on sale at Vida e Caffè stores and bookshops, has a comprehensive selection of cultural listings, as well as wine festivals, sporting events, art exhibitions, lectures and new places to eat.

Tickets for most of the venues and performances listed in this chapter are available from Computicket (☎083 915 8000, ⓦcomputicket.com). You'll find that most ticket prices are very reasonable at R90–150.

THEATRE AND MUSICALS

10

Cape Town's premier physical theatre company, **Magnet** (ⓦmagnettheatre.co.za), produces consistently excellent, politically conscious, non-didactic physical theatre. Some productions collaborate with **Jazzart** contemporary dance and theatre company (ⓦjazzart.co.za) where you'll see the finest black dancers in town, who have forged a fusion of Western and African dance in their work.

Artscape D.F. Malan St ☎021 410 9838, ⓦartscape .co.za. Cape Town's most central and largest arts venue, where major productions are staged. Catch some contemporary dance, ballet or opera here, with some adventurous new dramas appearing periodically. Don't be intimidated by the monumental 1970s apartheid architecture.

Baxter Theatre Centre Main Rd, Rondebosch ☎021 685 7880, ⓦbaxter.co.za. This mammoth brick theatre complex – its design inspired by Soviet Moscow's central train station – is the cultural heart of Cape Town, mounting an eclectic programme of innovative plays, comedy festivals, jazz and classical concerts and kids' theatre. It's the first place to check out what's on when you hit town.

Fugard Theatre Corner of Caledon and Harrington sts ☎021 461 4554, ⓦthefugard.com. Great new initative on the east side of town in the old District Six, with a cross-section of interesting productions that are well worth checking out. The venue, a stylishly renovated church, has a very nice ambience for a pre- or post-show drink.

Maynardville Open Air Theatre On the corner of Church and Wolfe sts, Wynberg ⓦmaynardville .co.za. Every year in Jan and Feb, an imaginative production of a Shakespeare play is staged by the cream of Cape Town's actors and designers under the summer stars in Maynardville Park. Some dance productions also take place here in the summer, but is not open the rest of the year.

COMEDY

Comedy has a well-established following, and is very popular, particularly with coloured Capetonians, making the mix of Afrikaans and cross-cultural inference potentially bewildering for outsiders. South Africa's best-known stage satirist is **Pieter Dirk Uys**, whose character **Evita Bezuidenhout**, South Africa's answer to Dame Edna Everidge, has relentlessly roasted South African society since apartheid days. He often performs in Cape Town, though the best place to catch him is on a dedicated day out, over the weekend, in Darling, an hour out of Cape Town. New generation home-grown comedians

CAPE TOWN'S FINEST

Athol Fugard is historically the best known of South African playwrights internationally, even producing fine work these days though a steady trickle of innovative **plays**, concerned with forging a new African or fusion theatre, has long out-sped the days of didactic protest theatre – most critically acclaimed are *Bosman and Lena* and *Master Harold and the Boys*. More controversial is the brilliant **Brett Bailey**, a white man more "township" than many blacks, who creates electrifying, chaotic visual and physical theatre with his company **Third World Bunfight** (ⓦthirdworldbunfight.co.za). The company does theatre productions, installations, house music shows and opera, mostly concerned with the post-colonial landscape of Africa. You're as likely to catch his works in Europe as you are in Cape Town (see their website for schedules), but it is worth grabbing a ticket for anything they're staging. Cape Town-born RSC actor **Sir Anthony Sher** is the city's most famous son, appearing almost annually in the mother city in some fabulous productions, including an African version of The *Tempest* in 2009 and Arthur Miller's *Broken Glass* at the Fugard Theatre in 2011.

As regards **musicals**, **David Kramer** and the late **Taliep Petersen** produced several hit shows, although Kramer is best known for his show *Kitaar Blues*, sung in Afrikaans with township and Cape rhythms. He doesn't perform often now (ⓦdavidkramer.co.za), but the soundtrack to *Kitaar Blues* is on sale from ⓦkalahari.net or the African Music Store, 134 Long St.

10

to look out for include **Marc Lottering**, a coloured Capetonian who derives his material from his own community; **Nik Rabinowitz**, an irreverent middle-class Jewish boy who uses his fluency in Xhosa to poke fun at cultural stereotypes; and **Riyaad Moosa**, a Muslim doctor-turned-comedian. If he is visiting from Gauteng, catch **Trevor Noah**, one of the most talented young South African stand-ups.

★ **Evita se Perron** Darling Station, Arcadia Rd, Darling ☎ 022 492 2831, 🌐 evita.co.za. An hour's drive north of Cape Town, on the R27, the town of Darling is well worth visiting for its camply converted train station, which plays host to the satirical shows of Pieter Dirk Uys. It makes for a great day out, and is a notable highlight of a stay in South Africa. Since it is dependent on Pieter Dirk Uys's schedule, check the website for dates.

Jou Ma Se Comedy Club The River Club, Liesbeek Parkway, Observatory 🌐 joumasecomedy.com.

A dedicated comedy venue in Cape Town, run by comedian Kurt Skoonraad, who has a regular Thursday-evening gig. Their website also carries info about any other comedy events and clubs in the city. Thurs 7–11pm.

On Broadway 44 Long St ☎ 021 424 1194, 🌐 onbroadway.co.za. One of the few venues committed to the city's small cabaret scene is this fun bar-restaurant with live performances, comedy and music for a big crowd every night of the week. Ticket prices are appealingly lower than mainstream venues. Daily 6.30pm–late.

CLASSICAL MUSIC

Classical music is thriving, albeit for small and elite audiences, and one of the best things you could take in on a visit to Cape Town is an **opera** (🌐 capetownopera.co.za). In all areas of the arts, there is a quest for fusion, which has given rise to some fascinating operas, usually with an almost totally black cast boasting some of the most superb voices in the country, a great statement about opera crossing cultural barriers and centuries. **Symphony concerts** are usually held at the City Hall and Baxter Theatre, and there are free **lunchtime concerts**, often showcasing the work of students from Cape Town University's South African College of Music, on Thursdays at 1pm at the Baxter Theatre or at the college itself (☎ 021 650 2640, 🌐 web.uct.ac.za/depts/sacm). Many recitals by visiting soloists and chamber ensembles are put on by an organization called **Cape Town Concert Series** (🌐 ctconcerts.co.za), and there are regular, and excellent performances in different churches, by Cape Town's only baroque ensemble, Camerata Tinta Barocca (🌐 ctbmusic.co.za).

CINEMA

Despite the fact that Cape Town is booming as a film-production centre, local feature films are scarce, though some excellent documentaries are produced. The daily newspapers are the best source to find out what's on at the movies. There are several **film festivals** of note: the International Documentary Festival in July (🌐 encounters.co.za), which features riveting South African documentaries in its line-up; the TRI Continental Film Festival in August/September (🌐 3continentsfestival.co.za), which has a strong developing world socio-political emphasis; and in September the Out in Africa South African Gay and Lesbian Film Festival (🌐 oia.co.za).

★ **Labia** 69 Orange St, or the Labia on Kloof, Lifestyles on Kloof Centre, Kloof St ☎ 021 424 5927, 🌐 labia .co.za. The retro Labia (Lah-bia) shows an intelligent mix of art films, cult classics and new releases, and is Cape Town's only independent cinema. It also has attractive ticket prices – half those of the mainstream cinemas.

Ster-Kinekor Cinema Nouveau Waterfront ☎ 082 16789, 🌐 www.sterkinekor.com; and Ster-Kinekor

Cinema Nouveau, Cavendish Sqaure Mall ☎ 021 657 5600. If you want to catch a movie, simply pitch up at the Waterfront or Cavendish Square. Each of these malls has two cinemas, one for mainstream popular releases, and a Cinema Nouveau, with an art-house selection, each showing films three times a day. Tickets are under R100, with cheap nights on Tuesdays.

Shopping

The V&A Waterfront is the city's most popular though mainstream shopping venue: it has a vast range of shops, the setting on the harbour is lovely and there's a huge choice of places to eat and drink when you need to refuel. The city centre also offers variety and, for some people's taste, an edgier and more interesting venue for browsing, especially if you're looking for collectables, antiques and secondhand books. The best area to find interesting South African crafts, music and gifts is definitely along Long Street, and the other central area for great shopping, browsing and eating is the Cape Quarter, accessed off Somerset Road in Green Point. If you're staying in the inner-city suburbs of Green Point and Sea Point, you'll find supermarkets and other functional shops along Main Road, while the City Bowl suburbs are served by the Gardens Shopping Centre.

ESSENTIALS

Opening hours Shops have traditionally opened from Monday to Friday 8.30am to 5pm, and Saturday until 1pm, though lots of supermarkets, bookshops and other specialist outlets are now open beyond 5pm and also on Sundays. That said, don't expect much to be open on Sunday afternoons, except at the Waterfront or Cavendish Square.

ARTS, CRAFTS AND JEWELLERY

Cape Town is not known for its indigenous arts and crafts, and many of the goods you'll buy here are from elsewhere in Africa, especially Zimbabwe and Zambia. There are several crafts outlets in the city centre and the V&A Waterfront, but you'll often pick up the same wares for a lot less money at the pavement markets scattered around town. Don't expect exotic West African-style affairs, however: Cape Town's markets are more like European or North American flea markets. Two of the most browsable streets for crafts, gifts and funky clothing are **Long Street** in the city centre, and Main Road in **Kalk Bay**. If you're after South African gold and diamonds, you'll find the Waterfront Mall one of the best places to browse – but price tags are high.

11 MARKETS

Blue Shed Craft Market Next to the Aquarium, V&A Waterfront; map p.62. Handmade products and African crafts; the location pushes up the prices. Mon–Sun 9am–6pm.

Cape Town Station Forecourt Adderley St; map p.49. Thronging ranks of market traders selling African crafts, as well as cheap Chinese goods, and not aimed at tourists – worthwhile for the downmarket city atmosphere rather than for the goods on offer. Mon–Fri 8am–5pm, Sat 8am–2pm.

Green Point Market Outside the stadium, Green Point; map p.88. A massive open-air market displaying everything from African arts and crafts to plants, car parts and anything home-made. Sun 9am–4pm.

Greenmarket Square Burg St; map p.62. City-centre open-air market on a cobbled square where you can pick up loads of presents to take home, from all over the continent. It's also the best place in town for colourful handmade Cape Town hippy gear and Tanzanian beach wraps (*kikois*). Mon–Fri 9am–4pm, Sat 9am–2pm.

Pan African Market 76 Long St; map p.49. A multicultural hothouse of township and contemporary art, artefacts, curios and crafts. There's also a café specializing in African cuisine, a bookshop, a Cameroonian hairbraider and a West African tailor. Mon–Fri 9am–5pm, Sat 9am–3pm.

Red Shed Craft Workshop Victoria Wharf, V&A Waterfront; map p.62. A market where some two dozen craftworkers make and sell ceramics, textiles, candles and jewellery, and where you can see glass-blowers at work. Mon–Sat 9am–9pm, Sun 10am–9pm.

Sivuyile Craft Centre Corner of NY1 and NY4, Guguletu, Cape Flats, phone for directions ☎ 021 637 8449. Township market attached to an information centre close to the N2 freeway, where beadworkers, wire-workers and other artists make traditional and modern crafts. Mon–Fri 8am–5pm, Sat 9am–1pm.

Victoria Road Market Camps Bay. Carvings, beads, fabrics and baskets sold from a roadside market spectacularly sited on a clifftop overlooking the Atlantic. Daily.

SHOPS

Africa Nova Cape Quarter, Waterkant St, De Waterkant; ⓦ africanova.co.za; map p.62. A better-than-average selection of ethnic crafts and curios as well as contemporary African textiles and artwork, with an emphasis on the individual and handmade. Mon–Sat 10am–5pm, Sun 10am–2pm.

African Image Victoria Wharf, V&A Waterfront; map p.49. One of the best places for authentic traditional and contemporary African arts and crafts, from fabrics and antique sculpture to beadwork, but goods are a little overpriced. More branches at the corner of Church and Burg sts, and Shop 6228 (opening times may vary). Daily 9am–9pm.

Ethno Bongo Mainstream Shopping Centre, Main Rd, Hout Bay ⓦ dolceandbanana.com. A charming shop in the main shopping centre in Hout Bay, selling wonderful and well-priced crafts, jewellery and accessories made from recycled metal and wood, and also quirky kaftans and ethnic clothing – highly recommended for unique gifts and souvenirs. Mon–Fri 9.30am–5.30pm, Sat 9.30am–4pm, Sun 10am–2pm.

Kalk Bay Gallery 62 Main Rd, Kalk Bay; map p.98. Graphics and engravings as well as African art and artefacts at reasonable prices, with the chance of picking up something very collectable. Mon–Fri 9am–5pm, Sat & Sun 9.30am–5pm.

Mike Cope Jewellery 5 St Heliers Rd, Muizenberg; ☎ 021 788 2083, ⓦ cope.co.za; map p.98. Call before visiting the home studio, just off the main road, of one of Cape Town's master jewellers. He'll be able to show you a small selection of bold, eye-catching work, often nature-inspired. By appointment.

CLOCKWISE FROM TOP LEFT OSTRICH EGGS FOR SALE; SHOPPING ON LONG STREET; BEACH TOWELS IN PE (P.243); TRIBAL MASK >

Montebello Craft & Design Centre 31 Newlands Ave, Newlands. A great selection of South African crafts, jewellery, beadwork, ceramics, woven goods, even musical instruments and garden items, in a centre where people from townships are trained to become artisans. Besides watching the craftsmen at work, you can eat here at the restaurant under the oaks. Mon–Fri 9am–4.45pm, Sat & Sun 9.30am–3pm.

Rose Korber Art Consultancy 48 Sedgemoor Rd, Camps Bay. This should be the first stop for the serious collector, with an exceptional selection of contemporary art and crafts, including ceramics and beadwork from around the continent. Mon–Fri 9am–5pm; weekends by appointment.

Zulu Azania 56a Church St city centre; map p.49. Tribal artefacts from all over Africa with some large and pricey pieces. It is also known for good-quality beadwork and terracotta drinking vessels. Mon–Fri 9am–4pm, Sat 9am–3pm.

BOOKS

South Africa has some very talented authors and you'll find good locally published novels and endless volumes on history, politics and natural history. **Exclusive Books** is the main chain you'll find in the airport and malls, while **Upper Long Street** has several secondhand book and specialist comic shops in close proximity, interspersed with inviting cafés, and there are a couple of notable independent bookshops.

★ **Book Lounge** 71 Roeland St ⓦ booklounge.co.za; map p.43. The most congenial central bookshop with comfy sofas and a downstairs café stocks an excellent selection of local books and imaginative list of imported titles, as well as running evening events with local intellectuals and writers. The website has listings of who's visiting. Mon–Fri 8.30am–7.30pm, Sat 9.30am–6pm, Sun 10am–4pm.

Clarke's Bookshop 211 Long St ⓦ clarkesbooks .co.za; map p.49. The best place in Cape Town for South African books has very well-informed staff who can help you find what you want among the huge selection of local titles covering literature, history, politics, natural history and the arts. It also deals in collectors' editions of South African books. Mon–Fri 9am–5pm, Sat 9am–1pm.

Exclusive Books Victoria Wharf, V&A Waterfront ⓦ exclus1ves.co.za; map p.62. Though small by British and American standards, the reasonably well-stocked shelves include magazines and a wide choice of coffee-table books on Cape Town and South African topics. There are other branches at Lower Mall, Cavendish Square, Claremont, Main Rd, and Constantia Village Shopping Centre, though their opening times may vary. Mon–Fri 9am–10pm, Sat 9am–11pm, Sun 10am–9pm.

Kirstenbosch Shop Kirstenbosch National Botanical Gardens; map p.71. A good selection of natural-history books, field guides and travel guides covering southern Africa, as well as a range of titles for kids. You don't need a Gardens ticket to browse. Daily 9am–6pm.

Wordsworth's Ground Floor V&A Waterfront; ⓦ wordsworth.co.za; map p.62. A good general bookshop, with a specialist travel section. Mon–Sat 9am–10pm, Sun 9am–9pm.

CDS AND RECORDS

African Music Store 134 Long St; map p.49. Small, upbeat, centrally located shop specializing in African music from around the continent. It also has a modest collection of instruments, such as shakers and thumb pianos. Mon–Fri 9am–5pm, Sat 9am–2pm.

Look & Listen Cavendish Square, Claremont ☏ 021 683 1810. Cape Town's largest music store, with a selection of all kinds of sounds, including good local jazz and a respectable selection from all over the African continent. Daily 9am–7pm.

Mabu Vinyl 2 Rheede St, Gardens; ☏ 021 423 7635; map p.73. The aficionado's choice for a great selection of secondhand CDs, vinyl and, even cassettes, of many genres. Mon–Thurs 9am–8pm, Fri 9am–7pm, Sat 9am–6pm, Sun 11am–3pm.

Musica Megastore V&A Waterfront ☏ 021 425 6300; map p.62. A megastore by international standards, with one of the best ranges of African music in the city, plus classical and jazz, pop and rock, and DVDs and video games. Daily 9am–9pm.

FOOD AND PROVISIONS

Self-catering is the cheapest way to eat in Cape Town and there are countless places where you can enjoy a terrific picnic. There are some excellent delicatessens, several of which are strung along Main Road, Green Point and Sea Point. You'll also find delicious food and some unusual fruit and vegetables at the more sophisticated farm stalls.

The larger branches of the better supermarkets have **fishmonger** counters where you can buy fresh fish, though by far the most atmospheric places to buy seafood are the Hout Bay and Kalk Bay harbours. Cape Town also has a sprinkling of stores specializing in **health foods** (see p.00) and modest selections of organic fruit and vegetables, the best choice being at the large branches of Woolworths. Supermarkets tend to have decent **wine** at competitive prices, but for more interesting labels, there are some first-rate specialist wine merchants. Otherwise, you can buy alcoholic beverages at bottle stores (the equivalent of the British off-licence), which generally keep normal shopping hours, although some stay open until 6.30pm.

DELIS AND FARMER'S MARKETS

Andiamo Cape Quarter Dixon St, De Waterkant ☎ 021 421 3688; map p.62. Italian deli where you can select from meats, cheeses, salads, dips, meze and fresh breads to take on your mountain walk. Phone ahead and they'll put the picnic together for you. Daily 9am–10pm.

Giovanni's 103 Main Rd, Green Point; map p.88. Excellent breads and delicious Italian foods to take away and – if temptation overcomes you – there's always the option of sitting down for a pavement coffee with a view onto Green Point Stadium. Daily 8.30am–9pm.

Melissa's Waterfront; map p.73. Highly delectable imported and local specialities, at a popular and gourmet deli with the option of eating in. Branches on Kloof St, Gardens and in Constantia Village. Not cheap, but always worth it. Daily 9am–9pm.

Neighbourgoods Market Old Biscuit Mill, 373–375 Albert Rd off Lower Main Rd. This is the best food experience of the week – walk around sampling artisanal cheeses and wood-fired breads, stopping for coffee or luxury beers, and marvelling at the array of fresh flowers, fruit and veg in a skylit Victorian warehouse. Not cheap, but it sells the best produce of its kind in the Cape, with a lively, sociable atmosphere. Sat 9am–2pm.

Organic Zone Lakeside Shopping Centre, Main Rd, Lakeside; map p.43. Always fresh and well-stocked organic fruit and veg, as well as grains, honey, breads and dairy products. Mon–Fri 9am–6pm, Sat 9am–2pm.

Quench Organic Deli 42 Lower Main Rd, Observatory. Organic restaurant and shop, where you can buy veggies and grains if you are self-catering, in a street also worth visiting for its trendy alternative shops and cafés. Mon–Fri 7.30am–5pm, Sat 7.30am–4pm.

Tokai Farmers Market Similar to the Neighbourgoods market (p.98), though smaller and less sophisticated, and in a rural setting. To get there, head south from the centre of town and take the Ladies Mile exit from the M3 onto Spaanschemacht. Head south again, and turn right into the forest at a signboard marked "The Range" on the Spaanschemacht Rd, just beyond Constantia Uitsig Wine Estate. Sat 9am–1pm.

FRESH FISH

Fish Market Mariner's Wharf, Hout Bay Harbour. Fresh seafood from South Africa's original Waterfront emporium, but slicker and less atmospheric than Kalk Bay Harbour. Mon–Fri 9am–5.30pm, Sat & Sun 9am–6pm.

Kalk Bay Harbour Harbourside, Kalk Bay; map p.98. Buy fresh fish directly from the fishermen and have it gutted and scaled on the spot. Your best bet is lunchtime, especially at weekends, though catches are dependent on several factors including the weather and rough seas.

SUPERMARKETS

Pick 'n Pay V&A Waterfront; Gardens Shopping Centre, Mill St, Gardens; Main Rd, Camps Bay; Main Rd, Observatory; Corner of Main and Campground rds, Claremont; Blue Route Mall, Tokai; Constantia Village, Main Rd, Constantia. Larger and cheaper than Woolworths (see p.98), this is one of the best places for groceries, with a good deli counter and a choice of prepared meals, including excellent-value ready-grilled whole chickens. Mon–Sat generally 8.30am–6pm, though the Waterfront and Observatory branches stay open later; on Sun all branches close at 2.30pm.

Woolworths Adderley St; V&A Waterfront; Cavendish Square Mall, Claremont; Blue Route Mall, Tokai; Constantia Village, Main Rd, Constantia; map p.62. Excellent for quality (and often pricey) fast-cook meals, fresh produce and cold foods, such as olives, hummus and various Mediterranean dips, and good wine. Daily 9am–6pm; Waterfront daily 9am–9pm.

WINE

Caroline's Fine Wines 62 Strand St and King's Warehouse, V&A Waterfront; map p.49. Caroline Rillema has been in the wine business since 1979 and stocks the Cape's finest and most exclusive wines. Mon–Fri 9am–5pm, Waterfront also Sat 9am–5pm.

11

GO GREEN

Cape Town's **Green Map** (Ⓦ www.greenmap.org) is a great source of information about ethical shopping, organic markets, delis, health shops and restaurants. They also have information on nature reserves and recycling initiatives, as well as green accommodation options and even city tours.

Vaughan Johnson's Dock Rd, V&A Waterfront ✆ 021 419 2121; map p.62. One of Cape Town's best-known wine shops, which has a huge range of labels from all over the country, though it can be a bit pricey. Mon–Fri 9am–6pm, Sat 9am–5pm, Sun 10am–5pm.

Wine Concepts Corner of Kildare and Main rds, Newlands; and Gardens Lifestyle Centre, Kloof St; ⓦ wineconcepts.co.za; map p.73. An excellent selection of South African and foreign wines from a knowledgeable and helpful outfit. Mon–Fri 10am–7pm, Sat 9am–5pm.

MALLS AND SHOPPING CENTRES

South African shopping tends to follow the American model, with **malls** where you can browse in a bookshop as well as bank, buy clothes and groceries and go to the movies. Malls always have several coffee shops and restaurants.

Blue Route Mall Tokai Rd, Tokai. A functional single-storey centre with branches of Checkers Hyper and Woolworths, handy if you're staying in Constantia or along the False Bay. Mon–Fri 9am–5.30pm, Sat & Sun 9am–3pm.

Cavendish Square Claremont station, Vineyard Rd, Claremont. An upmarket multistorey complex, the major shopping focus for the southern suburbs, and with a cinema showing art-house movies. Mon–Thurs & Sat 9am–6pm, Fri 9am–9pm, Sun 10am–4pm.

Constantia Village Shopping Centre Main Rd, Constantia. A small exclusive mall including two large supermarkets, post office and general, practical shopping facilities. Mon–Sat 9am–5pm, Sun 9am–2pm.

Gardens Shopping Centre Mill St, Gardens; map p.43. Small shopping mall in the City Bowl, very close to the Company's Gardens and city centre, with a large supermarket, excellent deli and most of the shops you'll need for anything practical. Mon–Fri 9am–6pm, Sat 9am–3pm; some shops also Sun 10am–2pm.

V&A Waterfront; map p.62. It would be possible to visit Cape Town and never leave the Waterfront complex, which has a vast range of upmarket shops packed into the Victoria Wharf Shopping Centre, including outlets of all the major South African chains, selling books, clothes, food and crafts, as well as two cinemas, one of them with art-house films. Mon–Sat 9am–9pm, Sun 10am–9pm.

11

NEWLANDS CRICKET GROUND

Sports and outdoor activities

One of Cape Town's most remarkable features is the fact that it melds with the Table Mountain National Park – a patchwork of mountains, forests and coastline – giving rise to myriad outdoor pursuits. In fact, there are few, if any, cities in the world where so many activities are so easily available and affordable. For land lovers, there's the obvious draw of hiking up the imposing faces of Table Mountain, as well as ubiquitous cycle paths and opportunities for horseriding. Surrounded by ocean coastline on all sides, it's not surprising that every watersport under the sun, from sea kayaking to surfing, is on offer, while the true daredevils can marvel at the aerial views of the city by launching off the Lion's Head on a paraglider. Alternatively, just let everyone else get on with it while you sink a few beers and watch high-calibre cricket, rugby or football – no denying it, South Africa is a sports-mad country.

PARTICIPATION SPORTS AND OUTDOOR ACTIVITIES

ABSEILING

Abseil Africa ☎ 021 424 4760, ⓦ abseilafrica.co.za. You can abseil off Table Mountain for around R695. A guided summit walk up Platteklip Gorge goes for R250.

BIRDWATCHING

Although Cape Town has fewer species of birds, compared to the east of the country, its pelagic population brings the number up to four hundred, including the highly endangered albatross. Pelagic trips by boat off the peninsula virtually guarantee four species of albatross. Good places for birdwatching include Lion's Head, Kirstenbosch Gardens and the Cape of Good Hope Nature Reserve, as well as at Kommetjie and Hout Bay.

Anne Grey ☎ 083 311 1140. Runs pelagic tours by boat if you're after the albatross and other rarities off the Cape coast.
Birding Africa ☎ 021 531 9148, ⓦ birdingafrica.com. Has a wealth of information on birding trips in Cape Town.

CYCLING

Cycling is very popular and is a great way to take in the scenery, though you have to be very vigilant about intolerant car drivers – cyclists are frequently knocked down.

Pedal Power Associates ☎ 021 689 8420, ⓦ www.cycletour.co.za. Organizes fun rides from Sept–May. Also has information on the annual, spectacular Argus Cycle Tour that takes place in March, 109km right around the peninsula, with 40,000 riders from all over the country as well as international entrants. Arterial routes are closed over much of Cape Town on that day, but it's well publicized beforehand.

GOLF

Cape Town has several well-maintained golf courses, all with relevant dress code and caddies. You can play for a fraction of what you might pay back home, in far better weather conditions.

Milnerton golf course Bridge Rd, Milnerton ☎ 021 552 1047. Tucked in between a lagoon and Table Bay, and boasts classic views of Table Mountain.

Westlake Golf Club Westlake Ave, Lakeside ☎ 021 788 2020, ⓦ westlakegolfclub.co.za. Situated at the southern end of the Constantia valley where the M3 south ends, with a mountainous backdrop, Westlake is one of the nicest courses to play on, with visitors always welcome.

GYMS

Virgin Active ☎ 086 020 0911, ⓦ virginactive.co.za. These gyms are upmarket, well appointed and dotted conveniently around the peninsula, all with large swimming pools and spotless changing rooms. Contact their call centre for current visitor rates, available for a day, week or month.

HEALTH SPAS

Most of Cape Town's luxury hotels have spas attached, which you can use as a day visitor, even if you are not staying there.

Twelve Apostles Hotel and Spa Victoria Rd, Camps Bay; daily 8am–8pm; ☎ 021 437 0677, ⓦ 12apostleshotel.com. Cape Town's most lavish spa in the most beautiful setting imaginable with mountain and ocean views. There are hot and cold plunge pools as well as all the usual treatments. They offer massage in the open air too.

The Vineyard Hotel Colinton Rd; daily 10am–8pm; ☎ 021 674 5005, ⓦ vineyard.co.za. A gorgeous garden setting with mountain backdrop and Zen-style decor make this a truly serene spot. The treatment rooms are decorated in silks and everything at the spa, like the rest of the hotel, is utterly elegant and pleasing.

HORSERIDING

Prices usually run at around R350 for a two-hour outride. If you are an intermediate or advanced rider, do find out if there are rides for experienced riders only, otherwise you may not get a canter.

Horse Trail Safaris Indicator Lodge, Skaapskraal Rd, Ottery, east of Wynberg across the M5 ☎ 021 703 4396, ⓦ horsetrailsafaris.co.za. Offers riding through the dunes to the coast, though you are only on the actual beach for ten minutes (2hr 30min; R350).

Sleepy Hollow Horse Riding Sleepy Hollow Lane, Noordhoek ☎ 021 789 2341 or ☎ 083 261 0104. Covers the spectacular Noordhoek Beach.

KAYAKING

Downhill Adventures On the corner of Kloof and Orange sts in the city centre ☎ 021 422 0388, ⓦ downhilladventures.co.za. Offers trips from Mouille Point or Simon's Town from R500 per half-day.

Real Cape Adventures ☎ 021 790 5611 or ☎ 082 556 2520, ⓦ www.seakayak.co.za. Offers a range of half- or full-day sea-kayaking packages that include trips around Cape Point, to the penguin colony at Boulders Beach and around Hout Bay.

MOUNTAIN BIKING

Day Trippers ☎ 021 511 4766, ⓦ daytrippers.co.za. Offers expert mountain-bike tours, including one from Scarborough to Cape Point. Downhill Adventures offers similar tours, including Tokai Forest.

12

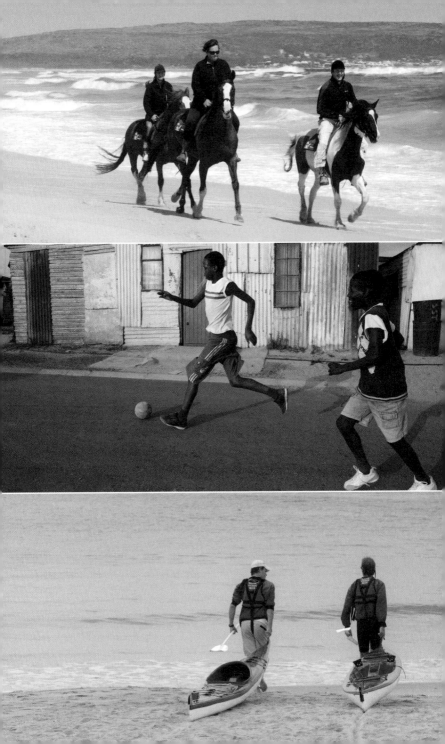

PARAGLIDING

Cape Town has great air thermals for paragliding: the usual spot is from Lion's Head, drifting down to Camps Bay.

Para-Taxi ☎082 966 2047, ⓦpara-taxi.com. Tandem jumps from R695.

Wallend-Air School ☎021 762 2441, ⓦwallendair .com. Peter Wallend, one of SA's paragliding champs, offers courses to get your paragliding licence.

ROCK CLIMBING

City Rock Indoor Climbing Centre 21 Anson Rd, Observatory ☎021 447 1326, ⓦcityrock.co.za. For practice walls, you'll find serious climbers at City Rock which has good facilities, including a small wall for children, and more challenging surfaces for teenagers.

High Adventure ☎021 689 1234 or ☎082 437 5145, ⓦhighadventure.co.za. This outfit will take you to unusual and unique locations depending on your ability. Packages are tailor-made, with a minimum of two people.

RUNNING

Two of the best places to jog are Newlands Forest up the mountain tracks, and along the Sea Point Promenade. The **Two Oceans Marathon**, every Easter Saturday (ⓦwww. twooceansmarathon.org.za) is one of the world's most exciting runs – athletes descend on the city from all corners of the globe to run the arduous 56km ultra-marathon around the peninsula.

SANDBOARDING

Downhill Adventures Orange St ☎021 422 0388, ⓦdownhilladventures.com. The pioneers of this ski-related adventure sport. Boards, boots and bindings are provided, as well as expert instruction for beginners. R550.

Sunscene Outdoor Adventures ☎021 783 0203, ⓦsunscene.co.za. Does sandboarding as well as surfing, and is good at teaching kids. Expect to pay from R500 for a day out.

SCUBA DIVING

While the Cape waters are cold, they're also good for seeing wrecks, reefs and magnificent kelp forests.

The Scuba Shack 289 Long St ☎021 424 9368, ⓦscubashack.co.za. Offers land and boat dives, from R520 for the dive and equipment, as well as dives in the Aquarium in the shark tank, or in the Kelp Forest, which teems with non-biting fish. You can also take an internationally recognized PADI Open Water diving qualification. If you don't want to dive, you can snorkel with Cape Fur Seals off the coast. Diving trips are cheaper with your own equipment.

SKYDIVING

The ultimate way to see Table Mountain and Robben Island is from a tandem jump 3000m up.

Skydive Cape Town ☎082 800 6290, ⓦskydivecapetown.za.net. Situated 30min from Cape Town along the R27 West Coast Rd, this is a long-established business offering reliable and good-quality dives for R1550.

SURFING

For information on competitions check out ⓦwavescape. co.za, the best place on the web for everything you want to know about surfing in SA, including what the waves are up to. Top surfing spots include Big Bay at Bloubergstrand (where competitions are held here every summer), Llandudno, Muizenberg and Long Beach near Kommetjie and Noordhoek. **Muizenberg** is the best place for beginners, with lessons frequently on the go, a strip of surf schools along the beachfront, gear for hire and surf shops selling all you might need. The car park pumps with surfers at the weekend, and you can get there by train.

Gary's Surf School ☎021 788 9839, ⓦgarysurf.com. A surfing school which has been there forever, offering a 2hr lesson including gear rental for R380, which guarantees to get you up and moving on the board in your first lesson.

Surf Shack ☎021 788 9286, ⓦsurfshack.co.za. Various packages including four lessons for a reasonable R800 per couple, plus gear rental. If you are staying for a week or longer, you can have a lesson every day at a reasonable cost.

SWIMMING

Sea swimming is best in False Bay, as it is far warmer than the Atlantic side, especially at Muizenberg and Fish Hoek beaches, as well as St James Pool. For swimming pools, try:

Long Street Baths Long St ☎021 400 3302; daily 7am–7pm. Cape Town's only public heated indoor pool, with steam and sauna facilities to warm up on winter days.

Newlands Swimming Pool Corner of Main and San Souci rds, Newlands ☎021 674 4197; Oct–Easter 9.30am–5pm; R15. An Olympic-sized chlorinated pool with trees, lawns, mountain views and a paddling pool for children.

Sea Point Swimming Pool Beach Rd ☎021 434 3341; summer 7am–7pm, winter unheated 8.30am–5pm R15. An Olympic-sized chlorinated seawater pool, right on the edge of the ocean with lovely lawns to laze on, and watch the ships go by.

WALKING

The best places for **easy walks** are in Kirstenbosch Gardens, Newlands Forest, along the Sea Point Promenade and the beaches. If you want to **hike**, however, and there are limitless opportunities, it's best, as a visitor to take a guided half-day or day trip. This is partly because of the unfamiliar terrain, and because there have been a small number of mugging incidents on the mountains over the years, involving unsuspecting tourists. For **Table Mountain safety** see p.141. Both operators below charge from R450 per person for a shorter hike, up to R900 for a full-day table-top ascent. Mike can also do trips of a couple of days out of town to the Cederberg wilderness area.

Guided by Mike ℗ 083 402 0288, @ guidedbymike @gmail.com. Experienced and very personable mountaineer, rock climber Mike Wakeford does trips up Table Mountain, Silvermine Reserve and Southern peninsula.

Margie ℗ 021 715 6136, ⓦ tablemountainwalks.co.za. Margie is a registered Table Mountain Guide who does the classic Table Mountain ascents, as well as other gorgeous routes on the peninsula. She will pick you up for free from your accommodation, and provide refreshments and lunch.

WINDSURFING AND KITESURFING

Langebaan, a 75min drive north of town, is one of the best spots, as the enormous lagoon offers better conditions than the ocean around Cape Town, which has a bigger swell and is choppier.

Cape Sport Centre, Langebaan ℗ 022 772 1114, ⓦ capesport.co.za. Does a variety of watersports and has accommodation along the same street. Prices for windsurfing start at R500 for a lesson and 2 hours on the water; a 2-day kitesurfing package costs from R2400 including gear and instruction.

YOGA AND PILATES

Cape Town is full of high-quality Yoga and Pilates studios, with internationally trained instructors that charge around half what you might pay back home.

Wynberg Pilates Studio 18 Mortimer Rd, Wynberg ℗ 021 797 2351, ⓦ pilatesafrica.co.za. The city's most experienced trainers for classes or individual tuition in a tranquil studio with a beautiful garden setting. The studio also offers Feldenkrais Method® and Gyrotonics®.

Karma Shala Yoga 117 Hatfield St, Gardens ℗ 082 642 5256, ℗ karmacalmer.co.za. Jim Harrington is one of the best-regarded teachers in Cape Town, with classes at the centrally located studio above, as well as in Hout Bay and Noordhoek.

SPECTATOR SPORTS

12

CRICKET

Newlands Cricket Ground 61 Campground Rd, Newlands ℗ 021 657 2003, ⓦ www.cricket.co.za. This is the city's cricketing heart. One of the most beautiful grounds in the world, Newlands nestles beneath venerable oaks and the elegant profile of Devil's Peak, and plays host to provincial, test and one-day international matches.

RUGBY

The Western Cape is one of the world's rugby heartlands, and the game is followed religiously here.

Newlands Rugby Stadium Boundary Rd, Newlands ℗ 021 659 4600, ⓦ www.wprugby.co.za. Provincial, international and Super 12 contests are fought on this hallowed turf.

FOOTBALL

For fixtures and results go to ⓦ beezsports.com, ⓦ psl.co.za. Though football matches aren't as well attended as cricket or rugby, Cape Town football is burgeoning with talent and received a huge boost post the 2010 FIFA World Cup. The dusty streets of the Cape Flats have produced superb young footballers such as Benni McCarthy (Porto, Ajax, Amsterdam, Celta Vigo) and Quinton Fortune (Atletico Madrid, Manchester United). The most ambitious and professional club in the city is Ajax (pronounced "I-axe") Cape Town (ⓦ ajaxct.com), jointly owned by its Amsterdam namesake, while the the most exciting games to attend are those between a local outfit and one of the Soweto glamour teams, Orlando Pirates and Kaizer Chiefs. Matches take place at **Green Point Stadium**, off Beach Rd and **Athlone Stadium**, off Klipfontein Rd, Athlone.

THE CAPE TOWN GAY PRIDE FESTIVAL

Gay and lesbian Cape Town

South Africa has the continent's most developed and diverse gay and lesbian scene – and Cape Town is its gay capital, on its way to becoming an African Sydney, attracting gay travellers from across the country and the globe. Cape Town is the only city in South Africa to have a dedicated gay village, De Waterkant, very centrally located with great cafés, accommodation and nightlife. Walk around the gay village and you'll always find a choice of places to drink or party. Furthermore, the country has the world's first pro-homosexual constitution: not only is homosexuality legal in South Africa between consenting adults of 18 or over, but the constitution outlaws any discrimination on the grounds of sexual orientation.

Outside the big cities, however, and even in Cape Town's townships, attitudes remain pretty conservative and homophobic, and open displays of affection by gays and lesbians are unlikely to go down well; many whites will find it un-Christian, while blacks will think it un-African. It's still especially hard for African and coloured gay men and women to come out. Homophobic attacks are still a threat whatever your ethnicity, so take care when venturing beyond the centre of Cape Town.

As you'd expect in a city where the great outdoors figures so prominently, there are a number of beaches popular with men, including **Clifton's Third Beach** (not Fourth Beach, which is family orientated; see p.89) which is great for body-ogling, and the nudist **Sandy Bay**, accessed from Llandudno beach (see p.90).

RESOURCES AND CONTACTS

Information Ⓦgaynetcapetown.co.za is aimed specifically at gay and lesbian travellers to the city, with restaurants and accommodation listings, as well as information about HIV and AIDS. Health4Men, 24 Napier St (Ⓦhealth4men.co.za) provides advice on how to access ARV treatment for men living with HIV.

Listings The best listings magazine is *Out Africa* magazine, available from the bars and restaurants in De Waterkant, and from GAP Leisure, on the corner of Napier and

Waterkant streets (Ⓦgapleisure.com), an agency that specializes in finding accommodation in both the Waterkant and countrywide.

Advice The Triangle Project (Ⓣ021 448 3812, Ⓦtriangle .org.za) is the longest established organization offering care and support for gay, lesbian, bisexual and transgender people including HIV testing, ARV advice and other medical services.

BARS AND CLUBS

Amsterdam Action Bar 12 Cobern St, off Somerset Rd, De Waterkant. Old-school gay bar (men only) with a more mature crowd, keen on full leathers. There's no disco but they have a pool table. Daily 4pm till late.

Bar Code 18 Cobern St, De Waterkant Ⓣ021 421 5305, Ⓦleatherbar.co.za. A leather, uniform and jeans bar with darkrooms and an outdoor deck. It's worth finding out what the evening's dress code is beforehand, in case they're having a themed night. Bouncers and a R50 entrance fee ensure it stays men only. Daily 10pm till late.

Beefcakes 40 Somerset Rd, Green Point Ⓣ021 425 9019, Ⓦbeefcakes.co.za. This is one seriously camp burger bar, with pink flamingo wallpaper and feathers, where you can build your own juicy burger, and wear a sequinned cowboy hat if you so wish. There is a range of live entertainment from Drag Divas to "Bitchy Bingo", on

varying nights, which go down as well as their delicious cocktails. Mon–Sat 11am till late, Sun 6pm–late.

Bronx Action Bar 22 Somerset Rd, cnr of Napier St, Green Point Ⓦbronx.co.za. Cape Town's most popular gay bar and longest standing dancefloor, the *Bronx Bar* is a wildly busy, nightly meat market with pumping pop music and bare-chested barmen, although women, straight and gay, are welcome. Daily 8pm till late.

Bubbles Bar 125a De Waterkant St, opposite Manhattan Ⓣ021 801 0501. Small, relaxed venue with a popular "cheap tequila" special during the week. Besides tequila, it's known as the Drag Show mecca, with shows from Wed to Sun run by delightful Drag Queen Lola Lou from France, now married to a South African. Daily 5pm–2am.

Cafe Manhattan 74 Waterkant St, De Waterkant, and 247 Main Rd, Sea Point Ⓦmanhattan.co.za. A buzzing

FESTIVALS

Cape Town hosts some fantastic festivals, the most famous being the hugely popular annual Mother City Queer Projects party (Ⓦmcqp.co.za), which has turned into a ten-day festival held each December between two public holidays (16–24). A cousin of Sydney's Mardi Gras festival, people dress as outrageously as possible according to the official yearly theme (past ones have included "Toolbox Project", "The Twinkly Sea Project" and "Lights, Camera, Action"). There's also an annual **gay pride festival** (Ⓦcapetownpride.co.za) that runs in mid to late February which has a small street parade in the city, but is best experienced for a number of fun events and parties, with some seminars on gay issues too, while the gay and lesbian **film festival** in April (see p.30), is a great exhibition of the latest in cinema. The Pink Loerie Festival (Ⓦpinkloerie.com) in late April is a good excuse to get out of town along the Garden Route to Knysna, with a suitcase of pink accessories to party in.

13

PILLOW TALK

Although most establishments in the city, especially in De Waterkant, have a relaxed attitude towards same-sex couples, a good number of **hotels** in CT are particularly accommodating.

4 on Varneys 4 Varneys Rd, Green Point ☎ 021 434 7167, ⓦ 4onvarneys.co.za. A little less extravagant than the other hotels recommended here, but still warm, welcoming and very comfortable, this guesthouse boasts a gorgeous plunge pool and wildflower terrace, not to mention big, soft beds, that offer some respite from the bustle of town. Of the three hotels recommended here, *4 on Varneys* is the most popular with women. <u>R900</u>

15 on Orange 15 Orange St, Gardens ☎ 021 430 5302, ⓦ africanpridehotels.com. This hotel oozes modern sophistication as decadent decorative flourishes, floor-to-ceiling windows, huge beds and marble baths are complemented with unwavering service. <u>R2400</u>

The Charles 137 Waterkant St ☎ 021 637 9706, ⓦ thecharles.co.za. A charming boutique guesthouse that stands out as an intimate and sumptuous place to stay in the pink village. The luxury open-plan suites, with sea or mountain views, are well worth the price tag, although the value carries through to the travellers rooms for more modest budgets. <u>R790</u>

bar-restaurant chain with an affordable and largely meat-orientated menu. The De Waterkant branch has an attractive terrace under oak trees, while the Sea Point branch, is ideal for people-watching on a busy street. Always bustling and lively, especially when the weather is good. Patrons of all genders and orientation will feel comfortable, though it is primarily a gay venue. Daily 10am–2am.

Crew Bar 30 Napier St, Green Point ☎ 021 418 0118. A fairly new addition to the scene, this stylish bar's topless barmen and sexy go-go dancers keep this place packed every weekend, with music starting off chilled and getting hotter and hotter as the night goes on – the verandas are *the* place to see and be seen in the summer. Daily 7pm till late.

★ **Lazari Food Gallery** Corner of Jarvis & Napier sts, Green Point ☎ 021 419 9555. Popular spot, great for coffee and cocktails – the best in the village – and the balcony is especially nice for people-watching. The food here's also a big draw as one of the best places in the village for vegetarians. Breakfast is served until 3pm and you can get ciabatta, meze and Mediterranean dishes too. Mon & Tues 8am–4pm, Wed–Sun 8am–10pm.

Navigaytion 22 Somerset Rd ⓦ navigaytion.co.za. Above *Bronx Action Bar,* and styling itself as slightly more exclusive, this popular club prefers less commercial dance music and is avowedly a place where gay men and boys, as well as adventurous straight men and women, can lose all their inhibitions on the dancefloor. Tues–Sun 5pm–2am.

Rosie's Corner of Waterkant and Chiappini sts, De Waterkant. An intimate bar attracting black and coloured guys – one of the few places in the village known for this – and women are also welcome. Drinks are quite a bit cheaper here than at the other bars, and its drag shows on Sunday nights are extremely popular. Daily 4pm–late.

SAUNA

The Hothouse 18 Jarvis St, Green Point ⓦ hothouse.co.za. A luxurious, men-only pleasure and total relaxation complex, and the only one of its kind in Cape Town, with all manner of jacuzzis and steam rooms, as well as a sundeck boasting superb views. There's also a bar, complete with fireplace. Entrance R90–110 depending on days and times. Mon–Wed noon–2am, Thurs noon–4am, Fri–Sun noon–6am.

THE ROCK POOLS, DE HOOP NATURE RESERVE

Cape Town for kids

Cape Town is an excellent place to travel with children. A love of the outdoors is inherent in most Capetonians and, as such, you'll find a multitude of activities and gardens to be enjoyed by the whole family, not to mention child-friendly restaurants and a couple of decent rainy-day options. See who can shriek the loudest as you descend into Crocodile Gorge at the Rantanga Junction theme park, or marvel at the jaw-dropping array of sea monsters at the Two Oceans Aquarium. For more of the outdoors, Cape Town's beaches are a classic and easy summer weekend family destination outing, while there are myriad nature reserves and parks to explore in search of the perfect picnic spot.

ESSENTIALS

Entrance fees Activities are either free or around half an adult ticket: children's prices in this chapter apply to under-12s, unless otherwise stated.

Car rental Companies will give you child seats if you ask for them in advance.

Resources A good **website** for finding out what's on is ⓦ capetownkids.co.za. For reputable babysitters or even nannies to accompany you on road trips, try Sitters4U (☎083 691 2009, ⓦ sitters4u.co.za) or Super Sitters (☎021 552 1220, ⓦ supersitters.net).

MUSEUMS AND THEME PARKS

14

Planet Kids 3 Wherry Rd, Muizenberg ☎021 788 3070, ⓦ planetkids.co.za. A great indoor play centre for kids up to 12, designed by an occupational therapist, which is loads of fun, as well as offering healthy snacks and a calmer environment than the usual plastic, sugar-crazed scene (R30/hr). With good assistants on hand, you can drop off your child for an hour, or have tea and a home-bake while you wait. All abilities welcome, with facilities for kids with special needs. Daily 10am–6pm.

Ratanga Junction Century City, signposted off N1 ☎086 120 0300, ⓦ ratanga.co.za. Popular and safe theme park with such thrilling rides as the Cobra, Crocodile Gorge and Monkey Falls. An easy and fun day out for parents as well as kids. Don't bring your own food – everything must be purchased on site. It's only open during

Cape school holidays, so call beforehand. The entry price (R130) gives you unlimited rides. Daily 10am–5pm.

Scratch Patch and Mineral World Dido Valley Rd, off Main Rd, Simon's Town ☎021 786 2020, and V&A Waterfront ☎021 419 9429. Over-3s can search for jewels, filling a bag with the reject polished gemstones that literally cover the floor (R15). At the Simon's Town venue you can also see one of the world's biggest gemstone tumbling plants in operation (Mon–Fri only). Daily 9am–5pm.

South African Museum and Planetarium See p.53. Great for rainy days, especially for 5- to 12-year-olds, who'll enjoy the four-storey whale well and African animal dioramas, as well as the dinosaur displays. The Discovery Room features live ants, massive spiders and a crocodile

BEACHES AND SWIMMING POOLS

Most of Cape Town's sandy **beaches** are pretty undeveloped, so it's best to take what you need in the way of food and drink with you. Get to the beach as early as possible so you can leave by 11am before the sun gets too strong, and to avoid the wind, which often gusts up in the late morning in summer.

On the False Bay seaboard, **Boulders Beach** (see p.102) is one of the few beaches to visit when the southeaster is blowing. It has safe, flat water, making it ideal for kids – and its resident penguin-breeding colony is an added attraction. **Fish Hoek** (see p.98) is one of the best peninsula beaches, with gentle waves that are warm in summer, a long stretch of sand and a playground. The paved Jager's Walk, which runs along the rocky coast here, is suitable for pushchairs and offers beautiful views of the Hottentots Holland Mountains. **St James** (see p.96) boasts a safe tidal pool with a small sandy beach and photogenic, if run-down bathing boxes, but gets seriously overcrowded on the weekend. From here you can walk to **Muizenberg** along a pushchair-friendly coastal pathway, with more views of distant mountains across the water.

The **Atlantic seaboard** is too cold for serious swimming, but does have some lovely stretches of sand, boulders and rock pools – and astonishing scenery. The beaches here are excellent for picnics, and on calm summer evenings idyllic for sundowners and sunsets. In the summer they're less windy than the False Bay beaches, but the afternoons are often baking hot. The closest stretch of coast to the centre ideal for prams – and rollerblading – is the paved **Sea Point Promenade**, stretching 3km from the lighthouse in Mouille Point to Sea Point Pavilion, with the draw of playgrounds and ice-cream sellers en route. The tidal pool and small rock pools of **Camps Bay** (see p.89) make this popular beach very child-friendly, and it's easily reachable from the centre by car or bus. Finally, the six-kilometre stretch of white sand from **Noordhoek** to **Kommetjie** (see p.91) provides fine walking, kite-flying and horseriding opportunities, with stupendous views of Chapman's Peak. If you're heading for Kommetjie, consider a spot of camel-riding at Imhoff Farm Village (see below).

As regards child-friendly swimming pools, **Newlands Pool** (see p.140) has a toddlers' pool and little playground in the large garden, while the marvellous **Sea Point Pool** at Sea Point Pavilion (see p.86) has two paddling pools for children and lawns to laze on, but is overcrowded on weekends, unless you go early or late in the day.

display. The planetarium has special children's shows over weekends and in school holidays. Discovery room Mon–Fri 10am–3pm, Sat & Sun 11am–4.30pm.

Two Oceans Aquarium See p.61. One of Cape Town's most rewarding museums, the aquarium features loads of interest to a wide range of ages. Apart from the excitement of just looking at the weird and wonderful sea creatures, kids can actually handle a few species in the touch pool – sometimes this includes a small shark or sea urchins – while the Alpha Activity Centre usually has puppet shows or face painting, as well as computer terminals where older kids can learn about marine ecology.

OUTDOOR AND PICNIC SPOTS

14

The Barnyard Farmstall Steenberg Rd (M42), next to Steenberg Estate, between Tokai Rd and the Ou Kaapse Weg. An excellent place for an outdoor snack or cup of coffee at a small farmyard, with ducks and chickens wandering around, and an unusually good kids' playground. Mon–Fri 8.30am–5pm, Sat & Sun 8am–5pm.

The Deer Park Cafe 2 Deerpark Drive, Vredehoek ☎ 021 462 6311. The most central, outdoor family venue, on the edge of a small park (sadly no deers) with swings and slides, and views across the suburb to Table Bay. While there is a kids' menu, the food for adults is thankfully sophisticated and imaginative, with plenty of fresh stuff, organic where possible. Sun–Tues 8.30am–4pm, Wed–Sat 8.30am–9pm.

Imhoff Farm Village Kommetjie Rd, opposite the Ocean View turn-off ☎ 021 783 4545, ⊛ imhofffarm. co.za. A conglomeration of activies including camel rides, pony rides, horseriding on the beach, paintball, farmyard petting zoo and reptile park. There's also a good café and farmers' shop. Daily 10am–5pm.

Kirstenbosch National Botanical Gardens See p.79. Top of the list for a family outing, with extensive lawns for running about, trees and rocks to climb and streams to paddle in. There's no litter, no dogs, it's extremely safe and you can push a pram all over the walkways; it's also great for picnics or to have tea outdoors at the café. For older kids there are short waymarked walks.

Newlands Forest 9km south of the centre, off the M3 to Muizenberg; free. Gentle walks in and around pine forests and streams on the wooded southern slopes of Table Mountain, with a flattish pathway suitable for pushchairs. It's good for picnics if you want to get out of the city and don't have time to go further afield. Safest at weekends and in the afternoons when the joggers and dog walkers are out. Use the access point off the M3 signposted "Forestry Office", where there's ample parking. Dawn–dusk.

Silvermine Nature Reserve See p.100. A good place to see *fynbos* vegetation at close quarters and stroll around the lake and picnic with small children; however, it is exposed, and not recommended in heavy winds or mist. For older children there are some mountaintop walks with relatively gentle gradients, which give spectacular views over both sides of the peninsula. Especially recommended is the hike to Elephant's Eye cave on Constantiaberg.

Tokai Forest Arboretum See p.84. The arboretum has good walks and mountain-biking trails, and a thatched teashop with outdoor seating. It's also a great place for young children to explore, with logs to jump off and a gentle walk to a stream. You have a good chance of spotting the Tokai baboon troupe here; but best of all it is sheltered from the wind.

VIEW ACROSS THE VINES, DELAIRE WINE ESTATE

The Winelands

Less than an hour from Cape Town, the Winelands is all about indulgence – eating, drinking and chilling. Each of the Western Cape's earliest European settlements, at Stellenbosch, Paarl, Franschhoek and Somerset West, has its own established wine route, packed with picture-perfect Dutch colonial heritage in the form of shimmering white, gabled homesteads, surrounded by vineyards and tall, slatey crags. To top it all off, the area has a disproportionate concentration of South Africa's stellar restaurants. Franschhoek is the smallest of the towns: a centre of culinary excellence draped in a heavily cultivated Provençal character. In a region of stunning settings, it has the best – at the head of a narrow valley. This is where you head if you're principally after a great lunch and a beautiful drive out of Cape Town.

Stellenbosch, by contrast, has some attractive historical streetscapes, a couple of decent museums, cafés and shops and, as far as great restaurants go, it gives Franschhoek stiff competition. One of the region's scenic highlights is the drive along the **R310** across the heady **Helshoogte Pass** between Stellenbosch and the R45 Franschhoek–Paarl road. **Paarl**, also a pretty drive from Stellenbosch, is a workaday farming town set in a fertile valley overlooked by stunning granite rock formations. Beyond, head to the sprawling town of **Somerset West** for its one simply outstanding drawcard: **Vergelegen**, by far the most stunning of all the Wineland estates.

GETTING AROUND   THE WINELANDS

All the wineries are an easy drive from Cape Town; if you're not staying overnight, you can visit up to three or four in a day. Use the **Metrorail** from Cape Town which serves Stellenbosch and Paarl (see p.23) with caution, as trains pass through rough areas of the Cape Flats. A handful of **buses** run to Stellenbosch and Paarl, but without your own transport it's best to visit the area's highlights on a **tour offered** by one of Cape Town's operators (see p.26).

ESSENTIALS

15

Activities Many wineries offer a lot more than wine-tasting – horseriding, for example, or meals and picnics in their grounds.

Seasons Summer is the best time to visit, when days are longer (as are opening hours), the vines are in leaf and there's activity at the wineries. In winter the wine has been made and there are fewer cellar tours, though the landscape is still gorgeous, and many of the region's upmarket guesthouses let their rooms at half-price.

Wine tasting Wine tasting and buying are supposed to be fun, so don't take them too seriously. If you aren't a wine buff, you'll often find staff at tasting rooms are happy to talk you through a wine. Most estates charge a fee for a wine-tasting session (anywhere up to R40) and some only have tastings at specific times; see the individual accounts for more details. Note also that some wineries are closed on Sundays.

TASTING THE FORBIDDEN FRUIT: SOUTH AFRICA'S WINES

South Africa is one of the world's top ten winemaking countries by volume. In 2010 it overtook France to become the **UK's biggest wine supplier**. Despite South Africa's having the longest-established New World winemaking tradition (going back over 350 years), this rapid rise is remarkable for having taken place within the past two post-apartheid decades. Before that, South Africa's isolation had led to a stagnant and inbred industry that produced heavy Bordeaux-style wines. After the arrival of democracy in 1994, winemakers began producing fresher, fruitier **New World wines**, but many quaffers still turned their wine-tasting noses up at them. It's over the last ten years that things have really started to rev up and some South African winemakers are finding their feet in wines that combine the best of the Old and New Worlds.

South Africa produces wines from a whole gamut of major cultivars. Of the **whites**, the top South African Sauvignon Blancs can stand up with the best the New World has to offer; among the **reds**, it's the blends that really shine. Also look out for red wine made from Pinotage grapes – a somewhat controversial curiosity unique to South Africa – which its detractors feel should stay on the vine. **Port** is also made, and the best vintages come from the Little Karoo town of Calitzdorp along the R62 (see p.238). There are also a handful of excellent **sparkling wines**, including Champagne-style, fermented-in-the-bottle bubbly, known locally as **méthode cap classique** (MCC).

The most enjoyable way to sample wines is by visiting wineries. The oldest and most rewarding wine-producing regions to tour are the **Constantia** estates in Cape Town (see p.81) and the **Winelands**; other wine-producing areas covered by this guide include **Walker Bay** around Hermanus (see p.167) and the **Little Karoo** along the R62 (see p.227). If you're serious about your wine tasting, think about buying the authoritative and annually updated *John Platter's South African Wine Guide* (also available as an iPhone app), which rates wines from virtually every producer in the country. *Wine* magazine, published every month and available from all newsagents, has useful features on wineries, places to eat, wine reviews, information on latest bottlings and a diary of events.

Stellenbosch

Dappled avenues of three-century-old oaks are the defining feature of **STELLENBOSCH**, 46km east of Cape Town – a fact reflected in its Afrikaans nickname Die Eikestad (the oak city). Stellenbosch's attractions lie principally in its setting and architecture, rooted in the seventeenth century, which make it a lovely place to simply wander around and one that's safe at night.

Stellenbosch today is the heart of the Winelands, having more urban attractions than either Paarl or Franschhoek, while at the same time being at the hub of the largest and oldest of the Cape **wine routes**. The city is also home to Stellenbosch University, Afrikanerdom's most prestigious educational institution, which does something to enliven the atmosphere. But even the heady promise of plentiful alcohol and thousands of students haven't changed the fact that at heart this is a conservative place, which was once the intellectual engine room of apartheid, and fostered the likes of Dr Hendrik Verwoerd, the prime minister who dreamed up apartheid (see p.54).

The tourist office is a good place to start your explorations. Heading east up this road, you'll soon reach a whitewashed block that was the **VOC Kruithuis**, the Dutch East India Company's powder magazine. From here, a right turn south down the side of the **Braak**, the large green occupying the centre of town, will take you past the **Rhenish Church** in Bloem Street, built in 1823 as a school for slaves and coloured people.

15

The Village Museum

18 Ryneveld St • Sept–Feb Mon–Sat 9am–5pm, Sun 10am–4pm; March–Aug Mon–Sat 9am–5pm, Sun 10am–1pm • R25

Stellenbosch's highlight, the extremely enjoyable **Village Museum**, cuts a cross section through the town's architectural and social heritage by means of four fortuitously adjacent historical dwellings from different periods. They're beautifully conserved and furnished in period style, and you'll meet the odd worker dressed in period costume.

Earliest of the houses is the homely **Shreuderhuis**, a vernacular cottage built in 1709, with a small courtyard garden filled with aromatic herbs, pomegranate bushes and vine-draped pergolas – bearing more resemblance to the early Cape settlement's European aesthetics than to modern South Africa.

Across the garden, **Blettermanhuis**, built in 1789 for the last Dutch East India Company-appointed magistrate of Stellenbosch, is an archetypal eighteenth-century Cape Dutch house, built on an H-plan with six gables. **Grosvenor House**, opposite, was altered to its current form in 1803, reflecting the growing influence of English taste after the 1795 British occupation of the Cape. The Neoclassical facade, with fluted pilasters supporting a pedimented entrance, borrows from high fashion then current at the heart of the growing empire. The more modest **O.M. Bergh House**, across the road, is a typical Victorian dwelling that was once similar to Blettermanhuis, but was

---

SIMON VAN DER STEL

One of the first actions of **Simon van der Stel**, after arriving at the Cape in November 1679 to take over as VOC commander, was to explore the area along the Eerste River (first river), where he came upon an enchanting little valley. Less than a month later it appeared on maps as Stellenbosch (Stel's bush), the first of several places dotted around the Cape, which the governor was to name after himself or members of his family; another was Simonsberg, overlooking the town. Charged by the Dutch East India Company directors in the Netherlands with opening up the Cape interior, Van der Stel soon settled the first **free burghers** in Stellenbosch. Within eight years, sixty freehold grants had been made; within the next two decades, Stellenbosch had established itself as a prosperous, semi-feudal society dominated by landowners, and in 1702 the Danish traveller, Abraham Bogaert, admired how it had "grown with fine dwellings, and how great a treasure of wine and grain is grown here". By the end of the eighteenth century there were over a thousand houses and some substantial burgher estates in and around Stellenbosch, many of which still exist.

"modernized" in the mid-nineteenth century on a rectangular plan, with a simplified facade without gables.

Dorp Street

Dorp Street, Stellenbosch's best-preserved historic axis, lies south of the museum and is well worth a slow stroll just to soak in the ambience of buildings, gables, oaks and roadside irrigation furrows.

Krige's Cottages

On Dorp St nos. 37–51, between Aan-de-Wagenweg and Krige sts

Look out for **Krige's Cottages**, an unusual terrace of historic townhouses. The houses were built as Cape Dutch cottages in the first half of the nineteenth century; Victorian features were added later, resulting in an interesting hybrid, with gables housing Victorian attic windows and decorative Victorian verandas with filigree ironwork fronting the elegantly simple Cape Dutch facades.

15

ARRIVAL AND DEPARTURE

STELLENBOSCH

By train Metrorail trains (☎0800 65 64 63, ⓦcapemetrorail.co.za) travel between Cape Town and Stellenbosch roughly every ninety minutes during the day, and take about an hour.

By bus Infrequent (and expensive) intercity buses from Cape Town and Port Elizabeth pass through Stellenbosch,

calling at the train station. The Baz Bus runs daily from Cape Town to Somerset West, where it drops passengers off at the BP filling station next to the *Lord Charles Hotel*. Some hostels operate shuttle services from there, but you need to arrange this beforehand.

INFORMATION AND TOURS

Tourist office The busy tourist office about 1km from the station at 36 Market St (Mon–Fri 8am–6pm, Sat 9am–4pm, Sun 9am–3pm; ☎021 883 3584, ⓦstellenboschtourism.co.za), provides basic information on local attractions.

Easy Rider Wine Tours Based at *Stumble Inn* backpacker lodge (see p.154), offers daytime packages to four wineries (R400), with cheese tasting at Fairview Estate and lunch thrown in.

ACCOMMODATION

Allegria Guest House Cairngorm Rd, Stellenbosch ☎021 881 3389, ⓦallegria.co.za. Small, well-run establishment on a country estate between two wine farms, 8km west of Stellenbosch. Under the warm proprietorship of hospitable Dutch couple Jan and Annemarie, the guesthouse offers six rooms with three levels of luxury, a swimming pool and great views. R1100

Banghoek Place 193 Banghoek Rd ☎021 887 0048, ⓦbanghoek.co.za. Slightly more upmarket sister hostel to *Stumble Inn* (see p.154), with mostly en-suite double, twin and triple rooms that offer terrific value, and also three small dorms. Discount packages available that include two nights' accommodation plus a wine tour. Dorms R120, doubles R400

De Oude Meul 10a Mill St (off Dorp St) ☎021 887 7085, ⓦdeoudemeul.com. Located in the middle of town on a fairly busy street, above an antique shop, these pleasant rooms are good value. Ask for a room at the back to ensure a quiet night's sleep. R850

Glenconner Jonkershoek Rd, 4km from the centre ☎021 886 5120, ⓔglenconner@icon.co.za; Both

self-catering and B&B options are available at these pretty farm cottages. The tranquil valley setting is spectacular, close to the walks in the Jonkershoek Nature Reserve. Breakfast can be taken under an old oak tree. R750

Natte Valleij On the R44, 12km north of town ☎021 875 5171, ⓦnattevalleij.co.za. Guests have a choice of a large cottage sleeping six, a smaller one-bedroom unit attached to an old wine cellar or an en-suite room with its own entrance. There's a swimming pool, and breakfast (included) is served on the veranda. R680

River Manor Boutique Hotel 6–8 The Ave ☎021 887 9944, ⓦrivermanor.co.za. Enjoy a totally romantic, if formal, stay in two historic houses with rose-petal-strewn beds, oil lamps, plush dressing gowns and wicker chairs to laze on in the sun around the pool, with spa facilities on site for extra pampering. R1900

Ryneveld Country Lodge 67 Ryneveld St ☎021 887 4469, ⓦryneveldlodge.co.za. Gracious late nineteenth-century building, now a National Monument and furnished with Victorian antiques. The rooms are spotless, with the

STELLENBOSCH

ACCOMMODATION

Allegria Guest House	8
Banghoek Place	2
De Oude Meul	6
Glenconner	4
Natte Vallej	1
River Manor Boutique Hotel	7
Ryneveld Country Lodge	3
Stumble Inn	5
Villa Merwe	9

RESTAURANTS & CAFÉS

Bukhara	3
Col'Cacchio	1
Moyo Spier	4
Terroir	6
Vida e Caffé	2
Volkskombuis	5

0   250
metres

two best rooms upstairs leading onto a wooden deck. There are also three family cottages, which sleep up to four, and a pool. **R900**

Stumble Inn 12 Market St ☏021 887 4049, ⓦstumbleinnstellenbosch.hostel.com. The town's best and longest standing hostel, spread across two houses that date from the turn of the last century and run by friendly, switched-on staff. Just down the road from

the tourist office, the hostel offers doubles and dorms and is also noted for its good-value tours. Dorms **R100**, doubles **R280**

Villa Merwe 6 Cynaroides Rd, Paradyskloof ☏021 880 1185, ⓦvillamerwe.co.za. Three immaculate and comfortable rooms in the owner's modern house, each with its own entrance and bathroom, with a lounge, pool and garden. It's a 5min drive from the centre. **R800**

EATING AND DRINKING

You'll be spoilt for choices of good places to eat in and around Stellenbosch – four of the town's establishments made the Eat Out (South African foodie Oscars) Top 10 restaurants in 2010. Many places have outdoor seating and, in the evenings, the student presence ensures a relaxed and sometimes raucous drinking culture.

Bukhara Corner of Dorp and Bird sts ☏021 882 9133, ⓦbukhara.com. Succulent North Indian dishes prepared in a kitchen behind a glass wall, in full view of diners. The prices are a little steep, though portions are large. Favourites include butter chicken and tandoori lamb chops. Service is excellent and the ambience relaxed (R100). Daily noon–3pm & Sat 6–10.30pm.

Col'Cacchio Shop 8, Simonsplein Centre, Plein St, ⓦcolcacchio.co.za. A better-than-average pizzeria, perfect for a quick bite and popular with students. Try the *Morituri* topped with bacon, chicken, feta, red pepper and avocado (R70). Daily noon–11pm.

Moyo Spier Spier Estate, Lynedoch Rd (R310) ☏021 809 1133, ⓦmoyo.com. An extravaganza of an eating place (one of four restaurants at Spier) in the gardens of one of the Western Cape's largest and most tourist-friendly wine estates. It's made to feel like a cross between an African village and a bedouin encampment, with seating for 1200 in gazebos, tents and tree houses, and the vast all-you-can-eat buffet brings together a dazzling array of flavours and dishes from across Africa. With live performance and optional face-painting thrown in, you can't help but enjoy yourself (R200). Daily noon till late.

★ **Overture** Hidden Valley Wine Estate, Annandale Rd, Stellenbosch ☏021 880 2646, ⓦdineatoverture. co.za. Top of the town in more ways than one, *Overture* looks down magnificently from the hills into the Annandale Valley – and it also bagged gold for South Africa's Best Chef, Best Restaurant and Best Service in the Eat Out 2010 Awards. Based on classical French cuisine, the dishes throw

up interesting contemporary twists. Select four-or-so courses (R350; R470 with wine) or sample the works with the eight-course tasting menu (R600; R750 with wine). Tues, Wed & Sun 12–3pm, Thurs & Fri 12–3pm & 6–10.30pm.

Terroir Kleine Zalze Wine Estate, Strand Rd (R44) ☏021 880 8167, ⓦkleinezalze.com. Some 12.5km from Stellenbosch on a wine and golf estate, *Terroir* has a surprisingly relaxed dining room (for a nationally fêted restaurant) and tables outside under shady oaks. The expensive French-inspired menu is based as far as possible on local seasonal produce, with signature dishes that include pork trotters and oxtail (R130). Mon–Sat 12.30–2.30pm & 7–9.30pm, Sun 12.30–2.30pm.

Vida e Caffé Corner of Bird and Kerk sts. Portuguese-style coffee shop in the middle of town, with a bustling atmosphere. Part of a national chain, it boasts excellent service and coffee and also a good bet for quick, inexpensive Portuguese-style sandwiches and rolls (R35). Mon–Sat 8am–5pm & Sun 9am–4pm.

Volkskombuis Aan-de-Wagenweg Off Dorp St ☏021 887 2121, ⓦvolkskombuis.co.za. Popular spot on the banks of the Eerste River, in a beautiful seventeenth-century Cape Dutch house. If you want to sample traditional Cape cuisine then this is the place to head, with starters that include *snoek* samosas and main courses such as Boland *bobotie* and braised oxtail (R100). Summer noon–2.30pm & 6.30–10pm; winter Mon–Sat noon–2.30pm & 6.30–10pm, Sun noon–2.30pm.

THE WINERIES

Stellenbosch was the first locality in the country to wake up to the marketing potential of a **wine route**. It launched its wine route in 1971, a tactic that has been hugely successful; today tens of thousands of visitors from all over the world are drawn here annually, making this the most toured area in the Winelands. Although the region accounts for only a fraction of South Africa's land under vine, its wine route is the most extensive in the country, approaching three hundred establishments; apart from the selection below (all of which produce creditable wines and are along a series of roads that radiate out from Stellenbosch) there are scores of other excellent places, which taken together would occupy months of exploration. All the wineries are clearly signposted off the main arteries.

Delaire Graff Estate On the Helshoogte Pass, 6km east of Stellenbosch along the R310 to Franschhoek ⓦdelairewinery.co.za. The highly regarded *Delaire Graff* restaurant has possibly the best views in the Winelands, looking through pin oaks across the Groot Drakenstein and Simonsig mountains and down into the valley. Outstanding wines aren't hard to find here as most of their output delivers the goods, most of them whites, but they also produce a great red blend. Tasting three wines R20, five wines R30, six wines R35. Mon–Sat 10am–5pm & Sun 10am–4pm; summer sundowners Fri & Sat 5–9pm.

Jordan Vineyards 11.5km west of Stellenbosch off the R310 ⓦjordanwines.com. A pioneer among the new-wave Cape wineries, Jordan's hi-tech cellar and modern tasting room is complemented by its friendly service. The drive there is half the fun, taking you into a *kloof* bounded by vineyards that get a whiff of the sea from both False Bay and Table Bay, which has clearly done something for its output – it has a list of outstanding wines as long as your arm and a highly rated restaurant. Tasting R25 for six wines, refundable with purchases. Daily 9.30am–4.30pm.

Morgenhof 4km north of Stellenbosch on the R44 ⓦmorgenhof.com. French-owned chateau-style complex on the slopes of the vine-covered Simonsberg, owned by Anne Cointreau-Huchon (granddaughter of the founder of Remy Martin cognac). Morgenhof has a light and airy tasting room with a bar, and delicious light lunches are served outside, topped off with ice cream on the lawns. They produce the excellent Morgehof Estate red blend and a couple of brilliant whites under the same label, while the Fantail range is their second, more affordable label. Tasting R20 for five wines. May–Oct Mon–Fri 9am–4.30pm, Sat & Sun 10am–3pm; Nov–April Mon–Fri 9am–5pm, Sat & Sun 10am–5pm.

Neethlingshof 6.5km west of Stellenbosch on Polkadraai Rd (the R306) ⓦneethlingshof.co.za. Centred around a beautifully restored Cape Dutch manor dating back to 1814, reached down a kilometre-long avenue of stone pines, Neethlingshof's first vines were planted in 1692. There's a restaurant, and for R95 you can try their "flash food" light lunch – pairings of six wines with six bite-sized takeaways (booking essential). The estate has two labels: Premium and Short Story reserve range, which consists of a Pinotage, a red blend and a flagship Noble Late Harvest white. Tasting R30 for six wines. Mon–Fri 9am–5pm, Sat & Sun 10am–4pm.

Overgaauw 6.5km west of Stellenbosch, off the M12 ⓦovergaauw.co.za. Notable for its elegant Victorian tasting room, this pioneering estate was the first winery in the country to produce Merlots, and it's still the only one to make Sylvaner, a well-priced, easy-drinking dry white. Tasting free. Mon–Fri 9am–5pm, Sat 10am–3.30pm.

Rustenberg Wines Rustenberg Rd, 5km north of Stellenbosch ⓦrustenberg.co.za. One of the closest estates to Stellenbosch, Rustenberg is also one of the most alluring, reached after a drive through orchards, sheep pastures and tree-lined avenues. An unassuming working farm, it has a romantic pastoral atmosphere, in contrast to its architecturally stunning, hi-tech tasting room in the former stables; the first vines were planted here in 1692, but the viniculture looks to the future. Their high-flyers include the Peter Barlow single vineyard Cabernet Sauvignon, John X Merriman red blend and a Chardonnay. There's a massive choice from their moderately priced Brampton range. Tasting free. Mon–Fri 9am–4.30pm, Sat 9am–1.30pm.

Simonsig Estate 9.5km north of Stellenbosch, off Kromme Rhee Rd, which runs between the R44 and the R304 ⓦwww.simonsig.co.za. The winery has a relaxed outdoor tasting area under vine-covered pergolas, offering majestic views back to Stellenbosch of hazy stone-blue mountains and vineyards. The first estate in the country to produce a bottle-fermented bubbly some three decades back, it also produces a vast range of first-class still wines. Tasting R25 for five wines and a bubbly. Mon–Fri 8.30am–5pm, Sat 8.30am–4pm, Sun 11am–3pm.

★ **Uva Mira** About 8km south of Stellenbosch, off Annandale Rd, which spurs off the R44, ⓦuvamira .co.za. Enchanting boutique winery that punches well above its weight, but worth visiting just for the winding drive halfway up the Helderberg. The highly original tasting room, despite being fairly recently built, gives the appearance of a gently decaying historic structure, and there are unsurpassed views from the deck across mountainside vineyards to False Bay some 50km away – on a clear day you can even see Robben Island. The Single Vineyard Chardonnay stands out and the red blend is also noteworthy. Tasting R20 for Cellar selection (four wines), R30 for Vineyard selection (two premier wines), R40 for all six wines. Mon–Fri 8am–5pm, Sat & Sun 10am–4pm.

15

Somerset West

The only compelling reasons to trawl out to the unpromising town of **SOMERSET WEST**, 50km east of Cape Town along the N2, are for **Vergelegen** on Loursford Road, and its immediate neighbour **Morgenster**, which are officially part of the Helderberg wine

THE HISTORY OF VERGELEGEN

Vergelegen represents a notorious episode of corruption and the arbitrary abuse of power at the Cape in the early years of Dutch East India Company rule. Built by Willem Adriaan van der Stel, who became governor in 1699 after the retirement of his father, Simon, the estate formed a grand Renaissance complex in the middle of the wild backwater that was the Cape at the beginning of the eighteenth century. Van der Stel acquired the land illegally and used Dutch East India Company slaves to build Vergelegen, as well as company resources to farm vast tracts of land in the surrounding areas. At the same time he abused his power as governor to corner most of the significant markets at the Cape. When this was brought to the notice of the bosses in the Netherlands, they sacked Van der Stel and ordered the destruction of Vergelegen to discourage future miscreant governors. It's believed that the destruction was never fully carried out and the current building is thought to stand on the foundations of the original.

15

route, but can easily be included as an extension to a visit to Stellenbosch, just 14km to the north.

Vergelegen

Daily 9.30am–4pm • R10 • **Wine tasting** R30 for six wines • **Restaurant** noon–2.30pm; ☎ 021 847 1346 • **Bistro** Nov–April 10am–4pm • **Picnics** Nov–April noon–2pm; essential to order these through restaurant in advance • ⓦ vergelegen.co.za

An absolute architectural treasure as well as an estate producing a stunning range of wines, Vergelegen was the only wine estate visited by the British queen during her 1995 state visit to South Africa – a good choice, as there's enough here to occupy even a monarch for an easy couple of hours.

The **interpretive centre**, just across the courtyard from the shop at the building entrance, provides a useful history and background to the estate. Next door, the **wine-tasting centre** offers a professionally run sampling with a brief talk through each label. They produce a vast range of wines, almost every one of which is excellent. In 2011 the Platter wine guide awarded four stars (out of five) or more to their Flagship range: Red 2004 (Bordeaux blend), White 2007 (Sauvignon Blanc/Sémillon blend) and Vergelegen V 2005 and 2006 (Bourdeaux blends); Premium range: Chardonnay 2009, Sauvignon Blanc 2010 and Cabernet Sauvignon-Merlot 2008; and Reserve range: Chardonnay 2009; Cabernet Sauvignon 2006; Cabernet Franc-Merlot 2006; Merlot 2007; Sémillon 2008; Sauvignon Blanc 2010; Shiraz 2007.

There's also a **restaurant** and a **bistro**, and **picnics** are available.

The homestead

The **homestead**, which was restored in 1917 to its current state by Lady Florence Phillips, wife of a Johannesburg mining magnate, can also be visited. Its pale facade, reached along an axis through an octagonal garden that flits with butterflies in summer, has a classical triangular gable and pilaster-decorated doorways. Massive grounds planted with chestnuts and camphor trees and ponds around every corner make this one of the most serene places in the Cape.

Morgenster

Mon–Fri 10am–5pm, Sat & Sun 10am–4pm • Tastings R20 • ⓦ www.morgenster.co.za

Apart from its exquisite rustic setting, the tasting room at **Morgenster**, Vergelegen's immediate neighbour, has a veranda that looks onto a lovely lake with hazy mountains in the distance. Its two stellar blended reds aside, the estate offers the unusual addition of olive tasting, with several types of olive and oil (including an award-winning cold-pressed extra virgin olive oil) and some delicious olive paste.

Paarl

Although **PAARL** is attractively ensconced in a fertile valley brimming with historical monuments, at heart it's a parochial *dorp*, lacking the sophistication of Stellenbosch or the striking setting and trendiness of Franschhoek. It is, however, a prosperous farming centre that earns its keep from the agricultural light industries – grain silos, canneries and flour mills – on the north side of town, and the cornucopia of grapes, guavas, olives, oranges and maize grown on the surrounding farms. Despite its small-town feel, Paarl has the largest municipality in the Winelands, with its most exclusive areas on the vined slopes of **Paarl Mountain** overlooking the town.

Brief history

In 1657, just five years after the establishment of the Dutch East India Company refreshment station on the Cape Peninsula, a party under Abraham Gabbema arrived in the Berg River Valley to look for trading opportunities with the Khoikhoi, and search for the legendary gold of Monomotapa. With treasure on the brain, they woke after a rainy night to see the glistening dome of granite dominating the valley, which they named **Peerlbergh** (pearl mountain), which in its modified form, Paarl, became the name of the town. Thirty years later, the commander of the Cape, Simon van der Stel, granted strips of the Khoikhoi lands on the slopes of Paarl Mountain to French Huguenot and Dutch settlers. By the time Paarl was officially granted town status in 1840, it was still an outpost at the edge of the Drakenstein Mountains, a flourishing

15

THE HISTORY OF AFRIKAANS

Afrikaans is South Africa's third mother tongue, spoken by fifteen percent of the population and outstripped only by Zulu and Xhosa. English, by contrast, is the mother tongue of only nine percent of South Africans, and ranks fifth in the league of the eleven official languages.

Signs of the emergence of a new southern African dialect appeared as early as 1685, when a VOC official from the Netherlands, complained about a "distorted and incomprehensible" Dutch being spoken around modern-day Paarl. By absorbing English, French, German, Malay and indigenous words and expressions, the language continued to diverge from mainstream Dutch, and by the nineteenth century was widely used in the Cape by both white and coloured speakers, but was regarded by the elite as an inferior creole, unsuitable for literary or official communication.

Ironically, it was the British defeat of the Afrikaner republics in the second Anglo-Boer War at the turn of the twentieth century that provided the catalyst for a mass white Afrikaans movement. The official British policy of anglicizing South Africa helped unite a demoralized white Afrikaner proletariat and elite against the common English enemy.

In 1905, **Gustav Preller**, a young journalist from a working-class Boer background, set about reinventing Afrikaans as a "white man's language". Substituting Dutch words for those with non-European origins, Preller began publishing the first of a series of populist magazines written in Afrikaans and glorifying Boer history and culture. In 1925 Afrikaans became recognized as an official language.

When the National Party took power in 1948, its apartheid policy went hand in hand with promoting the interests of white Afrikaners, which they did through a programme of **uplifting poor whites**. Despite there being more coloured than white Afrikaans speakers, the language became associated with the **apartheid** establishment. When the government tried to enforce Afrikaans as the sole medium of instruction in African schools, the policy led directly to the **Soweto uprising** in 1976, which marked the beginning of the end for Afrikaner hegemony in South Africa. The repression of the 1970s and 1980s and the forced removals of coloureds and blacks led many coloured Afrikaans speakers to adopt English in preference to their tainted mother tongue.

There are few signs, though, that Afrikaans will die out. Under the new constitution, language rights are protected, which means that Afrikaans will continue to be almost as widely used as before, except now it is as much with coloured as white people that the future of the *taal* (language) rests.

wagon-making and last-stop provisioning centre. This status was enhanced when the first **rail line** in the Cape connected it to the peninsula in 1863. Following in the spirit of the first Dutch adventurers of 1657, thousands of treasure-seekers brought custom to Paarl as the gateway to the interior during the diamond rush of the 1870s and the gold fever of the 1880s.

The town holds deep historical significance for the two competing political forces that forged modern South Africa. **Afrikanerdom** regards Paarl as the hallowed ground on which their language movement was born in 1875 (see box, p.42), while for the **ANC** (and the international community), Paarl will be remembered as the place from which Nelson Mandela made the final steps of his long walk to freedom, when he walked out of **Groot Drakenstein Prison** (then called Victor Verster) in 1990.

Paarl's best-preserved historical frontage is along oak-lined **Main Street,** which stretches for some 2km – not ideal for strolling, especially on a hot day.

Paarl Museum

303 Main St • Mon–Fri 9am–5pm, Sat 9am–1pm • R5

Housed in a handsome, thatched Cape Dutch building with one of the earliest surviving gables (1787) in the "new style", characterized by triangular caps, the contents of the **Paarl Museum** don't quite match up to its exterior. It does include some

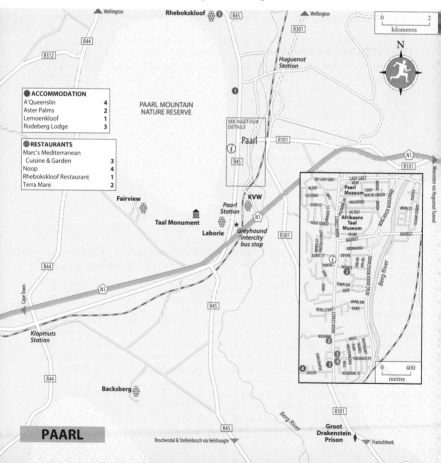

PAARL

HORSE AND QUAD-BIKE TRAILS

Hopping into the saddle and trotting off through the countryside offers a great alternative to seeing the Winelands from behind a restaurant table. At Rhebokskloof, you can do both.

Wine Valley Horse Trails ☎ 021 869 8687 or ☎ 083 226 8735, ⓦ horsetrails-sa.co.za. This company based at Rhebokskloof, offers one- to four-hour equestrian trails for novices and experts through the surrounding countryside – a choice spot for some riding. Prices start from R300 for a one-hour trail. Longer trails are restricted to experienced riders, but a four-hour package of a ride plus a conducted wine tasting at the estate is available for novices. They also do quad-bike trails which start at R200 for a half-hour trail.

reasonably enlightening panels on the architecture of the town, and several eccentric glass display cases of Victorian bric-a-brac. Post-apartheid transformation has introduced some coverage of the indigenous Khoisan populations of the area and the changes that came with European colonization, including slavery.

15

Taal Monument

South along Main Street past the head office of the KWV, follow signs to the right up the slope of the mountain • Daily 9am–5pm • Free

The only other sight of any interest in Paarl itself is the grandiose **Taal Monument**, the controversial memorial to the Afrikaans language, standing just outside the centre on the top of Paarl Mountain. The monument used to be as important a place of pilgrimage for Afrikaners as the Voortrekker Monument in Pretoria, although when it was erected in 1973 detractors joked that monuments were usually erected to the dead. From the coffee and curio shop you can admire a truly magnificent panorama across to the Cape Peninsula and False Bay in one direction and the Winelands ranges in the other.

Groot Drakenstein (Victor Verster) Prison

Roughly 9km south of the N1 as it cuts through Paarl, along the R301 (the southern extension of Jan van Riebeeck St)

The **Victor Verster Prison**, renamed **Groot Drakenstein** in 2000, was Nelson Mandela's last place of incarceration. It was through the gates at Victor Verster that Mandela walked to his freedom on February 11, 1990, and it was here that the first images of him in 27 years were bounced around the world (under the Prisons Act, not even old pictures of him could be published during his imprisonment). The working jail looks rather like a boys' school fronted by rugby fields beneath hazy mountains, and there's something bizarre about seeing a prison sign nonchalantly slipped in among all the vineyard and wine-route pointers.

ARRIVAL AND DEPARTURE
PAARL

By bus Daily Greyhound intercity buses from Cape Town (1hr) stop at the Monument Shell Garage, on the corner of Main Road and South Street, about 2km from the tourist office.

By train Metrorail and Spoornet services from Cape Town (18 daily; 1hr 15min) pull in at Huguenot Station in Lady Grey Street at the north end of town, near to the central shops.

INFORMATION

Tourist office Corner of Main and Plantasie streets (Mon–Fri 8am–5pm, Sat 9am–2pm & Sun 10am–2pm; ☎ 021 872 0860, ⓦ paarlonline.com). The tourist office has a good selection of maps and can help with booking accommodation.

ACCOMMODATION

A'Queenslin 2 Queen St ☎ 021 863 1160, ⓔ aqueenslin@ telkomsa.net. Two en-suite rooms with their own entrances and garden spaces, and three double rooms that share a bathroom, in a split-level family home set in a quiet part of town, bounded on one side by vineyards and towered over by Paarl Rock. Limited self-catering is possible – there's a fridge and microwave. R450

Aster Palms 3 Patriot St ☎ 021 872 0895,

ⓦasterpalms.co.za. Hospitable B&B in a 1920s house a couple of blocks from the tourist office, with four airy double rooms and a lovely back garden with a solar-heated swimming pool. **R550**

Lemoenkloof 396a Main St ☎021 872 3782, ⓦwww .lemoenkloof.co.za. A comfortable and tranquil, independent guesthouse in a National Monument, with

1820s Cape Dutch and Victorian features, a TV and fridge in each room and a secluded swimming pool. **R920**

Rodeberg Lodge 74 Main St ☎021 863 3202, ⓦrodeberglodge.co.za. Plain period furnishings give the en-suite rooms in this huge, centrally located Victorian townhouse a cool, spacious feel. Ask for a room at the back if traffic noise bothers you. **R540**

EATING AND DRINKING

A working town, Paarl has none of the Winelands foodie pretensions of Franschhoek or Stellenbosch, but you'll find a number of places along the main street for a decent snack and coffee or a meal, as well as a couple of outstanding places in the surrounding countryside, with great views of the vineyards and mountains.

Marc's Mediterranean Cuisine & Garden 129 Main St ☎021 863 3980, ⓦmarcsrestaurant.co.za. One of Paarl's most popular casual restaurants, *Marc's* dishes up a moderately priced, simple but tasty menu that includes paella, Lebanese meze, couscous, seafood and lamb, served in a converted historic house with a large outdoor area dotted with sun umbrellas and lemon trees (R100). Mon–Sat noon–2.30pm, 6.30–9.30pm, Sun noon–2.30pm.

Noop 127 Main St, ⓦnoop.co.za. This supercool pavement wine bar has a dauntingly long menu and equally long list of wines by the glass. They have some great takes on simple favourites such as burgers, biryanis and pies, inspired, says the owner, by the old French stockpot (R70). Mon–Fri 11am–11pm, Sat 10am–3pm.

The Victorian Rhebokskloof winery, Rhebokskloof

Minor Rd ☎021 869 8386, ⓦrhebokskloof.co.za. Intimate outdoor establishment recommended for the outstanding setting as well as the food. Overlooking a lake, it has a shaded terrace for summer lunches and gourmet meals. Meat is the house speciality done with thrilling combinations of flavours, both Cape and international. It's also a good place for morning or afternoon teas, and they can prepare picnics on the lawns outside (R75). Mon & Sun 9.30am–5.30pm, Tues–Sat 9.30am–9pm.

Terra Mare 90a Main St ☎021 863 4805. Italian- and Mediterranean-influenced dishes, such as Karoo lamb chops with spring rolls or pasta and pesto, using local ingredients and infused with considerable flair. The glass and steel restaurant has great sweeping views of the Paarl Valley (R110). Tues–Sat 10am–2pm & 6–10pm, Sun 10am–2pm.

THE WINERIES

There are a couple of notable wineries in Paarl itself, but most are on farms in the surrounding countryside. Boschendal, one of the most popular of these, is officially on the Franschhoek wine route (see p.162), but is in easy striking distance of Paarl. Most of the wineries have at least one restaurant, often more, which are generally of a high standard.

Backsberg Estate 22km south of Paarl on Simondium Rd (WR1) ⓦbacksberg.co.za; map p.158. Notable as the first carbon-neutral wine estate in South Africa, Backsberg produces some top-ranking red blends, and a delicious Chardonnay, in its Babylons Toren and Black Label ranges. Outdoor seating, with views of the rose garden and vineyard on the slopes of the Simonsberg, makes this busy estate a nice place to while away some time. There's also a restaurant and a maze to get lost in. Tasting R15 for five wines. Mon–Fri 8am–5pm, Sat & Sun 9.30am–4.30pm.

Fairview Suid Agter Paarl Rd, on the southern fringes of town ⓦfairview.co.za; map p.158. One of the most fun of all the Paarl estates (especially for families), with a resident population of goats who clamber up the spiral tower, featured in the estate's emblem, at the entrance. A deli sells sausages and cold meats for picnics on the lawn, and you can also sample

and buy the goats', sheep's and cows' cheeses made on the estate. As far as wine tasting goes, Fairview is an innovative, family-run place, but it can get a bit hectic when the tour buses roll in. Tasting cheese selection R15; six wines and cheese selection R25; eight wines plus cheese and olive oil selection R60. Mon–Fri 8am–5pm, Sat 9am–4pm, Sun 10am–4pm.

Laborie Taillefert St ⓦlaboriewines.co.za; map p.158. One of the most impressive Paarl wineries, all the more remarkable for being right in town. The beautiful manor is fronted by a rose garden, acres of close-cropped lawns, historic buildings and oak trees – all towered over by the Taal Monument. There's a truly wonderful tasting room with a balcony that jetties out over the vineyards trailing up Paarl Mountain, as well as a great restaurant with terrace seating under oaks with gobsmackingly good views of the town vineyards and mountains. Their flagship is the Jean Taillefert Shiraz and among a number of other wines is

their Pineau de Laborie, a dessert wine made from pinotage grapes laced with Pinotage brandy. Tasting R25. Dec–March Mon–Sat 9am–5pm, Sun 10am–5pm; Nov–April Sun 11am–3pm.

Rhebokskloof Signposted off the R45, 11.5km northwest of Paarl ⦿rhebokskloof.co.za; map p.158. A highly photogenic wine estate, a popular wedding venue, and a great place to bring kids, Rhebokskloof sits at the foot of sculptural granite *koppies* overlooking a shallow *kloof* that borders on the mountain nature reserve. The estate's renowned restaurant (see p.000) overlooks an artificial lake with swans. For those too young to legally imbibe, there's a kids' playground, pony rides and remote-controlled boats on the lake among the extensive offerings. Horse and quad-bike trails for adults are also operated from Rhebokskloof (see box, p.159). And of course, there's the wine, with Shiraz being where they make a mark. Tasting R50 for five wines. Daily 9am–5pm.

Franschhoek

If indulgence is what the Winelands is really about, then **Franschhoek** is the place that does it best. Despite being a fairly small *dorp*, it has managed to establish itself as the culinary capital of the Western Cape, if not the whole country. Its late Victorian and more recent Frenchified rustic architecture, the terrific setting (it's hemmed in on three sides by mountains), the vineyards down every other backstreet and some vigorous myth-making have created a place you can really lose yourself in, a set piece that unashamedly draws its inspiration from Provence.

Brief history

Between 1688 and 1700 about two hundred French Huguenots, desperate to escape religious persecution in France, accepted a Dutch East India Company offer of passage to the Cape and the grant of lands. They made contact with the area's earliest settlers, groups of Khoikhoi herders. Conflict between the French newcomers and the Khoikhoi followed familiar lines, with the white settlers gradually dispossessing the herdsmen, forcing them either further into the hinterland or into servitude on their farms. The establishment of white hegemony was swift and by 1713 the area was known as *de france hoek*. Though French-speaking died out within a generation because of explicit Company policy, many of the estates hereabouts are still known by their original French names. **Franschhoek** itself, 33km from Stellenbosch and 29km from Paarl, occupies parts of the original farms of La Cotte and Cabrière and is relatively young, having been established around a church built in 1833.

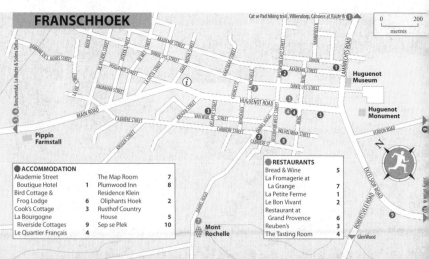

FRANSCHHOEK

● ACCOMMODATION		
Akademie Street	The Map Room	7
Boutique Hotel	1	Plumwood Inn	8
Bird Cottage &		Residence Klein	
Frog Lodge	6	Oliphants Hoek	2
Cook's Cottage	3	Rusthof Country	
La Bourgogne		House	5
Riverside Cottages	9	Sep se Plek	10
Le Quartier Français			

● RESTAURANTS	
Bread & Wine	5
La Fromagerie at	
La Grange	7
La Petite Ferme	1
Le Bon Vivant	2
Restaurant at	
Grand Provence	6
Reuben's	3
The Tasting Room	4

ACTIVITIES AROUND FRANSCHHOEK

HIKES

The best **hike** in the vicinity is the Cat se Pad (Cat's Path), which starts on your left just under a kilometre from the museum as you head out of town up the Franschhoek Pass. The walk leads into *fynbos* with proteas, and gives instant access to the mountains surrounding the valley, with good views. The first two-kilometre section gets you to the top of the pass, and you can keep going for another 10km in the direction of Villiersdorp (though you don't actually reach it).

EQUESTRIAN TOURS

A great way to take in the beauty of Franschhoek (and some wine) is in the saddle – a couple of operators offer guided **equestrian tours.** Prices of wine-tasting tours include the wine.

Delta Crest Stables Contact Rayanne ☎083 300 4368. Based at Solms Delta Wine Estate for three -hour wine-tasting rides (R350) that take in Solms Delta and Allée Bleue wineries; scenic outrides are R170 an hour.

Paradise Stables Roberstsvlei Rd ☎021 876 2160, ⓦparadisestables.co.za. Visit the same wineries, but do it over four hours (2hr 30 min in the saddle; R550) on the back of a thoroughbred Arab pony; their outrides are R200 an hour.

15

The Huguenot Museum and the monument
Mon–Sat 9am–5pm & Sun 2–5pm • R10

Driving through Franschhoek, you can't fail to miss the **Huguenot Memorial Museum** thanks to its location next to the town's most obvious landmark, the **Huguenot Monument**. Set in a prime position at the head of Huguenot Road, where it forms a T-junction with Lambrecht Street, the monument consists of three skinny interlocking arches, symbolizing the Holy Trinity. The museum gives comprehensive coverage of Huguenot history, culture and of their contribution to modern South Africa.

Museum van de Caab
Sun–Thurs 9am–5pm, Fri & Sat 9am–6pm • Free • ⓦsolms-delta.co.za

Twelve kilometres north of Franschhoek along the R45, at the Solms Delta Wine Estate, the highly recommended **Museum van de Caab** gives a condensed and riveting slice through South African vernacular history as it happened on the farm and its surrounds. Housed alongside the atmospherically understated tasting room in the original 1740s gabled Cape Dutch cellar, the display begins with Stone Age artefacts found on the site and goes on to trace the arrival of the aboriginal Khoisan people, their colonization by Europeans, the introduction of slavery and how this eventually evolved into the apartheid system and its eventual demise.

ARRIVAL AND DEPARTURE   FRANSCHHOEK

By car There's no public transport to Franschhoek or in the town itself. From Stellenbochs take the R310 heading north, then east out of town. The route winds through the beautiful Helshoogte Pass, with a bunch of first-class wineries lining the mountainside along the way. Roughly 16km from Stellenbosch the R310 hits a T-junction with the R45, where you should turn east (right) and take the road for 18km to Franschhoek.

INFORMATION

Tourist office 70 Huguenot Rd (May–Aug Mon–Fri 9am–5pm, Sat & Sun 9am–4pm; Sept–April Mon–Fri 9am–6pm, Sat & Sun 9am–5pm; ☎021 876 3603, ⓦfranschhoek.org.za). Just north of the junction with Kruger Street, it has some excellent maps of the village and its winelands.

ACCOMMODATION

On the whole, guesthouse accommodation here is pricey, but the rooms are of high quality and frequently in unparalleled settings; budget accommodation is hard to find, but there are a couple of reasonably priced self-catering cottages (listed here).

★ Akademie Street Boutique Hotel 5 Akademie St ☎021 876 3027, ⓦaka.co.za. Luxury guesthouse offering total privacy in each of its tastefully decorated and spacious suites set in beautiful gardens. Facilities include free wi-fi access, DVDs and CDs, a fridge stocked with free drinks and a long, saltwater swimming pool. Gourmet breakfasts with regional specialities are served poolside by the charming hosts who'll happily recommend a restaurant for dinner and book a table for you. R2600

Bird Cottage and Frog Lodge Verdun Rd, 4.5km from town ☎021 876 2136, ⓔcindy@kingsley.co.za. Two artistically furnished cottages that each sleep four, surrounded by beautiful indigenous gardens close to the mountains. This is about as remote as you'll find this close to Franschhoek as well as being thoroughly laidback and exceptional value. R460

Cook's Cottage Corner of De La Rey and Van Wyk sts ☎021 876 4229, ⓦexplorersclub.co.za. Accommodation in a spacious and beautifully decorated two-storey Victorian house, in the centre of town with two bedrooms and a huge open-plan kitchen, dining room and lounge with a fireplace. R1600

La Bourgogne Riverside Cottages Excelsior Rd ☎021 876 3245, ⓦlabourgogne.co.za. Six simply but very tastefully furnished converted labourers' cottages set in indigenous gardens along a river. The working farm presses their own oil and produces wines, including the highly rated Progeny Sémillon, from the surrounding plum and olive groves and vineyards. R800

★ Le Quartier Français 16 Huguenot Rd ☎021 876 2151, ⓦwww.lequartier.co.za. A magical place with suites (two with their own private walled garden and pool) and huge rooms decorated with sunny fabrics, all arranged around herb and flower gardens and a swimming pool.

Child-friendly. Has one of the consistently best restaurants in the country (see opposite). R3700

The Map Room Cabrière St ☎021 876 4229, ⓦexplorersclub.co.za. Imaginatively decorated self-catering cottage in the centre of the village. Two raised ground-floor bedrooms, one of them enormous, sleep up to four people, with the living space upstairs. Folding glass doors open onto a terrace with vineyard and mountain views. R1700

Plumwood Inn 11 Cabrière St ☎021 876 3883, ⓦplumwoodinn.com. Unfailingly excellent boutique guesthouse, which makes a break from Franschhoek's Francophilia with its ethnic African-inspired decor. Detail is everything – from the custom-made cotton tablecloths to the luxurious beds covered with a sea of cushions, and impeccable service. R1150

Residence Klein Oliphants Hoek 14 Akademie St ☎021 876 2566, ⓦkleinoliphantshoek.co.za. Entering this atmospheric, eight-roomed guesthouse in a former two-storey Victorian mission station, you will be struck by the massive reception room with soaring ceilings. The classrooms and missionary's quarters have been turned into bedrooms of varying size and luxury. Breakfast is taken in the terrace, overlooking a formal herb and rose garden. R1240

Rusthof Country House 12 Huguenot St ☎021 876 3762, ⓦrusthof.com. Modern eight-roomed guesthouse along the main drag (although it doesn't feel like it) within spitting distance of some of Franschhoek's top restaurants. Rooms open onto a rose garden, and the service is superb. R1700

Sep se Plek Excelsior Rd ☎083 459 9534, ⓔladboer@ mweb.co.za. Possibly the only bargain you'll find in Franschhoek in the form of three fully equipped, two-bedroom cottages on the edge of a small tranquil tree-lined lake on a working fruit farm. R400

EATING AND DRINKING

Eating and drinking is what Franschhoek is all about, so plan on sampling at least one or two of its excellent **restaurants**, some of which rate among the Cape's best. Franschhoek's cuisine tends to be French-inspired, but includes salmon trout as a local speciality. Restaurants in town are concentrated along Huguenot Road, but there are a number of excellent alternatives in the more rustic environment of the surrounding wine estates. Booking is essential.

Bread & Wine Moreson Farm, Happy Valley Rd, La Motte ☎021 876 3692, ⓦmoreson.co.za. Signposted off the R45, this is a genial and child-friendly venue surrounded by lemon orchards and vineyards, specializing in charcuterie accompanied by breads and the estate's own wines (R130). Daily noon–3pm.

La Fromagerie at La Grange 13 Daniel Hugo St ☎021 876 2155. Sample platters of South African cheeses accompanied by local wines in the gardens here, overlooking vineyards, or sit down for tea or lunches that include savoury tarts, terrines and soufflés. On summer weekends this family-friendly spot becomes a buzzing jazz

venue (R80). Daily noon–4pm.

La Petite Ferme Franschhoek Pass Rd ☎021 876 3016, ⓦlapetiteferme.co.za. Gorgeous views across a vineyard-covered valley and an equally outstanding lunch menu both contribute to the never-ending stream of accolades and diners, from home and abroad. Local heritage is here, but always with a twist, in dishes such as *kudu* fillet medallions with courgette and couscous roulade. Meals are served with wines from the restaurant's cellar (R130). Daily noon–4pm.

Le Bon Vivant 22 Dirkie Uys St ☎021 876 2717, ⓦlebonvivant.co.za. Well-priced and consistently excellent establishment serving two- to- five-course nouvelle cuisine set meals as well as an a la carte menu with a splash of Dutch influence (R130). Mon, Tues, Thurs–Sun noon–3pm & 6.30pm till late.

Reuben's 19 Huguenot Rd ☎021 876 3772, ⓦreubens. co.za. Chic, minimalist decor and a relaxed ambience set the tone at one of Franschhoek's top restaurants (one of only two in town nominated for Eat Out's Top 10), with an inspired, eclectic menu that varies from day to day. Venison features big and there's always poultry, lamb, pork, seafood and a vegetarian option, all spiced up with a touch of Indian, Japanese and other Asian accents (R130). Daily noon–3pm & 7–9pm.

The Restaurant at Grande Provence Grande Provence Estate, Main Rd ☎021 876 8600, ⓦwww.

grandeprovence.co.za. Great lunchtime venue on an historic estate with tables under shady oaks and seriously stylish country cuisine. Indoors, the dining room oozes relaxed elegance with its smart leather upholstery (R170). Daily noon–2.30pm & 7–9.30pm.

★ **The Tasting Room at Le Quartier Français** 16 Huguenot Rd ☎021 876 2151, ⓦwww.lequartier. co.za. The place that made Franschhoek synonymous with food yonks ago, and has never put a foot wrong since, is irrepressibly one of South Africa's very best restaurants, offering excellent formal evening meals and relaxed lunches with a contemporary, global flavour. There are always vegetarian options and delicious desserts (R130). Daily 7–10pm.

THE WINERIES

15

Franschhoek's wineries are small enough and sufficiently close together to make it a breeze to visit two or three in a morning. Heading north through town from the Huguenot Monument, you'll find most of the wineries signposted off Huguenot Road and its extension, Main Road; the rest are off Excelsior Road and the Franschhoek Pass Road.

Boschendal Pniel Rd, just after the junction of the R45 and R310 to Stellenbosch ⓦboschendalwines .com. One of the world's longest-established New World wine estates, Boschendal draws busloads of tourists – 200,000 visitors a year – with its impressive Cape Dutch buildings, tree-lined avenues, restaurants and cafés and, of course, its wines. Of their six labels the Pavilion range delivers high-class, well-priced plonk (Shiraz-Cabernet Sauvignon, Rosé and a white blend); but their top ranges consistently deliver with classy wines like the Cecil John Reserve Shiraz and sauvignon Blanc, and their Reserve range Cabernet Sauvignon, Shiraz and Bordeaux-blend Grande Reserve. Informal tasting R20 for five wines; conducted tasting R30. Daily Oct–March 8.30am–6pm; April–Sept 8.30am–4.30pm.

Cabrière at Haute Cabrière About 2km from town along the Franschhoek Pass Rd ⓦcabriere.co.za. Atmospheric winery notable for its Pinot Noirs and colourful wine-maker Achim von Arnim, whose presence guarantees an eventful visit; try to catch him or, more commonly now, his son Takuan, when they demonstrate *sabrage* – slicing off the upper neck of a bubbly bottle with a French cavalry sabre. Cabrière is noted for its top-notch Pierre Jourdan range of sparkling wines and it specializes in Pinot Noir and blends made with the cultivar. Tasting R10 per wine or R30 for five. Mon–Fri 9am–4.30pm, Sat 10am–4pm, Sun 11am–4pm.

GlenWood Robertsvlei Rd, signposted off the R45 ⓦwww.glenwoodvineyards.co.za. Small winery in a beautiful setting that produces outstanding wines year after year. Although only ten-or-so minutes' drive from the village throng, it feels surprisingly remote, and vineyard and cellar tours are frequently conducted by the owner. Their flagship is the Chardonnay Vigneron's Selection, but

they also produce some excellent Shiraz and a Merlot. Tasting R30 (three whites and three reds). Mon–Fri 11am–4pm plus Sept–April Sat & Sun 11am–3pm.

Mont Rochelle Dassenberg Rd ⓦwww.montrochelle .co.za. Set against the Klein Dassenberg, Mont Rochelle has one of the most stunning settings in Franschhoek and an unusual cellar in a converted nineteenth-century fruit-packing shed, edged by eaves decorated with fretwork, stained-glass windows and chandeliers. Chardonnay is what they do best here, but don't overlook their also stellar Sauvignon Blanc and Syrah. Tasting R25. Daily 10am–6pm.

★ **Solms Delta** 13km north of Franschhoek along the R45 ⓦsolms-delta.co.za. Pleasantly bucolic Solms Delta produces unusual and consistently outstanding wines, which, on a summer's day, you can taste under ancient oaks at the edge of the vineyards with a picnic. Half the profits from the wines produced go into a trust that benefits residents of the farm and the Franschhoek Valley. The Solms-Wijn de Caab range includes the consistently great Hiervandaan (an unusual blend for these parts dominated by Shiraz, and including Carignan, Mourvèdre and Viognier grapes) and the even more highly rated Amalie (vine-dried Grenache Blanc and Viognier).Tasting R10 (refunded if you buy wine). Fri & Sat 9am–6pm, Sun–Thurs 9am–5pm.

Stony Brook Vineyards About 4km from Franschhoek, off Excelsior Rd ☎021 876 2182, ⓦstonybrook.co.za. Family-run boutique winery, with just 140,000 square metres under vine, that produces first-rate wines, including its acclaimed flagship Ghost Gum Cabernet Sauvignon, which takes its name from a magnificent old tree outside the house and informal tasting room. Tastings are convivial affairs conducted by the owners; R20. Mon–Fri 10am–3pm & Sat 10am–1pm.

The Whale Coast and Overberg Interior

From roughly July to November, southern right whales can be seen in the warm, sheltered bays of the Western Cape, and the southern Cape coast is prime territory for sightings. The Whale Coast, as the section from roughly Kleinmond to De Hoop has come to be known, is close enough for an easy outing from Cape Town, and yet is surprisingly undeveloped, with the exception of popular Hermanus, heralded as the whale capital of South Africa. The Overberg Interior – the stretch as far as Swellendam, along the N2 towards the Garden Route – is dominated by the towns of Greyton, a peaceful, oak-lined country town 35km off the main road, and Swellendam itself, brimming with historical guesthouses and decent restaurants as well as the Bontebok National Park.

Hermanus

On the edge of rocky cliffs and backed by mountains 112km east of Cape Town, **HERMANUS** sits at the northernmost end of **Walker Bay**, an inlet whose protective curve attracts calving whales as it slides south to the promontory of Danger Point. The town trumpets itself as the whale capital of South Africa, and to prove it, an official whale crier (purportedly the world's only one) struts around armed with a mobile phone and a dried kelp horn through which he yells the latest sightings. The hype aside, the bay on which Hermanus sits does provide some of the finest shore-based whale-watching in the world and, even if there are better spots nearby, the town is the best geared-up for tourists to enjoy it. There is still the barest trace of a once-quiet cliff-edge fishing village around the historic harbour and in some understated seaside cottages, but for the most part the town has gorged itself on its whale-generated income that has produced modern shopping malls, supermarkets and craft shops.

   Main Road, the continuation of the R43, meanders through Hermanus, briefly becoming Seventh Street. **Market Square**, just above the old harbour and to the south of Main Street, is the closest thing to a centre, and it's here you'll find the heaviest concentration of restaurants, craft shops and flea markets – the principal forms of entertainment in town when the whales are taking time out.

The Old Harbour Museum

At the Old Harbour • Mon–Sat 9am–4.30pm, Sun noon–4pm • R20

Just below Market Square is the **Old Harbour Museum** where, among the uncompelling displays, you'll find lots of fishing tackle and some sharks' jaws. Outside, a few colourful boats, used by local fishermen from the mid-eighteenth to mid-nineteenth centuries, create a photogenic vignette in the tiny harbour.

16

The Cliff Path

An almost continuous five-kilometre cliff path through coastal *fynbos* hugs the rocky coastline from the old harbour to Grotto Beach in the eastern suburbs. For one short

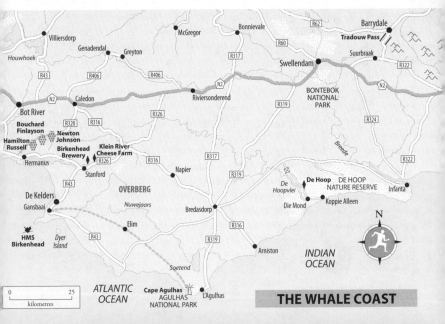

stretch the path heads away from the coast and follows Main Street before returning to the shore. This is the path along which there are excellent viewing spots of whales, and you can do as little or as much of the walk as you like.

Fernkloof Nature Reserve

Theron St • Dawn–dusk • Free

On the east side of town, off Main Road, the **Fernkloof Nature Reserve** encompasses fifteen square kilometres of mountainous terrain and offers sweeping views of Walker Bay. This highly recommended wilderness area is more than just another nature reserve on the edge of town – it has some 40km of **waymarked footpaths**, including a 4.5km circular nature trail. Visiting is an excellent way to get close to the astonishing variety of delicate montane coastal *fynbos* (over a thousand species have been identified in the reserve), much of it flowering species that attract scores of birds, including brightly coloured sunbirds and sugarbirds endemic to the area.

New Harbour

A couple of kilometres west of town along Westcliff, the **New Harbour** is a working fishing harbour, dramatically surrounded by steep cliffs, projecting a gutsy counterpoint to the more manicured central area. Whales sometimes enter the harbour – and there's nowhere better to watch them than from the *Harbour Rock* (see p.171).

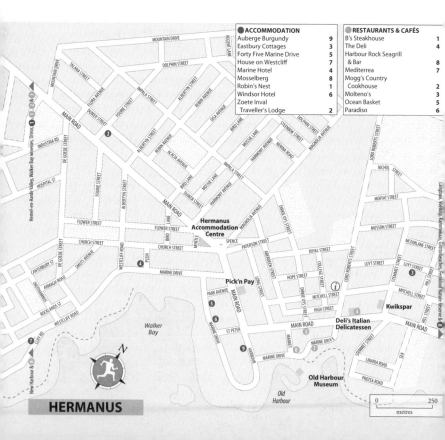

● ACCOMMODATION	
Auberge Burgundy	9
Eastbury Cottages	3
Forty Five Marine Drive	5
House on Westcliff	7
Marine Hotel	4
Mosselberg	8
Robin's Nest	1
Windsor Hotel	6
Zoete Inval Traveller's Lodge	2

● RESTAURANTS & CAFÉS	
B's Steakhouse	1
The Deli	4
Harbour Rock Seagrill & Bar	8
Mediterrea	7
Mogg's Country Cookhouse	2
Molteno's	3
Ocean Basket	5
Paradiso	6

HERMANUS

Rotary Way

On the eastern edge of Hermanus, **Rotary Way** is a fantastic ten-kilometre drive that follows the mountain spine through beautiful montane *fynbos* offering sweeping views of the town, the Hemel-en-Aarde Valley and Walker Bay from Kleinmond to Danger Point. To get there from town, turn right just after the sports ground, and take a track straddled by a pair of white gateposts labelled "Rotary Way". The road is tarred for part of the way, then becomes a dirt track, eventually petering out altogether, which means you have to return the same way.

Wine Village

Hemel-en-Aarde Village, at the junction of R43 and R320 • Mon–Sat 9am–6pm & Sun 10am–3pm • ☎ 028 316 3988, ⓦ wine-village.co.za

Hermanus has possibly the best wine shop in South Africa, the **Wine Village**, with a staggering selection of labels from all the country's various wine-producing districts, covering a vast price range. This is the place to stock up just before flying out – or have some cases shipped.

ARRIVAL AND DEPARTURE   HERMANUS

By car There are two routes to Hermanus, 125km from Cape Town. It's more direct to take the N2 and head south onto the R43 at Bot River (a 1hr 30min drive), but the winding road that hugs the coast from Strand, leaving the N2 just before Sir Lowry's Pass, is the more scenic and one of the best coastal drives in South Africa (2hr).

By bus The national Baz Bus (☎ 021 439 2323) drops off at Bot River, where you can arrange to be collected by your backpacker hostel. Two shuttles – Bernadus (☎ 028 316 1093 or ☎ 083 658 7848) and Splash (☎ 028 316 4004) – ply the route between Hermanus and Cape Town (1hr 30min). They are effectively a taxi service, operating on demand, so you need to book in advance. The journey one way costs roughly R700.

16

INFORMATION

Tourist office At the old station building in Mitchell Street (Mon–Sat 9am–5pm, plus summer Sun 10am–3pm; ☎ 028 312 2629, ⓦ hermanus.co.za). Helpful place, with maps, useful brochures about the area and an internet café. It operates a free accommodation-finding service and can take bookings for boat-based and aerial whale-watching, as well as shark-cage diving trips.

Whale festival During the last week in September the town puts on a fun show of anything that's got a whale connection, even tenuously. To find out what's on – events range from ecology talks to classical recitals – check ⓦ whalefestival.co.za.

ACCOMMODATION

The most popular coastal destination outside Cape Town, Hermanus is awash with accommodation. If you want something a little more countrified, head off to Stanford, twenty minutes' drive away around the curve of the bay, though there are no beaches. Alternatively, head further along the coast to Gansbaai (see p.173), an ugly place, but one with great whale viewing in season from the windows of any sea-facing room.

SWIMMING AND BEACHES

East of the Old Harbour, just below the *Marine Hotel*, a beautiful tidal pool offers the only **sea swimming** around the town centre's craggy coast; it's big enough to do laps. For **beaches**, you have to head out east across the Mossel River to the suburbs, where you'll find a decent choice, starting with secluded **Langbaai**, closest to town, a cove beneath cliffs at the bottom of Sixth Avenue that has a narrow strip of beach and is excellent for swimming. **Voe"lklip**, at the bottom of Eighth Avenue, has grassed terraces, toilets, a nearby café for tea and is great for picnics if you prefer your sandwiches unseasoned with sand. Adjacent is **Kammabaai**, with the best surfing break around Hermanus, and 1km further east, **Grotto Beach** (which despite its name is not a rocky cove), marking the start of a twelve-kilometre curve of dazzlingly white sand that stretches all the way to De Kelders.

Auberge Burgundy 16 Harbour Rd ☎ 028 313 1201, ⊕ auberge.co.za. A Provençal-style country house in the town centre, projecting a stylish Mediterranean feel. The rooms are light and airy with imported French fabrics, and a lavender garden. R1300

Eastbury Cottages 36 Luyt St ☎ 028 312 1258, ⊕ eastburycottage.co.za. Three very reasonably priced, fully equipped self-catering cottages close to the *Marine Hotel*. Prices vary depending on group size, and you can add breakfast for R60. R450

Marine Hotel Marine Drive ☎ 028 313 1000, ⊕ www .marine-hermanus.co.za. This 5-star Relais & Chateaux Hotel provides an opportunity to treat yourself to pure luxury. The seafront rooms are tastefully decorated and surrounded by lush gardens, while the sun lounge, bar, restaurant and spa are suitably decadent. R4200

Forty Five Marine Drive 45 Marine Drive ☎ 028 312 3610, ⊕ hermanusesplanade.com. Cliffside self-catering apartments of varying sizes next to the *Windsor Hotel*, with terrific views across the bay. Or you can choose a more affordable and child-friendly option at the *Esplanade*, also on the seafront of Marine Drive, in self-catering duplex units or cottages. Dorms R180, cottages R350

WHALE-WATCHING

The Southern Cape, including Cape Town, provides some of the easiest and best places in the world for **whale-watching**. You don't need to rent a boat or take a pricey tour to get out to sea; if you come at the right time of year, whales are often visible from the shore, although a good pair of binoculars will come in useful for when they are far out.

All nine of the great whale species of the southern hemisphere pass by South Africa's shores, but the most commonly seen off Cape Town are **southern right whales** (their name derives from being the "right" one to kill because of their high oil and bone yields and the fact that, they float when dead). Southern right whales are black and easily recognized from their pale, brownish **callosities**. These unappealing patches of raised, roughened skin on their snouts and heads have a distinct pattern on each animal, which helps scientists keep track of them.

Female whales come inshore to calve in sheltered bays, and stay to nurse their young for up to three months. **July to October** is the best time to see them, although they start appearing in June and some stay around until December. When the calves are big enough, the whales head off south again, to colder, stormy waters, where they feed on enormous quantities of plankton, making up for the nursing months when the females don't eat at all. Though you're most likely to see females and young, you may see **males** early in the season boisterously flopping about the females, though they neither help rear the calves nor form lasting bonds with females.

What gives away the presence of a whale is the blow or spout, a tall smoky plume which disperses after a few seconds and is actually the whale breathing out before it surfaces. If luck is on your side, you may see whales **breaching** – the movement when they thrust high out of the water and fall back with a great splash.

THE WHALE COAST'S HOTTEST WHALE SPOTS

In **Hermanus**, the best vantage points are the concrete cliff paths that ring the rocky shore from New Harbour to Grotto Beach. There are interpretation boards at three of the popular vantage points (Gearing's Point, Die Gang and Bientang's Cave). This is, however, the most congested venue during the whale season – at their worst, the paths can be lined two or three deep with people – though there are equally good spots elsewhere along the Walker Bay coast. Aficionados claim that **De Kelders** (see p.173), some 39km east of Hermanus, is even better, while **De Hoop Nature Reserve** (see p.180), east of Arniston, is reckoned by some to be the ultimate place along the entire southern African coast for whale-watching, though doesn't have the easy access to Cape Town that Hermanus does.

Several **operators** offer boat trips from Hermanus, all essentially offering the same service. For starters try Hermanus Whale Cruises (☎ 028 313 2722, ⊕ hermanus-whale-cruises.co.za) which is a coloured fishing village community project. Boats go out five times daily from the New Harbour, for the two-hour trip (June–Dec; R550). Boat trips also go from Kleinbaai at Gansbaai, in the summer to view birds, seals and perhaps dolphins and the odd whale, while in winter prices double to see whales. Marine Dynamics (☎ 028 384 0406, ⊕ whalewatchsa.com) is a reputable operator, and does shark-cage diving as well. Whale-watching trips go out daily from Kleinbaai at 9.15am, 11.45am and 2.15pm (2hr 30min; R450 in summer, R900 in winter).

Boats must give a fifty-metre berth to whales, but if a whale approaches a boat, the boat may stop and watch it for up to twenty minutes.

16

WALKER BAY WINERIES

Some of South Africa's top **wines** come from the **Hemel-en-Aarde Valley** along a few gravel kilometres of the **R320** to Caledon, which branches off the main road to Cape Town 2km west of Hermanus. Several small **wineries** are dotted along the same road and are worth popping into for their intimate tasting rooms and first-class wines, with views of the stark scrubby mountains just inland. All **wine tasting** is free unless you're in a group of more than six people.

Hamilton Russell Winery Off R320, Hemel-en-Aarde Road (see website for full directions), Mon–Fri 9am–5pm, Sat 9am–1pm; ☎028 312 3595, ⊛hamiltonrussellvineyards .com is the longest established of the Walker Bay wineries and produces some of South Africa's priciest wines. Adjacent to Hamilton Russell, towards Caledon, **Bouchard Finlayson** (Mon–Fri 9am–5pm, Sat 9.30am–12.30pm; ☎028 312 3515, ⊛bouchardfinlayson.co.za) is another establishment with a formidable reputation, and a wider range of wines than its neighbour. Furthest from town is **Newton Johnson** (Mon–Sat 9am–4pm; ☎028 312 3862, ⊛newtonjohnson.com), 8km from the Hemel-en-Aarde turn-off; its estate restaurant, *Heaven* (Tues–Sun 11am–3pm), is rated for a good blackboard-menu lunch and superb views.

House on Westcliff 96 Westcliff Rd ☎028 313 2388, ⊛westcliffhouse.co.za. This B&B is situated just out of the centre near the new harbour and boasts six bedrooms in a classic Cape-style house with a protected, tranquil garden and a solar-heated pool and jacuzzi. All rooms are en suite and have their own entrance off the garden. R800

Mosselberg Tenth Ave, Voelklip ☎086 111 9000, ⊛mosselberg.co.za. Five-star, five-roomed guesthouse right at the beach with a mellow atmosphere and superbly designed spaces. It's worth checking out during low season, when rooms are far cheaper. R2800

Robin's Nest 10 Meadow Ave ☎028 316 1597. Three fully equipped, self-catering studio flats above a garage in a garden, 4km west of the centre. Reached through the Hemel-en-Aarde shopping village, these purpose-built, two-storey flats sleep two and have good mountain views. R450

Windsor Hotel 49 Marine Drive ☎028 312 3727, ⊛windsorhotel.co.za. This seafront hotel offers a full range of accommodation right on the cliff edge. It's ideally situated in the centre of Hermanus and guests have sea views from the dining room, lounges and almost half of the bedrooms. R1360

Zoete Inval Travellers Lodge 23 Main Rd ☎028 312 1242, ⊛zoeteinval.co.za. A quiet and relaxing hostel, with a distinct lack of party vibe, comprising dorms, doubles and family suites and extras such as good coffee, a jacuzzi and fireplace. They'll organize all tours and outings, and arrange transport to and from the Baz Bus drop-off in Bot River. Dorms R120, doubles R400

16

EATING AND DRINKING

Seafood is the obvious thing to eat in Hermanus – and you'll find plenty of restaurants serving it – though the views are generally better than the food. **Book well ahead** at weekends; without a booking, you can always get fish and chips at the harbour, while grub features large at the **market** held every Saturday morning on Market Square. Here you'll find excellent cheeses from Bot River as well as fresh pasta, pesto, marinated cheeses, muffins, hummus and baked goods.

B's Steakhouse Hemel-en-Aarde Village ☎028 316 3625. A friendly and buzzing independent steakhouse serving brilliantly prepared, reasonably priced, slabs of beef (they hasten to tell punters they don't do burgers). Its formidable wine list and child-friendliness makes it an obvious choice for families, and they get endless repeat visits (R90). Tues–Sun noon–10pm.

The Deli Main Rd ☎028 313 2137. This friendly café with a cheerful, local vibe, makes a great spot for coffee, breakfasts or a light lunchtime meals. Their cheese soufflé is recommended (R50). Daily 8am–5pm, Sat & Sun 8am–2pm.

Harbour Rock Seagrill & Bar New Harbour ☎028 312 2920. This very busy, trendy restaurant serves up fish and chips and other seafood dishes; stunning views from the cliffs make it an excellent place for sundowners and sushi. It's always packed and has occasional live music, which make Friday nights quite raucous (R90). Summer daily 9am –10pm; winter Mon–Fri noon –3pm, Sat & Sun 9am–10pm.

Mediterrea 83 Marine Drive ☎028 313 1685. Great gourmet restaurant with good views of Walker Bay. The Mediterranean-style food is expensive, but you pay for the location right on the seafront, and its heavyweight reputation – booking is essential in season (R130). Mon–Sun 7–10pm, Sun 12.30–2.30pm.

Molteno's Viljoen St, On Rus ☎028 316 2658. Friendly staff, reasonable prices, generous portions and consistently reliable Italian-style food make this a good bet, though it is out of town and without a sea view (R100). Mon, Wed–Sat 6–10pm, Sun noon–2.30pm.

★ **Mogg's Country Cookhouse** Hemel-en-Aarde Valley, 12km from Hermanus along the R320 to Caledon ☎028 312 4321. A most unlikely location for one of Hermanus's most successful restaurants – a farm cottage – with superb views across the valley. *Mogg's* is an intimate place that's always full and unfailingly excellent, serving whatever country-cooking surprises take the fancy of chefs Jenny Mogg and her daughter Julia. Booking essential (R90). Wed–Sun noon–2.30pm, plus Fri & Sat 7–9.30pm.

Ocean Basket Fashion Square, 137 Main Rd ☎028 312 1313. As part of a reasonably priced and consistently reliable seafood chain, this restaurant is so popular customers are queuing out the door, thanks in no small part to its fabulous setting (R65). Daily 11.30am–2.30pm & 6–9pm.

Paradiso Ristorante Italiano 83 Marine Drive ☎028 313 1153. Situated behind the village square, near the water in a zone of tourist restaurants, this Italian place does veal, chicken and prawn dishes, besides delicious pizza and pasta (R75). Mon–Fri noon–5pm & 5.30–10pm, Sat & Sun 11.30am–10pm.

Stanford

East of Hermanus the R43 takes a detour inland around the attractive Klein River Lagoon, past the village of **STANFORD**, fifteen minutes away and 155km from Cape Town. This historic village, established in 1857, has become something of a refuge for arty types seeking a tranquil escape from the urban rat race. To keep visitors racing around Stanford, the hamlet's residents have created an **arts and crafts route** that takes in over a dozen artists' studios. But apart from the town's excellent microbrewery, Stanford's principal attraction is its travel-brochure streetscape of simple **Victorian architecture** that includes limewashed houses and sandstone cottages – as well as an Anglican church – with thatched roofs that glow under the late afternoon sun.

The Klein River

The town's northern boundary is the attractive Klein River, with a couple of great places to stay out of town along the river, as well as a boat trip and the chance to take to the water yourself in a kayak. There's rich birdlife in and among the rustling reed beds lining the riverbanks where you stand a chance of spotting the flashy malachite kingfisher. Boat trips run by Platanna River Cruises (☎084 583 5389; R100) will help you spot birds. For canoe or kayak rental, try Ernie (☎083 310 0952); he also does two- to three-hour boat trips by arrangement.

Birkenhead Brewery

Just across the R43 from Stanford along the R326 • Free tasting tours Wed–Sun 11am–3pm • Open for lunch Wed–Sun 10am–4pm

Although the **Birkenhead Brewery** bills itself as a "craft brewery estate", the gleaming stainless-steel pipes and equipment inside soon dispel any images of bloodshot hillbillies knocking up a bit of moonshine on the quiet. This is a slick operation and a great place to go for a pub lunch or buy beers, which put those of SAB, South Africa's big brewing near-monopoly, in their place.

ARRIVAL AND INFORMATION
STANFORD

By car Stanford is 155km from Cape Town. Take the Hermanus off-ramp from the N2 (about 90km from Cape Town), and follow the R43 for another 65km through Hermanus to Stanford.

Tourist office Main Road (Mon–Fri 8am–4pm & Sat 10am–12pm; ☎028 341 0340, ⒲stanfordinfo.co.za). Can help with booking accommodation, and there is also a brochure for a walkabout you can do, taking in the various historical houses in the village. They can provide information on wineries to visit and other activities.

ACCOMMODATION

B's Cottage 17 Morton St ☎028 341 0430, ⒲stanford -accommodation.co.za. A small, open-plan, self-catering thatched house, sleeping two, in an English-style country garden. It's popular and central, so book well ahead. <u>R450</u>

Klein River Cheese Farm Cottage On the R326, 7km from Stanford ☎028 341 0693. This is a charming

STANFORD CHEESE AND WINE

Two kilometres beyond Birkenhead brewery, and 7km from Stanford, is the **Klein River Cheese Farm** (Mon–Fri 9am–5pm, Sat 9am–1pm), which offers tastings of its famous Gruyÿre, Leiden, Colby and Dando cheeses. Buy one of its picnic baskets to have under the trees next to the river (Sept 15–May 15 daily 11am–3pm).

As everywhere else in the Cape, more and more vineyards are opening, *fynbos* giving way to grapes, but Stanford's best wine is sold from **Raka** (Mon–Fri 9am–4.30pm, Sat 10am–2.30pm), 17km from town along the R326. To visit other wineries, consult the tourist office for a map of wine routes.

three-bedroomed/two-bathroomed Victorian cottage on the river, complete with a fireplace for the winter. There's a minimum stay of two nights. R410

Mosaic Farm 10km from the centre, exit from Queen Victoria St ☏028 313 2814, ⒲mosaicfarm.net. You'll find stone, canvas and thatch self-catering chalets on the river here, with 4km of lagoon frontage and canoeing and walks on the farm. They also run the half-board *Lagoon Lodge* on the same site (R2800), which has a luxury safari lodge feel. They can make you up picnic lunches and dinners for a bit extra. R800

★ **Stanford River Lodge** 4km from the centre, exit from Queen Victoria St ☏028 341 0444 or ☏082 378 1935, ⒲stanfordriverlodge.co.za. Sunny, spacious and modern self-catering cottages with river and mountain views. It's a lovely, upmarket spot with river swimming and canoeing in summer. Owners John and Valda Finch will show you a good time, and provide breakfast for a bit extra. R700

EATING

Madres Ktchen Robert Stanford Estate, 1km outside Stanford ☏028 341 0647. Farm-style eating with menu changing daily. Home-made bread, pies, pâtés and cheeses, plus some South African signature dishes and wines from their own estate (which they also sell in their on-site shop). It is great for children, with lawns, a jungle gym and dam (R70). Thurs–Tues 8am–4pm.

★ **Mariana's Bistro and Home Deli** Du Toit St ☏028 341 0272. The innovative and reasonably priced country food served at this Victorian cottage is good enough to draw Cape Town gourmands out for the day. Food and wines are local, and many of the vegetables are picked from owners Mariana and Peter's garden. You'll need to book a couple of months beforehand, though cancellations are always a possibility. No children under 10 (R75). Thurs–Sun noon–4pm.

Stanford Gallery Art Café Queen Victoria St. You can enjoy espressos and cake, and the best pizza in Stanford surrounded by artworks by local artists at this pleasant café. There are daily specials too, including fish from Gansbaai (R70). Tues–Sun 8am–9pm.

16

Gansbaai

GANSBAAI, 175km from Cape Town, is a workaday place, economically dependent on its fishing industry and the seafood canning factory at the harbour. This gives the place a more gutsy feel than the surrounding holiday lands, but there's little reason to spend time here unless you want to engage in **great white shark safaris**, Gansbaai's other major industry. It is an appropriately competitive and cut-throat business with operators engaged in a blind feeding frenzy to attract punters. Boats set out from Gansbaai to **Dyer Island** (see box, p.176), east of Danger Point, where great white sharks come to feed on the resident colony of seals.

De Kelders

A suburb of Gansbaai, **DE KELDERS** is a treeless blob of bland holiday homes and ostentatious seafront mansions on the cliffs staring across Walker Bay to Hermanus. Its rocky coast, though, provides outstanding whale-watching and there is access to a beautiful, long sandy beach at the Walker Bay Nature Reserve.

Walker Bay Nature Reserve and the Klipgat Strandloper Caves

Access is at the end of Cliff Rd • R25

You can clamber over rocky sections and walk for miles along the beach at the **Walker**

Bay Nature Reserve, known by everyone as "Die Plat". Swimming is very dangerous though, and it's best not to venture in more than knee-high. From the car park, a path leads down to the **Klipgat Strandloper Caves**, excavated in the early 1990s, when evidence was unearthed of modern human habitation from 80,000 years ago. The caves became unoccupied for a few thousand years, after which they were used again by Khoisan people 20,000 years ago. Shells, middens, tools and bones were uncovered; some of these are now displayed in the South African Museum in Cape Town (see p.53). From the caves, the waymarked **Duiwelsgats hiking trail** goes east for 7km as far as Gansbaai and is a good way to explore the coastline, which can also be accessed at a number of other points.

ARRIVAL AND INFORMATION GANSBAAI

By car Gansbaai is 175km from Cape Town. Take the Hermanus off-ramp from the N2 (about 90km from Cape Town), and follow the R43 for another 85km through Hermanus, Stanford, De Kelders and Gansbaai.

Tourist office Mon–Fri 9am–1pm & 2–5pm, Sat 10am–2pm; ☎ 028 384 1439, ⓦ gansbaaiinfo.com.

ACCOMMODATION

Cliff Lodge 6 Cliff St ☎ 028 384 0983, ⓦ clifflodge .co.za. A stylish seafront guesthouse, perched on the cliffs of De Kelders, with breathtaking views from all four luxurious bedrooms and a spacious penthouse suite, plus a deck for whale-watching and a pool for your own splashing. R1500

★ **Crayfish Lodge** Killarney St ☎ 028 384 1898, ⓦ www.crayfishlodge.net. This is the top stay in town; a palatial guesthouse with sea views and an individual patio or courtyard for all five rooms. If you're treating yourself, go for the upstairs suites with jacuzzis. A path leads down to a rocky beach with a channel for bathing or there's a heated swimming pool. R1920

Ama-Krokka 28 Vyfer St ☎ 028 384 2776, ⓦ ama-krokka.co.za. This homely B&B is situated nice and near to the beach. The house boasts a pool and the two suites have their own patio, and come with a microwave so you can have a stab at self-catering. Much more interesting, however, is that the owners will let you make a braai. R900

EATING AND DRINKING

Benguela On corner of Church & Harbour sts ☎ 028 384 2120. Upmarket crisp interior offering a range of specialities – seafood, meat and vegetarian – every plate picture perfect and, surprisingly, the meat dishes surpass the fish. The desserts are recommended, prices reasonable and the host Jonathan is very welcoming and friendly (R90). Mon–Fri 6–10pm, Sat & Sun 11am–2.30pm & 6–10pm.

Coffee on the Rocks Cliff St ☎ 028 384 2017. A small bistro that does great coffee, cakes and light meals, with a deck in an unsurpassed position for whale-watching, and leisurely Sunday roasts. Booking is absolutely essential as it is very popular (R65). Wed–Sun 10am–5pm.

Gansbaai Fisheries Gansbaai Harbour. Over the counter traditional fresh fish and chips, while you watch the fishing boats come in (R45). Daily 9am–5pm.

★ **Grootbos Nature Reserve** ☎ 028 384 8000. This is the culinary highlight of the area – fine dining traditional cuisine with a modern twist, at this delightful eco-lodge. What's more, it's extremely reasonable for the quality of food you receive. They run a set menu only; a three-course lunch will set you back R155, while the six-course dinner is R320. Dinner is R320 (see box opposite). Daily 1–3pm and 6.30–9pm.

Danger Point

Danger Point, the southernmost point of Walker Bay, is where British naval history was allegedly made. True to its name, the Point lured the ill-fated HMS *Birkenhead* onto its hidden rocks on February 26, 1852. As was the custom, the captain of the troopship gave the order "Every man for himself". Displaying true British pluck, the soldiers are said to have lined up in their ranks on deck where they stood stock-still, knowing that if one man broke ranks it would lead to a rush that might overwhelm the lifeboats carrying women and children to safety. The precedent of "women and children first", which became known as the **Birkenhead Drill**, was thus established, even though 445 lives were lost in the disaster.

Cape Agulhas and around

Along the east flank of the Danger Point promontory, the rocky and shallow coastline with heavy swells and strong currents makes this one of South Africa's most treacherous stretches of coast – one that has claimed over 250 wrecks and around 2500 lives. Its rocky terrain also accounts for the lack of a coastal road from Gansbaai and Danger Point to **Cape Agulhas**, the southernmost tip of Africa.

The plain around the southern tip of South Africa has been declared the **Agulhas National Park** to conserve its estimated two thousand species of indigenous plant and marine and intertidal life as well as a cultural heritage which includes shipwrecks and archeological sites – stone hearths, pottery and shell middens have been discovered.

The actual tip of the continent is marked by a rock and plaque about 1km from the landmark of Agulhas Lighthouse, towards Suiderstrand. Following the dirt road to **Suiderstrand** itself takes you to some beautiful, undeveloped beaches with rock pools to explore, and is definitely the best part of Agulhas.

L'AGULHAS, the rather windblown settlement associated with the southern tip, consists of a small collection of holiday houses and a few shops. It's a much quieter coastal destination than anywhere along the Garden Route. The centre of Agulhas, if you can call it a centre, is along Main Road, where you'll find a couple of restaurants, small supermarket and a craft shop.

Agulhas Lighthouse

Lighthouse Daily 9am–5pm • R20 • **Restaurant** ☎ 028 435 7580 • Daily 9am–10pm, closed Sun eve

The red and white Agulhas Lighthouse commissioned in 1849, offers vertiginous views from its top, reached by a series of steep ladders. The appeal of lonely lighthouses on rocky edges beaming out signals to ships at night, is explored through interesting exhibits about lighthouses around South Africa. It's worth absorbing the lighthouse atmosphere at the **restaurant**, but stick to tea and *koeksisters* – the food is no draw.

16

Struisbaai

Struisbaii is little more than a small collection of holiday homes, about 6km east of Agulhas along the R319, with an attractive harbour and long sandy beaches. Its main draw, however, is the recommended sundowner or dinner spot, *Pelican's* (see p.176) at the harbour.

ARRIVAL AND DEPARTURE   AGULHAS

By car Agulhas is 230km from Cape Town. Take the N2 to Caledon (115km), then the R316 to Bredasdorp, where the road splits; the more westerly branch (the R319) continuing 43km on to Agulhas, while the other fork leads to Arniston. The drive takes you through rolling farmlands where you are almost certain to see South Africa's national bird, the elegant and endangered blue crane, feeding in the fields. Both the small towns of Napier and Bredasdorp en route have appealing cafés and restaurants to tempt you to break the journey.

GROOTBOS PRIVATE NATURE RESERVE

Set among the hills 6km before De Kelders, *Grootbos Private Nature Reserve* (☎ 028 384 8000, ⓦgrootbos.com) is an exceedingly tasteful, luxurious eco-lodge that offers whale-watching safaris and guidance into Cape flora and fauna, as well as very good horseriding excursions. Even if you can't stay – and it is undoubtedly the top stay along the Whale Coast – you can visit for the day and enjoy absolutely superb gourmet meals (breakfast, lunch and dinner) at surprisingly reasonable rates, though you'll need to book ahead. Full board including all activities is R3000 per person per night with a minimum stay of two nights.

INFORMATION

The Tourist information centre at the Agulhas Lighthouse is very good (Mon–Sun 9am–5pm; ☎028 435 7185, ⓦwww.discovercapeagulhas.co.za). It produces an excellent guidebook *Discover Cape Agulhas* (free) which is useful if you want a map to explore several new vineyards and wineries that have opened up in the area – the Wine Boutique (☎082 567 7858) in the Main Road next to *Angelo's Trattoria* stocks wines of the region.

ACCOMMODATION

Agulhas Country Lodge Main Rd ☎028 435 7650, ⓦagulhascountrylodge.com. The lodge is a rather grand stone building perched halfway up a hillside. All rooms have sea views from private balconies, and some from the beds themselves; excellent, if pricey, seafood dinners provide another inducement to stay. R1400

Cape Agulhas Backpackers Corner of Duiker & Main rds ☎082 372 3354, ⓦcapeagulhasbackpackers.com. The only budget place around Agulhas has camping, dorms, doubles and self-catering cottages with a pool, garden and good bedding throughout. It's run by a couple who are big on helping you enjoy the outdoors and will organize boating, surfing lessons, kiteboarding, horseriding and other activities around Struisbaai, and also arrange pick-ups from Botrivier or Swellendam for those without their own transport. Camping R50, dorms R100, doubles R320

★ **Pebble Beach** Suiderstrand, follow signs to the Southern Tip of Africa and then 4km beyond for Pebble Beach ☎028 435 7270 or ☎082 774 5008, ⓦpebble-beach.co.za. Uniquely positioned on the edge of the Agulhas National Park, with kilometres of undeveloped beach to explore to the west, this sea-facing guesthouse run by Chris and Peta has two en-suite rooms in a modern thatched house, featuring white beds and wooden floors. The scent of *fynbos* wafts in from the dunes. Guests also have the choice of a special upstairs bedroom with bath and large balcony overlooking the sea. R790

Southernmost B&B On the corner of Van Breda and Lighthouse sts ☎028 435 6565, ⓦsouthermost.co.za; closed in winter. A well-loved and rather dilapidated historic beach cottage, run by welcoming Meg, opposite the tidal pool with an indigenous garden sloping down to the water's edge. It is an easy walk from here to the centre to get an evening meal. R700

EATING

Agulhas Country Lodge Main Rd ☎028 435 7650. Pricey but very good four-course set menu (R295) and seafood dinners for a special night out (from around R150). Book in advance, and try for a table at the window as it's a little dark inside. The lodge also opens for slap-up breakfasts. Daily 8.15–10am & 7.30–10pm.

Agulhas Seafoods Main Rd. The fish and chips at *Agulhas Seafoods* are so succulent and delicious that Capetonians have been known to travel all the way out here to enjoy them (R55). Mon–Sat 11.30am–7pm, Sun 11.30am–3pm.

Pelican's Struisbaai, Hawe Rd, ☎072 742 5824.

16

DYER ISLAND AND SHARK ALLEY

How a black American came to be living on an island off South Africa in the early nineteenth century is something of a mystery. But, according to records, **Samson Dyer** arrived here in 1806 and made a living collecting guano on the island that subsequently took his name.

Dyer Island is home to substantial **African penguin** and **seal breeding colonies**, both of which are prized morsels among great white sharks. So shark-infested is the channel between the island and the mainland at some times of year that it is known as **Shark Alley**, and these waters are used extensively by operators of great white viewing trips. If you go on a trip, you'll be safely contained within a sturdy boat or cage. This is a luxury that a group of West African castaways could not afford when, in 1996, they found themselves washed up here as the Taiwanese merchant vessel they were riding on sank en route to the Far East. One of them drowned, but the rest (amazingly) survived five days at sea, including a stint down Shark Alley, clinging to pieces of timber and barrels.

TOUR OPERATORS

African Wings ☎028 312 2701, ⓦafricanwings .co.za. This operator, based in Hermanus sells popular whale-watching plane flights over the bay. A two-hour flight for two to six people costs from R3700.

Marine Dynamics and Dyer Island Cruises Geelbek St, Kleinbaai, between De Kelders and Gansbaai ☎028 384 0406, ⓦwhalewatchsa.com. Whale sightings by boat and shark-cage diving, around Dyer Island. Trips are 2hr 30min long, and preceded by an introductory talk. R790 per person.

ELIM MISSION STATION

A good reason to venture along the network of dirt roads that crisscrosses the Whale Coast interior is to visit **ELIM**, a Moravian mission station 40km northwest of Agulhas, founded in 1824. The whole village is a National Monument of streets lined with thatched, whitewashed houses and fig trees. Tours, arranged by the tourist office in Church Street (Mon–Sat 9am–12.30pm & 1.30–5pm; ☎028 482 1806) take in the oldest house in the settlement, the church, the restored water mill where wheat is still ground, and the pottery studio. There's also a memorial commemorating the **emancipation of slaves** in 1834, the only such monument in South Africa; its presence reflects the fact that numerous freed slaves found refuge in mission stations like Elim. The only **accommodation** is the community-run *Elim Guesthouse* (☎028 482 1715; R400; dinner available on request), a newly renovated 1901 thatched home.

Struisbaai's best seafood grill restaurant, well situated at the harbour. It's a lovely spot to watch the sun go down with a chilled glass of wine, although it can get uncomfortably busy in peak season (R85). Daily 9am–10pm.

Pot Pouri Main Rd. Outdoor seating under umbrellas and a well-stocked curio & craft shop are a good enough reason to have a light lunch or coffee here. Toasted sandwiches, greek salad, tea and cake (R60). Mon–Sat 9am–5pm. R45

Zuidste Kaap 99 Main Rd ☎028 435 7838. You'll get straightforward, no-frills cooking in this elegant thatched restaurant. It has a lovely ambience with an airy, open feel, but sadly no sea views. Recommended dishes include *eisbein*, stuffed chicken breasts and line fish (R80). Daily 10am–10pm.

16

Arniston

After the cool deep blues of the Atlantic to the west, the azure of the Indian Ocean at **ARNISTON** is startling, made all the more dazzling by the white dunes interspersed with rocky ledges. Reached on the R316, 24km southeast of Bredasdorp, and 220km from Cape Town, this is one of the best places to stay in the Overberg – if you want nothing more than beach life. The colours may be tropical, but the wind can howl unpredictably here, as anywhere else along the Cape coast, and when it does, there's nothing much to do. The village is known to locals by its Afrikaans name, Waenhuiskrans ("wagon-house cliff"), after a cliff containing a huge cave 1500m south of town (see below), which trekboers reckoned was spacious enough for a wagon and span of oxen (the largest thing they could think of). The English name derives from a British ship, the *Arniston*, which hit the rocks here in 1815.

The shallow seas, so treacherous for vessels, provide Arniston with the safest swimming waters along the Whale Coast. You can swim next to the slipway or at **Roman Beach**, the main swimming beach, just along the coast as you head south from the harbour.

Kassiebaai

A principal attraction of Arniston is **Kassiesbaai**, a district of starkly beautiful limewashed cottages, now declared a National Monument and home to coloured fishing families that have for generations made their living here. But Kassiesbaai sits a little uneasily as a living community, as it's also a bit of a theme park for visitors stalking the streets with their cameras. Heading north through Kassiesbaai at low tide, you can walk 5km along an unspoilt beach unmarred by buildings until you reach an unassuming fence – resist the temptation to climb over this, as it marks the boundary of the local testing range for military material and missiles.

Arniston Caves

Heading south of the harbour for 1500m along spectacular cliffs, you'll reach the vast **cave** after which the town is named. The walk is worth doing simply for the

> ## TOURS
>
> For tours of the region, to Arniston or Agulhas and other scenic areas, you can take a full-day tour with Coastal Tours from Agulhas (R480; Ⓦ www.coastaltours.co.za) or with Pieter in Swellendam from Fynbus Tours(☎ 028 514 3303 or ☎ 083 621 8503, Ⓦ www.fynbus.co.za). They will drive you to the major sites, and organize the day depending on the interests of the group involved. This is the best way to see the region without your own car.

fynbos-covered dunes you'll cross on the way. From the car park right by the cave, it's a short signposted walk down to the dunes and the cave, which can only be reached at low tide. The rocks can be slippery and have sharp sections, so be sure to wear shoes with tough soles and a good grip.

ARRIVAL AND TOURS   ARNISTON

By car Arniston is 225km from Cape Town. Take the N2 to Caledon (115km), take the R316 to Bredasdorp, where the road splits; take the 316 for 25km to Arniston.
Tours There is no public transport to Arniston, so if you don't have our yown car, you can take a full-day tour with

Coastal Tours from Agulhas (R480, ☎ 028 435 6903, Ⓦ www.coastaltours.co.za) or with Fynbus Tours in Swellendam (☎ 028 514 3303 or ☎ 083 621 8503, Ⓦ www.fynbus.co.za).

ACCOMMODATION

The holiday accommodation is in the new section of town, adjacent to the traditional fishing village quarter of Kassiebaai, where you'll find a number of exclusive holiday homes all built in a whitewashed, thatched-roof cottage style. You will not find pumping nightlife or adrenaline-packed attractions here, only an azure sea, peace and quiet.

Arniston Lodge 23 Main Rd ☎ 028 445 9175, Ⓦ arnistonlodge.co.za. In the residential area, this B&B offers four rooms in a two-storey thatched home with a pool. The upstairs rooms have views and better bathrooms than those downstairs. R620
Arniston Resort Signposted 300m from the centre along the main road into Arniston ☎ 028 445 9620. You can pitch your own tent or stay in one of the four- or six-bed en-suite bungalows here. The cheaper, older ones don't provide linen, and you'll pay a bit more to have all the mod cons including TV. The place can get crowded and very noisy over weekends and during peak season. R400
Arniston Seaside Cottages Huxham St, signposted as you arrive from Bredasdorp ☎ 028 445 9772,

Ⓦ www.arniston-online.co.za. A series of attractive and modern self-catering establishments built in the style of traditional fisherman's cottages with limewashed walls and thatched roofs. Clean and bright, they're well situated a few minutes' walk from the beach and come fully equipped. R560
Arniston Spa Hotel Beach Rd ☎ 028 445 9000, Ⓦ arnistonhotel.com. Dominating the seafront, this luxurious spa hotel boasts every comfort, including a spa with massage and beauty treatments. The best rooms have a fireplace, or a balcony with sea views. If it's way out of your budget, go during the week or in winter when prices drop. It is one of the best-set beach hotels in the country, and the only one in town. R2150

EATING AND DRINKING

Arniston Hotel Beach Rd. Outdoor seating to take in the sea views, and does blowout breakfasts, and pleasing fresh fish dinners. It also holds the town's only bar, which serves burgers and the like and has sport on TV. Daily 8–10am & 7–10pm.
Kassiesbaai Craft Shop ☎ 028 445 9760. The Arniston fishermen's wives can cook up a three-course traditional fisherman's meal with a catch of the day in a small eating area at the craft shop; booking in advance is essential. They cater on demand and are very laidback

and friendly, but getting hold of them can be a little hit and miss (R60).
Willeen's Meals Arts and Crafts House C26, Kassiesbaai ☎ 028 445 9995. This is an authentic fisherman's cottage where you'll be served traditional Cape Malay meals by family members. You can try *bobotie*, a seafood platter (R100) or fried fish. They have a BYO booze policy, though soft drinks are available. You can also just have tea and scones in the garden that boasts sea views. Daily 8am–10pm.

16

De Hoop Nature Reserve

Daily 7am–6pm • R30

De Hoop is the **wilderness highlight** of the Western Cape and one of the best places in the world for land-based whale-watching. No need to take a boat or use binoculars – in season you'll see whales blowing or breaching – leaping clear of the water – or perhaps slapping a giant tail. Although the reserve could technically be done as a day-trip from Agulhas, Arniston or Swellendam, you'll find it far more rewarding to come here for a night or more. The Whale Trail hike is one of South Africa's best walks and among the finest wildlife experiences in the world (see box, p.182).

The breathtaking coastline is edged by bleached sand dunes standing 90m high in places, and rocky formations that at one point open to the sea in a massive craggy arch. The flora and fauna are impressive, too, encompassing 86 species of mammal, 260 different birds and 1500 varieties of plants. July to October is the best time, notably August and September for highest numbers, but you stand a very good chance of a sighting from June through to November. Inland, rare **Cape mountain zebra**, **bontebok** and other **antelope** congregate on a plain near the reserve accommodation.

ARRIVAL AND TOURS

DE HOOP NATURE RESERVE

By car De Hoop is signposted off the N2, the Spitskop Rd, 13km west of Swellendam, the quickest route from Cape Town. Alternatively, if you are in the Overberg, take the signposted dirt road that spurs off the R319 as it heads out of Bredasdorp, 50km to its west.

Tours Without your own car, you can take a full-day tour with Coastal Tours from Agulhas (R480; ⓦwww .coastaltours.co.za) or with Pieter in Swellendam from Fynbus Tours (☎028 514 3303 or ☎083 621 8503, ⓦwww.fynbus.co.za). As the ex-manager of Bontebok National Park, he knows his stuff.

ACCOMMODATION

Accommodation within the National Park is available through the De Hoop Collection, and varies from camping to luxurious cottages. Outside the park are a couple of options, but if you can get a place inside, it is preferable as the journey to the coastline is shorter. There are a couple of different locations within the park, the most convenient is at De Opstel where the information office and restaurant is located, a twenty-minute drive from the coast.

De Hoop Cottages ☎021 422 4522, ⓦdehoopcollection.co.za. You'll find an array of options here, none of them especially cheap, starting with camping in a sheltered spot. The range continues through different-sized cottages and rondavels. Best of all, if you're a group of six you could take the renovated, splendidly isolated beach house at Koppie Alleen, on the beach itself. The site couldn't be more thrilling, overlooking a bay full of whales and huge rock pools. Camping R295; cottage R600; Koppie Alleen R4800

Verfheuwel Farm Off the road signposted Whale Trail and Potberg ☎028 542 1038 or ☎082 767 0148, ⓔverfheuwel@whalemail.co.za. This cottage accommodation, attached to the main farmhouse, is run by hospitable Afrikaner farming folk who can bring dinner to your cottage if you ask in advance. It sleeps a couple, with beds in the living area for children. The garden is beautiful and has a swimming pool. If *Verfheuwel* is full, owner Matti can direct you to other friends and relatives in the area with farm accommodation. R500

EATING

There are **no food supplies** at De Hoop, bar a small shop selling basics, so be sure to stock up with everything before you come. The one restaurant is the *Fig Tree* (☎028 542 1254; 12–3pm & 7–8.30pm; R185) which is close to the reception and open daily.

The Overberg interior

Just off the N2, **Caledon** merits a quick visit for its refreshing hot springs, while a few towns are worth visiting for a night or two. Closer to Cape Town, **Greyton** makes a perfect weekend break, with enough good food, walks and lounging in garden cafés to occupy you for a couple of nights. Nearby, South Africa's oldest mission station, **Genadendal**, a six-kilometre excursion west of Greyton, is also worth a look around. **Swellendam**, further along the N2 is often treated as the first night stop along the

Garden Route, but can be used as a base to visit **De Hoop Nature Reserve** for the day, or to see some antelope and ostriches in the **Bontebok National Park** a few kilometres away.

Caledon

The first impression of **CALEDON**, some 111km east of Cape Town on the N2, is of huge, cathedral-like grain silos that dwarf its church spires. It's worth a stop to indulge in its hot spring, or if you fancy a flutter the next-door casino kitted out with scores of slot machines lined up inside the large gambling hall and a number of gaming tables.

Caledon Spa

Tues–Sat 8am–7pm • R150 • ☎ 028 214 5100

The natural, hot brown water that flows through the spa here offers a gamut of physical indulgences. It is wonderfully relaxing and rejuvenating and the views from the hottest waterfall pools over the farmlands are lovely. Saunas and steam room are all included in the price but bring your own towels.

Greyton

GREYTON, a tranquil village 46km north of Caledon, and 145km from Cape Town, is a favourite weekend destination for Capetonians, based around a core of Georgian and Victorian buildings, shaded by grand old oaks and tucked away at the edge of the Riviersonderend (meaning "river with no end") Mountains. With good guesthouses, it is a great place to unwind, stroll and potter about in the handful of galleries, antique shops and cafés and sample locally produced Von Geusau Belgian chocolates and cakes. It also boasts some great hikes, most notably the superb **Boesmanskloof Traverse** trail, which crosses the mountains to a point 14km from McGregor.

16

ARRIVAL AND DEPARTURE
GREYTON

The best route is to take the signposted, sealed R406 from the N2, just west of Caledon and 105km from Cape Town. Follow the R406 for 30km. Ignore any other signs to Greyton on the N2, they are for unsealed, difficult roads. Allow two to two and a half hours for the journey.

INFORMATION

Greyton Tourism Bureau 29 Main St, along the main road as you come into town (Mon–Sat 9am–2pm; ☎ 028 254 9414, ⓦ greyton.net). Has lists of accommodation and is helpful.

Horseriding You can do excellent horseriding trails just outside Greyton through orchards and mountain paths, on very good horses, contact Clive from *Blue Hippo* (☎ 083 776 1922).

ACCOMMODATION

It's worth staying somewhere with a fireplace if you're here in winter, as it can be cold in this mountainous terrain, and conversely look for a pool in summer. Most places charge more for a one-night stay, as it is primarily a weekend destination, and there's little accommodation to be found in the lower price ranges.

Auberge Greyton Corner of Oak St and Main Rd ☎ 028 254 9192. Simple, uncluttered farm-style rooms – if you're planning on hiking and just need a bed for the night or two, this place is ideal. R350

Barnards Boutique Hotel 16 Main Rd ☎ 028 254 9394, ⓦ barnardshotel.co.za. Modern and comfortable rooms in a new and fashionable establishment with a lovely pool and a great bar. The cheaper doubles above the bar are more functional, while the duplexes at the back are quieter and have some self-catering facilities too. R600

★ **Blue Hippo Tipi Village** 4km outside Greyton ☎ 028 254 9595, ⓦ bluehippo.co.za. Huge, comfortable

tipis equipped with two double futons on a magnificent farm just outside town. There is a river and dam ideal for swimming, as well as recommended horseriding, and a good a communal kitchen. This is a great place for kids. R300

High Hopes 89 Main Rd ☎ 028 254 9898, ⓦ highhopes .co.za. One of the best B&Bs in town, in a beautiful country-style home set in large gardens with a swimming pool. Besides four rooms, there's a self-contained unit with a kitchen, which can be taken on a B&B or self-catering basis. They have a variety of therapies, including massage, on offer and bikes for hire, too. Substantial midweek discounts. R800

ON THE WHALE TRAIL

Only moderately difficult, the five-day, four-night, self-guided **Whale Trail** (☏0861 227 362 8873, ⓦcapenature.co.za) follows a spectacularly beautiful route from the Potberg Mountains 55km along the deserted coast to Koppie Alleen. To go in whale season, though, you'll need to book a year in advance and take any date offered. Bookings are for a minimum of six and maximum of twelve people (with no children under 8), and you pay for six even if there are just two of you. Prices are about R1000 per person and include supplies, which are portered to each night's accommodation – comfortable cottages, each in splendid isolation. For the duration of the trail you see only your own group, and no other people or signs of habitation at all.

EATING AND DRINKING

The town has a short Saturday **market** at the corner of Main Road and Cross Market Street (10am–noon), to which locals bring their produce: organic vegetables, fabulous and well-priced cheeses, decadent cakes, breads, biscuits and preserves. Food at the restaurants tends to be quite sophisticated and creative nouvelle cuisine.

Abbey Rose Main Rd ☏028 254 9470. Nice garden setting, with a deck and the delightful rose garden that the name might suggest, to enjoy salads or tea and scones. Food is hearty and uncomplicated; try the oxtail stew and the bread and butter pudding (R80). Wed–Sat noon–3pm & 7.30–9pm, Tues 7.30–9pm.

Barnard's Boutique Hotel 16 Main Rd ☏028 254 9394. Nice setting for a sundowner, or champagne, with wine and tapas on the veranda or by the fireplace inside. The food accent is contemporary country such as caramelized onion with gnocchi. The big screen at the pub draws sports fans and there are pavement braziers in the evening, livening up the street (R100). Daily 8am–10pm.

Oak and Vigne Café DS Botha St ☏028 254 9037. An extremely popular restaurant situated in an old cottage with an oak-shaded terrace where you can savour teas and gourmet lunches daily – including North African lentil soup with baguettes and a variety of home-made ice creams,

including one with locally made Geusau chocolate, for dessert. While they don't serve wine, you can buy some wine from the adjoining wine shop (R60). Daily 8am–5pm.

Peccadillo's 23 Main Rd ☏028 254 9066. You're unlikely to eat better than at this bistro, with seasonal blackboard specials. Reasonable prices for food with a strong Mediterranean influence; try the local trout dishes, or fish pie with capers. A good place to try boutique wines which the owner collects from Winelands excursions. Children can be accommodated (R85). Thurs–Mon noon–2pm & 7.30–10pm. R85

Via's Deli 31 Main Rd ☏028 254 9190. Vegetarian lunches in a building which was once the general dealer's, with a guesthouse at the back, *Via's* is a reliable outlet for deli food and organic vegetables, as well as free-range meat. The freshly squeezed carrot and apple juice, and smoothies are recommended. The wholesome organic food is absolutely fresh and seasonal, and you can sit out on the veranda (R50). Tues–Sun 9am–4pm.

Genadendal

GENADENDAL, 6km from Greyton was founded in 1737 by Moravians, and is definitely worth a wander about. The village's focus is around **Church Square**, dominated by a very Germanic church building dating back to 1891. The old bell outside dates back to the eighteenth century, when it became the centre of a flaming row between the local farmers and the mission station. The scrap broke out when missionary Georg Schmidt annoyed the local white farmers by forming a small Christian congregation with impoverished Khoi – who were on the threshold of extinction – and giving refuge to maltreated labourers from local farms. What really got the farmers' goat was the fact that while they, white Christians, were illiterate, Schmidt was teaching native people, whom they considered uncivilized, to read and write. The Dutch Reformed Church, under the control of the Dutch East India Company, waded in when Schmidt began baptizing converts, and prohibited the mission from ringing the bell, which called the faithful to prayer.

In 1838 Genadendal established the first teacher training college in the country, which the government closed in 1926, on the grounds that coloured people didn't need tertiary education and should be employed as workers on local farms – a policy that effectively ground the community into poverty. In 1995, in recognition of the mission's role, Nelson Mandela renamed his official residence in Cape Town "Genadendal".

Today, the population of this principally coloured town numbers around four thousand people, adhering to a variety of Christian sects – no longer just Moravianism. The **Mission Museum** adjacent to Church Square (Mon–Thurs 9am–1pm & 2–5pm, Fri 9am–3.30pm, Sat 9am–noon; free) is moderately interesting, as is a wander through the town, down to the rural graveyard, spiked with old tombstones.

Swellendam and around

On the N2, 97km east of Caledon and 220km from Cape Town, **SWELLENDAM** is an attractive historic town at the foot of the Langeberg. With one of the best country museums in South Africa, it's a congenial stop along the N2 between Cape Town and the Garden Route. And because of its ample supply of good accommodation and its position – poised between the coastal De Hoop Nature Reserve and the Langeberg – it's a suitable base for spending a day or two exploring this part of the Overberg, with the **Bontebok National Park**, stomping ground of an attractive type of antelope, close at hand to the south.

South Africa's third-oldest white settlement, Swellendam was established in 1745 by **Baron Gustav van Imhoff**, a visiting Dutch East India Company bigwig. He was deeply concerned about the "moral degeneration" of burghers who were trekking further and further from Cape Town and out of Company control. Of no less concern to the baron was the loss of revenue from these "vagabonds", who were neglecting to pay the company for the right to hold land and were fiddling their annual tax returns. Following a brief hiccup in 1795, when burghers declared a "free republic" (quickly extinguished when Britain occupied the Cape), the town grew into a prosperous rural centre known for its wagon-making, and for being the last "civilized" port of call for trekboers heading out into the interior. The income generated from this helped build Swellendam's gracious homes, many of which went up in smoke in the fire of 1865, which razed much of the town centre.

The town is built along a very long main road with no traffic lights; it's most attractive at either end, with a mundane shopping area in the middle. The eastern end is dominated by the museum complex and tourist information, and is nearest to the mountain reserve for hiking or horseriding. This is also the area where you'll find the backpacker lodge.

Oefeningshuis

36 Voortrek St

The only building in the centre to survive the town's 1865 fire is the Cape Dutch-style **Oefeningshuis**, which now houses the tourist office. Built in 1838, it was first used as a

---

THE BOESMANSKLOOF TRAVERSE

The fourteen-kilometre **Boesmanskloof Traverse** takes you from gentle **Greyton** across the Riviersonderend mountain range to the glaring Karoo scrubland around the town of **McGregor** (see p.227). No direct roads connect the two towns; to drive from one to the other involves a circuitous two-hour journey.

The classic way to cover the Traverse is to walk from Greyton to **Die Galg** (14km from McGregor), where people commonly spend the night, returning the same way to be fit to contend with a lot of strenuous uphill walking. If you're based in Greyton and don't want to do the whole thing, walk to **Oak Falls**, 9km from town, and back. Composed of a series of cascades, it's the highlight of the route, its most impressive feature being a large pool where you can rest and swim in cola-coloured water. You may walk the first 5km of the trail without a permit, but to complete the whole you will need a **permit** (R35/person/day). Over weekends, the trail gets extremely full and permits must be arranged in advance through the Greyton Tourism Bureau.

place for religious activity, then as a school for freed slaves, and has surreal-looking clocks with frozen hands carved into either gable end, below which there's a real clock above the entrance.

Dutch Reformed Church

11 Voortrek St

The unmissable **Dutch Reformed Church**, dating from 1910, incorporates Gothic windows, a Baroque spire, Renaissance portico elements and Cape Dutch gables into a wedding cake of a building that agreeably holds its own, against the odds, and certainly still draws a good crowd on Sundays.

Drostdy Museum

18 Swellegrebel St • Mon–Fri 9am–4.45pm, Sat & Sun 10am–3.45pm • R20

On the east side of town, a short way from the centre, is the excellent **Drostdy Museum**. It's a collection of historic buildings arranged around large grounds, with a lovely nineteenth-century Cape garden. The centrepiece is the *drostdy* itself, built in 1747 as the seat of the *landdrost*, a magistrate-cum-commissioner sent out by the Dutch East India Company to control the outer reaches of its territory. The building conforms to the beautiful limewashed, thatched and shuttered Cape Dutch style of the eighteenth century, but the furnishings are of nineteenth-century vintage. From the rear garden of the *drostdy* you can stroll along a path and across Drostdy Street to **Mayville**, a middle-class Victorian homestead from the mid-nineteenth century with an old rose garden.

16 ARRIVAL AND DEPARTURE · SWELLENDAM

By car Swellendam is a 220km drive from Cape Town, on the N2 from Cape Town.
By bus Coaches run between Cape Town and Port Elizabeth via Swellendam, including the Baz Bus, which pulls in opposite the *Swellengrebel Hotel* in the centre of town. Tickets for coaches can be purchased from Oasis Supermarket across the road.

INFORMATION

Tourist office 22 Swellengrebel St, in one of the museum buildings (Mon–Fri 9am–5pm, Sat & Sun 9am–2pm; ☎ 028 514 2770, ⓦ www.swellendamtourism.co.za). Very switched-on, providing frank and helpful advice about local attractions and can book accommodation.

ACCOMMODATION

Anyone who enjoys the atmosphere of historic houses will be spoilt for choice in Swellendam, where places to stay in Cape Dutch and Georgian houses are ten a penny, and rates tend to be pretty reasonable.

★ **Augusta de Mist** 3 Human St ☎ 028 514 2425, ⓦ augustademist.com. A 200-year-old homestead with three beautifully renovated cottages, two garden suites and a family unit, mostly with fireplaces and all with percale linen, and altogether luxurious and stylish. A rambling terraced garden and a pool complete the picture. There is a good restaurant on site, but you need to book a meal in advance. **R1000**

★ **Cypress Cottage** 3 Voortrek St ☎ 028 514 3296, ⓦ cypress-cottage.co.za. The seven charming rooms here are great value, decorated with antiques in the back garden of a grand house. The house is one of the oldest in town and the friendly owner a brilliant gardener. **R700**

Eenuurkop Huisie 8km from town on the Ashton Rd ☎ 028 514 1447. Two self-catering cottages, one with three bedrooms, the other with one, in a stunning setting with great views and access to mountain walks. **R650**

Hermitage Huisies 3km from town on R60 to Ashton ☎ 028 514 2308 or ☎ 082 380 2080, ⓦ www .wildebraam.co.za Two restored labourers' self-catering

HORSERIDING

If you have never ridden before, you could have a really good time ambling in forests and mountains at the eastern edge of town, securely seated in a western-style saddle. **Two Feathers Horse Trails** (☎ 082 494 8279, ⓦ twofeathers.co.za) offers riding by the hour from R200.

cottages, sleeping four or five people, plus a flatlet for two, on a smallholding with a duck pond and grazing sheep and horses, ideal for families. You'll find a couple more cottages on the farm next door, *Wildebraam* (same contact details). Both are a little more upmarket. If you want to ride, you can arrange in advance to be taken up the mountain, plus there is berry picking in Nov & Dec and a liquor-tasting cellar at *Wildebraam*. **R470**

Klippe Rivier Homestead Signposted off the western end of town ☎028 514 3341, ⓦklipperivier.com. Swellendam's most formal and luxurious accommodation, in a beautiful 1825 Cape Dutch homestead with utterly comfortable country-style bedrooms, downstairs with walled-in herb gardens, or upstairs loft rooms with mountain views. There is also a secluded honeymoon cottage with its own garden; a saltwater swimming pool, gorgeous gardens and fabulous breakfasts included in the price. No under-8s. **R1200**

Lulu's B&B 10 Voortrek St ☎028 514 2202 or ☎082 343 4648. A well-run and centrally located B&B with three en-suite rooms and a self-catering loft apartment (sleeping up to eight people) above. It is the cheapest deal in town, if you are not after an elegant guest house experience. **R400**

Swellendam Backpackers 5 Lichtenstein St ☎028 514 2648 or ☎082 494 8279, ⓦswellendambackpackers .co.za. Swellendam's only hostel is a friendly place, well situated near the Marloth Nature Reserve and museum, with a large campsite, dorms and decent doubles; staff can also arrange activities including horseriding and hiking permits for Marloth. Children are welcome, as there's lots of space, and while this isn't a big party place, there is a bar conveniently on the premises. Camping **R50**, dorms **R90**, doubles **R410**

Swellendam Country Lodge 237 Voortrek St ☎028 514 3629, ⓦswellendamlodge.com. Six garden rooms with separate entrances, reed ceilings and elegant, uncluttered decor in muted hues. There's a veranda for summer days, as well as a swimming pool and well-kept garden. **R920**

EATING

De Kolonie 26 Swellengrebel St. Set in a historic thatched building at the Museum complex, this is a good place to rest your legs and have a salad, sandwich or a traditional Afrikaans-styled dish (R80). Mon–Sat 9am–5pm.

The Old Gaol Coffee Shop Church Square, 8a Voortrek St ☎028 514 3847. A great place with indoor and outdoor seating where you can get milk tart in a copper pan and *roosterkoek*, traditional bread made on an open fire, with nice fillings (R40). Daily 8.30am–5pm.

Pennantwing Café and Gift Shop 5 Swellengrebel,

near the bridge, east end. This café has the best coffee in town with great scones and cakes, combined with the opportunity to browse around unusual, locally-made crafts and art pieces (R50). Daily 8.30am–4.30pm.

Woodpecker Deli Voortrek St, west end ☎028 514 2924. Pizzas, pasta, soups, sandwiches and light meals are on the menu here plus great burgers. This is a good choice if you are in town for one night and don't want a formal or expensive meal (R70). Mon–Sat 9.30am–9pm, Sun 9.30am–3pm.

Bontebok National Park

Daily 7am–7pm, May–Sept till 6pm • R30 • ☎028 514 2735

Just 6km south of Swellendam along the Breede River, **Bontebok National Park** is a compact, 28-square-kilometre reserve at the foot of the Langeberg range that makes a relaxing overnight stop in self-catering cottages, between Cape Town and the Garden Route. The park was established in 1931 to save the Cape's dwindling population of bontebok, an attractive antelope with distinctive cappuccino, chocolate-brown and white markings on its forehead and hindquarters. By 1930, hunting had reduced the number of animals to a mere thirty. Their survival has happily been secured and there are now three hundred of them in the park, as well as populations in other game and nature reserves in the province. There are no big cats in the park, but **mammals** you might encounter include rare Cape mountain zebra, red hartebeest and grey rhebok, and there are more than 120 **bird species**. It's also a rich environment for **fynbos**, with nearly five hundred species here, including erica, gladioli and proteas. Apart from game viewing, there are opportunities to swim in the Breede River, hike a couple of short nature trails and fish.

ACCOMMODATION	BONTEBOK NATIONAL PARK

★ **Bontebok National Park** ☎028 514 2735, ⓦwww.sanparks.org. Self-catering accommodation is available in ten, fully equipped chalets; the best have river

views. There is a campsite with very clean washing facilities – the sites without their own electricity supply are cheaper. Camping **R180**, chalets **R775**

The Garden Route

The Garden Route, a slender stretch of coastal plain on the N2 between Mossel Bay and Storms River Mouth, has a legendary status as South Africa's paradise – reflected in local names such as Garden of Eden and Wilderness. This soft, green, forested swath that stretches nearly 200km is cut by rivers that tumble down from the mountains to the north, tumbling to its southern rocky shores and sandy beaches. The Khoikhoi herders who lived off its natural bounty considered the area a paradise, calling it Outeniqua ("the man laden with honey"). Their Eden was quickly destroyed in the eighteenth century with the arrival of Dutch woodcutters, who had exhausted the forests around Cape Town and set about doing the same in Outeniqua, killing or dispersing the Khoikhoi and San in the process.

17

Birds and animals suffered too from the encroachment of Europeans. In the 1850s, the Swedish naturalist Johan Victorin shot and feasted on the species he had come to study, some of which, including the endangered narina trogon, he noted were both "beautiful and good to eat".

Despite the dense appearance of the area, what you see today are only the remnants of one of Africa's great **forests**; much of the indigenous hardwoods have been replaced by exotic pine plantations, and the only milk and honey you'll find now is in the many shops servicing the Garden Route coastal resorts. **Conservation** has halted the wholesale destruction of the indigenous woodlands, but a huge growth in tourism and the influx of urbanites seeking a quiet life in the relatively crime-free Garden Route towns threaten to rob the area of its remaining tranquillity.

The Garden Route coast is dominated by three inlets – Mossel Bay, the Knysna lagoon and Plettenberg Bay – each with its own town. Oldest of these and closest to Cape Town is **Mossel Bay**, an industrial centre of modest charm, which marks the official start of the Garden Route. **Knysna**, though younger, exudes a well-rooted urban character and is the nicest of the coastal towns, with one major drawback – unlike **Plettenberg Bay**, its eastern neighbour, it has no beach of its own. A major draw, though, is the **Knysna forest** covering some of the hilly country around Knysna.

Between the coastal towns are some ugly modern holiday developments, but also some wonderful empty beaches and tiny coves, such as **Victoria Bay** and **Nature's Valley**. Best of all is the **Tsitsikamma National Park**, which has it all – indigenous forest, dramatic coastline, the pumping **Storms River Mouth** and South Africa's most popular hike, the **Otter Trail**.

Most visitors take the Garden Route as a journey between Cape Town and **Port Elizabeth** (see p.243), dallying for little more than a day or two for shopping, sightseeing or a taste of one of the many adventure sports on offer. The rapid passage cut by the excellent N2 makes it all too easy to have a fast scenic drive – and end up disappointed because you don't see that much from the road. To make the journey worthwhile, you'll need to slow down, take some detours off the highway and explore a little. To avoid having to drive the N2 in both directions, consider flying one of the legs (see p.24) or tackling the interior **Route 62** (see p.227).

GETTING AROUND THE GARDEN

The **Garden Route** is probably the best-served stretch of South Africa for **transport**. If time is tight, you may want to go by **air** to George at the west end of the Garden Route, served by scheduled flights from Cape Town and Port Elizabeth.

BY BUS

Baz Bus Most user-friendly among the public transport options is the daily Baz Bus (see p.24) service between Cape Town and Port Elizabeth (☎021 439 2323, Skype Bazbus Reservations ⓦbazbus.co.za), which picks up passengers daily in Cape Town (7.15–8.30am) and Port Elizabeth (6.45–7.30am). It provides a door-to-door service within the central districts of all the towns along the way, and has the advantage over the large intercity lines that it will happily carry outdoor gear, such as surfboards or mountain bikes. Although the buses take standby passengers if there's space available, you should book ahead to secure a seat.

Intercity buses Intercape, Greyhound and Translux intercity buses (see p.24) from Cape Town and Port Elizabeth are better for more direct journeys, stopping only at Mossel Bay, George, Wilderness, Sedgefield, Knysna and Storms River (the village, but not the Mouth, which is some distance away). These buses often don't go into town, letting passengers off at petrol stations on the highway instead.

Mossel Bay

MOSSEL BAY, a mid-sized town 397km east of Cape Town, gets a bad press from most South Africans, mainly because of the huge industrial facade it presents to the N2. Don't panic – the historic centre is a thoroughly pleasant contrast, set on a hill

17

overlooking the small working harbour and bay, with one of the best **swimming** beaches along the southern Cape coast and an interesting museum. The bay's **sharks** are the principal drawcard for visitors, but it's also a springboard for numerous other adventure activities. The town takes on a strong Afrikaans flavour over Christmas, when Karoo farmers and their families descend in droves to occupy its caravan parks and chalets.

Brief history

Mossel Bay bears poignant historical significance as the place where indigenous Khoi cattle herders first encountered the Europeans in a bloody spat that symbolically set the tone for five hundred years of race relations on the subcontinent. A group of Portuguese mariners under Captain **Bartholomeu Dias** set sail from Portugal in August 1487 in search of a sea route to the riches of India, and months later rounded the Cape of Good Hope. In February 1488, they became the first Europeans to make landfall along the South African coast, when they pulled in for water to the safety of an inlet they called Aguado de So Bras ("watering place of St Blaize"), now Mossel Bay. The Khoikhoi were organized into distinct groups, each under its own chief and each with territorial rights over pastures and water sources. The Portuguese, who were flouting local customs, saw it as "bad manners" when the Khoikhoi tried to drive them off the spring. In a mutual babble of incomprehension the Khoi began

---

GARDEN ROUTE ADVENTURE ACTIVITIES: THE HIGHLIGHTS

The Garden Route is no longer just a place for sun-soaking or communing with nature. Now adrenaline-junkies go expressly to throw themselves off bridges, to gape into the jaws of great white sharks and to freewheel down scary mountain passes. The choice is broad – and widely spread across the entire length of the Garden Route. To help you plan, here are some highlights.

Abseiling Drop down a cliff face at the private Featherbed Nature Reserve (see box, p.206), the entrance to the Knysna lagoon, or along the Kaaimans River gorge in Wilderness (p.198).

Blackwater Tubing Get wet and wild riding the rapids of the Storms River gorge (p.225)

Bungee jumping The world's highest commercial jump is at Bloukrans Bridge (p.217).

Canopy tours and zip-lining Swing from tree to tree in an indigenous forest, 30m above the forest floor, or zing over waterfalls and across a river gorge (see box, p.225)

Hiking There's a terrific circular one-day hike along the edge of the Robberg Peninsula (p.219), with a chance of seeing whales, dolphins and seals. Otherwise, there are quite a few longer and more challenging trails to attempt; see box, p.222.

Horseriding Sit cowboy-style in a deep saddle at *Southern Comfort Western Horse Ranch*, between Knysna and Plettenberg Bay (p.207). Or head out with an English saddle through African countryside near Plettenberg Bay, for *fynbos* and forest trails.

Mountain biking Tear down the hair-raising Swartberg Pass, starting out from Knysna or Oudtshoorn (p.227), or pedal your way in a slightly calmer fashion

round the Homtini Cycle Route in the Knysna forest (p.207).

River boat Go for a leisurely ferry ride down the spectacular Keurbooms River estuary where bird life is in abundance (p.217).

Sandboarding Pit yourself against the "Dragon Dune", the longest runnable stretch of sand in South Africa, just outside Mossel Bay (p.197).

Scenic excursions The Outeniqua Power Van, a diesel-powered, single cab train climbs into the Outeniqua Mountains along the train tracks east of George (p.197). With your own transport, try taking the old road just east of The Crags, winding your way down the fantastically scenic route to Nature's Valley (p.221).

Whale, dolphin and shark encounters Take to the water on a well-informed eco-tour that could encounter a variety of whales and dolphins at Plettenberg Bay (p.216), or enter a shark cage for a first-hand encounter with Jaws at Mossel Bay (p.194).

Wildlife spotting There's family fun in the forest, looking for apes from around the world at Monkeyland (p.220) or avifauna at the adjacent Birds of Eden; or coming face to face with the world's largest land mammal at the Elephant Sanctuary (p.220) and the Knysna Elephant Park (p.211).

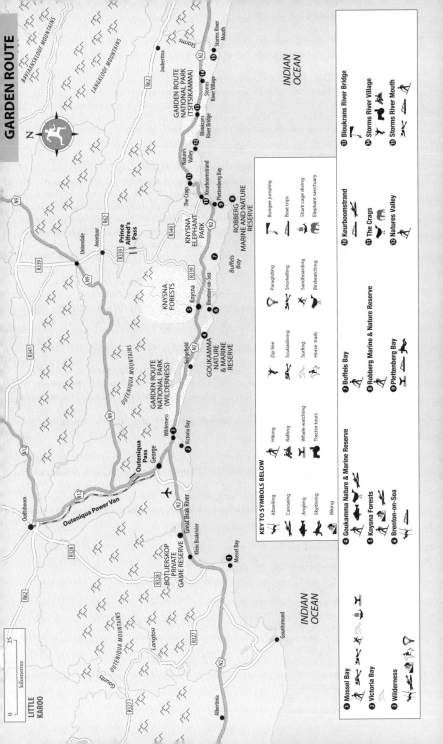

17

stoning the Portuguese, who retaliated with crossbow fire that left one of the herders dead.

Bartholomeu Dias Museum Complex

Mon–Fri 9am–4.45pm, Sat & Sun 9am–3.45pm • R10, entry onto Dias caravel additional R15

Mossel Bay's main urban attraction is the **Bartholomeu Dias Museum Complex**, housed in a collection of historic buildings well integrated into the small town centre, all near the tourist office and within a couple of minutes' walk of each other.

The Maritime Museum

The highlight is the **Maritime Museum**, a spiral gallery with displays on the history of European, principally Portuguese, seafaring, arranged around a full-size replica of Dias' original caravel. The ship was built in Portugal and sailed from Lisbon to Mossel Bay in 1987 to celebrate the five hundredth anniversary of Dias' historic journey. You can't fail to be awed by the idea of the original mariners setting out on the high seas into terra incognita on such a small vessel – particularly as the crew were accommodated above deck with only a sailcloth for protection against the elements.

Post Office Tree

Sixteenth-century mariners used to leave messages for passing ships in an old boot under a milkwood tree somewhere around the designated **Post Office Tree**, just outside the Maritime Museum; the plaque claims that "this may well" be the same tree. You can post mail here in a large, boot-shaped letterbox and have it stamped with a special postmark.

Shell Museum and Aquarium

Of the remaining exhibitions, the **Shell Museum and Aquarium**, next to the Post Office Tree, is the only one worth taking time to visit. This is your chance to see some of the beautiful shells found off the South African coast, as well as shells from around the world. Exhibits include a history of the use of shells by humans and a fascinating display of living shellfish including cowries with their inhabitants still at home.

Santos Beach

A short walk north down the hill from the Maritime Museum gets you to **Santos Beach**, the main town strand, and purportedly the only north-facing beach in South Africa – which gives it exceptionally long sunny afternoons. Adjacent to the small town harbour, the beach provides some of the finest swimming along the Garden

---

FYNBOS

Early Dutch settlers were alarmed by the lack of good timber on the Cape Peninsula's hillsides, which were covered by nondescript, scrubby bush they described as *fijn bosch* (literally "fine bush"), now known by its Afrikaans name **fynbos** (pronounced "fayn-bos"). You'll encounter *fynbos* all over Cape Town and the Garden Route, especially on the mountainsides; despite its rather unpromising grey-green appearance from afar, if you get into the *fynbos* at any time of year (spring and summer are best), you'll encounter countless beautiful little flowering shrubs. *Fynbos* is remarkable for its astonishing variety of plants, its 8500 species making its habitat one of the world's biodiversity hot spots. The Cape Peninsula alone, measuring less than 500 square kilometres, has 2256 plant species (nearly twice as many as Britain, which is 5000 times bigger). The four basic types of *fynbos* plants are **proteas** (South Africa's national flower); **ericas**, amounting to six hundred species of heather; **restios** (reeds); and **geophytes**, including ground orchids and the startling, flaming-red disas, which can be seen in flower on Table Mountain in late summer.

17

Route, with uncharacteristically gentle surf, small waves and a depth perfect for practising your crawl.

The Point
East of the harbour, the coast bulges south towards the **Point**, which has several restaurants and a popular restaurant bar (see p.192) with a deck at the ocean's edge, from which you may see dolphins cruising past along a surreal five-hundred-metre rocky channel known as the aquarium, which is used as a natural **tidal pool**.

St Blaize Lighthouse and Cape St Blaize Cave
A couple of hundred metres to the south of the harbour, atop some cliffs, the **St Blaize Lighthouse**, built in 1864, is still in use as a beacon to ships. Below it, the **Cape St Blaize Cave** is both a marvellous lookout point and a significant archeological site. A boardwalk leads through the cave past three information panels describing the history of the interpretation of the cave as well as the modern understanding of it. In 1801 Sir John Barrow insisted that **shells** found at the site had been brought by seagulls, while others argued that they were relics of human habitation. It turned out that Barrow's opponents were right, but it wasn't till 1888 that excavations uncovered **stone tools** and showed that people had been using the cave for something close on 100,000 years. The path leading up to the cave continues onto the Cape St Blaize trail (see p.194).

ARRIVAL AND GETTING AROUND

MOSSEL BAY

Intercity Bus Greyhound, Intercape and Translux buses stop at Shell Voorbaai Service Station on the N2, 7km from the centre, at the junction of the national highway and the road into town.

Destinations: Cape Town (6–7 daily; 5hr 30min); George (6–7 daily; 45min); Knysna (6–7 daily; 1hr 15min); Oudtshoorn (1–2 daily; 1hr 15min); Plettenberg Bay (6–7

daily; 2hr 15min); Port Elizabeth (6–7 daily; 4hr 30min).

Baz Bus The N2 bypasses Mossel Bay and, of all the buses, only the daily Baz Bus comes right into town, dropping you off at *Mossel Bay Backpackers* and *Park House Lodge*.

Taxi The town itself is small enough to negotiate on foot, but should you need transport, Jordaan runs a **taxi** service (☏ 082 673 7314).

INFORMATION

Tourist office Corner of Church and Market streets (Mon–Fri 8am–6pm, Sat & Sun 9am–4pm; ☏ 044 691 2202, ⓦ visitmosselbay.co.za). Bang in the centre, the tourist

information office has shelves of brochures about Mossel Bay and the rest of the Garden Route, and a map of the town.

ACCOMMODATION

Edward Charles 1 Sixth Ave ☏ 044 691 2152, ⓦ edwardcharles.co.za. An upmarket two-storey guesthouse in a central location overlooking Santos Beach with a swimming pool. There are fifteen en-suite rooms and courtesy shuttle to take you to town if you don't have your own car. R850

Huijs Te Marquette 1 Marsh St ☏ 044 691 3182, ⓦ marquette.co.za. Twelve guest rooms in a very well-run establishment near the Point. The decor is simple but half the suites have doors opening out onto a patio garden and the swimming pool. R760

Mossel Bay Backpackers 1 Marsh St ☏ 044 691 3182, ⓦ mosselbayhostel.co.za. Well-run lodge with squeaky clean rooms, only 300m from the sea and attached to *Huijs Te Marquette* (see above). They also do adventure activity bookings and there's a swimming pool in the garden. Dorms R120, doubles R320

Park House Lodge 121 High St ☏ 044 691 1937, ⓦ parkhouse.co.za. Top-notch budget accommodation in twenty rooms distributed across three buildings, one of which is a beautiful nineteenth-century sandstone manor house. Some rooms have private entrances leading onto the lush garden. Dorms R160, doubles R440

Protea Hotel Mossel Bay Bartholomeu Dias Museum Complex, Market St ☏ 044 691 3738, ⓦ proteahotels.com/mosselbay. Opposite the tourist office, in an old Cape Dutch manor house, this quaint place in the town centre overlooks Santos Bay and the harbour. Breakfast is served at *Café Gannet*, Mossel Bay's nicest restaurant (see p.192). R1100

CAMPING

De Bakke George Rd just back from the beach ☏ 044 691 2915, ⓦ mosselbaymun.co.za. There's camping at

17

this municipal caravan site right next to Santos Beach, in walking distance of the town centre. There are also good one- and two-bedroom self-catering chalets. Camping R65, chalet R390
Point Caravan Park Point Rd ☎ 044 690 3501.

Beautifully situated along the rocky point with views of the sea. Although there's a tidal pool it's not as nice as the bay's main beach for swimming, but it is close to the start of the St Blaize hiking trail. Caravan R170

EATING AND DRINKING

You don't come to Mossel Bay for the food, but there are a number of reasonable places to eat, some of them with superb sea views. The small Point Village shopping development at the north end has a couple of inexpensive to mid-priced family restaurants, opening daily from the morning until 11pm-ish.

Café Gannet Market St ☎ 044 691 1885, ⓦ oldposttree .co.za. Close to the Bartholomeu Dias Museum Complex, Mossel Bay's smartest restaurant does straightforward seafood dishes at a moderate price, served in a stylish garden with glimpses across the harbour; good spot for sundowners (R100). Daily 7am–11pm.
Delfino's Espresso Bar and Pizzeria Point Village ☎ 044 690 5247. Pasta, pizza and steak as well as decent coffee all at reasonable prices, with great views of the sea. Try their scrambled egg and bacon pizza for a breakfast that will set you up for the day (R60). Daily 7am–11pm.
Jazzbury's 11 Marsh St ☎ 044 691 1923,

ⓦ jazzburys.co.za. Traditional South African dishes, such as *bobotie*, Karoo lamb and mixed ostrich grill served with maize meal and sweet potato, at a relaxed venue that's popular with locals. There's seating inside the atmospheric stone building as well as alfresco (R135). Daily 6–11pm.
King Fisher Point Village ☎ 044 690 6390, ⓦ thekingfisher.co.za. A relaxed joint that, as its name suggests, specializes in seafood from humble fish and chips to lobster thermidor and everything in between. There's also a kids' menu. Its position above *Delfino's*, means it has excellent views (R120). Daily 10.30am–5pm & 6–11.30pm.

Robinson Pass to Oudtshoorn

The Eight Bells R1100 • ☎ 044 631 0000, ⓦ eightbells.co.za

Heading inland towards Oudtshoorn from Mossel Bay on the R328 takes you over the forested coastal mountains over the **Robinson Pass** into the desiccated Little Karoo. Close to the top, 35km from Mossel Bay, and a compelling stop for a meal or drink, is the *Eight Bells Mountain Inn*, a firm favourite with well-heeled families wanting a fully catered hotel-style holiday with all sorts of activities laid on for children, and rest time for adults. The atmosphere is friendly and it's superbly run with special meals and meal times for younger children, horseriding, swimming, tennis and walking. Out of school holidays it remains a restful stopoff with lovely gardens and extensive grounds.

Botlierskop Private Game Reserve

About 7km north of Little Brak River • ☎ 044 696 6055, ⓦ botlierskop.co.za

There are no serious Big Five game reserves in the Western Cape and certainly none that can offer anything like you'll get on a safari in the Kruger or a stay in one of the reserves near Port Elizabeth at the eastern end of the Garden Route. Having said that, Botlierskop is probably the best safari you're going to find this close to Cape Town. There's nothing wild about it, but the tented accommodation does work hard at providing the atmosphere and you will mostly (although not always) see lions in their huge enclosure, and there's a good chance of spotting rhinos, elephants, giraffes and antelope too. The whole package is professionally put together and includes a number of activities for both day and overnight visitors.

ACCOMMODATION   BOTLIERSKOP

Accommodation is in a range of tented suites – luxury, deluxe, executive and family – with prices to match the number of bells and whistles laid on. All are decorated in a colonial style and have decks and fabulous views. The price includes full board and high tea with the elephants and two game drives. R2331

17

George

There's little reason to visit **GEORGE**, 66km northeast of Mossel Bay, unless you need what a big centre offers – airport, hospital and shops – and it does lie conveniently halfway between Cape Town and Port Elizabeth. If you're pushed for time, flying here drops you right at the western end of the Garden Route.

MOSSEL BAY ACTIVITIES

The town is also a springboard for other popular **activities**, including skydiving, surfing instruction, sandboarding and deep-sea fishing, all of which can be booked through the Garden Route Adventure Centre at *Mossel Bay Backpackers* (☎044 691 3182, ⓦgardenrouteadventures.com).

DIVING AND SNORKELLING

There are several rewarding diving and snorkelling spots around Mossel Bay, and full facilities, including Open Water certification courses (around R2400) and one-off dives. If you haven't the time or inclination to go the whole hog, you can take a scuba crash course (R500) that allows you to go out on a dive with an instructor. These aren't tropical seas, so don't expect clear warm waters, but with visibility usually between 4m and 10m you stand a good chance of seeing octopus, squid, sea stars, soft corals, pyjama sharks and butterfly fish.

Electro Dive ☎044 690 3402 or ☎082 561 1259, ⓦelectrodive.co.za. This outfit rent out gear and provides shore-based and boat-based dives (R300/340 including kit), and also offers parasailing and jetskiing.

HIKING

On the mainland you can check out the coast on the **St Blaize** hiking trail, an easy fifteen-kilometre walk (roughly 4hr each way; a map is available from the tourist office) along the southern shore of Mossel Bay. The route starts from the Cape St Blaize Cave, just below the lighthouse at the Point, and heads west as far as Dana Bay, taking in magnificent coastal views of cliffs, rocks, bays and coves.

SANDBOARDING AND SURFING

Mossel Bay is one of the best places in the country for sandboarding: the dunes are big, the sand is moist and fine and you pay roughly half what you would in Cape Town.

Billeon Surf and Sandboarding At the Surf Factory in Fields St ☎044 691 3811 or ☎082 97 11 405, ⓦbilleon.com. You can take trips with these guys to the so-called "Dragon Dune", which they claim, at 320m, is the longest runnable stretch of sand in the country. The activity is suitable for all levels, from beginner to extreme – the dune tends to run faster during the winter months. They also offer surfing instruction, and Mossel Bay has a good beach break suitable for novices. All gear is included in the price for both activities (R350/person; group discounts available).

SHARK ENCOUNTERS

Great white sharks are a major reason many visitors come to Mossel Bay, which has one of the southern coast's more reputable **shark-cage diving** operations.

White Shark Africa On the corner of Church and Market sts ☎044 691 3796, ⓦwhitesharkafrica .com. One of the better shark-cage operations in the country, they'll let you watch from a boat or go underwater in a cage for R1300 (R1000 for South Africans). The best months for sightings are March to November, but at no time are encounters guaranteed.

WHALE-WATCHING AND SEAL ISLAND CRUISES

The Romonza Hourly 10am–3pm, peak season 10am–4pm; R120, ☎044 690 3101. Cruises around Seal Island, about 10km northwest of Santos Beach, to see the African penguin and seal colonies can be taken on the *Romonza*, a medium-sized yacht that launches from the yacht marina in the harbour. The *Romonza* is also the only registered vessel allowed to run boat-based whale-watching cruises (R600; 2–3 hr) in Mossel Bay. As elsewhere along this coast, the whale season is variable with southern rights appearing from June till late October. If you're extremely lucky, you may also see a humpback whale.

A large inland town, George is a five-kilometre detour northwest off the N2, and 9km from the nearest stretch of ocean at Victoria Bay. Sadly, all that's left of the forests and quaint character that moved Anthony Trollope, during a visit in 1877, to describe it as the "prettiest village on the face of the earth" are some historic buildings.

17

The Dutch Reformed Church
Davidson St
The most notable of the historic buildings is the beautiful **Dutch Reformed Church**, at the top end of Meade Street. Completed in the early 1840s, the church is definitely worth a stop if you happen to be passing through, with its elegantly simple classical facade, Greek-cross plan with an impressive centrally placed pulpit and wonderful domed ceiling, panelled with glowing yellowwood.

St Mark's Cathedral
Cathedral St
St Mark's Cathedral, consecrated in 1850, is also worth seeing, but unlike the Dutch

---

PRESIDENT BOTHA AND APARTHEID'S LAST STAND

Pieter Willem Botha believed that by setting up a powerful "Imperial Presidency" in South Africa he could withstand the inevitable tide of democracy. A National Party hack from the age of 20, Botha worked his way up through the ranks, getting elected as an MP in 1948 when the first apartheid government took power. He was promoted through various cabinet posts until he became **Minister of Defence**, a position he used to launch a palace coup in 1978 against his colleague, Prime Minister John Vorster. Botha immediately set about modernizing apartheid, modifying his own role from that of a British-style prime minister, answerable to parliament, to one of an executive president taking vital decisions in the secrecy of a President's Council heavily weighted with army top brass.

Informed by the army that the battle to preserve the apartheid status quo was unwinnable purely by force, Botha embarked on his **Total Strategy**, which involved reforms to peripheral aspects of apartheid and the fostering of a black middle class as a buffer against the ANC, while pumping vast sums of money into building an enormous military machine that crossed South Africa's borders to bully or crush neighbouring countries harbouring groups opposed to apartheid. South African refugees in Botswana and Zimbabwe were bombed, Angola was invaded, and arms were run to anti-government rebels in Mozambique, reducing it to ruins – a policy that has returned to haunt South Africa with those same weapons now returning across the border and finding their way into the hands of criminals. Inside South Africa, security forces enjoyed a free hand to murder, maim and torture **opponents of apartheid**.

Botha's intransigence led to his greatest blunder in 1985, when he responded to international calls for change by hinting that he would announce significant reforms at his party congress that would irreversibly jettison apartheid. In the event, the so-called **Rubicon speech** was a disaster, as Botha proved to have insufficient steel to resist pressure from white right-wing extremists. The speech shrank away from meaningful concessions to black South Africans, the immediate result of which was a flight of capital from the country and intensified sanctions. Perhaps worst of all for the apartheid regime, the **Chase Manhattan Bank** refused to roll over its massive loan to South Africa, leaving the country an uncreditworthy pariah.

Botha blustered and wagged his finger at the opposition through the late 1980s, while his bloated military sucked the state coffers dry as it prosecuted its dirty wars. Even National Party stalwarts realized that his policies were leading to ruin, and in 1989, when he suffered a stroke, the party was quick to replace him with **F.W. de Klerk**, who immediately proceeded to announce reforms.

Botha lived out his unrepentant retirement near George, declining ever to apologize for any of the brutal actions taken under his presidency to bolster apartheid. Curiously, when he died in 2006, he was given an uncritical, high-profile state funeral, broadcast on national television and attended by members of the government, including then-president, Thabo Mbeki.

17

ACTIVITIES IN BOTLIERSKOP

Overnight visitors who stay for two nights can swap a game drive for a horseride; and if you stay three nights you can have a helicopter flip as one of your activities. Over and above this, activities are charged for and are also available to **day visitors**; these include game drives (R395); **elephant-back rides** (R550); **horserides** (R200 an hour); and **helicopter flips** (R280).

Reformed Church, which is open to the public, it can only be visited by appointment. Ask at the tourist office for bookings (see below).

ARRIVAL AND INFORMATION

GEORGE

By air Kulula, 1Time and SAA each fly between Johannesburg and the small George airport, 10km west of town on the N2, at least once daily (1hr 50min). SAA also flies here at least once a day from Cape Town (50min). Most tourists flying in rent a car from one of the rental companies here and set off down the Garden Route.

Intercity buses Intercape, Translux and Greyhound intercity buses pull in at George station, adjacent to the railway museum.

Destinations: Cape Town (6–7 daily; 6hr); Knysna (6–7 daily; 1hr); Mossel Bay (6–7 daily; 45min); Oudtshoorn (3–4 daily; 1hr 30min); Plettenberg Bay (6–7 daily; 1hr 30min); Port Elizabeth (6–7 daily; 4hr 30min).

Baz Bus drops off at *Outeniqua Backpackers* on Merriman Street on its daily run between Cape Town and Port Elizabeth.

INFORMATION

Tourist office 124 York St (Mon–Fri 7.45am–4.30pm, Sat 9am–1pm; ☎044 801 9295, ⓦ visitgeorge.co.za). The George tourist office can provide town maps and help with accommodation bookings.

ACCOMMODATION

10 Caledon Street 10 Caledon St ☎044 873 4983, ⓦ 10caledon.co.za. The pick of the mid-priced B&Bs, in a spotless guesthouse in a quiet street, featuring balconies with mountain views and a garden. The owners are superb hosts and prive an excellent breakfast. The B&B is an easy walk to the city centre. **R800**

Die Waenhuis 11 Caledon St ☎044 874 0034, ⓦ www .diewaenhuis.co.za. Mid-nineteenth-century home that has retained its period character with eleven spacious en-suite rooms, a beautiful garden and gracious hosts. English breakfasts, included in the price, are served in a sunlit dining room. **R700**

Fairview Historic Homestead 36 Stander St ☎082 226 9466, ⓦ fairviewhomestead.com. Stately Cape Georgian homestead with five B&B rooms filled with lovely Victoriana and set in extensive, beautiful formal gardens. Despite the obvious attention to detail, there's nothing

precious about this welcoming, child-friendly establishment. **R650**

Mount View Resort & Lifestyle Village York St ☎044 874 5205, ⓦ mountviewsa.co.za. Modern complex that lacks much character, but offers great value in its one-, two- and three-bedroom chalets and rondavels. The gardens are well-kept and pleasant and the complex also houses a wellness and beauty salon, a ten-pin bowling alley and a pool hall. **R390**

Outeniqua Backpackers 115 Merriman St ☎082 316 7720, ⓦ outeniqua-backpackers.com. Friendly hostel in a bright and airy suburban house with comfortable dorms and doubles, some with mountain views. There's a swimming pool, they rent out bikes and provide free airport pick-ups. The Baz Bus pulls in here. Dorms **R120**, doubles **R400**

EATING AND DRINKING

Het Vijfde Seizoen 3 Maitland St ☎044 870 7320. Belgian-influenced international-fusion cuisine with some traditional South African touches at a cosy restaurant attached to a guesthouse. Dishes include Flemish-style mussel pot, Moroccan lamb shanks on a bed of couscous and Cape Malay lamb pot (R85). Mon 8–10am, Tues–Sat 8–10am, noon–3pm & 6.30pm till late. Sun (booking essential) noon–3pm.

Kafe Serefe 60 Courtenay St ☎044 884 1012. Hugely popular venue that does South African cuisine which, like

the belly dancing on Wednesday and Friday nights, comes with a Turkish twist. Meat is the speciality, whether oven-roasted lamb in a red wine sauce or pork with goat's cheese and a brandy fig sauce. There's also a good choice of mezze, if you're after something lighter (R80). Mon 10am–4.30pm, Tues–Fri 10am–4.30pm & 7pm till late, Sat 10.30am–2.30pm.

La Capannina 122 York St ☎044 874 5313. Italian restaurant that in addition to excellent pizzas and pasta, has other tricks up its sleeve such as beef fillet on a bed of polenta and distinctly un-Italian fare such as ostrich jambalaya with a hint of curry (R80). Mon–Fri noon–2pm & 6–10pm, Sun 6–10pm.

The Old Town House Corner of York and Market sts ☎044 874 3663. Lovely ambience in this original town house, which specializes in venison and beef and where the food is well cooked with attention to detail in an intimate setting. Despite the place's carnivorous inclination,

vegetarians are catered for (R90). Mon–Fri 12.30–3pm & Mon–Sat 6–10pm.

Zanzibar Sports Café Corner of York and Courtenay sts. Next to the museum, in two old railway carriages, *Zanzibar's* big screen, Sunday deck parties, Monday metal nights – and of course lashings of the amber nectar – makes it a popular spot for some action. Mon–Sat 11am till late.

17

Victoria Bay

Some 9km south of George and 3km off the N2 lies the minuscule hamlet of **VICTORIA BAY**, on the edge of a small sandy beach wedged into a cove between cliffs, with a grassy sunbathing area, safe swimming and a tidal pool. During the December holidays it packs out with day-trippers, and rates as one of the top **surfing** spots in South Africa. Because of the cliffs, there's only a single row of buildings along the beachfront, with some of the most dreamily positioned guesthouses along the coast (and therefore some of the priciest for what you get).

ARRIVAL AND DEPARTURE   VICTORIA BAY

By car Arriving by car, you'll encounter a metal barrier as you drop down the hill to the bay, and you'll have to try and park in a car park that's frequently full (especially in summer). If you're staying at one of the B&Bs, leave your

car at the barrier and collect the key from your lodgings to gain access to the private beach road.

By bus The daily Baz Bus, which provides the only transport to Victoria Bay, drops passengers at the *Vic Bay Surf Lodge*.

ACCOMMODATION

Land's End Guest House The Point, Beach Rd ☎044 889 0123, ⒲www.vicbay.com. En-suite rooms in what claims to be "the closest B&B to the sea in Africa", as well as self-catering accommodation a few doors away at *Bay House*, which sleeps four and *Sea Cottage*, which sleeps five. R1035

Sea Breeze Holiday Resort Along the main road into the settlement ☎044 889 0098, ⒲seabreezecabanas .co.za. A variety of budget self-catering units, including

modern two-storey holiday huts and wooden chalets, sleeping two, four or eight people. The huts have no sea views, but it's an easy stroll to the beach. R750

Victoria Bay Surf Lodge Behind the restaurant as you arrive in Vic Bay, 80 seconds from the beach ☎072 593 1741, ⒲vicbaysurflodge.com. Former municipal workers' accommodation transformed into a squeaky clean backpacker lodge that sleeps up to 26 in dorms or private rooms (only available off-peak). They also run the adjacent

---

THE OUTENIQUA POWER VAN

Sadly South Africa's main-line railways are slowly dying. Sad, because the iron road passed through some of the most beautiful, and otherwise most inaccessible, parts of the country. The Garden Route's train line, for one, penetrated some of the region's most impenetrable and visually stunning back country making the Cape Town to Port Elizabeth run one of the great railway journeys of the world. That ended when some of the tracks were washed away and never replaced. Until 2010, you could still travel on the tourist Outeniqua Choo-Tjoe steam train that chugged between George and Mossel Bay. That too has gone – wiped away by government bean counters, who regard it as financially unviable.

Fortunately you can still get a taster of the line on the **Outeniqua Power Van**, a single cab diesel-powered train that trails into the Outeniqua Mountains just outside George. The train stops at a scenic site for picnic before returning to the town. En route you pass through forest, negotiate passes and tunnels and will see waterfalls, *fynbos* and (if you're lucky) wildlife.

BOOKING

The train departs from the Outeniqua Transport Museum, 2 Mission Rd, George (☎082 490 5627, ⒠opv@mweb.co.za; Mon–Sat on demand – booking essential; R100) and the trip takes two and a half hours. Bring refreshments, picnic lunch, sunglasses, a hat and a warm jacket.

17

Lank Small Surf Shop, which rents out all the gear you might need to make the most of the water: surfboards, bodyboards, wet suits, snorkelling kit and fishing equipment. Dorms R120, doubles R300

The Waves 6 Beach Rd ☎ 044 889 0166, ⓦ www .thewavesvictoriabay.co.za. Three comfortable and pleasantly furnished B&B suites, all with sea views and opening onto a patio, in a high-ceilinged Victorian house, as well as three self-catering units, which come with stoves, microwaves and fridges. R1500

EATING

The only places to buy **food** are a small beachside kiosk (selling light refreshments) and a restaurant, which delivers to a tee just what a casual beach café ought to: a relaxed atmosphere that feels right in flip-flops and shorts and an unpretentious menu covering standards such as toasted sandwiches, fish and chips and burgers. If you're up for something more exotic and don't want to cook, the resort's B&Bs are served by Mr Delivery, a company that will collect from about ten fast-food joints in George and will also fetch groceries and even DVDs.

Wilderness

East of Victoria Bay, across the Kaaimans River, the beach at **WILDERNESS** is so close to the N2 that you can pull over for a quick dip with barely an interruption to your journey, though African wilderness is the last thing you'll find here. Wilderness village earned its name, so the story goes, after a young man called Van den Berg bought the property in 1830 for £183 as a blind lot at a Cape Town auction. When he got engaged, his fiancée insisted that their first year of marriage should be spent out of town in the wilderness, so he romantically (or perhaps opportunistically) named his property Wilderness and built a hut on it.

If the hut still exists, you'll struggle to find it among the sprawl of retirement homes, holiday houses and thousands of beds for rent in the vicinity. The beach, which is renowned for its long stretch of sand, is backed by tall dunes, rudely blighted by holiday houses. Once in the water, stay close to the shoreline: this part of the coast is notorious for its unpredictable currents.

INFORMATION
WILDERNESS

Wilderness's tiny village centre, on the north side of the N2, has a **petrol station**, a few shops, restaurants and a **tourist office** in Milkwood Village Mall, Beacon Road, off the N2 opposite the Caltex Garage (Mon–Fri 7.45am–4.30pm, Sat 9am–1pm; ☎ 044 877 0045, ⓦ george.org.za).

ACCOMMODATION

The Albatross Sixth Ave, take South St exit off the N2 ☎ 044 877 1716. A B&B in an elevated position that gives it great views and makes for perfect dolphin-watching from its balconies. Of the three colour-coordinated rooms (pink, blue and ocean) only one has sea views. It's an easy walk to the beach down a boardwalk. R600

Fairy Knowe Backpackers 6km from the village, follow signs from the N2 east of Wilderness ☎ 044 877 1285, ⓦ wildernessbackpackers.com. The oldest home (built 1897) in the area, with a wraparound balcony and set in the quiet woodlands near the Touws River, though nowhere near the sea. The Baz Bus drops off here. Dorms R100, doubles R300

Island Lake Holiday Resort Lakes Rd, 2km from the Hoekwil/Island Lake turn-off on the N2 ☎ 044 877 1194, ⓦ islandlake.co.za. Camping and self-catering rondavels that sleep four on one of the quietest and prettiest spots on the lakes. The rondavels are basic one-room affairs with kitchenettes equipped with hotplates, microwaves and utensils, but you share communal washing and toilet facilities. Camping R185, rondavel R370

Mes-Amis Homestead Buxton Close, signposted off the N2 on the coastal side of the road, directly opposite the national park turn-off ☎ 044 877 1928, ⓦ mesamis.co.za. Nine double rooms, each of which has its own terrace, offering some of the best views in Wilderness. Rooms are elegantly furnished with crisp white bedding and curtains and there are luxurious touches such as bathrobes and espresso machines in each room. R1300

The Tops Hunts Lane, on a hill about 500m from the tourist office ☎ 044 877 0187 or ☎ 083 631 2339, ⓦ thetops.co.za. A hotel comprising four airy en-suite bedrooms (that have breakfast included in the price), three of which have sea views and French doors opening

RIGHT TSITSIKAMMA NATIONAL PARK (P.221) >

17

ACTIVITIES IN WILDERNESS

Black Horse Trails Contact Lindsay ☎ 082 494 5642, ⓦ blackhorsetrails.co.za. Runs mountain and forest horseriding tours (R250 for 90min or R390 for 3hr).
Cloudbase Paragliding Adventures ☎ 044 877 1414, ⓦ cloudbase-paragliding.co.za. To see it all from the air, sign up the a recommended tandem paragliding jump that starts from R450 for a minimum of fifteen minutes. You'll only be taken up when the weather offers absolutely safe conditions. They also offer a one-day introductory course for R950.
Eden Adventures ☎ 044 877 0179 or ☎ 083 628 8547, ⓦ eden.co.za. Offers daily kloofing adventures (8am–1pm, R475) and abseiling (1.30–4.30pm, R365); a full day taking in both activities costs R750. Explore the river yourself by renting a two-seater canoe from them (R70/hr).

onto a deck, as well as four self-catering studio flats (R900). **R650**
Wilderness Bush Camp Heights Rd (follow Waterside Rd west for 1600m up the hill) ☎ 044 877 1168, ⓦ boskamp.co.za. Six self-catering timber units with loft bedrooms, thatched roofs and ocean views. The camp, set on a hillside amidst *fynbos* wilderness, is part of a conservation estate that you're free to roam around. **R300**

EATING

The Girls George Rd ☎ 044 877 1648, ⓦ thegirlsrestaurant.co.za. Deservedly one of the most popular restaurants in the village fuses classic French fare, such as steak tartare, with North African flavours and Middle Eastern dishes. The prawns are fantastic, they do a mean steak and vegetarians get a decent look in (R140). Tues–Sun 6pm till late.
Palms 3km from town at The Palms Wilderness Guest House, Owen Grant Rd ☎ 044 877 1420, ⓦ palms-wilderness.com. A moderately priced changing four-course set menu with a limited choice that focuses on game and fish. Seating is either indoors under thatch or alfresco under umbrellas. Mon–Sat 7–9pm.
Pomodoro Corner of George and Layla rds ☎ 044 877 1403. Good pastas and pizzas are among the Italian standards at this trattoria that's a popular family venue with a pleasant ambience. For something more substantial try the lamb shanks slow roasted in the pizza oven (R75). Daily 7.30am–10.30pm.
Wilderness Grille George Rd. A casual venue offering an informal something that might include smoked salmon omelette, pizza or steak. Seating outside under parasols or, in winter, indoors by the fire. A good spot for breakfast (R70). Daily 8am–11pm.

Garden Route National Park: Wilderness Section

Reception open 24hr • ☎ 044 877 0046 • R80

Stretching east from Wilderness village is the **Wilderness Section of the Garden Route National Park**, an inappropriate name, as it never feels very far from the N2. It's the **forests** you should come for, and the 16km of inland waterways; the variety of habitats here includes coastal and montane *fynbos* and wetlands, attracting 250 species of **birds** – as well as many holiday-makers.

ACCOMMODATION
WILDERNESS SECTION

There are two **restcamps**, *Ebb and Flow North*, and *Ebb and Flow South*, both on the west side of the park and clearly signposted off the N2.

Ebb and Flow North right on the river, is cheap, old-fashioned and away from the hustle. It offers camping, fully equipped two-person bungalows with their own showers, and ones with communal washing and toilet facilities. **R280**

Ebb and Flow South has camping and modern accommodation in spacious log cottages on stilts and brick bungalows for up to four people. There are also en-suite forest huts with communal kitchens for two people. **R540**

ACTIVITIES

Canoeing You can also navigate the Touw River from the restcamp down to the beach in a canoe, which can be hired from Eden Adventures (see box above).
Hiking There are five waymarked trails in the Wilderness Section of between two and five kilometres. A map of the trails, which also shows the location of three bird hides, is available at reception or you can download it from the SANParks website (ⓦ sanparks.org).

Sedgefield

17

The drive between Wilderness and Sedgefield gives glimpses on your left of dark-coloured lakes which eventually surge out to sea, 21km later, through a wide lagoon at **SEDGEFIELD** a pleasantly old-fashioned holiday village – one of the last of its kind along the Garden Route – a few kilometres off the road, with miles of beautiful beaches. In fact so proud is Sedgefield of its lack of pizzazz, that the village has had itself registered as a "slow town", affiliated to the Cittaslow towns of Italy with its emblem a tortoise.

The entertainment highlight of Sedgefield's week is the **Wild Oats Community Farmers' Market** (Sat 8–11.30am), along the N2 on the west side of town, just before Swartvlei lake, where you can pick up groceries and tasty nosh, such as preserves, cheeses, pickles and cured meats as well delectable takeaway finger foods.

Sedgefield can be used as a base from which to explore Goukamma Nature and Marine Reserve and the western extent of Groenvlei, a freshwater lake that falls within the reserve's boundaries.

ARRIVAL AND DEPARTURE

SEDGEFIELD

Intercity buses Greyhound, Intercape and Translux buses stop in the middle of the village at the Sedgefield Garage, Main Road, a service road running parallel to the N2, which passes through the town's shopping area.

Destinations: Cape Town (6–7 daily; 8hr); Knysna (6–7 daily; 20 min); Mossel Bay (6–7 daily; 40min); Plettenberg Bay (6–7 daily; 50min); Port Elizabeth (6–7 daily; 4hr); Storms River Bridge (6–7 daily; 2hr).

ACCOMMODATION

Coral Reef Guesthouse 28 Coral Reef Crescent, Cola Beach, Sedgefield ☎ 044 343 3133, ⓦ coralreef.co.za. Two double rooms, a triple and a family unit, all brightly decorated, two minutes' walk from the beach. Some rooms have balconies with views of the ocean across the dunes. There's a saltwater pool and a comfortable chill-out area. R700

Ganzvlei Cottage 12km east of Sedgefield along the N2 ☎ 083 373 3880, ⓔ cmeterlerkamp@ganzvlei.co.za. Exceptional rustic retreat in a hundred-year-old cottage on Ganzvlei dairy farm. The cottage is effectively on an island, cut off on three sides from the rest of the property by the oxbowing Goukamma River, and on the fourth by massive dunes that abut the Goukamma Nature Reserve (see p.202). There's no electricity – lighting is by paraffin lamps and generator, and cooking is on a wood stove – and transport to the cottage is via a pont across the water. The

cottage has three bedrooms, sleeps six and must be taken for a minimum of three nights. R500

★ **Teniqua Treetops** 23km northeast of Sedgefield ☎ 044 356 2868, ⓦ teniquatreetops.co.za. This is a genuinely unique and romantic retreat among the boughs of virgin forest between Sedgefield and Knysna, a patch including four kilometres of woodland walks and a river with pools for swimming. Luxury tents are raised on timber decks, where, if you feel so inclined, you can leave the flaps open and wake up to dappled light filtering through the leaves; one unit is wheelchair accessible. Apart from being a chilled-out hideout, this is a fascinating example of sustainable living in practice: not a single tree was felled to build *Teniqua*; recycled materials were used where possible; water is gravity fed; showers are solar-heated; and toilets use a dry composting system that preserves precious water. R1045

ACTIVITIES IN GOUKAMMA

Apart from angling and birdwatching, the Goukamma offers a number of self-guided activities, including safe **swimming** in Groenvlei.

There are several day-long hiking trails that enable you to explore different habitats. A **beach walk**, which takes around four hours one way, traverses the 14km of crumbling cliffs and sands between the Platbank car park on the western side of the reserve and the Rowwehoek one on the eastern side. Alternatively, you can go from one end of the reserve to the other via a slightly longer **inland trek** across the dunes. There's also a shorter circular walk from the reserve office through a milkwood forest.

You can **canoe** on the Goukamma River on the eastern side of the reserve; a limited number of **canoes** can be hired from the office during the week or at the gate over the weekend. Single/double canoes R60/100 a day.

17 ## Goukamma Nature Reserve
Daily 8am–6pm • R30, overnight visitors no extra charge • ☎ 044 383 0042

An unassuming sanctuary of around 220 square kilometres, Goukamma ranges from near Sedgefield and stretches east to Buffalo Bay (also known as Buffels Bay) to take in Groenvlei lake and approximately 18km of beach frontage, some of the highest vegetated dunes in the country, and walking country covered with coastal *fynbos* and dense thickets of milkwood, yellowwood and candlewood trees.

The area has long been popular with anglers. Away from the water, you stand a small chance of spotting one of the area's **mammals**, including bushbuck, grysbok, mongoose, vervet monkeys, caracals and otters. Because of the diversity of coastal and wetland habitats, over 220 different kinds of **birds** have been recorded here, including fish eagles, Knysna louries, kingfishers and very rare African black oystercatchers. Offshore, southern right whales often make an appearance during their August to December breeding season, and bottlenose and common dolphins can show up at any time of year.

ARRIVAL AND DEPARTURE   GOUKAMMA

Two roads off the N2 provide access to the reserve. The entrance and office are on the Buffalo Bay side accessed via the **Buffalo Bay** road, halfway along which is the reserve office. There are no public roads within the reserve. At the westernmost side, a dirt road that runs down to Platbank Beach takes you past the tiny settlement of **Lake Pleasant** on the south bank of Groenvlei, which consists of little more than a hotel and holiday resort.

ACCOMMODATION

There are two fully equipped bush camps on the Groenvlei side of the reserve and three thatched rondavels on the east side. Book through CapeNature (🖥 capenature.co.za). Over weekends, expect to pay roughly 25 percent more than prices quoted.

Groenvlei Timber bush camp set in a milkwood forest with two double-storey sleeping units, each with two bedrooms, one with a double and the other two single beds. A walkway leads to a jetty where two double canoes are moored for guests' use. R580

Mvubu Thatched timber and reed bush camp on stilts at the edge of Groenvlei in a stand of milkwood trees. There are two en-suite bedrooms, both of which have doors opening onto a deck that overlooks the lake. Up to four people R670

Rondavels Three basic double units at the Buffalo Bay side of the reserve that sleep four to five people. Each has a double bed and single or bunk beds and the rondavels overlook the river and estuary. R280

Knysna

South Africa's 1990s tourist boom rudely shook **KNYSNA** (pronounced "Nize-na") from its gentle backwoods drowse, which for decades had made it the hippy and craftwork capital and quiet retirement village of the country. The town, 102km east of Mossel Bay, now stands at the hub of the Garden Route, its lack of ocean beaches compensated for by its hilly setting around the **Knysna lagoon**, its handsome **forests**, good opportunities for **adventure sports**, a pleasant **waterfront development** – and some hot marketing.

Knysna's distinctive atmosphere derives from its small historic core of Georgian and Victorian buildings, which gives it a character absent from most of the Garden Route holiday towns. Coffee shops, craft galleries, street traders and a modest nightlife add to the attractions, and you may find yourself tempted to stay longer than just one night. That the town has outgrown itself is evident from the cars and tour buses that, especially in December and January, clog Main Street, the constricted artery that merges with the N2 as it enters the town.

Knysna wraps around the lagoon, with its oldest part – the town centre – on the northern side. The lagoon's narrow mouth is guarded by a pair of steep rocky promontories called **The Heads**, the western side being a private nature reserve and the eastern one an exclusive residential area (confusingly, it's also called The Heads), along dramatic cliffs above the Indian Ocean.

17

Main Street, which used to be the hub of Knysna, lost some of its status as the heart of the town with the development of the waterfront area. But it has begun fighting back, with extensive redevelopment that has brought with it trendy coffee shops, restaurants and shops.

Brief history

At the beginning of the nineteenth century, the only white settlements outside Cape Town were a handful of villages that would have considered themselves lucky to have even one horse. Knysna, an undeveloped backwater hidden in the forest, was no exception. The name comes from a Khoi word meaning "hard to reach", and this remained its defining character well into the twentieth century. One important figure was not deterred by the distance – **George Rex**, a colourful colonial administrator who placed himself beyond the pale of decent colonial society by taking a coloured mistress. Shunned by his peers in Britain, he headed for Knysna at the turn of the nineteenth century in the hope of making a killing shipping out hardwood from the lagoon.

By the time of Rex's death in 1839, Knysna had become a major **timber centre**, attracting white labourers who felled trees with primitive tools for miserly payments, and looked set eventually to destroy the forest. In 1872, **Prince Alfred**, on his visit to the Cape, made his small royal contribution to this destruction when he took a special detour here to hunt elephants. The forest only narrowly escaped devastation by far-sighted and effective conservation policies introduced in the 1880s.

By the turn of the twentieth century, Knysna was still remote, and its forests were inhabited by isolated and inbred communities made up of the impoverished descendants of the woodcutters. As late as 1914, if you travelled from Knysna

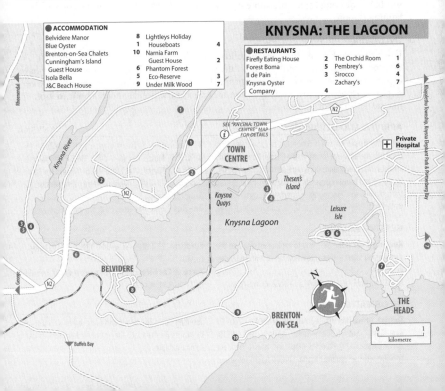

KNYSNA: THE LAGOON

● ACCOMMODATION

Belvidere Manor	8	Lightleys Holiday	
Blue Oyster	1	Houseboats	4
Brenton-on-Sea Chalets	10	Narnia Farm	
Cunningham's Island		Guest House	2
Guest House	6	Phantom Forest	
Isola Bella	5	Eco-Reserve	3
J&C Beach House	9	Under Milk Wood	7

● RESTAURANTS

Firefly Eating House	2	The Orchid Room	1
Forest Boma	5	Pembrey's	6
Il de Pain	3	Sirocco	4
Knysna Oyster		Zachary's	7
Company	4		

N2

Rheenendal

Knysna River

George

N2

N2

TOWN CENTRE

SEE "KNYSNA: TOWN CENTRE" MAP FOR DETAILS

Knysna Quays

Thesen's Island

Knysna Lagoon

Leisure Isle

BELVIDERE

BRENTON-ON-SEA

Buffels Bay

THE HEADS

Private Hospital

Khayalethu Township, Knysna Elephant Park & Plettenberg Bay

0   1
kilometre

17

TOWNSHIP TOURS AND HOMESTAYS

Get a taste of Knysna's townships by joining one of the warts-and-all tours operated by **Eco Afrika**. Tours go to five areas, where you'll be given some historical background and get a chance to walk around and chat to people. You can also include lunch with a township family as part of the package (an additional R50 paid directly to your hosts). Tours daily 9.30am & 2pm; R350; booking essential (☎082 558 9104).

Eco Afrika also arrange **homestays** in one of the shanty towns within the townships, where you stay with a family in a corrugated iron shack (R150 paid to your hosts). The tour operator will drop you off and pick you up the next morning.

---

to George you would have to open and close 58 gates along the 75-kilometre track. Fifteen years on, the passes in the region proved too much for **George Bernard Shaw**, who did some impromptu off-road driving and crashed into a bush, forcing Mrs Shaw to spend a couple of weeks in bed at Knysna's *Royal Hotel* with a broken leg.

Knysna Quays and Thesen's Island
About 500m south of Knysna Tourism, at the end of Grey St

The **Knysna Quays** are the town's waterfront complex and yacht basin. Built at the end of the 1990s, this elegant two-storey steel structure with timber boardwalks resembles a tiny version of Cape Town's V&A Waterfront. Here you'll find a mix of hotels, clothes and knick-knack shops and a couple of good eating places, some with outdoor decks, from which you can watch yachts drift past.

Riding on the success of the Quays, **Thesen's Island**, reached by a causeway at the south end of Long Street, has some stylish shops and places to eat, on the edge of the lapping lagoon.

The beaches

Don't come to Knysna for a beach holiday: the closest beach is 20km from town at **Brenton-on-Sea**. A tiny settlement on the shores of Buffels Bay, it does admittedly have a quite exceptional beach. In the opposite direction from Knysna, the closest patch of sand is at **Noetzie**, a town known more for its eccentric holiday homes built to look like castles than for its seaside.

ARRIVAL AND DEPARTURE   **KNYSNA**

Intercity buses Knysna is connected to Cape Town, Port Elizabeth and all major towns on the Garden Route by daily services on Greyhound, Intercape and Translux buses. Intercape and Translux buses drop passengers off at the old train station in Remembrance Avenue opposite Knysna waterfront; Greyhound stops at the Toyota Garage, 9 Main Rd. **Destinations** between Knysna and: Cape Town (6–7 daily; 8hr); Mossel Bay (6–7 daily; 1hr); Plettenberg Bay (6–7 daily; 30min); Port Elizabeth (6–7 daily; 3hr 30min); Sedgefield (6–7daily; 30min) Storms River Bridge (6–7 daily; 1hr 30min).

Baz Bus The Baz Bus drops off at *Knysna Backpackers*.

GETTING AROUND

Renting a car is the best way to explore Knysna and the surrounding forest – there are a number of rental agencies in town.

Avis Long and Fichat sts ☎044 382 2222, ⓦavis.co.za.

Europcar 23 Trotter St ☎044 382 2733, ⓦeuropcar. co.za.

Tortoise Car Hire, 23 Uil St, Sedgefield ☎044 343 2991, ⓦtortoisecarhire.co.za.

INFORMATION

Tourist office Knysna Tourism, 40 Main St (Mon–Fri 8am–5pm, Sat 8.30am–1pm; ☎044 382 5510, ⓦvisitknysna.co.za) Provides maps and runs a desk for booking activities around Knysna – including cruises to and abseiling down The Heads and bungee jumping from the Bloukrans River Bridge. They can also help with booking accommodation.

17

ACCOMMODATION

The best places to stay in Knysna are away from the main road, with views of the lagoon and The Heads. Out of town there are some excellent establishments as well as reasonably priced self-catering cottages right in the forest. For somewhere quieter on the lagoon, make for the western edge at Brenton-on-Sea.

TOWN CENTRE AND KNYSNA QUAYS

Knysna Backpackers 42 Queen St ☎ 044 382 2554, ⓦ knysnabackpackers.co.za; map p.205. Spotless, well-organized hostel in a large, rambling and centrally located Victorian house that has been declared a National Monument. This tranquil establishment has five rooms rented as doubles (but able to sleep up to four people) and a dorm that sleeps eight. Dorms R90, doubles R280

Protea Hotel – Knysna Quays Waterfront Drive ☎ 044 382 5005, ⓦ proteahotels.com; map p.205. A 122-room, nautically themed luxury hotel in a fabulous spot on the waterfront, within walking distance of the centre. Rooms either have views of the lagoon and the yacht basin or of the train station; breakfast not included. R1630

Wayside Inn Pledge Square, 48 Main Rd ☎ 044 382 6011, ⓦ www.waysideinn.co.za; map p.205. A smart overnight stop right in the centre done out in sisal matting, wicker furniture and white linen on black wrought-iron bedsteads. A continental breakfast is served in your room or on the deck outside. R780

EASTERN SUBURBS, LEISURE ISLE AND THE HEADS

Cunningham's Island Guest House 3 Kingsway, Leisure Isle ☎ 044 384 1319, ⓦ islandhouse.co.za; map p.203. Purpose-built two-storey, timber-and-glass guesthouse with eight suites, decked out in dazzling white relieved by a touch of blue and some ethnic colour (stripey cushions and African baskets). Each room has its own entrance leading to the garden, which has a swimming pool shaded by giant strelitzias. Stylish and comfortable, its only drawback is the lack of views. R760

Isola Bella 21 Hart Lane, Leisure Isle ☎ 044 384 0049, ⓦ isolabella.co.za; map p.203. You can't help

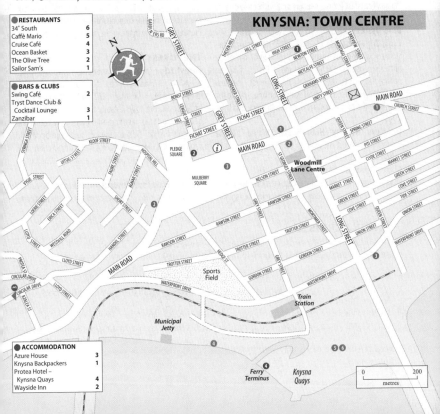

KNYSNA: TOWN CENTRE

RESTAURANTS	
34° South	6
Caffè Mario	5
Cruise Café	4
Ocean Basket	3
The Olive Tree	2
Sailor Sam's	1

BARS & CLUBS	
Swing Café	2
Tryst Dance Club & Cocktail Lounge	3
Zanzibar	1

ACCOMMODATION	
Azure House	3
Knysna Backpackers	1
Protea Hotel – Kynsna Quays	4
Wayside Inn	2

0 200 metres

17

but gasp at the views of The Heads through the huge windows of this imposing guesthouse at the lagoon's edge. You'll either love or loathe the mildly operatic decor – repro furniture, lots of oil paintings and some floral fabrics. Either way, the rooms are undeniably luxurious. Breakfast is served on the spectacularly positioned balcony overlooking the water. R3320

Under Milk Wood George Rex Drive, The Heads ☎ 044 384 0745, ⓦ milkwood.co.za; map p.203. Luxury self-catering accommodation on the lagoon at the foot of The Heads with its own private beach – safe for swimming – and terrific views of the mountains and water. The two-bedroom self-catering units with their own sun decks, are surrounded by milkwood trees; rates vary depending on whether the unit is on the lagoon, the hillside or between. There are also two B&B rooms. B&B R910, self-catering unit 1700

WEST OF TOWN

Azure House 65 Circular Drive ☎ 044 382 1221, ⓦ azurehouse.com; map p.205. Lime-washed whites, blues and pale yellows are the signature colours in these upmarket self-catering rooms, each en suite, with a small lounge. Breakfast (extra) is served on a wicker tray on your private balcony overlooking the lagoon. R850

Blue Oyster Corner of Rio and Stent sts ☎ 044 382 2265, ⓦ blueoyster.co.za; map p.203. Hospitable three-storey, vaguely Greek-themed B&B set high on one of the hills that rise up behind Knysna, offering fabulous panoramas across the lagoon to The Heads. The four comfortable double rooms, of which the ones on the top floor have the best views, are done out in white and blue. R940

Lightleys Holiday Houseboats Moored at the Belvidere turn-off from the N2 ☎ 044 386 0007, ⓦ houseboats.co.za/knysna; map p.203. For something different, you can rent fully equipped houseboats for groups of two, four or six that boast interiors resembling those of caravans and allow you to explore the lagoon's

20km of navigable water. R1450

★ **Narnia Country Guest House** Signed off Welbedacht Lane, 3km west of Knysna ☎ 044 382 1334, ⓦ www.narnia.co.za; map p.203. On a hillside with views of the lagoon, this is an immensely fun stone and rough-hewn timber farmhouse in a glorious garden. Two en-suite B&B rooms upstairs have their own balconies and swinging chairs, and are decorated in a rustic-chic style, as is a comfortable semi-detached two-bedroom cottage downstairs which has a lounge, fireplace and kitchenette. The Pool House (so called either because it opens onto a swimming pool or because its spacious lounge has its own pool table) sleeps two (R1050). Walks on the property include one down to a small lake. R1200

Phantom Forest Eco-Reserve Phantom Pass Rd, west of town off the N2 ☎ 044 386 0046, ⓦ phantomforest. com; map p.203. Breathtaking, tranquil forest lodge making extensive use of timber and glass, set on a hill in indigenous forest, with fabulous lagoon views. African fabrics and pure cotton linen reinforce the sense of unbridled luxury. Timber boardwalks wind through the forest to connect the suites to the main buildings, which feature a safari-style dining room, an open-air hot tub, a massage suite and a jacuzzi. The swimming pool teeters on the edge of the hill, cocooned by vegetation, with vervet monkeys frolicking in the forest canopy. R3400

THE FOREST

Forest Edge Cottages Rheenendal turn-off, 16km west of Knysna on the N2 ☎ 082 456 1338, ⓦ forestedge.co.za; map p.208. Ideal if you want to be close to the forest itself, these traditional, two-bedroom cottages have verandas built in the vernacular tin-roofed style. Self-contained, fully equipped and serviced, they sleep four. Forest walks and cycling trails start from the cottages, and you can also rent mountain bikes. R650

Southern Comfort Western Horse Ranch 3km along the Fisanthoek Rd, 17km east of Knysna en route to

---

KNYSNA CRUISES

One of the most pleasant activities around Knysna is a **cruise** across the lagoon to The Heads. Knysna Featherbed Company (☎ 044 382 1693, ⓦ knysnafeatherbed.com) runs a number of trips a day from Knysna Quays to The Heads, the shortest of which take 75 minutes (R85). For travel beyond The Heads, you can take a sailing trip (1hr 30min; R250) and a sunset cruise (2hr 30min; R490) with delicious food and wine. The only way to reach the private **Featherbed Nature Reserve** on the western side of the lagoon is on a four-hour Featherbed Nature Tour (R420), which includes the boat there, a 4WD shuttle to the top of the western Head and a buffet meal. There's a slightly shorter version (3hr 30min) which excludes the meal. **Bookings** are essential, and can be made at the kiosk on the north side of Knysna Quays; **departures** are from the Waterfront Jetty and municipal jetty on Remembrance Avenue, 400m west of the quays and station.

17

THE FOREST ON WHEELS, WATER AND FOOT

Eleventh-hour **conservation** has ensured that some of the hardwoods have survived to maturity in reserves of woodland that can still take your breath away. A number of walks have been laid out in several of the forests – yet the effects of the nineteenth-century timber industry means that all these reserves are some distance from Knysna itself and require transport to get to. **Knysna Forest Tours and Mountain Biking Africa** (Tony Cook ☎082 783 8392, ⓦmountainbikingafrica.co.za, ⓦknysnaforesttours.co.za) is an adventure company offering guided forest and coastal **hikes, mountain biking and canoe trips** in the area as well as birdwatching and fly-fishing. You can also combine two activities into a full-day trip. Half-day hikes start at R400 per person and biking trips at R530, including refreshments.

Plettenberg Bay ☎044 532 7885, ⓦschranch.co.za; map p.208. Very basic double rooms, dorms and a tree house, on a farm adjacent to the eastern section of the Knysna forest; staff can pick you up from the N2. Horseriding (one-hour ride R200, two-hour ride R300) – and massages for the saddle-weary – are on offer. You can self-cater or take the meals provided. Dorms R100, doubles R260

BELVIDERE AND BRENTON-ON-SEA

Belvidere Manor Duthie Drive, Belvidere Estate ☎044 387 1055, ⓦbelvidere.co.za; map p.203. A collection of tin-roofed repro Victorian cottages, nicely positioned on the water's edge. The only accommodation in

this exclusive leafy area, with its lush gardens and replica Norman church, built in the 1850s. R2340

Brenton-on-Sea Chalets C.R. Swart Drive, Brenton beachfront ☎044 381 0081, ⓦabalonelodges.co.za; map p.203. A 15min drive from Knysna and overlooking the long curve of Brenton beach, which swings round to Buffels Bay, these three-bedroom, self-catering chalets sleep six people, and are well equipped and comfortably furnished. R780

J&C Beach House 116 Watsonia Ave, Brenton ☎044 381 0107, ⓦjcbeachhouse.co.za; map p.203. Simple and elegant rooms, each with views of the ocean from the balcony. You can sun yourself at the pool or on nearby Brenton beach. R900

EATING

As far as food goes, **oysters** are an obvious choice, with the Knysna Oyster Company here being one of the world's largest oyster farms, but you'll also find a lot of good restaurants catering to other palates and one or two excellent coffee shops. With so many forests, waterways and beaches, you may be tempted to have a **picnic**, and there's no shortage of tempting deli food in town.

34° South Knysna Quays ⓦ34-south.com; map p.205. An outstanding, deli, café, restaurant, bar, sushi joint with imported groceries, home-made food and an extensive menu that includes seafood in all its guises whether *peri-peri* calamari heads, red Thai curry mussel pot or game fish salad; from here you can watch the drawbridge open to let yachts sail through (R90). Daily 8.30am–10pm.

Caffé Mario Knysna Quays ☎044 382 7250; map p.205. An intimate Italian waterside restaurant with outdoor seating, and *paninoteca* and *tramezzini* on its snack menu as well as great pizza and pasta. The food is consistently great and excellent value (R70). Daily 7.30am–10pm.

Cruise Café Featherbed Ferry Terminal, off Waterfront Drive; map p.205. A relaxed place that fuses African and Asian flavours to bring forth starters such as *bobotie* spring rolls. Main courses include Karoo lamb with mint and cranberry reduction and some great seafood offerings. The

waterside deck here is one of the best places in town to sink a drink while watching the setting sun (R120). Daily 11am–3pm & Mon–Sat 5–11pm.

Firefly Eating House 152a Old Cape Rd ☎044 382 1490, ⓦfireflyeatinghouse.com; map p.203. Relaxed little bistro whose fiery-red decor and sparkling fairy lights match the mid-priced spicy menu. Dishes draw their inspiration from Malaysia, Thailand and East and South Africa. Recommended if you like it hot (R70). Tues–Sun 6.30–10pm.

Forest Boma Phantom Forest Eco-Reserve, Phantom Pass Rd ☎044 386 0046; map p.203. Eating is secondary to being in one of the most beautiful places in South Africa, in a forest with views of the whole estuary. The six-course Pan-African set menu ranges from kudu and prune sosatie with herb polenta to pan-fried ostrich in black cherry sauce and Knysna cheese, and tempting desserts such as brandy snap baskets (R290). Daily 6.30–8.30pm.

17

Ile de Pain Thesen Island, ⓦiledepain.co.za; map p.203. A trendy restaurant in an artisan bakery, that does salads, baguettes, oysters and pastas, written up on a blackboard. Try the thick crusty bread baked in a wood-fired oven with butter and preserve for breakfast or settle for one of the delicious pastries with coffee (breakfast R20–60, lunch R45–90). Tues–Sat 8am–3pm & Sun 9am–1.30pm.

Knysna Oyster Company Thesen Island; map p.203. Run by the firm of the same name, in operation since 1949, this restaurant serves oysters harvested by the parent company from beds in the Knysna River Estuary. Don't worry if you're not an oyster eater – they also serve steaks, chicken and freshly caught fish (R90). Daily 9am–5pm (closes 9pm in high season).

Ocean Basket Knysna Mall, corner of Main Rd and Grey St; map p.205. A predictable but reliable family-friendly seafood restaurant chain with everything from freshly caught fish to not-at-all-bad hake and chips, at reasonable prices (R80). Mon–Thurs noon–10pm, Fri–Sun noon–11pm.

The Olive Tree 12 Wood Mill Lane, Main Rd; map p.205. This local favourite offers a great buffet lunch, cooked on the day. Choice depends on the whim of the chef

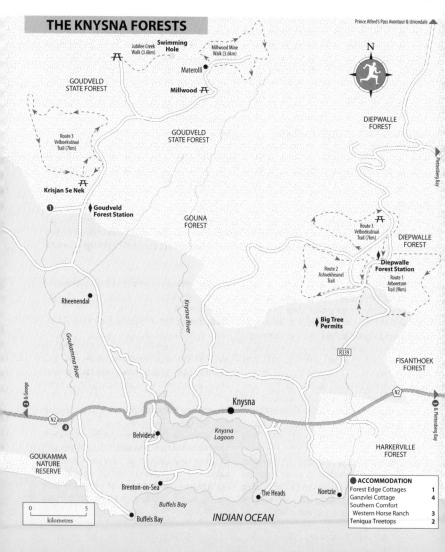

THE KNYSNA FORESTS

Prince Alfred's Pass Avontuur & Uniondale

N

GOUDVELD STATE FOREST

Jubilee Creek Walk (3.6km)
Swimming Hole
Millwood Mine Walk (3.6km)
Materolli
Millwood

GOUDVELD STATE FOREST

Route 3 Velboeksdraai Trail (7km)

DIEPWALLE FOREST

Krisjan Se Nek

1 Goudveld Forest Station

GOUNA FOREST

Route 3 Velboeksdraai Trail (7km)

Route 2 Ashoekheunel Trail

DIEPWALLE FOREST

Diepwalle Forest Station
Route 1 Arboretum Trail (9km)

Rheenendal

Knysna River

Big Tree Permits

R339

FISANTHOEK FOREST

Goukamma River

2 & George

N2

Knysna

N2

3 & Plettenberg Bay

Plettenberg Bay

N2

4

Belvidere

Knysna Lagoon

HARKERVILLE FOREST

GOUKAMMA NATURE RESERVE

Brenton-on-Sea

The Heads

Noetzie

Buffels Bay

Buffels Bay

INDIAN OCEAN

0   5
kilometres

● ACCOMMODATION	
Forest Edge Cottages	1
Ganzvlei Cottage	4
Southern Comfort Western Horse Ranch	3
Teniqua Treetops	2

and the availability of ingredients. The well-priced spread can consist of spicy chickpeas, chicken wings – you name it – and a range of fresh salads. Dinners are strongly Mediterranean-influenced. Excellent for vegetarians (R50). Mon & Tues 8am–4pm, Wed–Fri 8am–4pm & 6.30pm till late, Sat 9am–1pm.

The Orchid Room Simola Hotel, 1 Old Cape Rd ☎044 302 9600, ⓦsimolaestate.co.za; map p.203. Good-value, family-friendly restaurant with fantastic views of the lagoon and The Heads at one of the town's poshest hotels. The a la carte menu is based on seasonal ingredients done with terrific sauces, and there's a sushi bar. The extensive Sunday buffet spread is very popular (R100). Daily 7–11am, noon–4pm & 6.30–11pm.

Pembrey's Brenton Rd, Belvidere ☎044 386 0005; map p.203. Small, unpretentious and highly rated restaurant that fuses country cooking with haute cuisine. You'll usually find venison, duck confit and prawns on the changing menu that's written up daily on a blackboard. Booking essential (R115). Wed–Sun 6.30pm till late.

★ **Sailor Sam's** Main Rd, opposite the post office; map p.205. A warm-hearted, old-fashioned chippy that offers incredible value, brilliant fish and chips and the cheapest oysters in town (don't tell a soul, but the delicious shellfish aren't local; they're shipped in from the West Coast). Mon–Sat 11am–8.30pm & Sun 11am–3pm.

Sirocco Thesen Harbour ⓦsirocco.co.za; map p.203. Self-consciously hip minimalist restaurant with loads of glass to make the most of its setting on the water's edge. Known for its seafood, especially prawns, *Sirocco's* menu also includes family-friendly fare such as burgers (R90). Daily noon till late.

Zachary's Pezula Resort Hotel and Spa, Lagoonview Drive, Eastern Head ☎044 302 3300, ⓦzacharys.co.za; map p.203. Fine dining at the only place in Knysna to be nominated in 2010 for an *Eat Out* Top 10 Award. Service is formal and the ambience larney, but the pitch-perfect food – South African with a global twist – is worth traipsing out for, if the prices don't deter you (R170). Daily 7–10.30am & 6.30–10pm.

DRINKING AND NIGHTLIFE

Knysna has perked up over the past decade, but it still isn't somewhere you come if your main aim is to get down. Having said that, there are one or two clubs in town that burn the midnight oil and where you may catch some live music or DJs.

Swing Cafe 3 Sun Centre, Templeman Square ⓦtheswingcafe.co.za; map p.205. One of the Garden Route's more serious live music venues, aimed at a mature audience and featuring local performers three nights a week (and every night during the December holidays). It

also has an all-day snack menu and decent bar food and drinks. Mon–Sat 9am till late.

Tryst Dance Club & Cocktail Lounge Opposite the fire station on Waterfront Drive ☎044 382 0590; map p.205. Knysna's hottest club is inhabited mainly by twentysomethings. Sink a few balls at their pool tables while you wait for the action to begin – it only really revs up at around 10 or 11 pm. Wed, Fri & Sat 9pm–4am.

Zanzibar Corner of St George's and Main sts ☎044 382 0386; map p.205. Knysna's longest-established nightclub

---

GOUDVELD HIKES

A number of clearly **waymarked hikes** traverse the Goudveld. The most rewarding (and easy going) is along **Jubilee Creek**, which traces the progress of a burbling brook for 3.5km through giant woodland to a gorgeous, deep rock pool – ideal for cooling off after your effort. It's also an excellent place to encounter **Knysna turacos** (formerly known as Knysna louries); keep an eye focused on the branches above for the crimson flash of their flight feathers as they forage for berries, and listen out for their harsh call above the gentler chorus provided by the wide variety of other birdlife here. You can pick up a **map** directing you to the creek from the entrance gate to the reserve; the waymarked trail is linear, so you return via the same route. There's a pleasant **picnic site** along the banks of the stream at the start of the walk.

A more strenuous option is the circular **Woodcutter Walk**, though you can choose either the three- or the nine-kilometre version. Starting at **Krisjan se Nek**, another picnic site not far past the Goudveld entrance gate, it meanders downhill through dense forest, passing through stands of tree ferns, and returns uphill to the starting point. The picnic site is also where the nineteen-kilometre **Homtini Cycle Route** starts, taking you through forest and *fynbos* and offering wonderful mountain views. Be warned though; you really have to work hard at this, with one particular section climbing over 300m in just 3km. The tourist office in town has maps of the area.

17

THE KNYSNA ELEPHANTS

Traffic signs warning motorists about elephants along the N2 between Knysna and Plettenberg Bay are rather optimistic: there are few indigenous pachyderms left and, with such an immense forest, sightings are rare. But such is the mystique attached to the **Knysna elephants** that locals tend to be a little cagey about just how few they number. By 1860, the thousands that had formerly wandered the once vast forests were down to five hundred, and by 1920 (twelve years after they were protected by law), there were only twenty animals left; the current estimate is three. Loss of habitat and consequent malnutrition, rather than full-scale hunting, seems to have been the principal cause of their decline. The only elephants you're guaranteed to see near Knysna are at the **Knysna Elephant Park** (see opposite) or the **Elephant Sanctuary** (see p.220), both near Plettenberg Bay.

occupies the premises of the Old Barnyard Theatre and blends everything from pop to commercial house and beyond. It continues with the Barnyard's tradition of occasional live acts that include bands, cabaret and comedy. Wed, Fri & Sat 9pm–2am.

DIRECTORY

Emergencies General emergency number from landline ❼ 107, from mobile phone ❼ 112; Police ❼ 044 302 6600; National Sea Rescue ❼ 082 990 5956.

Hospital Life Knysna Private Hospital, Hunters Drive (❼ 044 384 1083), is well run and has a casualty department.

The Knysna forests

The best reason to come to Knysna is for its **forests**, shreds of a once magnificent woodland that was home to **Khoi** clans and harboured a thrilling variety of wildlife, including elephant herds. The forests attracted European explorers and naturalists, and in their wake woodcutters, gold-diggers and businessmen like George Rex, all bent on making their fortunes here.

The French explorer Francois Le Vaillant was one of the first Europeans to **shoot and kill** an elephant. The explorer found the animal's feet so "delicious" that he wagered that "never can our modern epicures have such a dainty at their tables". Two hundred years later, all that's left of the Khoi people are some names of local places. The legendary Knysna elephants have hardly fared better and are teetering on the edge of certain extinction.

Goudveld State Forest

Just over 30km northwest of Knysna • Daily sunrise–sunset • R15

The beautiful **Goudveld State Forest**, just over 30km northwest of Knysna, is a mixture of plantation and indigenous woodland. It takes its name from the gold boom (*goudveld* is Afrikaans for goldfields) that brought hundreds of prospectors to the mining town of **Millwood** in the 1880s. The six hundred small-time diggers who were here by 1886, scouring out the hillsides and panning Jubilee Creek for alluvial gold, were rapidly followed by larger syndicates, and a flourishing little town quickly sprang up, with six hotels, three newspapers and a music hall.

However, the singing and dancing was shortlived and bust followed boom in 1890 after most of the mining companies went to the wall. The ever-hopeful diggers took off for the newly discovered Johannesburg goldfields, and Millwood was left a deserted **ghost town**. Over the years, its buildings were demolished or relocated, leaving an old store known as Materolli as the only original building standing. Today, the old town is completely overgrown, apart from signs indicating where the old streets stood. In **Jubilee Creek**, which provides a lovely shady walk along a burbling stream, the holes scraped or blasted out of the hillside are still clearly visible. Some of the old mine works have been restored, as have the original

reduction works around the cocopan track, used to carry the ore from the mine to the works, which is still there after a century.

The forest itself is still lovely, featuring tall, indigenous trees, a delightful valley with a stream, and plenty of swimming holes and picnic sites.

ARRIVAL AND DEPARTURE — GOUDVELD STATE FOREST

To get here from Knysna, follow the N2 west toward George, turning right onto the Rheenendal road just after the Knysna River, and continue for about 25km, following the Bibby's Koep signposts until the Goudveld sign.

Diepwalle Forest

Just over 20km northeast of Knysna • Daily 6am–6pm • R15

The **Diepwalle Forest**, just over 20km northeast of Knysna, is the last haunt of Knysna's almost extinct elephant population, although the only elephants you can expect to see here are on the painted markers indicating the three main hikes through these woodlands. However, if you're quiet and alert, you do stand a chance of seeing vervet monkeys, bushbuck and blue duiker.

Diepwalle ("deep walls") is one of the highlights of the Knysna area and is renowned for its impressive density of huge trees, especially **yellowwoods**. Once the budget timber of South Africa, yellowwood was considered an inferior local substitute in place of imported pine, and found its way into the structure, floorboards, window frames and doors of thousands of often quite modest nineteenth-century houses in the Western and Eastern Cape. Today, its deep golden grain is so sought after that it commands premium prices at the annual auctions.

The three main hiking routes cover between 7km and 9km of terrain, and pass through flat to gently undulating country covered by indigenous forest and montane *fynbos*. If you're moderately fit, the hikes should take 2hr to 2hr 30min. The nine-kilometre **Arboretum trail**, marked by black elephants, starts a short way back along the road you drove in on, and descends to a stream edged with tree ferns. Across the stream you'll come to the much-photographed **Big Tree**, a six-hundred-year-old Goliath yellowwood. The easy nine-kilometre **Ashoekheuwel trail**, marked by white elephants, crosses the Gouna River, where there's a large pool allegedly used by real pachyderms. Most difficult of the three hikes is the rewarding seven-kilometre **Velboeksdraai trail**, marked by red elephants, which passes along the foothills of the Outeniquas. Take care here to stick to the elephant markers, as they overlap with a series of painted footprints marking the Outeniqua trail, for which you need to have arranged a permit to use (see p.215). Just before the Veldboeksdraai picnic site stands another mighty yellowwood regarded by some as the most beautiful in the forest.

ARRIVAL AND DEPARTURE — DIEPWALLE FOREST

To get there from Knysna, follow the N2 east towards Plettenberg Bay, after 7km turning left onto the R339, which you should take for about 16km in the direction of Avontuur and Uniondale.

INFORMATION

Forest station The station is 10.5km after the tar gives way to gravel and provides a map for the park's trails, all of which begin here.

Knysna Elephant Park

Daily 8.30am–5pm • Free • ☎ 044 532 7732, knysnaelephantpark.co.za

Heading east from Knysna along the N2 for 20km, you come to the **Knysna Elephant Park**. The park was established in 1994 to provide a home for abandoned, orphaned and abused young elephants, and opened to the public in 2003. The youngest of its charges are reared by park staff, who hand-feed them forty litres of baby formula a day, and sleep next to them at night.

17

Self-catering The park offers accommodation in upmarket self-catering units, which, as the management points out, are "situated on the second level of the elephant *boma* and as a result the sounds of the elephants and the cleaning of their stalls in the morning will be audible". R1260

ACTIVITIES

Tours The most popular activity on offer are the roughly hour-long tours, which leave every half-hour (daily 8.30am–4.30pm; R190). During the tour you'll get the chance to touch and feed one of the pachyderms. You can also take a two-hour ride on an elephant or a guided nature walk of the same duration alongside one (R815; booking essential).

Plettenberg Bay

Over the Christmas holidays, forty thousand residents from Johannesburg's wealthy northern suburbs decamp to **PLETTENBERG BAY** (usually called Plett), 33km east of Knysna, and the flashiest of the Garden Route's seaside towns. It's wise to give it a miss at this time, with prices doubling and accommodation impossible to find. Yet, during low season, sipping champagne and sucking oysters while watching the sunset from a bar can be wonderful – the banal suburban development on the surrounding hills somehow doesn't seem so bad because the bay views really are stupendous. Nevertheless it remains an expensive place to stay, with no cheap chalets or camping. For these you'll have to go to nearby **Keurbooms**. Further afield, the deep-blue **Tsitsikamma Mountains** drop sharply to the inlet and its large estuary, providing a constant vista to the town and its suburbs. The bay generously curves over several kilometres of white sands separated from the mountains by forest, which makes this a green and temperate location with rainfall throughout the year.

Plett's town **centre**, at the top of the hill, consists of a conglomeration of supermarkets, swimwear shops, estate agents and restaurants aimed largely at the holiday trade. Visitors principally come for Plett's **beaches** – and there's a fair choice. Southeast of the town centre on a rocky promontory is **Beacon Island**, dominated by a 1970s hotel, an eyesore blighting a fabulous location.

The beaches

Beacon Island Beach, or **Main Beach**, right at the central shore of the bay, is where

---

PLETT'S ATTRACTIONS

Southern right whales appear every winter, and are a seriously underrated attraction, while **dolphins** can be seen throughout the year, hunting or riding the surf, often in substantial numbers. **Swimming** is safe, and though the waters are never tropically warm they reach a comfortable temperature between November and April. River and rock **fishing** are rewarding all year long. One of the Garden Route's best short **hikes** covers a circuit round the Robberg Peninsula – a great tongue of headland that contains the western edge of the bay.

On the east of the bay lies the seaside resort of **Keurboomsstand** and beyond that **The Crags** (both of them more or less suburbs of Plett) with its trio of wildlife parks: **Monkeyland, Birds of Eden** and the **Elephant Sanctuary** (see p.220) are all worth a visit, especially if you're travelling with kids. If you're keen on walking and the outdoors, and want to schedule in at least one long walk somewhere in the country during your holiday, the Garden Route provides some fine possibilities, and you'll find a couple of excellent options around Plett (see p.219), which also tend to get less booked out than the more popular trails around Tsitsikamma National Park (see p.221).

the fishing boats and seacats anchor a little out to sea. The small waves here make for calm swimming, and this is an ideal family spot. To the east is **Lookout Rocks**, attracting surfers to the break off a needle of rocks known as the Point and the predictable surf of **Lookout Beach**, to its east, which is also one of the nicest stretches of sand for bathers, bodysurfers or sun lizards. Lookout Beach has the added attraction of a marvellously located restaurant (see p.219), from which you can often catch sight of **dolphins** cruising into the bay. From here you can walk several kilometres down the beach towards Keurbooms (see p.214) and the **Keurbooms Lagoon**.

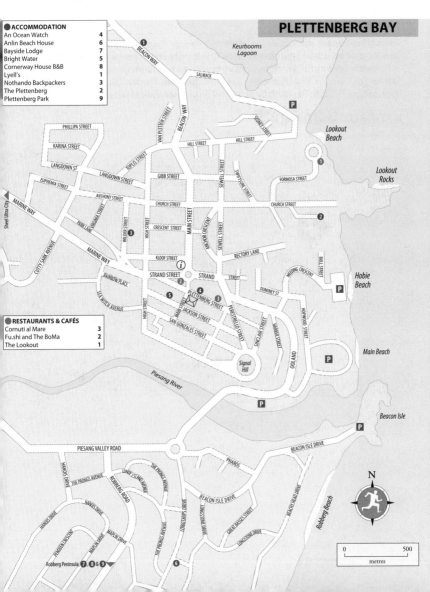

PLETTENBERG BAY

● ACCOMMODATION
An Ocean Watch	4
Anlin Beach House	6
Bayside Lodge	7
Bright Water	5
Cornerway House B&B	8
Lyell's	1
Nothando Backpackers	3
The Plettenberg	2
Plettenberg Park	9

● RESTAURANTS & CAFÉS
Cornuti al Mare	3
Fu.shi and The BoMa	2
The Lookout	1

N

| 0 | | 500 |
| metres |

17

Keurboomstrand

Some 14km east of Plettenberg Bay by road, across the Keurbooms River, is the uncluttered resort of **KEURBOOMSTRAND** (Keurbooms for short), little more than a suburb of Plett, sharing the same bay and with equally wonderful beaches, but less safe for swimming. The safest place to take the waves is at **Arch Rock**, in front of the caravan park, though **Picnic Rock beach** is also pretty good. A calm and attractive place, Keurbooms has few facilities, and if you're intending to stay here you should stock up in Plett beforehand. One of Keurbooms' highlights is **canoeing** or, if you feel less energetic, taking a ferry ride or motorboat up the Keurbooms River (see box, p.217).

ARRIVAL AND DEPARTURE

PLETTENBERG BAY

Intercity bus Intercape, Greyhound and Translux intercity buses stop at the Shell Ultra City petrol station, just off the N2 in Marine Way, 2km from the town centre. Destinations: Cape Town (6–7 daily; 7hr 30min); George (6–7 daily; 1hr 30min); Knysna (6–7 daily; 1hr 30min); Mossel Bay (6–7 daily; 2hr 15min); Port Elizabeth (6–7 daily; 2hr 30min). As there's no transport around town, if you don't have your own car, you'll need to arrange for your guesthouse to collect you.

Baz Bus The Baz Bus drops passengers off at accommodation in town.

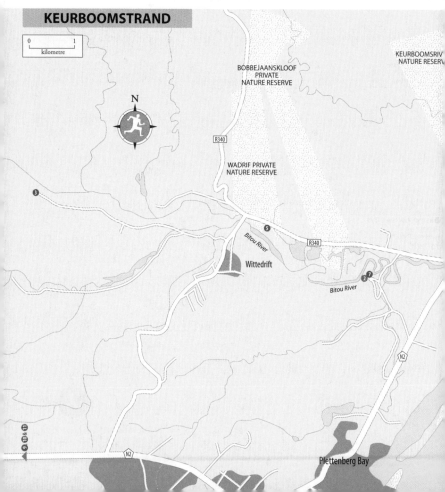

KEURBOOMSTRAND

INFORMATION

Tourist office Shop 35, Mellville Corner, Main Street (Mon–Fri 8.30am–5pm, Sat 9am–1pm; ☎ 044 533 4065, ⓦ plettenbergbay.co.za). The tourist office has maps of the town and may be able to help with booking accommodation.

HIKING

The waymarked **hikes** listed below are two to five days long. You'll need to carry all your food, a sleeping bag for use in the communal hiking huts (mattresses are provided), lightweight cooking utensils and stove, and waterproofs. You should also wear proper worn-in hiking boots.

Harkerville Coastal Trail Start and end: Harkerville Forestry Station, 12km west of Plettenberg Bay, signposted off the N2; Distance: 26.5km; Duration: two days; Permit and booking: ☎ 044 302 5606, ⓔ nagamsom@sanparks.org; Cost: R160 per person + daily conservation fee R18. Closer to the roads, this circular trail doesn't feel as remote as the Otter trail (see below) but is a good second-best, taking in magnificent rocky coastline, indigenous forest and *fynbos*. Lots of rock scrambling and some traversing of exposed, narrow ledges above the sea is required, so don't attempt this if you're unfit or scared of heights. Monkeys, baboons and fish eagles are commonly seen, and you may also spot dolphins or whales.

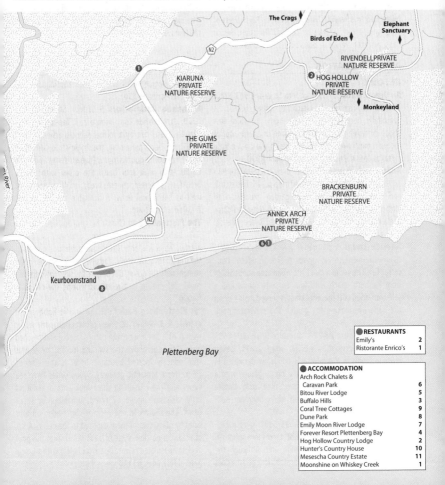

The Crags

Elephant Sanctuary

Birds of Eden

① RIVENDELL PRIVATE NATURE RESERVE

KIARUNA PRIVATE NATURE RESERVE

② HOG HOLLOW PRIVATE NATURE RESERVE

Monkeyland

THE GUMS PRIVATE NATURE RESERVE

BRACKENBURN PRIVATE NATURE RESERVE

ANNEX ARCH PRIVATE NATURE RESERVE

⑥①

Keurboomstrand

⑧

Plettenberg Bay

● RESTAURANTS	
Emily's	2
Ristorante Enrico's	1

● ACCOMMODATION	
Arch Rock Chalets & Caravan Park	6
Bitou River Lodge	5
Buffalo Hills	3
Coral Tree Cottages	9
Dune Park	8
Emily Moon River Lodge	7
Forever Resort Plettenberg Bay	4
Hog Hollow Country Lodge	2
Hunter's Country House	10
Mesescha Country Estate	11
Moonshine on Whiskey Creek	1

17

WHALE- AND DOLPHIN-WATCHING

Elevated ocean panoramas give Plettenberg Bay outstanding vantages for watching **southern right whales** during their breeding season between June and October. An especially good vantage point is the area between the wreck of the *Athene* at the southern end of Lookout Beach and the Keurbooms River. The Robberg Peninsula is also excellent, looming protectively over this whale nursery and giving a grandstand view of the bay. Other good town viewpoints are from Beachy Head Road at Robberg Beach; Signal Hill in San Gonzales Street past the post office and police station; the *Beacon Island Hotel* on Beacon Island; and the deck of the *Lookout* restaurant on Lookout Beach. Outside Plett, the Kranshoek viewpoint and hiking trail offers wonderful whale-watching points along the route. To get there, head for Knysna, taking the Harkerville turn-off, and continue for 7km. It's also possible to view the occasional pair (mother and calf) at Nature's Valley, 29km east of Plett on the R102, and from Storms River Mouth. The relationship between man and the whale has been fraught and often brutally one-sided. Fortunately, today the imbalance is being addressed (see p.219).

Outeniqua Trail Start: Beervlei (the old forest station – eight overnight huts); directions are given when you book; End: Harkerville Forestry Station, 12km west of Plettenberg Bay; Distance: 108km; Duration: seven days (shorter versions possible); Permit: ☎ 044 302 5606; Cost: R84 per person per day. The main draw here is the indigenous forest, including giant yellowwood trees, pine plantations and gold-mining remains at Millwood in the Goudveld State Forest.

ACCOMMODATION

IN TOWN

An Ocean Watch 21 Plettenberg St ☎ 044 533 1700, ⓦ anoceanwatchguesthouse.co.za; map p.213. A beautifully decorated beach-style home in which just about everything is shimmering white or cream. Four of the six rooms have sea views (for which you'll pay a little extra) as does the heated swimming pool. R990

Anlin Beach House 33 Roche Bonne Ave ☎ 044 533 3694, ⓦ anlinbeachhouse.co.za; map p.213. Two stylish and comfortably kitted out garden studios with kitchenettes, and a larger family unit with three bedrooms and a kitchen, in a garden setting close to Robberg Beach. Units are serviced daily. R1110

Bayside Lodge 5 Sanganer Ave ☎ 044 533 0601, ⓦ baysidelodge.co.za; map p.213. Modern two-storey brick house in a quiet suburban area about 500m from Robberg beach with four en-suite rooms and a self-contained cottage. Breakfast is served inside or on the patio overlooking the garden and saltwater pool. R900

Cornerway House B&B 61 Longships Drive ☎ 044 533 3190, ⓦ cornerwayhouse.co.za; map p.213. Seven en-suite rooms in a comfortable bungalow decorated in English cottage style and set in a pretty garden with a swimming pool. All rooms have their own private entrances. There's also a lovely three-bedroom self-catering cottage. R990

Lyell's 59 Beacon Way ☎ 044 533 5692; map p.213. Three sparkling white en-suite B&B rooms in a suburban house, plus a budget self-catering unit. Although the rooms don't have sea views the upstairs lounge area does have 180-degree vistas of the ocean and lagoon. B&B R600, self-catering 550

Nothando Backpackers 5 Wilder St ☎ 044 533 0220, ⓦ nothando.com; map p.213. Top-notch child-friendly hostel run by a former schoolteacher. A 5min walk from Plett's main drag, the single-storey suburban house has seven double rooms (five en suite) and three dorms (two with four beds, the other with eight). Breakfast (of cereal, cheese, bread, muffins, yogurt as well as bacon and eggs) is available for R35. Dorms R130, doubles R400

The Plettenberg 40 Church St, Lookout Rocks ☎ 044 533 2030, ⓦ plettenberg.com; map p.213. Plett's prestige hotel is a large, luxurious establishment with all the trimmings you'd expect and offering unbeatable views straight onto the ocean. But despite the sky-high rates you could still end up in a room overlooking the car park. R4000

★ **Plettenberg Park** Near the end of Robberg Rd ☎ 044 533 9067, ⓦ www.plettenbergpark.co.za; map p.213. Set in a private nature reserve and perched on a cliff edge above the swirling Indian Ocean, this stupendously located boutique hotel is the obvious choice for a romantic getaway. Seven suites have sea views and the remaining three look onto a beautiful little lake surrounded by *fynbos* inhabited by small game. The shower in one room is surrounded on four sides by glass, two of them exposed to the ocean. A set of meandering timber steps leads down from the pool deck to an isolated private beach far below with a lovely natural rock pool. R5120

ACTIVITIES

BUNGEE JUMPING & SKYDIVING

Bloukrans Bungy ☎042 281 1458, ⓦfaceadrenalin.com. If you fancy swinging through the air, then pull in at Tsitsikamma Forest Village, 20km east of The Crags and Monkeyland turn-off along the N2, where you'll find the registration office for the world's highest commercial bungee jump. The jump takes place off the 216-metre Bloukrans River Bridge, 2km beyond the village down a signposted road that also brings you to a viewpoint. There's no need to book ahead for the jump, which costs R690 (including video) for the seven-second descent. For the not so brave there's a mesh catwalk over the jump site (R100).

Skydive Plettenberg Bay ☎082 905 7440, ⓦskydiveplett.com. If you fancy a bit of an adrenaline rush, you can go tandem skydiving (no experience required) with these guys, who charge R1600 for a jump, with the option of paying extra for a DVD or video of the event.

CANOEING

If you can tear yourself away from the beach, canoeing up the Keurbooms River gives an alternative perspective on the area.

CapeNature on the east side of the Keurbooms River Bridge along the N2 ☎044 533 2125. This outfit rents fairly basic craft (R130, per day for a two-person canoe).

ELEPHANT ENCOUNTERS

The Knysna Elephant Park (see p.211) and Elephant Sanctuary (see p.220) offer the opportunity of close encounters with the large mammals.

FERRY TRIPS AND MOTORBOATING

Be sure to bring a picnic for any of the boat trips; the river is dotted with little beaches that are a good place to stop for a swim and walk. The indigenous forest comes right down to the river edge, and the journey gets better the higher up you go, the gorge narrowing and the pleasure boats and waterskiers now left behind.

Keurbooms River Ferries signposted on the east side of the Keurbooms River Bridge ☎044 532 7876, ☎082 487 3355 for motorboat rental, ⓦferry.co.za. The company runs guided upriver boat trips (R120) with knowledgeable guides skilled at

spotting rare birds, and also rents out motorboats (R350/half-day, R500/full day).

TOWNSHIP TOURS

Ocean Blue Central Beach ☎044 533 5083 or ☎083 701 3583, ⓦoceanadventures.co.za. Ocean Blue arranges relaxed tours into Plett's township with a guide who is a member of the community. Outings cost R150 per person and all the takings go into a development trust, which among other things, pays teachers' salaries and funds a crèche.

WHALE- AND DOLPHIN-WATCHING

A number of outfits run trips to see whales from the water, offering the chance of close encounters with a variety of whales and several dolphin species. Only **permitted whale watchers** are allowed to go within 50m of a whale; everyone must maintain a distance of 300m. In Plett, only Ocean Safaris and Ocean Blue (listed below) hold permits. Air-based trips have the additional attraction of spectacular aerial views of bays and river inlets.

Dolphin Adventures Central Beach ☎083 590 3405, ⓦdolphinadventures.co.za. Sea kayaking is one of the best ways to watch whales, and this outfit offers unforgettable trips with experienced and knowledgeable guides in two-person kayaks (2hr–2hr 30min; R250, children R150, including all equipment). Out of whale season it's still worth going out to see dolphins and seals.

Ocean Blue Central Beach ☎044 533 4897 or ☎083 701 3583, ⓦoceanadventures.co.za. Sea-kayaking (R300) and boat-based whale-watching (R650) are among the offerings of this licensed outfit, which also runs township tours (see below).

Ocean Safaris Shop 3, Hopwood St ☎044 533 4963, ⓦoceansafaris.co.za. Tailor-made cruises from a licensed whale-watching company. Apart from southern rights, the trips run into common, bottlenose and humpback dolphins, as well as Bryde's and humpback whales – and the occasional minke and killer whale. The Close Encounter with Whales outing costs R650 per person and virtually guarantees sightings between July and November; the Discovery Cruise, which costs R400, is principally a dolphin-viewing excursion.

ROBBERG BEACH AND WEST OF PLETT

Coral Tree Cottages Off the N2, 11km west of Plettenberg Bay ☎044 532 7822, ⓦcoraltreecottages .co.za; map p.214. High-quality, spacious thatched

cottages sleeping up to four, though unfortunately the roar of the N2 is never absent. The on-site mini-water park, swings, trampolines and climbing frames as well as a 3.5km quad bike forest trail are added attraction for children. **R600**

17

Hunter's Country House Off the N2, 10km west of Plett on the way to Knysna ☏ 044 532 7818, ⊛ hunterhotels.com; map p.214. Set in a woodland area, this is one of the best upmarket places to stay on the Garden Route, with an emphasis on country comfort rather than seaside glitz. Garden-suite accommodation is in thatched cottages set in well-established gardens, each with an open fireplace, private patio, underfloor heating and a/c, while the forest suites are larger and more sumptuous, each with its own private pool. **R2890**

Masescha Country Estate 1km north off the N2, signposted 12km west from Plettenberg Bay ☏ 044 532 7647, ⊛ masescha.co.za; map p.214. Six units, from a small self-catering chalet to a five-bedroom house, on an aquaponic farm with pleasant gardens and a forest. This is a good option for families and couples alike, and has a swimming pool. **R400**

KEURBOOMSTRAND AND EAST OF PLETT

Arch Rock Chalets and Caravan Park Arch Rock ☏ 044 535 9409, ⊛ archrock.co.za; map p.214. Seventeen fully equipped chalets some with one and the others with two bedrooms. Apart from the forest chalets and log cabins, which are set back among trees, the rest are close to the beach and have sea views. **R610**

Bitou River Lodge Bitou Valley Rd (the R340), about 4km from the N2 ☏ 044 535 9577, ⊛ bitou.co.za; map p.214. Great value in a lovely spot on the banks of the Bitou River, the five bedrooms at this intimate establishment are comfortable but unfussy and rooms overlook a pretty garden with a lily pond. Rate includes use of canoes on the river. **R1150**

Buffalo Hills Rietvlei Rd, Wittedrif Village ☏ 044 535 9739, ⊛ buffalohills.co.za; map p.214. Farm-turned-game-lodge on the banks of the Bitou River, a 15min drive from Plett. Although this is no substitute for seeing the big five at one of the major game reserves, it nonetheless provides a thoroughly entertaining experience. The package includes a game drive and guided walk on which you stand a chance of seeing rhino, buffalo, giraffe, bontebok, zebra and a number of other antelope. Accommodation is throughout an old-style African farmhouse, a stone cottage and luxury walk-in tents, pitched on their own decks, with spa baths. **R1800**

Dune Park Keurboomstrand Rd, leading off the N2 and running along the shore to Keurbooms ☏ 044 535

9606, ⊛ www.dunepark.co.za; map p.214. Luxury hotel whose airy bedrooms with crisp white linen are simple and stylish and two-bedroom self-catering cottages built on top of high dunes to provide great views (R750) within spitting distance of the sea. **R695**

Emily Moon River Lodge Rietvlei Rd, off the N2 (turn off at Penny Pinchers) ☏ 044 533 2982, ⊛ emilymoon. co.za; map p.214. That the owner of this highly imaginative and luxurious lodge, perched on a ridge looking across the Bitou Wetlands, is a dealer in ethnic art is plain to see. The place is not only littered with Batonga sculptures and Swazi crafts, it has in places been constructed out of artworks, such as the intricate Rajastani arched screen that is the entrance to the magnificently sited restaurant. Each of its chalets jetties out of the hillside to offer views from a private deck (and bathroom) of the oxbowing Bitou, along which small game can occasionally be seen. There is a family suite that sleeps four in which kids are accommodated at a very discounted rate. **R2540**

Forever Resort Plettenberg Bay 6km east of Plett and signposted off the N2 near Keurboomstrand ☏ 044 535 9309, ⊛ foreverplettenberg.co.za; map p.214. A sizeable family resort, with camping on the shady banks of the Keurbooms River, away from the sea, and a range of self-catering log cabins some with river views. Canoes and motorboats are available to rent, and there's a swimming pool. **R675**

Hog Hollow Country Lodge Askop Rd, 18km east of Plettenberg Bay (turn south off the N2 at the signpost) ☏ 044 534 8879, ⊛ hog-hollow.com; map p.214. A touch of luxury on a private reserve where each of the chalets, done out in earthy colours and spiced up with African artefacts, has a bath or shower and its own wooden deck with vistas across the forest and Tsitsikamma Mountains; superb food is served as well. From here you could hike for a couple of hours through forest to Keurbooms beach, or drive there in 15min. **R3040**

Moonshine on Whiskey Creek 14km east of Plettenburg Bay along the N2, signposted north of the N2 ☏ 044 534 8515 or ☏ 072 200 6656, ⊛ whiskeycreek. co.za; map p.214. Fully equipped bungalows, three wooden cabins and one creatively renovated labourer's cottage, nestled in indigenous forest, with a children's play area. One of the best reasons to come here is the access to a secluded natural mountain pool and waterfall at the bottom of the nearby gorge. **R590**

EATING AND DRINKING

Restaurants come and go in Plett at a similar lick to the tides, but one or two long-standing establishments have managed to remain afloat. Locally caught fresh **fish** is the thing to look out for. And because the town is built on hills, you should generally expect **terrific views**.

Cornuti al Mare Seaview Properties, 1 Perestrella St ☏ 044 533 1277, ⊛ cornuti.co.za; map p.213. Fantastic

pizzas – the best along the Garden Route – and also great pasta dishes that won't break the bank, topped off with endless views of sea and sky (R90). Daily noon–10pm.

Emily's Rietvlei Rd, off the N2 (turn off at Penny Pinchers) ☎044 533 2982; map p.214. Boutique restaurant attached to *Emily Moon's Lodge* that many regard as the best in the area, offering stunning views of the Bitou Wetland and classical French cuisine with an edge. There's no set menu as everything is based on what seasonal ingredients are locally available on the day, but there's always a choice of five or six starters and mains with a small range of desserts. Booking is essential (R100). Tues to Sun noon–3pm and daily 6.30–10pm.

Fu.shi and **The BoMa** The Upper Deck, 3 Strand St; map p.213. Two eateries rolled into one right in the centre, surrounded by picture windows to make the most of the elevated views. As its name suggests *Fu.shi*'s menu is Asian fusion, featuring sushi and various coquettishly named dishes – Nuggets of Pleasure (wasabi prawns with cashew salad), Flights of Fantasy (sliced duck breast with pak choi) and Concubine's Whisper (chilli chocolate fondant with pistachio brittle). The *BoMa* is a cocktail bar-cum-breakfast and-snack joint. Daily noon–5pm & 6–9.30pm.

The Lookout Lookout Beach ☎044 533 1379, ⓦlookout.co.za; map p.213. Marvellous bay views – if you're lucky, you'll see whales and dolphins rollicking in the surf – at this casual bar-restaurant focusing on seafood, including crayfish. They also do meat, poultry, pasta, salads and English breakfasts (R100). Daily 9am–11pm.

Ristorante Enrico Main Beach, Keurboomstrand; map p.214. Great, mid-priced Italian standards – thin-based pizzas, pasta and veal – to enjoy alfresco on the beach or in the stylish indoor restaurant. Daily 11.30am–10.30pm.

Robberg Marine and Nature Reserve

Daily Feb–Nov 7am–5pm; Dec & Jan 7am–8pm • R25

One of the Garden Route's nicest walks is the four-hour, nine-kilometre circular route around the spectacular rocky peninsula of **Robberg**, 8km southeast of Plett's town centre. Here you can completely escape Plett's development and experience the coast in its wildest state, with its enormous horizons and lovely vegetation. Much of the walk takes you along high cliffs, from where you can often look down on seals surfacing near the rocks, dolphins arching through the water and, in winter, whales further out in the bay.

If you don't have time for the full circular walk, there is a shorter two-hour hike and a thirty-minute ramble.

WHALING AND GNASHING OF TEETH

For conservationists, the monumental 1970s eyesore of the *Beacon Island Hotel* may not be such a bad thing, since previously the island was the site of a whale-processing factory established in 1806 – one of some half-dozen such plants erected along the Western Cape coast that year. Whaling continued at Plettenberg Bay until 1916. Southern right whales were the favoured species, yielding more oil and **whalebone** – an essential component of Victorian corsets – than any other. In the nineteenth century, a southern right would net around three times as much as a humpback caught along the Western Cape coast, leading to a rapid decline in the southern right population by the middle of the nineteenth century.

The years between the establishment and the closing of the Plettenberg Bay factory saw worldwide whaling transformed by the inventions of the Industrial Revolution. In 1852, the explosive harpoon was introduced, followed by the use of steam-powered ships five years later, making them swifter and safer for the crew. In 1863, Norwegian captain Sven Foyn built the first modern whale-catching vessel, which he followed up in 1868 with the **cannon-mounted harpoon**. In 1913 Plettenberg Bay was the site of one of seventeen shore-based and some dozen floating factories between West Africa and Mozambique, which that year between them took about ten thousand whales.

Inevitably, a rapid decline in humpback populations began; by 1918, all but four of the shore-based factories had closed due to lack of prey. The remaining whalers now turned their attention to fin and blue whales. When the South African fin whale population became depleted by the mid-1960s to twenty percent of its former size, they turned to sei and sperm whales. When these populations declined, the frustrated whalers started hunting minke whales, which at 9m in length are too small to be a viable catch. By the 1970s, the South African whaling industry was in its death throes and was finally put out of its misery in 1979, when the government banned all activity surrounding whaling.

17

By car There's no public transport to the reserve; if you're staying at a backpacker lodge, ask about their transfers, which are generally reasonably priced. To drive there, take Strand Street towards Beacon Isle, turn right into Piesangs Valley Road, and 200m further on turn left into Robberg Road. Follow the airport signs, continuing for 3.5km, and look out for the Robberg turn-off to your left.

INFORMATION

The trails Maps indicating these are available at the reserve gate when you pay to enter. You'll need sturdy walking shoes, as the terrain is rocky and steep in parts, and the walk involves some serious rock-hopping on the west side. Bring a hat and a bottle of water, as there's no drinking water for much of the way and no tearooms.

The Crags

From Keurbooms, look out for the BP petrol station, then take the Monkeyland/Kurland turn-off and follow the Elephant Sanctuary/ Monkeyland signs for 2km

The Crags, 2km east of Keurboomstrand, comprises a collection of smallholdings along the N2, a bottle store and a few other shops on the forest edge, but the reason most visitors pull in here is for the **Elephant Sanctuary**, **Monkeyland** and **Birds of Eden**.

Elephant Sanctuary

Daily 8am–5pm · **Trunk-in-Hand programme** daily between 8am–noon & 1.30–3.30pm · R295 · **Elephant rides** R670 · ☎ 044 534 8145, ⓦ elephantsanctuary.co.za

The **Elephant Sanctuary** offers a chance of close encounters with its half-dozen pachyderms, all of whom were saved from culling in Botswana and the Kruger National Park. On the popular one-hour Trunk-in-Hand programme you get to walk with an elephant, holding the tip of its trunk in your hand and also to feed and interact with it. The programme includes an informative talk about elephant behaviour; fifteen-minute elephant-back rides are among the other packages on offer.

Monkeyland

Daily 8am–5pm · Free entry to viewing deck · **Safaris** R125 · **Combined ticket** with Birds of Eden R200 · ⓦ monkeyland.co.za

Monkeyland, 400m beyond the Elephant Sanctuary, brings together primates from several continents, all of them orphaned or saved from a dismal life as pets. The place is a sanctuary, so none of the animals has been taken from the wild – and most wouldn't have the skills to survive there. Life is made as comfortable as possible for them and they are free to move around the reserve, looking for food and interacting with each other and their environment in as natural a way as possible. For your own safety and that of the monkeys, you are not allowed to wander around alone. **Guides** take visitors on walking "safaris", during which you come across water holes, experience a living indigenous forest and enjoy chance encounters with creatures such as ringtail lemurs from Madagascar and squirrel monkeys from South America.

The safaris are entertaining and also feature an informed **commentary** covering issues such as the differences between monkeys and apes, primate communication and social systems. One of the sanctuary's highlights is crossing the Indiana Jones-esque **rope bridge** (at 128m, it's purportedly the longest such bridge in the southern hemisphere) spanning a canyon to pass through the upper reaches of the forest canopy, where a number of species spend their entire lives. For **refreshments** or meals, there's a restaurant with a forest deck at the day lodge.

Birds of Eden

Daily 8am–5pm · R125 · **Combined ticket** with Monkeyland R200

Under the same management as Monkeyland and right next door, **Birds of Eden** is a huge bird sanctuary, which took four years to create. Great effort was taken to place netting over a substantial tract of virgin forest with as little impact as possible. The result is claimed to be the largest free-flight aviary in the world. As with Monkeyland,

17

most of Birds of Eden's charges were already living in cages and are now free to move and fly around within the confines of the large enclosure (so large in fact that you can easily spend an hour slowly meandering along its winding, wheelchair-friendly, wooden walkway).

Although it has come in for some criticism for cutting off local birds from their traditional turf and disrupting some migration routes, the result is quite remarkable, with little lakes, waterfalls and a wonderful **suspension bridge** along the way. Most of the birds are exotics, some impossibly brightly coloured (such as the incandescent scarlet ibis from South America and golden pheasant from China), but you'll also see a number of locals, such as the Knysna lourie and South Africa's national bird, the blue crane. Watch out for the cheeky cockatoos that may alight on your shoulder and steal buttons from your shirt or beads from round your neck. A **restaurant** by one of the lakes sells light meals and liquid refreshments.

Tsitsikamma

The **Tsitsikamma section** of the Garden Route National Park, roughly midway between Plettenberg Bay and Port Elizabeth, is the highlight of any Garden Route trip. Starting from just beyond Keurboomstrand in the west, the section extends for 68km into the Eastern Cape along a narrow belt of coast, with dramatic foamy surges of rocky coast, deep river gorges and ancient hardwood forests clinging to the edge of tangled, green cliffs. Don't pass up its main attraction, the **Storms River Mouth**, the most dramatic estuary on this exhilarating piece of coast. Established in 1964, Tsitsikamma is also South Africa's oldest marine reserve, stretching 5.5km out to sea, with an **underwater trail** open to snorkellers and licensed scuba divers.

Tsitsikamma has two sections: **Nature's Valley** in the west and **Storms River Mouth** in the east. Each section can only be reached down a winding tarred road from the N2 (apart from hiking, there's no way of getting from one to the other through the park itself). Nature's Valley incorporates the most low-key settlement on the Garden Route, with a fabulous sandy beach stretching for 3km. South Africa's ultimate hike, the five-day **Otter Trail** (see box, p.222), connects the two sections of the park.

The nearest settlement to Storms River Mouth, some 14km to its north at the top of a steep winding road, is the confusingly named **Storms River Village**, which is outside the national park and some distance from any part of the river. While Storms River Village makes a convenient base for adventure activities in the vicinity and day-trips down to Storms River Mouth, the experience is very different from staying overnight at the coast.

Nature's Valley

Nature's Valley, at the western end of Tsitsikamma Section of the Garden Route National Park, extends inland into a rugged and hilly interior incised with narrow valleys and traversed by a series of footpaths. It also incorporates a pleasantly old-fashioned settlement on the stunningly beautiful Groot River Lagoon with 20km of beach. Bypassed by the N2, and by intercity buses and tour parties, Nature's Valley, 29km east of Plettenberg Bay, down the lovely winding Groot River pass (along which you'll often encounter baboon troops), is the supreme destination if you're after a relaxed retreat along the Garden Route.

Walks

There are plenty of good **walks** at Nature's Valley, many starting from the national park campsite, 1km north of the village, where you can pick up maps and information about birds and trees. One of the loveliest places to head for is **Salt River Mouth**, 3km west of Nature's Valley, where you can swim and picnic – though you'll need to ford

17

the river at low tide. This walk starts and ends at the café at Nature's Valley. Also recommended is the circular six-kilometre **Kalanderkloof trail**, which starts at the national park campsite, ascends to a lookout point, and descends via a narrow river gorge graced with a profusion of huge Outeniqua yellowwood trees and Cape wild bananas. There is also a more serious, 60km hike from Nature's Valley to Storms River Bridge (see box below).

ARRIVAL AND DEPARTURE   NATURE'S VALLEY

By car There is no public transport to Nature's Valley and the only way of getting there is by car, taking the beautiful Groot River Pass road that winds down through riverine forest from the N2, 2km east of the Crags. Nature's Valley is at the bottom of the pass, 11km after the turn-off. The road continues from Nature's Valley and rejoins the N2 after

9km, just west of the Bloukrans River Bridge. The detour is well worth taking in its own right – the last relic of the meandering Garden Route as it was before the N2 sped through it – with a reasonable chance of encountering baboons and vervet monkeys along the way.

INFORMATION

The *Nature's Valley Trading Store* (see opposite) is effectively the village centre and acts as an informal but excellent, **information** bureau. If you're **self-catering**, stock up on supplies before you get to Nature's Valley, since their supplies are basic.

ACCOMMODATION

Accommodation in Nature's Valley itself is pretty limited, which contributes to its low-key charm, but you'll find some choice options on the road leading off the N2 into the village, just before the switchbacks begin. Other than the below, if you are self-catering you may wish to contact Meyer van Rooyen (☎ 082 772 2972) who handles a number of houses in and around Nature's Valley.

THE NATURE'S VALLEY AND STORM'S RIVER HIKES

Dolphin Trail *Start: Storms River Mouth, Garden Route National Park (Tsitsikamma); End: Sandrif River Mouth; Distance: 20km; Duration: two and a half days; Booking:* ☎ *042 281 1607 extension 219,* ⊛ *dolphintrail.co.za; Cost: R4620 per person, including food, accommodation and permits.* This is the Garden Route's luxury trail. Backpacks are transported to overnight stops where you're greeted with comfortable accommodation and cooked meals. The terrain through the Tsitsikamma National Park is breathtaking, covering the rugged coastal edge and the natural forest. The price includes a guide, a boat trip up the Storms River Gorge and a 4WD drive through the Storms River Pass.

Otter Trail *Start: Storms River Mouth; End: Nature's Valley; Distance: 42km; Duration: five days; Booking: Through South African National Parks, up to twelve months in advance (* ☎ *012 426 5111,* ⊜ *reservations@sanparks.org). The maximum number of people on the trail is twelve; Cost: R755 per person.* The Otter trail is South Africa's oldest and deservedly most popular hike. If you're desperate to walk the Otter trail and have been told that it is full, don't despair – a single person or a couple do stand a chance of getting in on the back of a last-minute cancellation, so it may be worth hanging out at the Mouth for a night or two. The coastal walk crossing rivers, tidal pools and indigenous forest. You may see dolphins, whales and seals, and the spoor of the Cape clawless otter – although virtually impossible to spot, the creatures are certainly around. The short stretches between log-hut nightstops mean you can take things slowly, and enjoy the vegetation and birds. The Bloukrans River has to be crossed by wading or swimming: go at low tide and waterproof your backpack. Some parts of the hike are steep, so you need to be fit.

Tsitsikamma Trail *Start: Nature's Valley; End: Storms River Bridge; Distance: 60km; Duration: two to six days; Permit: MTO Ecotourism* ☎ *042 281 1712,* ⊛ *mtoecotourism.co.za/tsitsikama.htm; Cost: R100 per person per night (porterage available for additional R550 per group of up to six per day).* Not to be confused with the Otter trail, this is an inland walk through indigenous forest, long stretches of open *fynbos* and the Tsitsikamma mountain range. Five overnight huts accommodate thirty people. It's not a difficult hike, and you won't cover more than 17km or so per day – although after heavy rains the rivers can be hard to cross.

17

WALKING AT STORMS RIVER MOUTH

Walking is the main activity at the Mouth, and at the visitors' office at the restcamp you can get **maps** of short, waymarked coastal trails that leave from here. These include steep walks up the forested cliffs, where you can see 800-year-old yellowwood trees with views onto a wide stretch of ocean. Most rewarding is the **three-kilometre hike** west from the restcamp along the start of the Otter trail to a fantastic **waterfall** pool at the base of fifty-metre-high falls where you can swim right on the edge of the shore. Less demanding is the kilometre-long **boardwalk stroll** from the restaurant to the suspension bridge to see the river mouth. On your way to the bridge, don't miss the dank *strandloper* (beachcomber) **cave**. Hunter-gatherers frequented this area between five thousand and two thousand years ago, living off seafood in wave-cut caves near the river mouth. A modest display shows an excavated midden, with clear layers of little bones and shells. The area's most famous and popular walks, however, are the Dolphin and Otter trails (see box opposite). **Swimming** at the Mouth is restricted to a safe and pristine little sandy bay below the restaurant, though conditions can be icy in summer if there are easterly winds and cold upwellings of deep water from the continental shelf.

Four Fields Farm Nature's Valley Rd; 3km from the N2 along the R102 and 6km from Nature's Valley ☎ 044 534 8708, ⓦ fourfields.iowners.net. A welcoming and charmingly unpretentious former dairy farm, less than 10min drive from the sea. Five en-suite bedrooms, simply furnished with beautiful old pieces, have French doors leading to their own private decks, which in turn open onto a lovely garden surrounded by fields. There's also a self-catering unit sleeping four (R720). R910

Froggy Pond Second house on the right as you enter Nature's Valley ☎ 044 531 6835, ⓦ www.cyberperk. co.za/naturesvalley/froggypond.htm. Self-catering accommodation in a two-storey timber and brick cottage. Downstairs is a self-contained flatlet with a double bedroom and living area (discounts for stays of 4 days or longer); upstairs are two double rooms with en-suite showers. R350

Lily Pond Lodge 102 Nature's Valley Rd; 3km from the N2 along the R102 and 6km from Nature's Valley ☎ 044 534 8767, ⓦ lilypond.co.za. Probably the most memorable accommodation in Nature's Valley, the lodge distinguishes itself through its sharp sense of style and its commitment to luxury. The four en-suite rooms have French doors opening onto private terraces, plus sound systems, TV and wi-fi access, while the two spacious luxury suites also have their own lounge, underfloor heating and

king-sized beds. There are three even more luxurious garden suites and a honeymoon suite that has its own private garden. R1380

Nature's Valley Guest House 411 St Patrick's Ave ☎ 044 531 6805, ⓦ naturesvalleyguesthouse.co.za. A well-located and well-priced B&B. Guests have use of a windsurfer, canoe and surfboard, and can set out from here on hikes along the beaches or through the forest. R580

Tranquility Lodge 130 Saint Michael's St (next to the shop) ☎ 044 531 6663, ⓦ tranquilitylodge.co.za. If Nature's Valley has a centre then this comfortable lodge, next to the village's only shop, is bang in the middle of it. A two-storey brick and timber building set in a garden that feels as if it's part of the encroaching forest, it is just 50m from the beach. Breakfast is served on an upstairs deck among the treetops. All rooms are en suite and there's also a larger honeymoon suite with a spa bath, double shower, fireplace and private deck. R1180

CAMPING

Nature's Valley restcamp 1km to the north of the village. Bookings through South African National Parks (see p.31), or if you're already in Nature's Valley, the camp supervisor ☎ 044 531 6700. Campsites tucked into indigenous forest, and basic two-person forest huts with communal ablution facilities. R365

EATING AND DRINKING

Nature's Valley Trading Store Forest and St Michael sts ☎ 044 531 6835. The only place in the village that does food and booze is a pretty informal and convivial spot for

seafood, steaks, burgers and toasted sandwiches, and provides the only nightlife – a large-screen TV – apart from gazing at the stars (R50). Daily 9.30am–8.45pm.

Storms River Mouth

55km east of Plettenberg Bay • Daily 7am–7pm • R100 • ☎ 042 281 1607

In contrast to the languid lagoon and long soft sands of Nature's Valley, **Storms River Mouth**, 55km from Plettenberg Bay, presents the elemental face of the Garden

17

Route, with the dark Storms River surging through a gorge to battle with the surf. Don't confuse this with **Storms River Village** just off the N2, which is nowhere near the sea.

ARRIVAL AND DEPARTURE   STORMS RIVER MOUTH

By car Storms River Mouth is 18km south of Storms River Bridge. Most people stop at the bridge, on the N2, to gaze into the deep river gorge and fill up at the most beautifully located petrol and service station in the country.
By shuttle You'll need your own wheels to get around

here as there's no public transport to the Mouth. However, *Tsitsikamma Backpackers* (see opposite) can arrange a shuttle service for their guests from Storms River Village to the Mouth (R100/person; minimum three passengers).

ACCOMMODATION

Sited on tended lawns, *Storms River Mouth Restcamp* (☎ 042 281 1607) is poised between a craggy shoreline of black rocks pounded by foamy white surf and steeply raking forested cliffs, and is the ultimate location along the southern Cape coast. It has a variety of accommodation, all with sea views, but each is heavily subscribed in season, so advance booking through **South African National Parks** is essential (see p.31). Two units have **disabled access**.

Camping The camping area is superbly located, just metres from where the surf breaks on the rocks. R235
Forest huts Two-person forest huts are definitely a notch up from camping and offer great value, although they are quite small and basic. Bedding and towels are provided, but you share washing and cooking facilities with other guests. R340

Chalets and Oceanettes Comfortable one-bedroom, fully equipped self-catering cabins mostly with two single beds, although some have doubles. They have their own kitchens and bathrooms. Oceanettes are right on the ocean's edge. R690
Family Cottages Similar to the chalets, but with two bedrooms and sleep four people. R1215

EATING

Tsitsikamma Restaurant The only place to eat at Storms River Mouth has such startling views that it can be forgiven its mediocre fare of traditional English breakfasts,

toasted sandwiches, burgers, pastas and steak. They also do a reasonable range of seafood dishes. Daily 8.30am–10pm. R100

Storms River Village

About a kilometre south of the national road, **STORMS RIVER VILLAGE** is a tranquil place crisscrossed by a handful of dirt roads and with a few dozen houses, enjoying mountain vistas. The main attraction of the village is as a centre for adventure activities, of which the canopy tour zip line is the really substantial drawcard (see box opposite).

ARRIVAL AND DEPARTURE   STORMS RIVER VILLAGE

Intercity buses Greyhound, Translux and Intercape intercity buses pull in on their daily hauls along the N2 between Cape Town and Port Elizabeth at the filling station at the Storms River Bridge, some 5km from the village.
Destinations: Cape Town (6–7 daily; 8hr 45 min); Knysna (6–7 daily; 1hr 20min); Mossel Bay (6–7 daily; 3hr); Plettenberg Bay (6–7 daily; 50min); Port Elizabeth (6–7 daily; 2hr 30min); Sedgefield (6–7daily; 1hr 40min).

Baz Bus The only transport into Storms River Village proper is on the Baz Bus, which pulls in at the backpacker hostels daily in each direction on its way between Cape Town and Port Elizabeth.
Shuttle bus Some of the backpacker hostels, among them *Tsitsikamma Backpackers* offer a free shuttle service to and from the bridge as well as shuttles to Storms River Mouth in the Garden Route National Park, the Bloukrans Bungee site, Nature's Valley and Plettenberg Bay.

ACCOMMODATION

The Armagh Fynbos Ave ☎ 042 281 1512, ⊕ thearmagh.com. A hospitable guesthouse in a beautiful garden that drifts off into the *fynbos*. The rooms include two budget rooms, three standard ones, two garden cottages and a honeymoon room, all of which open onto the garden. There's also a decent restaurant. R75, cottage R1450

At the Woods Guest House 49 Formosa St, along the main drag into town ☎ 042 281 1446, ⊕ atthewoods .co.za. Friendly, modern guesthouse that's the nicest place in town, with traditional reed ceilings and large, comfortable rooms with king-sized beds and French doors that open onto garden verandas, or upstairs, onto private

17

STORMS RIVER ACTIVITIES

Storms River Village makes a good base for numerous local adventure activities as well as those further afield.

Blackwater Tubing *Tube 'n Axe Backpackers* operate trips down the Storms River gorge, where during the high-water season (generally winter) you ride the river and its rapids buoyed up by a small inflatable.

Boat trips SANParks (☎ 042 281 1607) runs trips (every 45min 9.30am–2.45pm; R66) about 1km up Storms River leaving from near the dive shop, just beneath the restaurant.

Mountain biking A 22km mountain trail winds through the forest on the edge of the village and offers terrific views of the river gorge and coastline. Tsitsikamma Backpackers rent out mountain bikes for the day (R100).

Quad biking Bikes can be rented for R350 an hour from Tsitsikamma Falls Adventures (☎ 042 5280 3770, ⓦ tsitsikammaadventure.co.za).

Woodcutters' Journey A relaxed jaunt organized by Storms River Adventures (☎ 042 281 1836, ⓦ stormsriver.com; teatime trip R140, lunch trip R200),

which has its headquarters next to the Storms River Village post office. The trip takes you down through the forest to the river along the old Storms River Pass in a specially designed trailer, drawn by a tractor.

Zipline Run by Storms River Adventures (see Woodcutters' Journey, above), the Canopy Tour (R450) through the treetops gives a bird's eye view of the forest as you travel 30m above ground along a series of interconnected cables attached to the tallest trees. The system has been constructed in such a way that not a single nail has been hammered into any tree. A faster, higher alternative, geared more to adrenaline junkies, is the zipline tour across the Kruis River at Tsitsikamma Falls Adventures (☎ 072 030 4367, ⓦ tsitsikammaadventure.co.za; R350), which at times is 50m above the ground and crisscrosses an awesome ravine, zipping over three waterfalls, with the longest slide measuring 211m.

decks with mountain views. Three-course home-cooked dinners can be arranged. **R990**

Tsitsikamma Backpackers 54 Formosa St ☎ 042 281 1868, ⓦ tsitsikammabackpackers.co.za. Well-run hostel, whose accommodation options include luxury tents set in a beautiful garden that claims environmentally friendly and fair-trade credentials. You can self-cater or order a reasonably priced breakfast or dinner and there's a bar. They offer a shuttle service to local attractions and pick up guests for free from the Storms River Bridge. Tents **R240**, dorms **R120**, doubles **R300**

Tsitsikamma Lodge A couple of kilometres east of town along the N2, 8km east of the Storms River Bridge ☎ 042 280 3802, ⓦ www.riverhotels.co.za/tsitsikamma. Thirty cosy, A-frame cabins with their own decks and connected by boardwalks that traverse beautifully kept gardens. Most cabins have their own

jacuzzi, and there are a number of forest walks. There's also a restaurant serving South African cuisine. **R1380**

Tsitsikamma Village Inn Darnell St, along the road into the village and left at the T-junction ☎ 042 281 1711, ⓦ village-inn.co.za. A charming, old-fashioned hotel – part of the huge Protea chain – in the village with 49 rooms in eleven cottages, each differently themed and surrounding a manicured garden. **R850**

Tube 'n Axe On the corner of Darnell and Saffron sts ☎ 042 281 1757, ⓦ tubenaxe.co.za. A wacky place that works hard to compete with the bright lights of Knysna and Plett by offering backpackers drumming nights, a pool table and loads of laughs. Accommodation, besides the usual dorms and doubles, includes two-person elevated tents. Tents **R150**, dorms **R125**, doubles **R300**

EATING AND DRINKING

De Oude Martha *Tsitsikamma Village Inn*, Darnell St. Totally acceptable, if unexceptional, hotel restaurant that serves up unpretentious breakfasts, lunches and dinners, and still dines out on the fact that the *New York Times* rated it the "best restaurant in the Tsitsikamma" in 1991 (R85). Daily 7am–10pm.

Rafters The Armagh, Fynbos Ave. The dinner menu has an emphasis on the local: South African cuisine using organic vegetables grown in the village, fish from Plettenberg Bay and meat sourced nearby. Cape Muslim sweet and mild curries feature big on the menu. They also do a set or a la carte breakfast and lunch (R100). Daily 8am–2.30pm & 6–8.30pm.

THE OSTRICH FARM, OUDTSHOORN

Route 62 and the Little Karoo

One of the most rewarding journeys in the Western Cape is an inland counterpart to the Garden Route (see Chapter 17) – the mountain route from Cape Town to Port Elizabeth, largely along the R62, and thus often referred to as Route 62. Nowhere near as well known as the coastal journey, this trip takes you through some of the most dramatic passes and poorts (valley routes) in the country and crosses a frontier of dorps (villages) and drylands. This "back garden" is in many respects more rewarding than the actual Garden Route, being far less developed, with spectacular landscapes, quieter roads and some great small towns to visit.

The central point is Oudtshoorn, but it's particularly worth breaking your journey before then, to explore the pretty towns of McGregor, Montagu and Barrydale.

Continuing east from Barrydale, the R62 landscape becomes more spare as you get into the **Little Karoo** (or Klein Karoo), a vast, khaki-coloured hinterland (the name is a Khoi word meaning "hard and dry") with low, wiry scrub and dotted with flat-topped hills. One unsung surprise along the way is **Calitzdorp**, a rustic little *dorp*, five hours' solid driving from Cape Town, down whose backstreets a few unassuming wine farms produce some of South Africa's best port. By contrast, the well-trumpeted attractions of **Oudtshoorn**, half an hour further on, are the ostrich farms and the massive **Cango Caves**, one of the country's biggest tourist draws. Less than 70km from the coast, with good transport connections, Oudtshoorn marks the convergence of the mountain and coastal roads and is usually treated as a leisurely day-trip away from the Garden Route. From Oudtshoorn, over the most dramatic of all passes in the Cape – the unpaved **Swartberg Pass**, 27km of spectacular switchbacks and zigzags through the Swartberg Mountains – is **Prince Albert**, a favourite Karoo village whose spartan beauty and remarkable light make it popular with artists; the village boasts a worthwhile gallery of the artists' work and some excellent accommodation.

Worcester

Worcester, the large functional hub of the region, is on the N1 just 110km from Cape Town, and worth a stop if you are interested in Cape flora. Worcester has little appeal for tourists, it is an agricultural centre at the centre of a wine-making region, consisting mostly of co-operatives producing bulk plonk, and for most travellers it marks the place to buy petrol and deviate from the N1 onto the scenic R62. However, if you are in need of a break, consider visiting the peaceful botanical gardens for tea, rather than sitting at the petrol station. An interesting nugget is that J.M. Coetzee, South Africa's most acclaimed writer internationally, grew up here, though nothing yet in the town makes mention of its famous son.

Karoo Desert Botanic Gardens

Daily 7am–7pm · R20 · Restaurant daily 9am–5pm · ☎ 023 347 0785

As you enter Worcester from Cape Town, signs point to the **Karoo Botanic Gardens**, a sister reserve to Kirstenbosch in Cape Town known for its show of indigenous spring flowers and succulents. Looking out over the gardens onto an attractive mountain backdrop, the pleasant **restaurant** here serves light meals. The best time to visit the gardens is from late July to early September when all the flowers people travel to see in Namaqualand, bloom here in profusion in purples, oranges and yellows. Three hiking trails meander through large wild areas, full of desert plants and prickly blooms, and in the winter, snow caps the dramatic backdrop of the Hex River mountain range.

McGregor

McGregor is an attractive small village, with whitewashed cottages that sparkle in the summer daylight amid the low scrub, vines and olive trees. Its quiet, relaxed atmosphere has attracted a small population of spiritual seekers and artists, and residents are urged to build in harmony with existing style and thus maintain the town's character. It makes a great weekend break from Cape Town, with a couple of decent restaurants, plenty of well-priced accommodation and a beautiful retreat centre with reasonably priced massage and other body-work. Spending a day wine tasting around McGregor and its environs is another drawcard, as long as it's not a Sunday when almost everything is closed.

McGregor gained modest prosperity in the nineteenth century by becoming a centre of the whipstock industry, supplying wagoners and transport riders with long bamboo

18

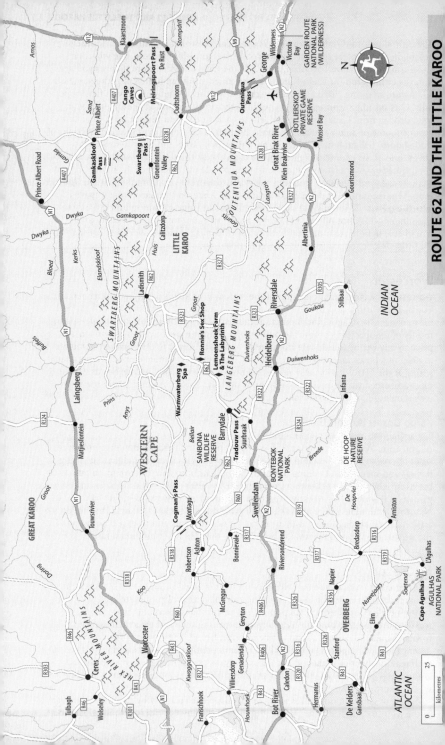

N

GARDEN ROUTE
NATIONAL PARK
(WILDERNESS)

N2

N9

Wilderness

George

Victoria Bay

BOTLIERSKOP
PRIVATE GAME
RESERVE

Mossel Bay

Outeniqua Pass

OUTENIQUA MOUNTAINS

Great Brak River
Klein Brakrivier

R328

Gourits

Gourikou

Langou

R327

N2

Gourtismond

INDIAN OCEAN

Albertinia

R305

Stilbaai

Riversdale

Goukou

R323

Heidelberg

N2

Duiwenhoks

Duiwenhoks

Infanta

R322

R322

DE HOOP
NATURE
RESERVE

De Hoopvlei

Breede

Amiston

R319

Bredasdorp

R316

R317

R339

L'Agulhas

Cape Agulhas

AGULHAS
NATIONAL PARK

Soetendal

Nuwejaars

OVERBERG

Napier

R316

R326

Elim

Stanford

R326

R43

De Kelders

Gansbaai

ATLANTIC OCEAN

Klaasstroom

R112

Amos

Stompdrif

De Rust

Meiringspoort Pass

Cango Caves

R407

Sand

Prince Albert

Gamkaskloof Pass

Swartberg Pass

Groenfontein Valley

R328

R62

Oudtshoorn

R112

Gamkapoort

Huis

Calitzdorp

LITTLE KAROO

Ladsmith

R62

Groot

Elandskloof

Kerks

SWARTBERG MOUNTAINS

R327

R321

Groot

Ronnie's Sex Shop

Lemoenshoek Farm
& The Labyrinth

R62

Warmwaterberg
Spa

LANGEBERG MOUNTAINS

Barrydale

SANBONA
WILDLIFE
RESERVE

Bellair

Tradouw Pass

Suurbraak

BONTEBOK
NATIONAL
PARK

R324

Swellendam

R60

N2

Riviersonderend

R317

Bonnievale

McGregor

R406

Genadendal

Greyton

R406

Villiersdorp

Kwaggaskloof

Bot River

Caledon

R320

R316

Hermanus

Houwhoek

R43

Prince Albert Road

N1

Comka

Gamka

R407

Dwyka

Dwyka

Bloed

Buffels

N1

Laingsberg

Prins

Anys

WESTERN CAPE

GREAT KAROO

Matjiesfontein

N1

R324

Touwsrivier

Groot

Doring

R318

R318

Montagu

Cogman's Pass

Ashton

Robertson

R318

Koo

R60

Worcester

HEX RIVER
MOUNTAINS

CERES
MOUNTAINS

R43

R321

R46

R303

Tulbagh

Wolseley

R46

R301

Ceres

Franschhoek

R43

0   25
kilometres

sticks for goading oxen. There aren't too many ox-drawn wagons today, and tourism, though developing, is still quite limited. One reason people come here is to walk the **Boesmanskloof Traverse** (see box, p.183), which starts 14km from McGregor and crosses to Greyton on the other side of the mountain. From McGregor you can walk a section of the trail, hiking to the main waterfall and back to the trailhead, which is a three- to four-hour round hike of exceeding beauty through the river gorge, or *kloof* in Afrikaans.

You'll find most of what you want down Voortrekker Street, McGregor's main thoroughfare, dominated by a Dutch Reformed church.

18

ARRIVAL AND DEPARTURE

MCGREGOR

By car McGregor, 180km from Cape Town and fifteen minutes to the south of Robertson, is at the end of a minor road signposted off the R60. Don't be tempted by an approach from the south which may look like a handy back route – you'd need a 4WD for this. Allow two and a half hours for the drive from Cape Town along the N1, turning onto the R62 at Worcester for Robertson.

INFORMATION

Tourist office Voortrekker Street (Mon–Fri 9am–1pm & 2–4.30pm, Sat & Sun 9am–1pm; ☎ 023 625 1954, ⓦ tourismmcgregor.co.za). The office can book you accommodation and issue permits for walking the whole Boesmanskloof Traverse or simply for the waterfall section (R30). They will also direct you to artists' studios in town, and to complementary health practitioners offering massage and yoga, and give you times of the daily meditation sessions at *Temenos Retreat Centre*.

ACCOMMODATION

The Barn Grewe St; book through the tourist office. Beautifully restored barn sleeping five in three rooms, with a Victorian bath, antique Cape furniture, fireplace and wood-burning stove. The barn is taken as a whole, which is a bit pricey if there are only two of you. **R1000**

Langewater Farm 2km outside town towards Boesmanskloof; book through the tourist office. Three no-frills, very reasonably priced self-catering cottages on a working farm. Ideal for families, with plenty of animals and space to run about. **R400**

McGregor Country Cottages Voortrekker St ☎ 023 625 1816, ⓦ mcgregor.org.za/countrycottages.php. Tranquil self-catering in a complex of cottages, both wheelchair and child friendly, with traditional reed ceilings and fireplaces, surrounded by gardens, orchards and vegetable patches. There's also a pool, and a separate honeymoon house is available and worth the price (R600). **R550**

McGregor Country House Voortrekker St ☎ 023 625 1656. B&B in a Victorian cottage on the main road with a pretty garden, three en-suite rooms, swimming pool and cosy Irish-style pub. Delicious continental breakfasts served by the friendly hostess Carol Smith. **R600**

Onverwacht At the trailhead of the Boesmanskloof Traverse ☎ 023 625 1667. Basic semi-equipped huts with spectacular views, no electricity and river pools for swimming – bring your own sleeping bag, towels and supplies. **R200**

Rhebokskraal Farm Cottages 2km south of town ☎ 023 625 1787, ⓔ rhebokskraal@hermann.co.za. Secluded cottages, each on a different part of this beautiful fruit, olive and grape farm, which is within easy reach of the restaurants in town. **R440**

★ **Temenos Country Retreat** On the corner of Bree and Voortrekker sts ☎ 023 625 1871, ⓦ temenos.org. za. Retreat centre with cottages dotted about beautiful gardens and walkways, a lap-length swimming pool, a library and meditation spaces. Breakfast is included and it's safe and peaceful – an ideal place for lone female travellers. **R700**

EATING AND DRINKING

Deli Girls Great for picnic supplies with homemade bread, smoked fish, cheese, chocolate and other tempting goodies; it also serves coffee and light lunches. You can sit on the back porch to savour home-made dishes, such as cottage pie and salad or tandoori pork chop (R50). Daily 9am–4.30pm.

Forty One Home-made preserves and organic fruit nectars for sale and it's good for daytime snacks and teas, with a veranda from which to watch the passing scene. You can feast on spareribs too (R80). Tues–Sat 10am–9pm.

Green Gables Mill House at the top of Voortrekker. The most formal of the establishments for a special dinner in an historical home, with a view over vineyards and cosy log fires in the winter (R100). Wed, Fri & Sat 7–9pm, booking essential.

★ **Tebaldi's at Temenos** Delicious tapas, cheeses, Italian fare and local wines served in a tranquil garden setting or at street-side tables, at the front of the village's well-known spiritual retreat centre. Try the butternut and sun-dried tomato soup (R80). Tues–Sun 9.30am–4.30pm, dinner Wed–Sat also 7–9.30pm.

Montagu

18

Some 190km from Cape Town, and 47km from McGregor, is **MONTAGU**, the centre of a major peach- and apricot-growing region whose soaring mountains with twisted red and ochre strata dominate the town with its pleasing Victorian architecture.

The town was named in 1851 after **John Montagu**, the visionary British Secretary of the Cape, who realized that the colony would never develop without decent communications and was responsible for commissioning the first mountain passes connecting remote areas to Cape Town. Montagu is best known for its **hot springs**, but serious **rock climbers** come for its cliff faces, which are regarded as among the country's most challenging. One of South Africa's top climbers runs *De Bos Guest Farm* (see below), which you could use as a base for climbing. You can also explore the mountains on a couple of trails or, easiest of all, on a tractor ride onto one of the peaks. Montagu is also conveniently positioned for excursions along both the Robertson and Little Karoo **wine routes**.

Highly photogenic, Montagu is ideal for seeing on foot, taking in the interesting buildings or simply enjoying the setting, with its mountains, valleys and farms.

Montagu Museum
41 Long St • Mon–Fri 9am–5pm, Sat & Sun 10.30am–12.30pm • R10

The best thing about the **Montagu Museum**, housed in a pleasant old church, is its herbal project, which traces traditional Khoisan knowledge about the medicinal properties of local plants. Also notice a style of flooring in these fruit-picking parts which uses embedded peachkernels for texture and many driveways use peach pips rather than gravel.

ARRIVAL AND DEPARTURE
MONTAGU

By car Montagu is 190km from Cape Town. Take the N1 from the capital as far as Worcester and then head southeast on the R60. The journey from Worcester (roughly 60km) takes you through Robertson and Ashton.

Buses to Montagu are restricted to a service from Belville in Cape Town via Paarl and Worcester, operated by Munniks (☎021 637 1850), departing Cape Town on Friday and returning on Sunday.

INFORMATION

Tourist office 24 Bath St (Mon–Fri 8am–6pm, Sat 9am–5pm, Sun 9.30am–5pm; ☎023 614 2471).

ACCOMMODATION

Even if you're here for the springs, it is far nicer to find somewhere to **stay** in town rather than at the spa, which amounts to little more than a large crowded resort, especially at weekends and school holidays.

Aasvoelkrans 1 Van Riebeeck St ☎023 614 1228, ⓦaasvoelkrans.co.za. Four exceptionally imaginative garden rooms at a guesthouse situated on an Arab thoroughbred stud farm, in a pretty part of town. R900

Cynthia's 3 Krom St ☎023 614 2760, ⓦwww .cynthias-cottages.co.za. Seven self-catering cottages dotted around the west side of town, all in old houses, with gardens and braai areas, and near the starting point for hiking trails. R320

De Bos Guest Farm 8 Brown St ☎023 614 2532, ⓦdebos.co.za. Camping, dorms and basic doubles on a farm at the western edge of town, run by rock climbers, where you can be taken on guided climbs, though you need to have your own gear and book in advance. There are also hikes on your doorstep, but you don't have to be into mountains to enjoy staying here. Camping R40, dorms R80, doubles R360

Montagu Rose Guest House 19 Kohler St ☎023 614 2681, ⓦmontagurose.co.za. In a modern home, with

18

MONTAGU SPRINGS RESORT

Signposted about 3km northwest of town on the R318, Montagu's main draw is the **Montagu Springs Resort** (daily 8am–11pm; R70; ⓦ montagusprings.co.za) Several chlorinated open-air pools of different temperatures and a couple of jacuzzis are spectacularly situated at the foot of the cliffs – an effect slightly spoilt by the neon lights of a hotel complex and fast-food restaurant. It's a fabulous place to take kids, but the weekends become a mass of splashing bodies: if you want a quiet time, go first thing in the morning or last thing at night. The temperatures in winter are not hot enough to be entirely comfortable, when you're better off heading to the springs at **Caledon** (p.181) or **Warmwaterberg** (p.234), which are much hotter, and in many respects preferable.

personalized service, all the rooms have baths and mountain views. It's well run and good value. <u>R700</u>

Montagu Springs Signposted off the R62, west of town ⓣ 023 614 1050, ⓦ montagusprings.co.za. Large resort with fully equipped self-catering chalets, some more luxurious than others, sleeping four. Prices go up by roughly a third at weekends and during school holidays. <u>R450</u>

Squirrel's Corner On the corner of Bloem and Jouberts sts ⓣ 023 614 1081, ⓦ squirrelscorner. co.za. A lovely B&B with four comfortable, spotless en-suite rooms in a friendly family house, as well as a garden suite situated two blocks from the main road. <u>R550</u>

EATING AND DRINKING

Farm stalls as you drive through Montagu on the R62 are worth stopping at for nibbles and local produce, and on Saturday mornings, don't miss the local **farmers' market** at the church, where you can get olives and olive oil, bread, cheese, almonds and dried fruit from the surrounding farms – all exceptionally well priced. In summer bags of peaches and apricots are often sold from backyards or along the roadside, for next to nothing.

Die Stal 8km out of town on the R318 ⓣ 082 324 4318. A thoroughly pleasant venue on a farm serving breakfast, lunches and teas, en route to the obligatory tractor ride. A good destination venue if you want to see something of the surrounding orchards and farmlands and sit on the porch (R60). Try their peppermint crisp tart. Tues–Sun 9am–5pm.

Jessica's 28 Bath St ⓣ 023 614 1805. Small and friendly, named after the proprietors' boxer dog and decorated with period dog prints. Here you'll get fairly pricey, refined, cosmopolitan bistro-style dishes and a top selection of Robertson wines; the cajun-roasted baby chicken on wild rice with *peri-peri* cream is recommended, as is the vegetable curry (R110). Daily 6.30–9.30pm, except Tues during winter.

Preston's Restaurant & Thomas Bain Pub Bath St ⓣ 023 614 3013. Small, intimate nightspot that remains open till late and is recommended for its pub rather than its food. It is primarily the local pub, and will stay open until the last customer leaves. Daily 11am–2.30pm & 5.30pm till late.

Templetons@Four Oaks 46 Long St ⓣ 023 614 2778. Pub and restaurant with meat and fish dishes, and a nice shady courtyard of a beautiful thatched house. Vegetarians can get a good spinach and goat's cheese ravioli while carnivores should enjoy the marinated lamb rump in a port sauce (R110). Summer daily 12.30–2.30pm & 6–9pm; winter Mon–Sat 6–9pm.

Barrydale

BARRYDALE, 240km from Cape Town, is perfect for a couple of days of doing very little other than experiencing small-town life in the Little Karoo, with good, reasonably priced accommodation, hot springs at **Warmwaterberg** or picnics along the Tradouw Pass. West of town you'll find big game – and correspondingly high rates – at the magnificent **Sanbona Wildlife Reserve**, though day visitors are not accepted.

Not yet on the tourist route, Barrydale nonetheless has a number of restaurants and decent places to stay, and the sixty-kilometre drive from Montagu offers spectacular mountain scenery. There's a distinct rural feel about Barrydale: vineyards line the main road, farm animals are kept on large plots of land behind dry-stone walling, and you'll find fig, peach and quince trees thriving in the dryness.

ARRIVAL AND DEPARTURE BARRYDALE

Allow three to three and a half hours for the journey from Cape Town, either taking the N1 and R62, or the N2, and cutting inland on the R324 just east of Swellendam for the lovely drive through Suurbraak and the Tradouw Pass. Both routes are equally recommended for the scenery and ease of travel.

INFORMATION

The R62 swings past the village, whose entrance is marked by a tiny **visitor information centre** (Mon–Fri 8.30am–1.15pm & 2–5pm; ☎ 028 572 1572). Turning off the R62 takes you along van Riebeeck Street, the main drag, with more pedestrians than cars, dominated by the ivory church and one **supermarket**, which houses an **ATM** and post office.

18

ACCOMMODATION

Goose and Gum Villiers St, phone for directions ☎ 028 572 1419, ✉ nigel@tugshill.co.za. Two tasteful, compact, self-catering cottages in a garden setting, at the home of Nigel and Linda, two Barrydale artists. One cottage has an outdoor shower and the garden leads to a dam with lots of birdlife. R250

★ **Tradouw Guest House** 46 van Riebeeck St ☎ 028 572 1434, ⌨ home.intekom.com/

tradouwguesthouse. One of the best accommodation places along the R62 is the friendly *Tradouw Guest House*, with four simple, homely rooms opening onto a courtyard shaded by vines where you can breakfast, and two onto the appealing large garden. Rates are extremely reasonable, and during the day you can eat at their on-site café or get a picnic. R550

EATING

Blue Cow Signposted off the eastern side of the R62. The setting, overlooking fields and a dam is restful and they do pleasant cakes and light meals. This is the best place if you are travelling with children and they need to run around. Mon–Sat 8am–5pm.

Clarke of the Karoo On R62. A great option for tasty steaks, *bobotie* and other hearty country fare, with a starter provided on the house. Their Karoo lamb curry or venison burger on ciabatta are recommended (R90). Mon–Sun 8am–5pm.

★ **Garden Café at the Tradouw Guest House** 46 Van Riebeeck St. A delightful spot, to watch the world go by from the veranda, feasting on real coffee, fresh salads, quiche and toasted bacon and egg sarnies, all served by the friendliest hosts in town (R60). Daily 8am–8pm.

Jam Tarts On R62. Of the several places strung along the R62, if you are driving through, rather than turning into Barrydale, the best place for coffee and light meals is *Jam Tarts*, where you can also pick up local olives and delicious jams with funky labels. Dishes include delicious soups, pizzas and other light meals. Tues–Sun 9am–9pm, Mon 6–9pm.

★ **Mez** On the corner of Van Riebeeck and Laing sts ☎ 028 572 1259. Excellent and reasonably priced Mediterranean food in the form of light tapas meals or their lamb speciality. Their bright-pink rose water ice cream served with pistachios and fresh mint is always delightful. Sit outside on the wooden benches for some street surveying, or inside where it's decorated with Persian rugs and batiks. Tues–Sat 6–10pm.

SHOPPING

A couple of **wine outlets** are worth a visit for tasting and buying, particularly the Southern Cape Winery in Van Riebeeck Street (Mon–Fri 8am–5pm, Sat 9am–3pm; ☎ 028 572 1012). Along the R62 itself, are interesting craft shops, as one would expect from an artistic community, and good cafés.

Sanbona Wildlife Reserve

R4800 • ☎ 028 572 1365, ⌨ sanbona.com

Twenty kilometres west of Barrydale, Sanbona Wildlife Reserve is the amalgamation

THE LABYRINTH

The Labyrinth, 15km east of Barrydale on a small farm at Lemoenhoek, is a beautiful outdoor maze based on one at Chartres Cathedral in France (by appointment only, with a donation to animal rehab; ☎ 028 572 1404). The circuit is demarcated by rose quartz stones and allows you to gaze at the mountains as you move through. On the same property is a Buddhist Peace Pagoda, a rather wonderful curiosity in this out-of-the-way place, at which you can stop off to visit.

18

WARMWATERBERG SPA

Thirty kilometres east of Barrydale (just beyond *Ronnie's Sex Shop*, a pub and well-known jokey landmark in the middle of nowhere), is **Warmwaterberg Spa** (☎ 028 572 1609, ⓦ warmwaterbergspa.co.za) a Karoo farm blessed with natural hot water siphoned into two, unchlorinated hot pools and surrounded by lush green lawns and lofty palms. Primarily aimed at South Africans, it gets rather crowded and noisy during school holidays and over weekends. Indeed, the best time of day to enjoy the baths is after dark, when the steam rises into the cold, starry Karoo sky.

Accommodation is basic, reasonably priced and all self-catering – in wooden cabins or rooms in the main farmhouse, each of which has an indoor spa bath (R535). There are also some campsites (R255), a bar and a restaurant serving dinners and breakfasts. Room rates start at R255 but are lowered on weekdays and during the school term.

of 21 farms that together create a massive wilderness area. The landscape is gorgeous – rocky outcrops, mountains and semi-desert vegetation with luxurious all-inclusive lodges, *Dwyka Tented Lodge* and *Gondwana Family Lodge*. *Dwyka* is closer to where most of the game is to be found and has the more spectacular setting, while *Gondwana* is great if you are travelling with kids. The price (see sight details on the previous page) includes two game drives a day, but, owing to the vegetation, the game is far sparser here than in the major game-viewing areas such as the Kruger National Park. Having said that, it is the only place in the Western Cape with free-roaming lions and cheetahs and there's a herd of elephants. Sanbona is worth considering only if you are set on seeing some big game and don't have time for Kruger. A two-night stay is recommended and day visitors are not allowed – check for specials and cheaper winter rates.

Oudtshoorn

From Barrydale, vineyards and orchards give way to arid mountains and rocky, treeless plains vegetated with low, wiry scrub, making for a dramatic journey onwards, and another spectacular, twisting pass. **OUDTSHOORN**, 420km from Cape Town and 180km from Barrydale, has been called the "ostrich capital of the

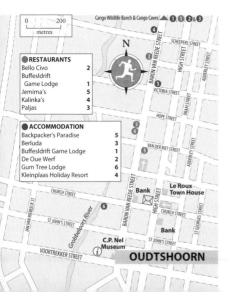

RESTAURANTS

Bello Civo	2
Buffelsdrift	
Game Lodge	1
Jemima's	5
Kalinka's	4
Paljas	3

ACCOMMODATION

Backpacker's Paradise	5
Berluda	3
Buffelsdrift Game Lodge	1
De Oue Werf	2
Gum Tree Lodge	6
Kleinplaas Holiday Resort	4

OUDTSHOORN

world"; the town's surrounds are indeed crammed with ostrich farms, several of which you can visit, and the local souvenir shops keep busy dreaming up 1001 tacky ways to recycle ostrich parts as comestibles and souvenirs. But Oudtshoorn has two other big draws: it's the best base for visiting the nearby **Cango Caves** (see p.237), and the town is known for its winter sunshine, when it can be raining on the Garden Route. It's boiling hot in summer, though, so make sure you have access to a pool, and nights in winter can freeze.

Oudtshoorn's town centre has little more than a couple of museums worth checking out if you've time to kill. The town's main interest lies in its Victorian and Edwardian sandstone buildings, some of which are unusually grand and elegant for a Karoo *dorp*.

Brief history

Oudtshoorn started out as a small village named in honour of Geesje Ernestina Johanna van Oudtshoorn, wife of the first civil commissioner for George. By the 1860s, **ostriches**, which live in the wild in Africa, were being raised under the ideal conditions of the Oudtshoorn Valley, where the warm climate and loamy soils enabled lucerne, the favourite diet of the flightless birds, to be grown. The quirky Victorian fashion for large feathers had turned the ostriches into a source of serious wealth, and by the 1880s hundreds of thousands of kilogrammes of feathers were being exported, and birds were changing hands for up to £1000 a pair – an unimaginable sum in those days. On the back of this boom, sharp businessmen made their fortunes, ignorant farmers were ripped off, and labourers drew the shortest straw of all. The latter were mostly coloured descendants of the Outeniqua and Attaqua Khoikhoi and trekboers, who received derisory wages supplemented by rations of food, wine, spirits and tobacco – a practice that still continues on some farms. In the early twentieth century, the most successful farmers and traders built themselves "feather palaces", ostentatious sandstone Edwardian buildings that have become the defining feature of Oudtshoorn.

18

C.P. Nel Museum

On the corner of Baron van Reede and Voortrekker sts • Mon–Sat 8am–5pm, Sat 9am–1pm • R15

The **C.P. Nel Museum** is a good place to start your explorations. A handsome sandstone building, it was built in 1906 as a boys' school, but now houses an eccentric collection of items relating to ostriches. It's worth a visit mainly for the story it tells of the town's feather boom and decline, and the contrast between ostrich design items of the past and gorgeous feather trimmings, compared to what you'll see in the tacky ostrich shops today.

Le Roux Town House

On the corner of Loop and High sts • Mon–Fri 9am–5pm • R15

Le Roux Town House is a perfectly preserved family townhouse, and the only way to get a glimpse inside one of the much-vaunted "feather palaces". The family's gracious, opulent style was enjoyed and appreciated by royalty and politicians alike during their visits here. The beautifully preserved furnishings were all imported from Europe between 1900 and 1920, and there is plenty to stroll around and admire, from the art nouveau glass panels inside to the corrugated iron verandas encircling the house.

Buffelsdrift Game Lodge

7km from Oudtshoorn • R180 • ☎ 044 272 0106

The **Buffelsdrift Game Lodge**, just out of town on the Cango Caves road, offers an exciting opportunity to get close to **elephants**. Book ahead for a really worthwhile experience where you get to stroke elephants under the guidance of their handlers, and watch them at training and play throughout the day. From the lodge's **restaurant** on the large dam, you are likely to see hippos, and may be lucky enough to see other animals coming to drink.

Cango Wildlife Ranch

Just outside town on the Cango Rd • Daily 8am–6pm • R110 • ☎ 044 272 5593

The other "wildlife" activity around Oudtshoorn is **Cango Wildlife Ranch**. Guided tours lead you past white tigers and cheetahs, crocodiles and other amazing creatures from other parts of Africa, and you can pay extra to be photographed touching the animals and reptiles, and even get into the pool with the crocodiles. Don't expect it to be thrilling, though; you'll be lucky if a crocodile so much as flicks its eyes while you're in there. The ranch offers a spectacle rather than authentic wildness, but it caters well for children who can frolic in water fountains or on climbing frames while you eat lunch.

18

OSTRICH TOURS

Many people come to Oudtshoorn to see, or even ride, **ostriches**. You don't actually have to visit one of the ostrich farms to view Africa's biggest bird, as you're bound to see flocks of them as you drive past farms in the vicinity or past truckloads of them on their way to the slaughterhouse (feathers being no longer fashionable, these days ostriches are raised for their low-cholesterol flesh). A number of show farms offer **tours**, which include the chance to sit on an ostrich (if you are under 70kg). Best of the bunch is **Cango Ostrich Farm** on the main road between Oudtshoorn and the Cango Caves, in the Schoemanshoek Valley, which takes tours every 20 min, where you can sit on a bird, stand on their unbreakable eggs and look at ostrich chicks. (45min; R70; ☎ 044 272 4623).

ARRIVAL AND DEPARTURE   OUDTSHOORN

By car Allow six hours from Cape Town for the 420km journey along the R62. Alternatively, take the N2 to George along the Garden Route and cut inland to Oudtshoorn on the N12.

By bus Intercity buses pull in at Queens Mall, off Voortrekker Street, across the river from the main road, Baron van Reede.

INFORMATION

Tourist office Baron van Reede Street, next to the *Queens Hotel* (Mon–Fri 8am–5pm, Sat 9am–12pm; ☎ 044 279 2532, ⓦ oudtshoorn.com). Good for information about the

caves, ostrich farms and local accommodation. The main road, Baron van Reede, has a Pick 'n Pay supermarket and an internet café.

ACTIVITIES

Backpacker's Paradise (see below) rents out bikes and also arranges spectacular adventurous cycling trips down

the Swartberg Pass, chaperoned with motor vehicle backup.

ACCOMMODATION

Oudtshoorn has a number of large **hotels** catering mainly to tour buses, plus plenty of good-quality B&Bs and guesthouses, a centrally located campsite with chalets, and one of the country's best-run backpacker lodges. Some of the nicest places to stay are in the attractive countryside en route to Cango Caves. The tourist office offers a free accommodation-booking service. **Rates** fall dramatically during the winter months following the week-long **Klein Karoo Nasionale Kunstefees** (KKNK; ⓦ absaknk.co.za), a major arts festival, mostly in Afrikaans, and street party in the March/April Easter holidays when people from all over the country take every bed in town.

Backpacker's Paradise 148 Baron van Reede St ☎ 044 272 3436, ⓦ backpackersparadise.net. A well-run two-storey hostel along the main drag, which makes an effort to go the extra few centimetres with three-quarter beds, en-suite doubles and family rooms as well as dorms. There are nightly ostrich, or veg-friendly, braais, too, and a daily shuttle from the Baz Bus drop-off in George to the hostel. The on-site adventure centre organizes cycle trips in the Swartberg Pass and there's a daily shuttle to the caves, ostrich farm and wildlife ranch. Dorms R110, doubles R350

Berluda On the R328, 15km from Oudtshoorn, en route to Cango Caves ☎ 044 272 8518, ⓦ berluda .co.za. An avenue of trees leads up to a fairly modern-looking farmhouse with five bedrooms and two self-catering cottages in a well-established garden. The friendly owners can organize ostrich farm tours on their property 8km away, and there is a pool to cool off in. R700

Buffelsdrift Game Lodge 7km from town on the road to the caves ☎ 044 272 0106, ⓦ buffelsdrift.com. The town's top stay, in luxurious en-suite safari tents overlooking a large dam with hippo in it, and a grand thatched dining area. Breakfast is included, and game drives or horseback rides to view rhino, buffalo, elephant, giraffe and various antelope can be included in a package, or paid for separately. R1055

★ **De Oue Werf** Signposted off the R328 to Cango Caves, 12km north of Oudtshoorn ☎ 044 272 8712, ⓦ ouewerf.co.za. Luxurious and well-priced garden rooms on a working farm, run by the very welcoming sixth generation of the family. Green lawns run down to a dam, which has a swinging slide and raft to play on, and lots of birdlife. A great option if you're visiting the caves and want to stay in the country. R900

Gum Tree Lodge 139 Church St ☎ 044 279 2528, ⓦ gumtreelodge.co.za. Six rooms in a peaceful B&B, conveniently a few minutes' walk from the centre, fronting onto a river with good birdlife. This is a good choice if you want a central location with a touch of country. R630

CAMPING
Kleinplaas Holiday Resort 171 Baron van Reede St ☎ 044 272 5811, ⓦ kleinplaas.co.za.

Well-run, spick-and-span shady camping and fully equipped self-catering brick chalets, conveniently close to town, with a swimming pool and launderette. The owners know the town well and will show you the ropes, and can provide breakfast for a little extra. Camping R185, chalets R380

18

EATING AND DRINKING

Oudtshoorn has a choice of several places to eat, mostly strung out along Baron van Reede Street and catering to the tourist trade, with the obligatory ostrich on the menu.

Bello Civo 146 Baron van Reede St ☎ 044 272 3245 Relaxed and reasonably priced Italian place with indoor and outdoor seating, making it easy with children. Besides pizza and pasta, there are some creative ostrich and other Italian-styled meaty offerings (R80). Mon–Sat 10am–11pm.

Buffelsdrift Game Lodge 7km out of town towards Cango Caves ☎ 044 272 0106. Have a great breakfast or lunch on a wooden deck overlooking the waterhole, and do a spot of game-viewing at the same time. The lodge is open to non-guests for meals, and you could combine it with an elephant encounter or other game activity (R80). Daily 7am–3pm.

Jemima's 94 Baron van Reede St ☎ 044 272 0808. An imaginative and good-value menu including

boerewors-stuffed ravioli, butternut cheesecake, game dishes and tasty, light food (R120). Mon–Fri 11am–3pm, daily 6pm till late.

★ **Kalinka's** 93 Baron van Reede St ☎ 044 279 2596. Sandstone house with a fountain outside, specializing in game dishes, with Russian black bread at every meal, and imported vodka. Service is good and food well presented, fresh, delicious and very expensive. The baked cardamom and date brandy pudding is great, and there are some creative choices for vegetarians. Book an outside table in the rose garden on summer evenings (R130). Daily 6–10pm.

Paljas 109 Baron van Reede St ☎ 044 272 0982. A good choice for ostrich steaks with a heavy emphasis on meat generally, in their Pan-African menu (R80). Daily 6–10pm.

Cango Caves

29km from Oudtshoorn • Daily 9am–4pm • R80 • ☎ 044 272 7410, ⓦ cangocaves.co.za

The **Cango Caves** number among South Africa's ten most popular attractions, drawing a quarter of a million visitors each year to gasp at their fantastic cavernous spaces, dripping rocks and rising columns of calcite. In the two centuries since they became known to the public, the caves have been seriously battered by human intervention, but they still represent a stunning landscape growing inside the Swartberg foothills. Don't go expecting a serene and contemplative experience, though: the only way of getting inside the caves is on a **guided tour** accompanied by a commentary.

San hunter-gatherers sheltered in the entrance caves for millennia before white settlers arrived, but it's unlikely that they ever made it to the lightless underground chambers. **Jacobus van Zyl**, a Karoo farmer, was probably the first person to penetrate beneath the surface, when he slid down on a rope into the darkness in July 1780, armed with a lamp. Over the next couple of centuries the caves were visited and pillaged by growing

CAVE TOURS

Two **tours** leave every hour. The one-hour Standard Tour (on the hour; R65) gets you through the first six chambers, but if you're an adrenaline junkie, the ninety-minute Adventure Tour (on the half-hour; R80) is a must; this takes you into the deepest sections open to the public, where the openings become smaller and smaller. Squeezing through tight openings with names like **Lumbago Walk**, **Devil's Chimney** and **The Letterbox** is not recommended for the overweight, faint-hearted or claustrophobic, and you should wear oldish clothes and shoes with a grip to negotiate the slippery floors.

numbers of callers, some of whom were photographed cheerfully carting off wagonloads of limestone columns.

In the 1960s and 1970s the caves were made accessible to mass consumption when a tourist complex was built, the rock-strewn floor was evened out with concrete, ladders and walkways were installed, and the caverns were subsequently turned into a kitsch extravaganza with coloured lights, piped music and an indecipherable commentary that drew hundreds of thousands of visitors each year. Even **apartheid** put its hefty boot in: under the premiership of Dr Hendrik Verwoerd, the arch-ideologue of racial segregation, a separate "non-whites" entrance was hacked through one wall, resulting in a disastrous through-draft that began dehydrating the caves. Fortunately, the worst excesses have now ended; concerts are no longer allowed inside the chambers, and the coloured lights have been removed.

18

ARRIVAL AND DEPARTURE
CANGO CAVES

By car The drive here from Oudtshoorn involves heading north along Baron van Reede Street, and continuing 32km along a signposted scenic, quiet road (R328) to the caves.

From the caves you can continue by car on the R328 to Prince Albert via the majestic Swartberg Pass.

INFORMATION

The **visitors' complex** includes an interpretive centre with quite interesting displays about geology, people and wildlife connected with the caves; the decent *Marimba* **restaurant**; and a souvenir shop. Below the complex you'll find shady picnic sites at the edge of a river that cuts its way into the mountains and along which there are hiking trails.

Calitzdorp

The tiny Karoo village of **CALITZDORP** hangs in a torpor of midday stillness, with its attractive, unpretentious Victorian streets and handful of wineries. There's nothing much to do here, apart from have tea, taste some wine and wander through the streets. Some of South Africa's best ports are produced at the three modest **wineries** signposted down side roads, a few hundred metres from the centre.

ARRIVAL AND DEPARTURE
CALITZDORP

By car Calitzdorp is 370km from Cape Town, 50km east of Oudtshoorn on the R62. If you're driving from the capital, allow for a five-hour drive with a lunch stop; this would be

a good halfway, overnight stop along the R62 if you are travelling between Cape Town and Port Elizabeth.

INFORMATION

Tourist office at the Shell Garage in Voortrekker Street (Mon–Fri 9am–5pm, Sat & Sun 10am–5pm ☎ 044 213 3775, ⓦ calitzdorp.co.za). Has some brochures about the

village and its surroundings, as well as information about the wineries and accommodation.

ACCOMMODATION

Die Dorpshuis Opposite the church ☎ 044 213 3453, ⓦ diedorpshuis.co.za. Airy, no-frills rooms in a nineteenth-century house that offer exceptional value. There is a convenient restaurant on-site that serves up reasonably priced sandwiches, teas and light meals as well as heavier traditional Karoo food, such as stews and lamb. Across the road from the church, you can be treated to bells ringing and organ recitals. R370
Port-Wine Guest House On the corner of Queen and Station sts ☎ 044 213 3131, ⓦ portwine.net. The

smartest and most comfortable guesthouse in town, in a renovated early nineteenth-century homestead overlooking the Boplaas Estate, with an attractive veranda. R840
Welgevonden Guest House St Helena Rd ☎ 044 213 3642, ⓦ welgevondenguesthouse.co.za. A comfortable and country-style guesthouse, on a small Chardonnay farm 300m from the main road. Four en-suite bedrooms in an 1880 outbuilding are furnished with brass or wooden bedsteads, patchwork quilts and wooden family heirloom furniture. R500

The Groenfontein Valley

A circuitous minor route diverts just east of Calitzdorp, signposted Groenfontein Retreat from the R62, and drops into the highly scenic **Groenfontein Valley**. The narrow dirt road twists through the Swartberg foothills, past whitewashed Karoo cottages and farms and across brooks, eventually joining the R328 to Oudtshoorn. Winding through these backroads is also an option to reach the Cango Caves (see p.234) and Prince Albert (see below), one of the best drives you'll ever do in South Africa. Many of the roads are unsealed but are perfectly navigable in an ordinary car if taken slowly.

18

| **ACCOMMODATION** | **GROENFONTEIN VALLEY** |

Kruis Rivier Guest Farm 17km off the R62 (signposted turn off 14km east of Calitzdorp) on a good, wide gravel road ☎ 044 213 3788, ⓦ kruisrivier.co.za. Homely cottages right underneath the mountains, with lovely streams and waterfalls, which make an excellent base for hiking. The owners, who have a policy of keeping prices absolutely affordable, will also do breakfast on request and provide braai packs, home-made bread and wood. **R400**

Red Stone Hills 6km off the R62 (signposted turn-off 14km east of Calitzdorp) ☎ 044 213 3783, ⓦ redstone .co.za. This place has four lovely period-furnished Victorian cottages on a working farm in a landscape full of red rock formations. The owners can provide dinner on request as

well as breakfast. Besides walking and cycling trails, there is birdwatching and four horses on the farm can be ridden. **R680**

★ **Retreat at Groenfontein** 20km from Calitzdorp and 59km from Oudtshoorn ☎ 044 213 3880, ⓦ groenfontein.com. This isolated Victorian colonial farmstead borders on the 2300-square-kilometre Swartberg Nature Reserve, an outstandingly beautiful area of gorges, rivers and dirt tracks. Accommodation is in deliciously comfortable en-suite rooms, each with its own fireplace, and rates include full board with vegetarians well catered for, and hospitable and helpful owners who turn every evening into a fine dinner party. **R1420**

Prince Albert

Isolation has left intact the traditional rural architecture of **PRINCE ALBERT**, an attractive little town 70km north of Oudtshoorn, and 400km from Cape Town, across the loops and razorbacks of the Swartberg Pass – one of the most dramatic drives and entries to a town imaginable. Although firmly in the thirstlands of the South African interior, on the cusp between the Little and Great Karoo, Prince Albert is all the more striking for its perennial spring, whose water trickles down furrows along its streets – a gift that propagates fruit trees and gardens. Visitors mostly come to Prince Albert for the drive through its two southerly gateways – the **Swartberg Pass** on the R328 and **Meiringspoort** on the N12, and to experience some Karoo life with the bonus of friendly natives and good arts, crafts and food.

EXPLORING WITH THE EXPERTS

STARGAZING

The Karoo sky is heaven for astronomers due to the lack of pollution and few lights, and you get some of the Southern Hemisphere's sharpest views of the firmament from here. One of the most exciting things you can do in Prince Albert, if not in South Africa, is to watch the **night skies** with resident astronomer Hans Daehne (new moon only; R250 for a lecture and viewing; ☎ 072 732 2950 ⓦ astrotours.co.za). Be sure to book far in advance for the right phase of the moon.

THE ROCK-ART SITES

You can also visit **rock-art sites** with one of the country's top paleontologists and archeologists, the now retired Dr Judy Maguire, on her farm at the start of the Swartberg Pass. It's a highly recommended way to spend an afternoon, but you'll need to book beforehand to arrange it (☎ 023 541 1713, ✉ questar@icon.co.uk). Making a donation to the town's museum is part of the deal.

18

GO TO HELL

Prince Albert is one of the best places to begin a trip into **Die Hel** (also known as Hell, The Hell or Gamkaskloof), a valley that's part of the Swartberg Nature Reserve. Die Hel is not on the way to anywhere and, although it doesn't look very far on the map, you'll need to allow two and a half hours in either direction to make the spectacular but tortuous drive into it along a dirt road. A 4WD isn't needed, but you should definitely not attempt the drive in the killing heat of December or January without air conditioning. Before attempting the trip, call Nature Conservation (☎044 802 5310), for an update on the condition of the roads.

The attraction of the place is the silence, isolation and birdlife. If you don't want to go it alone, contact Lisa from *Onse Rus* B&B, who organizes tours, for a minimum of two people. You can get picked up if you want to hike a section of the road (4–12km), instead of driving it.

There's **accommodation** here in the form of spick-and-span Nature Conservation cottages (R550; ☎021 659 3500). The valley has no electricity supply, and no shops or any other facilities, though you can order picnic baskets and cooked breakfasts and dinners from Annetje Joubert, a third-generation kloof dweller (☎023 541 1107).

Prince Albert is small enough to explore on foot and you'll find everything you want on the main road. The essence of the town is in the fleeting impressions that give the flavour of a Karoo *dorp* like nowhere else: the silver steeple of the Dutch Reformed church puncturing a deep-blue sky and residents sauntering along or progressing slowly down the main street on squeaky bikes.

Prince Albert Gallery,
57 Church St • Mon–Fri 10am–4pm, Sat & Sun 10am–1pm • Free

The town's beauty has attracted a number of artists to live here, and you'll find the excellent **Prince Albert Gallery**, in an airy Victorian building where you can browse or purchase paintings, sculpture, beadwork, jewellery, ceramics and etchings by local artists. There is also a small **café**.

ARRIVAL AND DEPARTURE — PRINCE ALBERT

By car From Cape Town allow 5–6 hours driving for the 420km trip. The fastest route and least scenic is along the N1, past Laingsburg, and involves no mountain passes; turn off onto the Price Albert Road. The most scenic route is along the R62 to Calitzdorp or Oudtshoorn, and along the R328 over Swartberg, the mighty, gravelled mountain pass that offers some of the best views in the Western Cape.

By train You can take the Cape Town–Johannesburg train to Prince Albert Road station, 45km from the hamlet, and arrange to be collected by your guesthouse, if they are willing. Be warned that the trains are often late, and Prince Albert Road station has absolutely no facilities or means of onward travel.

INFORMATION

Tourist office Church Street (Mon–Fri 9am–5pm, Sat 9am–noon; ☎023 541 1366, ⊛patourism.co.za). Has maps with accommodation, restaurants and craft shops, and can point you to other activities in the area.

Internet access You'll find wi-fi at the *Lazy Lizard* in Church Street which also does good light lunches at reasonable prices.

ACCOMMODATION

There's plenty of stylish accommodation in Prince Albert, mostly in historic limewashed and thatched Karoo cottages, Cape Dutch homesteads or colonial Victorian houses.

Cactus Blue Cottages Behind the National Centre opposite the Swartberg Hotel ☎072 464 1240, ⊛www .princealbert.org.za/cactusblue.htm. Two modern, funky cottages full of space, light and pleasing colours, overlooking a small vineyard. There is a stripey day bed to loll on, a collection of DVDs to watch, and a double mattress on an outside deck if you fancy a night under the stars. R600

Dennehof Guest House Off Christina de Wit St, on the outskirts of town ☎023 541 1227, ⊛dennehof .co.za. Five rooms – the best two with spa baths – in a homestead that is a National Monument. Moutain-biking and hiking trips are offered by the guesthouse; you're driven up the Swartberg, and descend the terrifying 18km on your own two wheels (R250). Renting a bike for a day around town is another, more sedate option (R75). R800

Hoogenoeg Holiday Houses ☎ 023 541 1455. The cheapest accommodation in town is run by Tannie ("Aunt") Alta, who rents out a number of sparsely furnished, old houses in Prince Albert, but bring your own feather duster, and linen if you are particular. R200

Karoo Lodge 66 Church St ☎ 023 541 1467 or ☎ 082 692 7736, ⓦ karoolodge.com. You'll find reasonably priced, spacious accommodation at this B&B, run by a hospitable couple who'll show you the ropes. Each of the suites, complete with pure cotton sheets and goosedown duvets, leads onto the pool and garden filled with crimson bougainvillea. R800

Karoo Views Margrieta Prinsloo Rd ☎ 023 541 1929, ⓦ karooview.co.za. Upmarket, comfortable self-catering in two modern Karoo-style cottages on the edge of town with views of the Swartberg and surrounding countryside, but close enough to walk into town. R700

Mai's Guest House 81 Church St ☎ 023 541 1188, ⓦ www.maisbandb.co.za. A comfortable stay is offered in the restored nineteenth-century house with great linen, a/c, lots of cats and a pool. A fab breakfast is served under the vines, dished up by a full-of-beans Irish owner. R800

★ **Onse Rus** 47 Church St ☎ 023 541 1380, ⓦ onserus .co.za. Cool, thatched B&B rooms attached to a restored Cape Dutch house, with welcoming and informed owners who serve you tea and chocolate or sponge cake on arrival, and do delicious home-made muesli and local yogurt breakfasts, as well as the usual eggs. They also run tours to Die Hel (see box opposite). R840

EATING

While Prince Albert is known more for its dramatic landscape than its food, there is at least one memorable restaurant, in an art gallery, and a couple of others where you can sip a coffee or beer and take in the village street life.

Café Albert 44 Church St ☎ 023 541 1175. You can tuck into tasty quiches, salads, scones, muffins and a variety of coffees on the *stoep* at this little café. Interesting dishes include kudu-steak-filled tortillas and home-made chicken pies (R50). Tues–Sun 8am–4pm.

★ **Gallery Café** Church St ☎ 082 749 2128. Imaginative dishes by passionate chef Brent, who creates a relaxed ambience above the gallery, with balcony seating – first choice for an evening in Prince Albert, and best booked beforehand. Vegetarians and vegans are catered for, there are delightful starters, meat dishes such as kudu,

springbok and chicken and home-made ice creams (R90). Daily 10am–10pm.

Karoo Kombuis 18 Deurdrift St ☎ 023 541 1110. Traditional dishes from this part of the country, with a home-cooked feel and meat galore. It has a nice atmosphere and is a little cheaper than the *Gallery* (R70). Mon–Sat 6–10pm.

Ladida Farmstall At the south end of the main road. Snacks, excellent dried fruit and rusks, as well as local olives which are among the best in South Africa. Daily 8am–5pm.

SHOPPING

Staying firmly in the realm of the handmade, Prince Albert is known for its **mohair products**: rugs, socks, scarves and other garments. Browse in Karoo Looms, 55 Church St next to the gallery which has some bright, funky designs or at Wolskuur Spinners, further down, for more traditional styles. The gallery itself is a rewarding shopping venue.

Gay's Guernsey Dairy at the southern end of town sells fantastic, award-winning **home-made cheeses**, which you can taste before buying, yogurts and cream. If you're travelling with children, you can take them to watch the milking at sunrise, and walk around the farm looking at other farm animals and activities (daily 7–9am & 4–6pm; free).

18

DONKIN STREET, PORT ELIZABETH

Port Elizabeth, Addo and the private reserves

Port Elizabeth, the Eastern Cape's commercial and industrial centre, is for many visitors, a place to start or end a trip along the Garden Route. On the western end of Nelson Mandela Bay (formerly Algoa Bay), the city is the transport hub of the Eastern Cape, well served by flights, trains, buses and car rental companies. Around an hour's drive inland is Port Elizabeth's biggest draw, Addo Elephant Park, the closest Big Five reserve to Cape Town, with virtually guaranteed sightings of elephants, and a good prospect of seeing other big game.

Port Elizabeth

As a city, **PORT ELIZABETH** (often referred to as **PE**) is pretty functional and easy enough to navigate. The industrial feel is mitigated by excellent and safe beaches, and should you end up killing time here, you'll find diversion in beautiful **coastal walks** a few kilometres from town and in the small **historical centre**. A couple of classically pretty rows of Victorian terraces still remain in the **Central** suburb on the hill above the bay, but most of the decent accommodation and eating options are in the beachfront suburbs of **Humewood** and **Summerstrand**.

Port Elizabeth's **city centre** is marred by a network of freeways that cuts a swath across the south of town, blocking off the city from the harbour. The city's white population retreated to the suburbs some time ago, leaving the centre to African traders and township shoppers. The **suburbs** offer little to draw you away from the beachfront, unless you're a shopaholic, in which case you should make a beeline for **Newton Park**, 5km west of the centre and home to the shopping malls of **Greenacres** and **The Bridge**. Further afield in **New Brighton**, you'll find Port Elizabeth's most important museum, the **Red Location Museum of the People's Struggle**, housed in a building that has won several awards.

19

Central suburb

The city's main street, which runs parallel to the freeway as it sweeps into town, has been renamed **Govan Mbeki Avenue** in honour of the veteran activist (father of Thabo Mbeki, South Africa's former president), who died in 2001. African traders dealing a pretty standard selection of crochet and leather goods line up along the

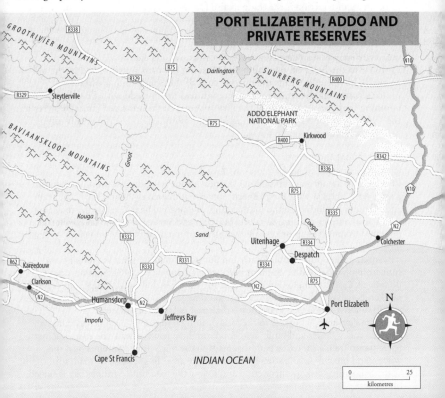

PORT ELIZABETH, ADDO AND PRIVATE RESERVES

pavements giving the precinct a lively feel, but it's not safe after dark. The symbolic heart of town is the **City Hall**, standing in **Market Square**, a large empty space surrounded by some striking mid-Victorian buildings, adjacent to the train and bus stations on the edge of the harbour. But the dejection of the quarter, under the grimy shadow of a flyover, conspires against it ever pumping any real life into the district.

Donkin Street

Heading west up hilly **Donkin Street**, you'll come upon a curious stone pyramid commemorating **Elizabeth Donkin**, after whom PE was named. Elizabeth was the young wife of the Cape's acting governor in 1820, Sir Rufane Donkin; she died of fever in India in 1818. As you stroll up Donkin Street, you could be forgiven for thinking you were in the wrong country, the wrong continent – the raked terrace of Victorian double-storey houses would look completely at home in any town on England's south coast. The nineteen **Donkin Houses**, built in the mid-nineteenth century and declared National Monuments in 1967, reflect the desire of the English settlers to create a home from home in this strange, desiccated land.

Nelson Mandela Metropolitan Art Museum

1 Park Drive • Mon–Fri 8.30am–5pm, Sat 9am–4.30pm, Sun 2–4.30pm • Free

The **Nelson Mandela Metropolitan Art Museum**, situated in two buildings framing the entrance to St George's Park, has a collection of contemporary local work, visiting exhibitions and a small shop selling postcards and local arts and crafts. Their Eastern Cape art section section is the thing to aim for, though they do have some minor European and oriental artworks.

South End Museum

On the corner of Humewood Rd and Walmer Boulevard • Mon–Fri 9am–4pm, Sat & Sun 2–5pm • Free

En route to the beaches, the **South End Museum** is worth a visit. Based in the old Seamen's Institute, it recalls the bygone days of the South End, a vibrant multicultural neighbourhood whose growth had much to do with PE's then booming harbour. As a result of the Group Areas Act it was razed street by street in the 1960s, save for a handful of churches and mosques. Today, the area is full of pricey townhouses.

The beachfront and around

Bayworld Museum and Snake Park daily 9am–4.30pm • R25 • ⓦ www.bayworld.co.za

PE's **beaches** are its main attraction. The beachfront strip, divided from the harbour by a large wall, starts at wide **King's Beach**, somewhat marred by a jumble of coal heaps and oil tanks behind it. To the southeast lies **Humewood Beach**, across the road from which is a complex housing **Bayworld Museum and Snake Park**. **Brookes Pavilion** next door and **Dolphin's Leap** nearby are complexes of restaurants, pubs and clubs with great views.

Beyond, to the south, **Hobie Beach** and **Summerstrand** are great for walking and sunbathing, with one dive operator based at the latter (see p.248). Summerstrand's **Boardwalk Casino Complex** has some pleasing shops, including an indigenous crafts market, cinemas and some reasonable restaurants.

Marine Drive continues 15km down the coast as far as the village of **Schoenmakerskop** (Schoenies to the locals), along impressive coastline that alternates between rocky shores and sandy beaches. From here you can walk the eight-kilometre **Sacramento Trail**, a shoreline path that leads to the huge-duned **Sardinia Bay**, the wildest and most dramatic stretch of coast in the area. To get there by road, turn right at the Schoenmakerskop intersection and follow the road until Sardinia Bay is signed, on the left.

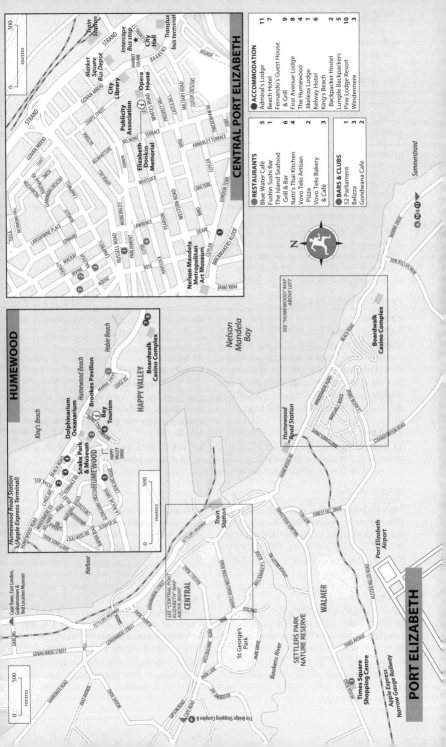

Red Location Museum of the People's Struggle

New Brighton suburb, 7km north of central Port Elizabeth, at the corner of Olof Palme and Singaphi sts • Tues–Fri 9am–4pm, Sat 9am–3pm • R12 • ☎ 041 408 8400

This modern, designer-built museum recalls the experiences of the residents of Red Location, Port Elizabeth's oldest African township, established in 1902. The settlement took its name from the rusted corrugated iron barracks – around which New Brighton developed – that had housed troops till the end of the Anglo-Boer War. A significant site of anti-apartheid resistance, New Brighton was the stomping ground of a number of significant South Africans, including Govan Mbeki, ANC stalwart and father of South Africa's former president, artist George Pemba, and internationally fêted actor John Kani. Red Location was the first place in South Africa to stage a passive resistance campaign against the pass laws (see p.260) and was the birthplace of the first cell of MK (the ANC's armed wing).

The museum is housed in a striking building awarded the 2006 Royal Institute of British Architects' **Lubetkin Prize** for the most outstanding work of architecture outside the European Union. Described by the judges as a "tour de force", the building wears an industrial-style saw-toothed roof that evokes the area's strong association with trade unionism. Inside, a dozen vast, rusted "**memory boxes**" contain exhibits exploring different themes related to the anti-apartheid struggle. The structures are inspired by the containers that migrant workers used to carry their most prized possessions. Four **permanent exhibitions** trace a century of Red Location's history from 1900.

ARRIVAL AND DEPARTURE — PORT ELIZABETH

BY PLANE

Port Elizabeth's **airport** (☎ 041 581 2984) is conveniently situated on the edge of Walmer suburb, 4km south from the city centre, and served by **kulula** (☎ 0861 585 852, ⓦ kulula.com) and **SAA** (☎ 041 507 1111, ⓦ flysaa.com). Taxis rank outside the airport and the major car rental companies are here too, best to arrange a car beforehand to ensure the best deal and have a car waiting for you.

BY TRAIN

The **train station** (☎ 041 507 2662) is centrally located on the Strand, connected only to Johannesburg, and the least used of any transport options to Port Elizabeth. You

will need to arrange to be met beforehand, as this downtown area is prone to crime.

BY BUS

Intercity buses Greyhound, Intercape and Translux buses stop at Greenacres shopping mall in Newton Park suburb, 3km from the centre, where you can arrange to met be by your hostel or B&B or get a taxi (see below). Destinations: Cape Town (6–7 daily; 12hr); Knysna (6–7 daily; 4hr 30min).

Baz Bus The Baz Bus will drop you off at any central location or accommodation.

INFORMATION

Tourist offices The Nelson Mandela Bay Tourism head office (Mon–Fri 8am–4.30pm; ☎ 041 582 2575, ⓦ nmbt. co.za) is on the corner of Mitchell Street and Walmer Boulevard, South End. There are also offices at the airport (daily 7am–7pm; ☎ 041 581 0456); Shop 48 at the Boardwalk, Marine Drive, Summerstrand (daily 8am–7pm; ☎ 041 583 2030); and Donkin Reserve Lighthouse Building, Belmont Terrace, Central (Mon–Fri 8am–4.30pm, Sat & Sun 9.30am–3.30pm; ☎ 041 585 8884).

GETTING AROUND

TOURS

If you're staying in Central, exploring the city on foot is a realistic possibility – try the self-guided **Heritage Walk**, shown on a map available at the tourist office. The best way to see Port Elizabeth, however, is on one of the excellent **bus tours**, which shed light on the culture and history of a city shaped by layers of political history. Calabash Tours (☎ 041 585 6162 or ☎ 084 552 4414, ⓦ calabashtours .co.za) is one of the best and operates "Real City Tours" by day and *shebeen* tours by night, as well as trips to Addo.

TAXIS

PE's **minibus taxis** run from town to the beachfront regularly, but are the least recommended way to travel. There are some **metered taxis** there but it's better to arrange something beforehand if you are arriving in the city by bus or train, as travellers wandering about aimlessly are easy targets. Try Hurter Taxis (☎ 041 585 5500) or Inner City Cabs (☎ 041 481 3687).

19

ACCOMMODATION

The obvious place to stay is the **beachfront**, with a vast choice of hotels, self-catering suites and hundreds of B&Bs. During the December and January peak holiday period the beachfront becomes the focus for most of the city's action, while February, March and April are much quieter yet offer perfect beach weather.

Admiral's Lodge 47 Admiralty Way, Summerstrand ☎041 583 1894 or ☎083 455 2072, ⓦadmiralslodge .co.za. Spacious and stylish rooms at a good B&B situated at the far end of Summerstrand, roughly 7km from the centre; airport transfers are available. There's a braai area, communal lounge, pool and a trampoline for the kids. R800

Beach Hotel Marine Drive, Humewood ☎041 583 2161, ⓦbeachhotel.co.za. Across the road from popular Hobie Beach, and sited at the centre of the beachside action, the hotel has a great patio bar overlooking the sea, offering snacks, cocktails and cold beer, and *The Crest*, a buffet restaurant. Ask about the weekend accommodation specials. Breakfast is extra, and you'll pay a little more for a room with a sea view. R1400

Fernando's Guest House & Grill 102 Cape Rd, Mill Park ☎041 373 2823, ⓔfernando@mweb.co.za. Purportedly South Africa's oldest guesthouse, in three separate Victorian houses decked out with period furniture and offering good value and a warm atmosphere, and continental breakfast included in the price. Traffic noise may put you off during the day, but evenings are quieter. R650

First Avenue Lodge 3 First Ave, Summerstrand ☎041 583 5173, ⓦwww.firstavenuelodge.co.za. Sixteen en-suite rooms close to the beach with their own entrances, offered on a B&B or self-catering basis, in a popular and pleasant establishment with a pool and chilling out area. R850

The Humewood 33 Beach Rd, Humewood ☎041 585 8961, ⓦwww.humewoodhotel.co.za. A large, old-fashioned hotel with more than a nostalgic hint of 1950s family seaside holidays. The rooms are large and feature wicker furniture and summery floral prints. Service is excellent and includes laundry facilities and babysitting. There's a good bar and sun deck. Airport transfers available. R950

Jikeleza Lodge 44 Cuyler St, Central ☎041 586 3721, ⓦhighwinds.co.za. Friendly backpacker place, recently renovated with dorms, doubles and a family room. Its adventure centre, High Winds, can help you sort out tour and travel bookings. They do tours around

Addo, as well as recommended combo tours to Addo and *Schotia* for the evening or night. Dorms R95, doubles R230

Kelway Hotel Brookes Hill Drive, Humewood ☎041 584 0638, ⓦthekelway.co.za. Stylish hotel kitted out with timber panelling, seagrass chairs and handcrafted wooden tables. Standard, luxury and family rooms are available, and breakfast is included. R1300

King's Beach Backpacker Hostel 41 Windermere Rd, Humewood ☎041 585 8113, ⓔkingsb@agnet. co.za. Spotless, well-established hostel, a block away from the beach, with camping facilities, dorms and double rooms, plus an outside bar and braai area. Although principally for self-catering, it lays on tea, coffee, bread and jams in the morning. The travel desk can book township and game park tours among others. Dorms R100, doubles R250

Lungile Backpackers 12 La Roche Drive, Summerstrand ☎041 582 2042, ⓦlungilebackpackers .co.za. Large and popular beachfront hostel with a sociable party vibe, situated in the heart of PE's beachfront nightlife strip. Perched on a hill, it has facilities for camping and a large lawn to relax on, twin rooms at the swimming pool or dorms inside the main house. Camping R50, dorms R120, doubles R310

Pine Lodge Resort Off Marine Drive, Humewood ☎041 583 4004, ⓦpinelodge.co.za. Right on the beach near the wonderful historic lighthouse and next to the Cape Recife Nature Reserve, where owls, mongooses and antelope make appearances. Accommodation is in the form of various log cabin units, some with full kitchens, sleeping from four to eight people. Besides a popular bar and restaurant, the lodge boasts a swimming pool, a gym and a games room. R950

Windermere 35 Humewood Rd, Humewood ☎041 582 2245, ⓦthewindermere.co.za. Stylish hotel with just eight suites, given an almost Zen-like feel through the subtle use of off-white to oatmeal tones contrasted with dark, choclatey hues and timber and granite surfaces. It's worth noting that the rooms with sea views don't have a higher price tag, so ask for one of those. R1500

EATING

The best area to trawl, both during the day and night, for an alfresco meal, rejuvenating coffee or tasty sandwich is **Richmond Hill**, close to Central, where the Art Deco buildings add to the quirky atmosphere, offsetting the overall industrial and functional quality of PE. Having a meal or drink along the **beachfront** is another obvious choice in a seaside town – wander about and see what takes your fancy.

19

Blue Waters Café Hobie Beach ☎ 041 583 4110. This pleasant restaurant has great sea views, good pasta and light snacks. Sipping an early evening cocktail on the terrace outdoors is recommended (R90). Daily 8am–9pm.

Fushin Sushi Bar Stanley on Bain, Richmond Hill ☎ 082 865 2707. Sit at the long counter for the most delicious sushi in town, as well as salads and eastern-influenced tapas-style small dishes (R75). Mon–Sun noon–10pm.

The Island Seafood Grill & Bar Pine Lodge Resort, Marine Drive ☎ 041 583 3789. This place enjoys an appealing setting in coastal dunes with wooden walkways and decking, and boasts a patio bar, ideal for enjoying a cocktail, and an indoor restaurant serving a decent range of snacks and full meals. Every dish is named after an island, and, though the food is nicely presented, the range spans a fairly predictable selection of pastas, burgers and so on (R80). Mon–Sat 11am–9pm, Sun 11am–8pm.

Natti's Thai Kitchen 5 Park Lane, Central ☎ 041 373 2763. Unfailingly excellent restaurant, which has been going for years, serving reasonably priced authentic Thai cuisine in a relaxed atmosphere, with a BYO alcohol policy. Mon–Sat 6.30pm till late.

Vov Telo Artisan Pizzeria 24 Bain St, Richmond Hill ☎ 041 585 8225. This industrial-chic restaurant with a pleasant outdoor patio serves up thin-based, wood-fired pizzas with interesting toppings, though the menu stretches to antipasti, salads, coffee and dessert. It's a fun and laidback place, and the eco-conscious owners are quick to tell you that the wood burned is from infestations of wattle and other Australian trees, which leach the soil (R60). Mon–Sat noon–10pm, Sun noon–9pm.

Vovo Telo Bakery and Café 16 Raleigh St, Richmond Hill ☎ 041 585 5606. This is a great place for breakfast and lunch, with Italian and French breads and pastries, real coffee and balcony seating. It's just round the corner from its sister pizzeria. Mon–Sat 7.30am–3pm.

DRINKING AND NIGHTLIFE

52 Parliament 52 Parliament St, Central. Late-night bar in a Victorian building decked out with interesting metal sculptures. DJs play house and other sounds, with occasional live music. Be warned, fights have been known to kick off. Wed, Fri & Sat 9pm till late.

Balizza Corner of Heugh Rd and 5th Ave at Times Square Shopping Centre, Walmer. With two bars, three lounges, two dancefloors and a range of cocktails and

shooters, plus DJs mixing recent house anthems and oldies, you're likely to have a good night out here. Mon–Sun 11am–2am.

Gondwana Cafe 2 Dolphin's Leap, Main Rd, Humewood. This place is great fun; a relaxed, racially mixed restaurant by day that doubles up as a club by night, plus jazz on Sunday afternoons. Tues–Sun 9am till late.

DIRECTORY

Cinema A reasonable range of popular films is screened at the Kine Park Cinema, 3 Rink St; Nu Metro, Walmer Park Shopping Centre, Walmer; Ster Kinekor in The Bridge shopping complex; or Cinema Starz at the Boardwalk Casino Complex.

Diving Although the Indian Ocean around PE isn't tropically clear and warm, the diving here is good, especially for soft corals. For dive courses try Pro Dive, at 189 Main Rd, Walmer (☎ 041 581 1144, ⊛ prodive.co.za),

which offers a one-day scuba-diving course and refresher courses.

Hospitals St George's (private), 40 Park Drive, Settlers Park ☎ 041 392 6111.

Pharmacy Mount Road Pharmacy, 559 Govan Mbeki Ave, is open daily until 11pm; ☎ 041 484 3838.

Post office Brookes Pavilion, Humewood, Mon–Fri 9am–3.30pm & Sat 8.30–11am.

Addo Elephant National Park

73km northeast of Port Elizabeth • Daily 7am–7pm • R140 • ⊛ addoelephantpark.com

Addo Elephant National Park is just 73km north of Port Elizabeth, and should be your first choice for a relaxing few days' excursion from PE, though it is close enough to town to take in on a day-trip. A Big Five reserve, it is undergoing an expansion programme that will see it become one of South Africa's three largest game reserves, d the only one including coastline.

u can drive around Addo yourself, but if you want to be taken around in open-
 Land Rovers and given a pampering safari experience, stay in one of the nearby
 eserves (see p.253). Another highly enjoyable way to roam the park is from
 se or elephant (see box, p.250).

CALL OF THE WILD

With the expansion programme under way, Addo's PR people are now talking in terms of a "Big Seven" reserve, as the denizens of the future coastal section (adjoining the Alexandra State Forest/Woody Cape section of the park) include **whales** and **great white sharks**. **Elephants** remain Addo's most obvious drawcard, but with the re-introduction in 2003 of a small number of **lions**, in two prides (big cats last roamed here over a century ago), as well as the presence of the rest of the Big Five – **buffalo**, **hippos** and **leopards** – it has become a game reserve to be reckoned with. **Spotted hyenas** were also introduced in 2003 as part of a programme to re-establish predators in the local ecosystem. Other species to look out for include **cheetah**, **black rhino**, **eland**, **kudu**, **warthog**, **ostrich** and **red hartebeest**.

One big attraction of Addo and these private reserves is that, unlike the country's other major game parks, they benefit from the fact that the Eastern Cape is **malaria-free**. And if you've driven out this way along the Garden Route and don't fancy heading back exactly the way you came, you've the option of returning to Cape Town via the inland **Route 62** (covered in chapter 18), branching off the N2 not far west of Port Elizabeth.

Wildlife watching

The Addo bush is thick, dry and prickly, making it difficult sometimes to spot any of the 450 or so elephants and other game; when you do, though, it's often thrillingly close up. The best strategy is to ask where the pachyderms and the other four of the Big Five have last been seen (enquire with staff at the park reception), and also to head for the waterhole in front of the restaurant to scan the bush for large grey backs quietly

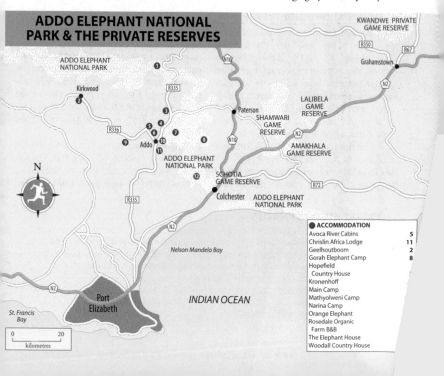

ADDO ELEPHANT NATIONAL
PARK & THE PRIVATE RESERVES

KWANDWE PRIVATE
GAME RESERVE

ADDO ELEPHANT
NATIONAL PARK

Kirkwood

Paterson

LALIBELA
GAME
RESERVE

SHAMWARI
GAME
RESERVE

AMAKHALA
GAME RESERVE

Addo

ADDO ELEPHANT
NATIONAL PARK

SCHOTIA
GAME RESERVE

Colchester   ADDO ELEPHANT
NATIONAL PARK

Grahamstown

Nelson Mandela Bay

INDIAN OCEAN

Port
Elizabeth

St. Francis
Bay

0   20
kilometres

● ACCOMMODATION
Avoca River Cabins   5
Chrislin Africa Lodge   11
Geelhoutboom   2
Gorah Elephant Camp   8
Hopefield
 Country House
Kronenhoff
Main Camp
Mathyolweni Camp
Narina Camp
Orange Elephant
Rosedale Organic
 Farm B&B
The Elephant House
Woodall Country House

moving about. The best way, though, is to go on a **guided game drive** in an open vehicle with a knowledgeable national parks driver.

ARRIVAL AND DEPARTURE
ADDO ELEPHANT NATIONAL PARK

Matyholweni Camp By far the most straightforward way of getting to Addo is via the southern gate, which is accessed off the N2 at the village of Colchester, 43km northeast of Port Elizabeth. From here, it's roughly 5km to Matyholweni.

Main Camp Situated north of Matyholweni, you can either take a slow, scenic drive through the park, which will take at least an hour, or use the R335 road that runs outside

the western flank of the park – take the N2 from Port Elizabeth east towards Grahamstown for 5km, branching off at the Addo/Motherwell/Markman signpost onto the R335 through Addo village.

Narina bush camp Narina bush camp is 22km north of Main Camp along a gravel road. The network of roads within the section of the park between Main Camp and Mathyolweni is untarred, but in good condition.

INFORMATION

Maps of the park are available at reception and indicate the location of picnic and braai sites. Until the park is consolidated (not imminent), you won't be able to reach the coastal section that includes the Alexandria State

Forest from inside the national park.

Eating The restaurant at Main Camp is open for three meals a day (daily 6am–8pm), while the shop is well stocked with food and drink.

TOURS

Guided tours can be booked in advance at the Main Camp or on the park's website. Two-hour outings leave throughout the day and cost R220 a person for day drives, R330 for sunset trips (including snacks and drinks), and R250 for night drives. The vehicles used are higher off the ground than a normal sedan to improve viewing opportunities.

★ **Hop-on guide** You can also hire the exclusive services of a hop-on guide who joins you in your own car for two hours for R150 and will direct you to where you will find game. If you don't have your own transport, Calabash Tours based in PE (see p.246) run day-trips here, as do most of the backpacker hostels.

ACCOMMODATION INSIDE THE PARK

Gorah Elephant Camp 9km west along the Addo Heights Rd leading from the N10 to Addo village ☎ 044 501 1111, ⓦ hunterhotels.com /gorahelephantcamp. Ultra-luxurious outfit based around a Victorian homestead decked out with the appropriate paraphernalia (mounted antelope skulls above the fireplace, evocative African landscapes, and tabletops so polished you can admire your reflection) and accompanied by a beautifully landscaped swimming pool. The suites are plush and there are opportunities to dine under the stars; meals are included in the price, as are game drives. R12700

Main Camp This is the oldest and largest of the National Parks camps. Besides camping facilities, there are forest

cabins that sleep two people and share cooking facilities in communal kitchens; and more luxurious two-person chalets (R900) with their own kitchenettes. Some of these units sleep up to four people (but the minimum charge is for two occupants). The cheapest accommodation available is in well-designed, spacious safari tents, perfect during the summer months, with decks right next to the perimeter fence. Camping R165, safari tents R420, forest cabins R550, chalets R900

Mathyolweni Camp National Parks accommodation in a dozen fully equipped self-catering chalets with showers, each sleeping two. Set in a secluded valley surrounded by thicket that supports a wealth of birdlife,

---

HORSES AND ELEPHANTS

Two-hour **horserides** suitable for the not-so-experienced (8am; R220) and three-hour rides for experienced equestrians (2pm; R310) leave from just outside the main gate and run along the exterior of the park fence (book at *Main Camp*). All-day rides in the beautiful Zuurberg section, where there is not much game, but scenery to make up for it, is available for experienced riders who need a head for heights (R300).

Elephant-back safaris are operated from a farm abutting the northern boundary of Addo (☎ 042 235 1400, ⓦ addoelephantbacksafaris.co.za), 90km from Port Elizabeth, off the R335, cost approximately R875 per person.

PREPARING FOR ADDO

If you're planning on staying in Addo, bear in mind that **reservations** are essential in the high season, and can be made through SANParks or, less than 72 hours in advance, directly with Addo (☎ 042 233 8600, ✆ sanparks.org/parks/addo). The area around the park is pretty much farmland, with few villages. As such, **meals** are provided by most of the accommodation options listed, unless you're self-catering at one of the camps. If you do want to take your own provisions, or just do your own thing one evening, you will need to head to Port Elizabeth, or Colchester, which is a 15min drive away from the park and has shops and a few basic places to eat.

19

and the chalets have nice viewing decks. There is no restaurant, so plan to self-cater, bring food from PE or Colchester. R825

Narina Camp This is a small National Parks bush camp in the mountainous Zuurberg section of Addo, comprising four safari tents that sleep four people and share ablution and cooking facilities; there is no restaurant here either, so bring your own provisions. Horseriding is available for an additional cost. R855

ACCOMMODATION JUST OUTSIDE THE PARK

Outside the park, but within easy striking distance, you'll find an abundance of private B&Bs and guesthouses, especially among the citrus groves of the Sundays River Valley. Many offer day and night drives in the game reserve.

Avoca River Cabins 13km northwest of Addo village on the R336 ☎ 042 234 0421 or ☎ 082 677 9920, ✆ www.gardenroute.co.za/addo/avoca. Reasonably priced B&B and self-catering accommodation on a farm in the Sundays River Valley. The range of self-catering spans from budget cabins to more comfortable thatched huts (some on the banks of the river); there are some pleasant walks to be had on the farm, and canoes are available to rent. R300

Chrislin Africa Lodge 12km south of Addo main gate, off the R336 ☎ 042 233 0022 or ☎ 082 783 3553, ✆ chrislin.co.za. Quirky B&B with thatched huts built using traditional Xhosa construction techniques, with a lovely *lapa* (courtyard) and pool, and hearty country breakfasts, as well as dinners on request. R800

★ **The Elephant House** 5km north of Addo village on the R335 ☎ 042 233 2462 or ☎ 083 799 5671, ✆ elephanthouse.co.za. Just minutes from Addo is one of the Eastern Cape's top places to stay, a stunning thatch-roofed lodge filled with Persian rugs and antique furniture that perfectly balances luxury with a supremely relaxed atmosphere. The eight bedrooms and six garden cottages open onto a lawned courtyard. Candlelit dinners are available, as are game drives (R650/person) into Addo and the surrounding reserves. R1200

Geelhoutboom 26 Market St, Kirkwood ☎ 042 230 1191, ✆ geelhoutboom.co.za. A great value and homely B&B in the shade of a large yellowwood tree, with a/c rooms just a 20min drive from Addo main gate. R550

Hopefield Country House 20km southwest of Addo main gate ☎ 042 234 0333, ✆ hopefield.co.za. An atmospheric 1930s farmhouse set in beautiful English-style gardens on a citrus farm. The five bedrooms are imaginatively furnished with period pieces in a style the owners (a pair of classical musicians who occasionally give impromptu concerts for guests) describe as "farmhouse eclectic". R1200

Kronenhoff On the R336 as you enter Kirkwood ☎ 042 230 1448, ✆ kronenhoff.co.za. Situated in a small farming town, this is a hospitable, high-ceilinged Cape Dutch-style home, with spacious suites, polished wooden floors, large leather sofas and a sociable pub. In summer the sweet scent of orange blossom carries from the surrounding citrus groves. R1050

Orange Elephant On the R335, 8km from the National Park gate ☎ 042 233 0023, ✆ addobackpackers.com. Budget accommodation at a comfortable hostel, whose management will help you organize outings into the surrounding game reserves, and is well known for its large portions of pub grub at its lively bar. Dorms R120, doubles R400.

Rosedale Organic Farm B&B On the R335, 1km north of Addo village ☎ 042 233 0404 or ☎ 083 329 8775, ✆ rosedalebnb.co.za. Very reasonably priced accommodation in six cottages on a certified organic farm that exports citrus fruits to the EU. Hosts Keith and Nondumiso Finnemore are seriously committed to sustainable farming and tourism – water for the cottages is solar-heated, the boilers for the outdoor showers are fired by uprooted exotic trees and, as far as possible, breakfasts consist of organic produce. Keith offers a free one-hour walking tour of the farm to guests, on which you can get all those nagging questions about the state of the world's food industry answered. R650

Woodall Country House About 1km west of Addo

main gate ☎042 233 0128, ⊛woodall-addo.co.za. Excellent luxury guesthouse on a working citrus farm with eleven self-contained suites and rooms. There's a swimming pool, gymnasium, spa and sauna (massages are available, and there's a resident beautician). A lovely sundowner deck overlooks a small lake full of swans and other waterfowl. Renowned for its outstanding country cuisine, its restaurant offers three- to six-course dinners. **R2400**

The Eastern Cape's private game reserves

Although driving through Addo can be extremely rewarding, nothing beats getting into the wild in an open vehicle with a trained guide – something the private reserves excel at. If you want the works – game drives, outstanding food, uncompromising luxury and excellent accommodation, you'll find it at top-ranking **Shamwari**, with prices rising over R5000 per person a day. If you're in this league it's also worth considering **Kwandwe Game Reserve**, another outstanding safari destination in the Eastern Cape, near Grahamstown.

If you're on a tighter budget or pushed for time, a good option is one of the day or half-day safaris that start at R600 per person offered by **Amakhala** and **Schotia**. Accommodation rates are listed as the cheapest for two people in high season, although specials and season variations may be available.

19

THE PRIVATE RESERVES

Amakhala Game Reserve Just 2km further along the N2 from the turn-off to Shamwari (see below) ☎042 235 1608, ⊛amakhala.co.za. A fantastic, family-friendly reserve stocked with the Big Five as well as cheetah, giraffe, zebra, wildebeest and antelopes. The Bushman's River meanders through the reserve allowing for canoe safaris and riverboat sundowner cruises. Safaris for day visitors must be booked in advance and include two game drives, a river cruise and lunch (R980). All accommodation comprises fabulous views, whether the fabulous farmhouse lodges or the camp with beds fashioned from restored ox wagons. **R4160**

★ **Kwandwe Private Game Reserve** On the R67, 34km north of Grahamstown and 160km from Port Elizabeth ☎011 809 4300, ⊛kwandwereserve.com. This the Eastern Cape's top wildlife destination, with 30km of Fish River frontage and the Big Five in attendance. Apart from twice-a-day game drives, Kwandwe's safari activities include guided river walks, canoeing on the Great Fish, rhino tracking and fascinating cultural tours with a resident historian. Children are well catered for with family game drives, bush walks and frog safaris. There are four lodges, ranging from a quintessential luxury thatched lodge to a stunning boutique-hotel-in-the-bush ingeniously designed with glass walls for panoramic views of the terrain. **R7800**

Lalibela Game Reserve 90km northeast of Port Elizabeth on the N2 to Grahamstown ☎041 581 8170, ⊛lalibela.co.za. An excellent mid-range choice, *Lalibela Game Reserve* is home to the Big Five and diverse flora and fauna. Safaris are included in the accommodation rate, along with all meals and drinks – you can dine on terrific Eastern

Cape food and contemporary cuisine. There are three fabulous lodges with private viewing decks, swimming pools and *bomas* to choose from, and they also offer an African drumming and dancing session. **R6400**

Schotia Game Reserve On the eastern flank of Addo ☎042 235 1436, ⊛schotia.com. *Schotia* is the smallest and the busiest of the private reserves, on account of the excellent value it offers. Although not (quite) a Big Five reserve, it's really only missing the ellies. Day visitors can arrange to be collected from Port Elizabeth or anywhere in the Addo vicinity; full-day safaris (R1200/person) involve a game drive through Addo and an evening game drive with lunch and dinner thrown in. If you're pushed for time or money you can opt for the afternoon game drive (R660/person). An overnight stay here is the cheapest among the private reserves; rates include a room in one of three bush lodges or eight double rooms plus game drives into Addo. You pay even less if you don't go into Addo, but it would be a travesty to miss the pachyderms. **R4000**

Shamwari Game Reserve 65km north of Port Elizabeth on the N2 ☎042 203 1111, ⊛shamwari.com. The largest and best known of the private reserves, *Shamwari* has cultivated a jetsetter fan base, hosting such celebrities as Tiger Woods and John Travolta. In 2010 it won the World's Leading Safari and Game Reserve Award at the World Travel Awards (tourism's Oscars) for the thirteenth year running. The accolades are justified in the reserve's diverse landscapes, requisite animals and high standards of game-viewing. Accommodation is in colonial-style, family-friendly *Long Lee Manor* or attractive (child-unfriendly) lodges and tented camps, furnished with every conceivable comfort. **R8470**

Contexts

History

Cape Town's history is complex and what follows is only a brief account of major events in the city's past. For more detailed coverage on both Cape Town's and South Africa's history in general, see the list in "Books".

Hunters and herders

Rock art provides evidence of human culture in the Western Cape dating back nearly 30,000 years. The artists were hunter-gatherers, known most commonly as **San**, a relatively modern term from the Nama language with roots in the concept of "inhabiting or dwelling", to reflect the fact these were South Africa's aboriginals. At one time they probably spread throughout sub-Saharan Africa, having pretty well perfected their **nomadic lifestyle** of hunting gathering, leaving them considerable time for artistic and religious pursuits. People lived in small, loosely connected bands comprising family units and were free to leave and join up with other groups.

About two thousand years ago, this changed when some groups in territory north of modern South Africa laid their hands on fat-tailed sheep and cattle from northern Africa, thus transforming themselves into **herding communities**, known as **Khoikhoi** or simply Khoi. The introduction of livestock had a revolutionary effect on social organization and introduced the idea of ownership and accumulation. Social divisions developed, and political units became larger, centring around a chief who would determine the allocation of pasturage among other important duties.

The Cape goes Dutch

Portuguese mariners, under the command of **Bartholomeu Dias**, first rounded the Cape in the 1480s, and named it Cabo de Boa Esperanza, the **Cape of Good Hope**. Marking their progress, they left an unpleasant set of calling cards all along the coast – slaves they had captured in West Africa and had cast ashore to trumpet the power and glory of Portugal with the aim of intimidating the locals. Little wonder then, that the first encounter of the Portuguese with the indigenous Khoikhoi along the Garden Route coast was not a happy one. It began with a group of Khoikhoi stoning the Portuguese for taking water from a spring without asking permission, and ended with a Khoikhoi man lying dead with a crossbow bolt through his chest.

It was another 170 years before any European settlement was established in South Africa. In 1652, a group of white employees of the **Dutch East India Company** (Verenigde Oostindische Compagnie or **VOC**), which was engaged in trade between the Netherlands and the East Indies, pulled into Table Bay to set up a refreshment station to revictual Company ships trading between Europe and the East. There were no plans at this time to set up a colony; in fact, the Cape post was given to the station commander **Jan van Riebeeck** because he had been caught with his hand in the till. Van Riebeeck dreamed up a number of schemes to keep "darkest Africa" at bay, including the very Dutch solution of building a canal that would cut the Cape

30,000 years ago	2000 years ago	1652 AD	1657
Hunter gatherers occupy Cape Peninsula.	Khoikhoi herders with fat-tailed sheep migrate from the north.	Dutch East India Company establishes supply station for trade ships sailing to Indies.	Company releases indentured labourers to farm as free burghers.

Peninsula adrift. In the end he had to satisfy himself with planting a **bitter almond hedge** (still growing in Cape Town's Kirstenbosch Gardens) to keep the natives at arm's length.

Despite Van Riebeeck's view that the indigenous Khoikhoi were "a savage set, living without conscience", from the start the Dutch were dependent on them to provide livestock, which were traded for trinkets. As the settlement developed, Van Riebeeck needed more **labour** to keep the show going, and bemoaned the fact that he was unsuccessful in persuading the Khoikhoi to discard the freedom of their herding life for him. Much to his annoyance, the bosses back in Holland had forbidden Van Riebeeck from enslaving the locals, and refused his request for slaves from elsewhere in the Company's empire.

Creeping colonization

Everyone at the Cape at this time was under stringent contract to the VOC, which effectively had total control over their activities and movements – a form of indentureship. But a number of Dutch men were released from their contracts in 1657 to farm as **free burghers** on land granted by the Company; they were now at liberty to pursue their own economic activities, although the VOC still controlled the market and set prices for produce. This annexation of the lands around the mud fort, which preceded the construction of the more solid Castle of Good Hope, ultimately led to the inexorable process of **colonization**.

The only snag was that the land granted didn't belong to the Company in the first place, and the move sparked the first of a series of **Khoikhoi–Dutch wars**. Although the first campaign ended in stalemate, the Khoikhoi were ultimately no match for the Dutch, who had the tactical mobility of horses and the superior killing power of firearms. Campaigns continued through the 1660s and 1670s and proved rather profitable for Dutch raiders, who on one outing in 1674 rounded up eight hundred Khoikhoi cattle and four thousand sheep.

Meanwhile, in 1658, Van Riebeeck had managed successfully to purloin a shipload of **slaves** from West Africa, whetting an insatiable appetite for this form of labour. The VOC itself became the biggest slaveholders at the Cape and continued importing slaves, mostly from the East Indies, at such a pace that by 1711 there were more slaves than burghers in the colony. With the help of this ready workforce, the embryonic Cape colony expanded outwards and trampled the peninsula's Khoikhoi, who by 1713 had lost everything. Most of their livestock (nearly fifty thousand animals) and most of their land west of the Hottentots Holland Mountains had been gobbled up by the VOC. Dispossession, and diseases like smallpox, previously unknown in South Africa, decimated their numbers and shattered their social system. By the middle of the eighteenth century, those who remained had been reduced to a condition of miserable servitude to the colonists.

Kaapstad

During the early eighteenth century, **slavery** became the economic backbone of the colony, which was now a rude colonial village of low, whitewashed, flat-roofed houses.

1658	1679	1710	1713	1795
First slaves brought to settlement.	Castle of Good Hope completed.	Slaves outnumber settlers.	Khoikhoi dispossessed of all livestock by Company and free burghers and reduced to servitude.	Company goes bust and English becomes official language when British take Cape.

Passing through in 1710, Jan van Riebeeck's granddaughter, Johanna, commented contemptuously that the settlement was "a miserable place. There is nothing pretty along the shoreline, the Castle is peculiar, the houses resemble prisons" and "one sees here peculiar people who live in strange ways".

Dutch global influence began to wane in the early 1700s, but by mid-century the Cape settlement had developed an independent identity and some little prosperity based on its pivotal position on the European–Far East trade route. People now began referring to it as "**Kaapstad**" (Cape Town) rather than "the Cape settlement", and by 1750 it had a thousand buildings, with over three thousand diverse inhabitants. Some of these were indigenous Khoikhoi people, but the largest number were VOC employees, dominated by an elite of high-ranking Dutch-born officials. The lower rungs were filled by the poor from all over Europe, including Scandinavia, Germany, France, England, Scotland and Russia, while slaves came from East Africa, Madagascar, India and Indonesia. There was also a transient population from passing ships, which by the second half of the century were largely manned by Indian, Javanese and Chinese crews. If nothing else, the constant **maritime traffic** injected some life into this intellectual desert, which couldn't boast a single printing press, let alone a newspaper. Entertainment consisted mainly of carousing, whoring and gambling.

Britain takes the Cape

By the 1790s the VOC was more or less bankrupt, and its control over the restive Cape burghers had become decidedly tenuous. As Dutch maritime influence declined, Britain and France were tussling for domination of the Indian Ocean. The outbreak of the French Revolution in 1789 and the establishment of a Francophile republic in the Netherlands a few years later made the **British** distinctly jittery about their strategic access to Cape Town. In August 1795, Rear-Admiral George Keith Elphinstone was sent in haste with four British sloops of war to secure Cape Town; by mid-September the ragtag Dutch garrison had capitulated.

The British occupation heralded a period of **free trade** in which exports from the Cape lifted off as tariffs were slashed, with the result that Cape wines, the largest Cape export, were meeting ten percent of British wine consumption by 1822. The tightly controlled and highly restrictive Dutch regime was replaced with a more tolerant government, which brought immediate **freedom of religion**, the abolition of the slave trade in 1808, and the **emancipation** of slaves in 1834.

Although British-born residents were a minority during the first half of the nineteenth century, their influence was huge, and Cape Town began to take on a British character through a process of cultural, economic and political dominance. **English** became the language of status and officialdom and by 1860 there were eight newspapers, six of them in English. A vibrant press fed a culture of **liberalism** which led Capetonians to thwart British attempts to transport convicts to the Cape (see box, p.44) – the first time since the American Revolution that an outpost of empire had successfully defied Whitehall. This gave the colonists the confidence to demand **self-government** and, in 1854, males, regardless of race, who owned property worth £25 or more won the right to vote for a lower house of parliament, which was based

1834	1864	1901	1899–1901
Emancipation of slaves leads many Dutch to leave Cape and establish two Boer republics.	Completion of Cape Town–Wynberg rail line facilitates development of outlying suburbs.	First segregated black location, Ndabeni, established after bubonic plague outbreak.	Britain defeats Afrikaner republics in Anglo-Boer War.

in Cape Town. A significant development of the second half of the nineteenth century was the rapid growth of **communications**, both within Cape Town and also into the interior, which reinforced the city's status as the principal centre of a Cape Colony that by now extended 1000km to the east. The road from Cape Town to Camps Bay across Kloof Nek was started in 1848, a telegraph line between Cape Town and Simon's Town was laid in 1860, but most significant of all was the introduction of steam. The first **rail line** from central Cape Town to Wynberg was completed in 1864, opening up the southern peninsula to the development of **middle-class suburbia**.

From backwater to breakwater

The development of an urban infrastructure wasn't enough to lift Cape Town from its backwater provinciality. That required the discovery in 1867 of the world's largest deposit of **diamonds** around modern-day Kimberley. Coinciding with this, the city's breakwater was started and the **harbour** was completed just in time to accommodate the massive influx of fortune-hunters, immigrants and capital into Cape Town en route to the diggings. More significant still was the **discovery of gold** around Johannesburg in the Boer-controlled South African Republic in the 1880s, which gave Cape Town a new significance as the gateway to the world's richest mineral deposits.

From the 1870s, growing middle-class self-confidence was reflected in the erection of grand **Victorian frontages** to the city centre's shops, banks and offices. Echoing Victorian London, this prosperous public facade hid a growing world of poverty, inhabited by immigrants, Africans and coloureds – people of mixed race (see box, p.42) who made up a cheap labour force. The degradation and vice that thrived in Cape Town's growing slums were disquieting to the Anglocentric middle class, which would have preferred Cape Town to be like a respectably homogenous Home Counties town, rather than a cultural melting pot.

As the twentieth century dawned, the authorities attempted to achieve a closer approximation to the white middle-class ideal by introducing laws to stem **immigration**, other than from Western Europe, while other statutes sought to protect "European traders" against competition from other ethnic groups. Racial segregation wasn't far behind, and an outbreak of bubonic plague in 1901 gave the town council an excuse to establish **Ndabeni**, Cape Town's first black location, near present-day Pinelands.

Industrialization and segregation

Apart from contributing to Cape Town's development as a trading port, the discovery of gold had more significant consequences for the city. By the end of the nineteenth century, a number of influential capitalists, among them **Cecil John Rhodes** (prime minister of the Cape from 1890 to 1897), were convinced that it would be a good idea to annex the two Boer republics to the north to create a unified South Africa under British influence. In 1899 Britain marched on the Boer republics, in what was rashly described by Lord Kitchener as a "teatime war", but became known

1910	1920s	1920s	1930s
Parliament comes to Cape Town when Afrikaner republics and British colonies (Cape and Natal) federate.	Agatha Christie surfs at Muizenberg.	Influx of Africans leads to building of segregated township Langa surrounded by barbed-wire fence.	Fascist Greys Shirts hang out at Koffiehuis café next to Groote Kerk in Adderley Street.

internationally as the **Anglo-Boer War**, Britain's most expensive campaign since the Napoleonic Wars. Eventually, three years later, the Anglo-Boer War ended with the Boers' surrender. What followed was nearly a decade of discussions, at the end of which the two Boer republics (the South African Republic and the Orange Free State) and two British colonies (the Cape and Natal) were federated in 1910 to become the **Union of South Africa**, Cape Town gaining a pivotal position as the **legislative capital** of the country.

Africans and coloureds, excluded from the cosy deal between Boers and Brits, had to find expression in the workplace, flexing their collective muscle on the docks in 1919, where they formed the mighty **Industrial and Commercial Union**, which boasted 200,000 members in its heyday. Cape Town began the process of becoming a modern industrial city and, with the building of the South African National Gallery, promoted itself as the urbane cultural capital of the country. Accelerated **industrialization** brought an influx of Africans from the rural areas and soon Ndabeni was overflowing. Alarmed that Africans were living close to the city centre in District Six and were also spilling out into the Cape Flats, the authorities passed the **Urban Areas Act**, which compelled Africans to live in what were named "locations" and empowered the city council to expel jobless Africans – measures that preceded apartheid by 25 years. In 1927, the new location of **Langa** (which ironically means "sun") was opened next to the sewage works. Laid out along military lines, with barrack-style dormitories for the residents, it was surrounded by a security fence.

World War II

During the 1930s Cape Town saw the growth of several fascist movements, the largest of which was the **Greyshirts**, whose favourite meeting place was the Koffiehuis (coffee house) next to the Groote Kerk in Adderley Street. Its members included Hendrik Verwoerd, a Dutch-born intellectual who became a fanatical Afrikaner Nationalist and South African prime minister from 1958 to 1966. When **World War II** broke out there was a heated debate in parliament, which narrowly voted for South Africa to side with Britain against Germany. Members of all South African communities volunteered for service, the **ANC** (founded in 1912) arguing that their support should be linked to full citizenship for blacks. Afrikanerdom was deeply divided and **Nazi sympathizers**, among them John Vorster (Verwoerd's successor as prime minister), were jailed for actively attempting to sabotage the war effort. *Die Burger*, Cape Town's Afrikaans-language newspaper, backed Germany throughout the war.

The war brought hardship, particularly to those at the bottom of the heap, leading to an increased influx of Africans and poor white Afrikaners from the countryside to the cities. This changed the demographics of the city of Cape Town, which lost its British colonial flavour and, for the first time in 150 years, had more black (mostly coloured) than white residents. New townships were built to accommodate the burgeoning African population.

Cape Town became a mixed bag of ad hoc official **segregation** in some areas of life while in others, such as on buses and trains, there was none.

1948	1952	1960	1962
National Party, with its former-Nazi members, wins election and goes full throttle on segregation.	Nelson Mandela leads defiance campaign against apartheid legislation.	Robert Sobukwe heads march from Langa against enforced carrying of passes by Africans.	Mandela, Sobukwe and ANC leadership imprisoned on Robben Island.

Apartheid and defiance

In postwar South Africa, ideological tensions grew between those pushing for universal civil rights and those whites who feared black advancement. In 1948 the **National Party** came to power, promising its fearful white supporters that it would reverse the flow of Africans to the cities. In Cape Town it introduced a policy favouring coloureds for certain unskilled and semi-skilled jobs, admitting only African men who already had work and forbidding the construction of family accommodation for Africans – hence turning the townships into predominantly male preserves.

During the 1950s the National Party began putting in place a barrage of laws that would eventually constitute the structure of apartheid. Early **onslaughts on civil rights** included the Coloured Voters Act, which stripped coloureds of the vote; the Bantu Authorities Act, which set up puppet authorities to govern Africans in rural reserves; the Population Registration Act, which classified every South African at birth as "white, Bantu or coloured"; the Group Areas Act, which divided South Africa into ethnically distinct areas; and the Suppression of Communism Act, which made anti-apartheid opposition (communist or not) a criminal offence. Africans, now regarded as foreigners in their own country, had at all times to carry **passes** – one of the most hated symbols of apartheid.

The ANC responded in 1952 with the **Defiance Campaign**, whose aim was the granting of full civil rights to blacks. A radical young firebrand called **Nelson Mandela** was appointed "volunteer-in-chief" of the campaign, which had a crucial influence on his politics. Up to that point he had rejected political association with non-Africans, but the campaign's interracial solidarity brought him round to the conciliatory inclusive approach for which he is now famous. The government swooped on the homes of the ANC leadership, resulting in the detention and then banning of over a hundred ANC organizers. Unbowed, the ANC pressed ahead with the **Congress of the People**, held near Johannesburg in 1955. At a mass meeting of nearly three thousand delegates, four organizations – representing Africans, coloureds, whites and Indians – formed a strategic partnership.

From within the organization, a group of Africanists criticized cooperation with white activists, leading to the formation in 1958 of the breakaway **Pan Africanist Congress** (PAC) under the leadership of the charismatic **Robert Mangaliso Sobukwe**. Langa township became a stronghold of the PAC, which organized peaceful **anti-pass demonstrations** in Johannesburg and Cape Town on March 21, 1960. Over a period of days, work stayaways spread to all Cape Town's locations, achieving a temporary nationwide suspension of the pass laws – the calm before the storm. As the protests gathered strength, the government declared a **State of Emergency**, sent the army in to crush the strike, restored the pass laws and banned the ANC and PAC. Nelson Mandela continued to operate in secret for a year until he was finally captured in 1962, tried and imprisoned – together with most of the ANC leadership – on **Robben Island**.

Soweto and the Total Strategy

With resistance stifled, the state grew more powerful, and for the majority of white South Africans, business people and foreign investors, life seemed perfect. The panic

1966	1976	1978	1981
Coloureds and Africans evicted from "white areas" and relocated to Cape Flats townships.	Police open fire on black school pupils opposing government, leaving 128 Capetonians dead.	Hawkish P.W. Botha becomes president in palace coup.	Botha moves Mandela to mainland prison, but also sends massed troops into townships to suppress rolling protest.

caused by the 1960 uprising soon became a dim memory and confidence returned. For black South Africans, poverty deepened – a state of affairs enforced by apartheid legislation.

In 1966 the notorious **Group Areas Act** was used to uproot whole coloured communities from many areas, including District Six, and to move them to the soulless **Cape Flats** where, in the wake of social disintegration, gangsterism took root (see box, p.82). It remains one of Cape Town's most pressing problems. Compounding the injury, the National Party stripped away coloured representation on Cape Town city council in 1972.

The **Soweto Revolt** of June 16, 1976, signalled the start of a new wave of anti-apartheid protest, when black youths took to the streets against the imposition of Afrikaans as a medium of instruction in their schools. The protests spread to Cape Town where, as in Jo'burg, the government responded ruthlessly by sending in armed police, who killed 128 and injured 400 Capetonians.

Despite naked violence, protest spread to all sections of the community. The government was forced to rely increasingly on armed police to impose order. Even this was unable to stop the mushrooming of new liberation organizations, many of them part of the broadly based **Black Consciousness movement**. As the unrest rumbled on into 1977, the government responded by banning all the new black organizations and detaining their leadership.

From the mid-1960s to the mid-1970s Prime Minister **John Vorster** had relied on the police to maintain the apartheid status quo, but it became obvious that this wasn't working. In 1978 he was deposed in a palace coup by his minister of defence, **P.W. Botha**, who conceived a complex military-style approach he called the **Total Strategy**. The strategy was a two-handed one of reforming peripheral aspects of apartheid, while deploying the armed forces in unprecedented acts of repression. In 1981, as resistance grew, Botha began contemplating change and moved Nelson Mandela and other ANC leaders from Robben Island to Pollsmoor Prison in mainland Cape Town. At the same time he poured ever-increasing numbers of troops into the townships.

In 1983 Botha concocted what he believed was a master plan for a so-called **New Constitution** in which coloureds and Indians would be granted the vote – in racially segregated chambers with no executive power. The only constructive outcome of this project was the extension of the Houses of Parliament to their current size.

Apartheid suffers a stroke

As President Botha was punting his ramshackle scheme in 1983, fifteen thousand anti-apartheid delegates met at Mitchell's Plain on the Cape Flats, to form the **United Democratic Front (UDF)**, the largest opposition gathering in South Africa since the Congress of the People in 1955. The UDF became a proxy for the banned ANC, and two years of strikes, boycotts and protest followed. As the government resorted to increasingly extreme measures, internal resistance grew and the international community turned up the heat on the apartheid regime. The Commonwealth passed a resolution condemning apartheid, the US and Australia severed air links, Congress passed disinvestment legislation and finally, in 1985, the Chase Manhattan Bank called in its massive loan to South Africa.

1983	1989	1989	1990
15,000 delegates form ANC proxy the United Democratic Front, leading to escalation of violence.	Botha rebuffs Mandela's appeal for negotiations to avert civil war.	Botha has stroke and is replaced by FW. De Klerk, who unbans ANC and releases Mandela.	Mandela walks free and makes first public speech from City Hall.

Botha declared his umpteenth **State of Emergency** and unleashed a last-ditch storm of tyranny. There were bannings, mass arrests, detentions, treason trials and torture, as well as assassinations of UDF leaders by sinister hit squads. At the beginning of 1989, **Mandela** wrote to Botha from prison describing his fear of a polarized South Africa and calling for negotiations. An intransigent character, Botha found himself paralysed by his inability to reconcile the need for radical change with his fear of a right-wing backlash. When he suffered a stroke later that year, his party colleagues moved swiftly to oust him and replaced him with **F.W. de Klerk**.

Faced with the worst crisis in South Africa's history, President de Klerk realized that repression had failed. Even South Africa's friends were losing patience, and in September 1989 US President George Bush Sr told de Klerk that if Mandela wasn't released within six months he would extend US sanctions. Five months later, de Klerk lifted the ban on the ANC, PAC, the Communist Party and 33 other organizations, as well as the release of Mandela.

On February 11, 1990, Cape Town's history took a neat twist when, just hours after being released from prison, **Nelson Mandela** made his first public speech from the balcony of City Hall to a jubilant crowd spilling across the Grand Parade, the site of the very first Dutch fort.

A tale of two cities

Four protracted years of negotiations followed, leading eventually to South Africa's current constitution. Following the country's first-ever democratic elections in 1994, Mandela voted in national elections for the first time in his life – and became South Africa's president. One of the anomalies of the 1994 election was that while most of South Africa delivered an **ANC landslide**, the Western Cape, purportedly the most liberal region of the country, returned the **National Party,** the party that implemented apartheid, as its provincial government. Politics in South Africa were not, it turned out, divided along a faultline that separated whites from the rest of the population as many had assumed; the majority of coloureds had voted for the very party that had once stripped them of the vote, regarding it with less suspicion than the ANC. Apart from the period between 2002 and 2006, when Capetonians elected an ANC mayor and administration, the Western Cape and its capital have consistently bucked South Africa's national trend of overwhelming ANC dominance.

During the ANC's first term in national government under Mandela (1994–1999), affirmative action policies and a racial shift in the economy led to the rise of a **black middle class**, but even so this represented a tiny fraction of the African and coloured population, and many people felt that transformation hadn't gone far enough. Indeed after nearly two decades of non-racial democracy, Cape Town is still a very divided city.

On the one hand the Mother City has been titivating itself for tourists and investors, helped by the establishment of the Cape Town Partnership in 1999, which has overseen the regeneration of the city centre. The post-apartheid period led to a wave of economic confidence expressed by investors in a number of monumental developments among them the megalomaniacal **Century City** (1997) in the northern suburbs, a garish retail, residential and office-complex that adopted Tuscan architecture and Venice-inspired canals. More tasteful was the expansion of the **V&A Waterfront** to include the

1994	2006	1997–2011
ANC wins election and Mandela becomes president, but Western Cape returns National Party provincial government.	Liberal Democratic Alliance takes control of Western Cape and Cape Town.	City constructs several prestige developments and regenerates centre.

hugely symbolic **Nelson Mandela Gateway** (2001), from where the ferry to Robben Island now embarks. In conjunction with South Africa's hosting of the 2010 FIFA World Cup, the iconic **Cape Town Stadium** (2009) went up on Green Point Common and Cape Town International Airport got a brand-new **Central Terminal Building** (2009), at last providing a facility that can cope with the city's expanding air traffic. To cap it all, the state-of-the-art **Cape Town Film Studio** (2010) was already attracting major projects by 2011.

On the other hand, as the biggest city within a thousand kilometres, Cape Town continued (and continues) to attract a steady **influx** of people seeking a better life, mostly from the rural Eastern Cape, but also from all over Africa, making it one of the subcontinent's fastest-growing Third World cities, with shacks proliferating wherever there are available open spaces in the townships. The city estimates that nearly a quarter of its households live in so-called "**informal dwellings**" or shacks. In 2005 the ANC national housing minister launched the **N2 Gateway Project,** to replace with brick buildings some of the shacks that lined the N1 from the airport to the city. Whether it was a serious attempt to alleviate the housing shortage or just grandstanding for the electorate and eye candy for tourists arriving by air in the Mother City is a moot point. Either way, **housing** is still one of the biggest problems facing the metropolis (and the whole of South Africa) and a growing one: between 1998 and 2008 Cape Town's housing **backlog** grew from 150,000 to 300,000.

The housing shortage means that hundreds of thousands of Capetonians have limited **access to services**, such as running water, waterborne-sewerage and electricity. It's also symptomatic of the city's slew of other problems: poverty, unemployment, rampant crime and high infection rates for HIV and TB. Planners project that within the next twenty years the city's **population** will grow from its present 3.5 million to anywhere between five and seven million inhabitants.

Industry has long been the route for urbanizing societies to rapidly create **employment**. But industrialization comes at an environmental cost and Cape Town's environment is one of its greatest assets: a tangible source of income and employment through tourism. But on its own it's not enough. The city's planners and politicians face some tough choices.

2008	**2010**	**2011**
Planners worry about growing housing backlog and that a quarter of Cape Town homes are shacks.	City stages glittering FIFA World Cup extravaganza in new Cape Town Stadium.	U2 plays to packed Stadium, while *zef*-rappers Die Antwoord take Cape Flats slang to the world.

Books

For a country with a relatively small reading public, South Africa generates a huge number of books, particularly novels, politics and history titles. Some of the South African published books may be tricky to find outside the country, but almost all those listed below are in print and should be available from the larger bookshops listed on p.134.

FICTION

Tatamkhulu Afrika *The Innocents*. Set in the struggle years, this novel examines the moral and ethical issues of the time from a Muslim perspective.

Mark Behr *The Smell of Apples*. Powerful first novel set in the 1970s recounts the gradual falling of the scales from the eyes of an eleven-year-old Afrikaner boy, whose father is a major-general in the apartheid army.

Andre Brink *A Chain of Voices*. Superbly evocative tale of Cape eighteenth-century life, exploring the impact of slavery on one farming family, right up to its dramatic and murderous end.

★ **J.M. Coetzee** *Disgrace*. A subtle, strange novel set in a Cape Town university and on a remote Eastern Cape farm, where the lives of a literature professor and his farmer daughter are violently transformed. Bleak but totally engrossing, this won the Booker Prize in 1999. Coetzee is something of a national treasure (see box below).

Achmat Dangor *The Z Town Trilogy* and *Bitter Fruit*. One of the best writers from Cape Town, Dangor sets his trilogy in a town much like it, during one of apartheid South Africa's many states of emergency, which have started to burrow in intricate ways into the psyches of his characters. *Bitter Fruit* is the story of the son of two anti-apartheid activists, and of an act of violence and injustice threading two generations, which is resurrected by the Truth and Reconciliation Commission. The book portrays a brittle family, a dysfunctional society, and how we address – or fail to address – the past's deepest wounds.

Damon Galgut *In a Strange Room*. The writer, some say, best placed to fill J.M. Coetzee's literary shoes, Damon

---

J.M. COETZEE

To read a **J.M. Coetzee** novel is to walk an emotional tightrope from exhilaration to sadness, with a sense throughout of being guided by a strong creative intellect and an exceptionally shrewd observer of human experience.

Coetzee's taut, measured style strikes some readers as cold and bloodless; he is relentlessly unsentimental, and plots tend to end on an unsettling note. But despite his reputation as a "difficult" writer, Coetzee never fails to involve us absolutely in the fates of his characters; in the words of Nadine Gordimer, Coetzee "goes to the nerve-centre of being".

Born in Cape Town in 1940, and trained as a linguist and computer scientist in South Africa and the US, Coetzee began to write fiction in the early 1970s. *Dusklands* and *In the Heart of the Country*, his first two novels, were dense and often overwrought dissections of settler psychology, but his prose reached a soaring maturity with *Waiting for the Barbarians* (1980), in which an imaginary desert landscape is the setting for a chilling exploration of the dynamics of imperial power.

In 1983 *The Life and Times of Michael K*, following the wanderings of a reclusive refugee across a future South Africa ravaged by civil war, won the Booker Prize. The novel ends with a passage of extraordinary beauty and subtlety, and stands as a postmodern masterpiece that now bears ironic testimony to South Africa's actual future. After *Michael K* came the novels *Foe*, *Age of Iron* and *The Master of Petersburg*, an anthology of criticism, *White Writing*, and a moving childhood memoir, *Boyhood*.

When Coetzee won an unprecedented second Booker Prize for *Disgrace* in 1999, he became famous beyond literary circles for the first time. This has meant exasperation for soundbite-hungry media hounds, since Coetzee abhors publicity – he chose not to attend the Booker Prize award ceremony and is notoriously cagey in social interactions. In 2002 Coetzee emigrated to Australia, where he lives in Adelaide.

Galgut has scooped several literary awards: *In a Strange Room* was shortlisted for the 2010 Man Booker Prize for fiction. Unusually for Galgut, it's set outside South Africa and describes in interchanging first and third person the global travels and relationships of a protagonist named, like the author, Damon. Quirky, beautifully written and highly readable.

Lily Herne *Deadlands*. South Africa's street-smart answer to Twilight follows the adventures and romance of seventeen-year-old Lele as she navigates the shattered, dystopian and zombie-infested suburbs of a post-apocalyptic Cape Town.

Rayda Jacobs *The Slave Book*. A carefully researched historical novel dealing with love and survival in a slave household in 1830s Cape Town, on the eve of the abolition of slavery.

Ashraf Jamal *Love Themes for the Wilderness*. The inhabitants of a bohemian subculture are lovingly observed in this funny and free-spirited novel set in mid-1990s Observatory.

Pamela Jooste *Dance with a Poor Man's Daughter*. The fragile world of a young coloured girl during the early apartheid years is sensitively imagined in this hugely successful first novel.

Alex La Guma *A Walk in the Night*. One of the truly proletarian writers that South Africa has produced, La Guma, before his long exile in Cuba, focused on the conditions of life in Cape Town, particularly the inner-city areas like District Six. His social realism is gritty yet poignant and it gives us many indelible portraits of Cape Town in the mid-twentieth century. A real historian of the city.

Anne Landsman *The Devil's Chimney*. A stylish and entertaining piece of magic realism about the Southern Cape town of Oudtshoorn in the days of the ostrich-feather boom.

Sindiwe Magona *Mother to Mother*. Magona adopts the narrative voice of the mother of the killer of Amy Biehl, an American student murdered in a Cape Town township in 1993. The novel is addressed to Biehl's mother, and is a

trenchant and lyrical meditation on the traumas of the past.

Deon Meyer *Thirteen Hours*. The latest offering from South Africa's hottest crime writer is, as usual, a riveting read, but may be uncomfortably close to the bone for some – one thread follows Detective Benny Griessel's quest to find and save the life of an American backpacker on the run from Cape Town gangsters after her travelling companion has been murdered.

Mike Nicol *Payback*. Hard-boiled thriller, one of several by established novelist Nicol (who has been compared to Elmore Leonard and Cormac McCarthy), follows a pair of gun-runners drawn back from retirement into Cape Town's dark underworld.

Patricia Schonstein Pinnock *Skyline*. Set in a crumbling apartment block in central Cape Town, Pinnock's novel examines a young girl's coming of age, her encounters with immigrants and refugees from Nigeria, Zimbabwe, Sudan and elsewhere in Africa, and the rising xenophobia in South Africa.

Richard Rive *Buckingham Palace, District Six*. The unique urban culture of District Six is movingly remembered in this short novel about the life of a now-desolate street and its inhabitants.

Linda Rode (ed) *Crossing Over*. Collection of 26 stories by new and emerging South African writers on the experiences of adolescence and early adulthood in a period of political transition.

Jann Turner *Heartland*. A white farmer's daughter and a black labourer's son are childhood companions on a Boland fruit farm; a betrayal occurs, and years later the boy returns from political exile, ready to stake his claim to the land. A hefty and ambitious popular novel.

Zoe Wicombe *You Can't Get Lost in Cape Town*. The author of a book of primarily short stories with a compelling title, Wicombe is remarkable for her sense of realism and the subtle way in which she produces work where social concern is transparent, humour is demonstrable, and yet which consents to none of the heavy-handed treatment anti-apartheid protest literature usually follows.

GUIDES AND REFERENCE BOOKS

G.M. Branch *Two Oceans*. Don't be put off by the coffee-table format; this is a comprehensive guide to southern Africa's marine life.

★ **Richard Cowling and Dave Richardson** *Fynbos: South Africa's Unique Floral Kingdom*. Lavishly illustrated coffee-table book. A fascinating layman's portrait of the fynbos ecosystem.

Mike Lundy *Best walks in the Cape Peninsula*. An invaluable, not-too-bulky book for casual walkers, offering plenty of possibilities for an afternoon's stroll. *Weekend Trails in the Western Cape* is the best guide to outings in the

Cape, with good maps, good advice and notes on flora and fauna.

L. McMahon and M. Fraser *A Fynbos Year*. Exquisitely illustrated and well-written book about the Western Cape's unique floral kingdom.

★ **Philip van Zyl** (ed) *John Platter South African Wines*. One of the best-selling titles in South Africa – an annually updated pocket book that rates virtually every wine produced in the country. No aspiring connoisseur of Cape wines should venture forth without it. Also available as a useful, but slightly flawed iPhone app.

HISTORY, POLITICS AND SOCIETY

★ **Vivian Bickford-Smith, Elizabeth van Heyningen and Nigel Worden** *Cape Town: The Making of a City* and *Cape Town in the Twentieth Century*. The first book is richly illustrated and exhaustively researched, and recounts the growth of Cape Town, from early Khoisan societies to the end of the nineteenth century. The second volume is a thorough and elegant account of modern Cape Town, which interweaves rich local history with international events.

Emile Boonzaier, Candy Malherbe, Andy Smith and Penny Berens *The Cape Herders: A History of the Khoikhoi of Southern Africa*. This accessible account of the Khoikhoi successfully explodes the many prejudices and myths that surround them and explores their way of life, their interaction with Europeans, and what remains of them today.

Andrew Brown *Street Blues*. Advocate, police-reserve sergeant and award-winning novelist, Brown paints a gritty, and sometimes witty, picture of life on the beat, tackling the mean streets of Cape Town.

Richard Calland *Anatomy of South Africa: Who Holds the Power*. An incisive dissection of politics and power in South Africa today, from one of the country's most respected commentators.

John Carlin *Playing the Enemy: Nelson Mandela and the Game that made a Nation*. Gripping account of Nelson Mandela's use of the 1995 rugby World Cup to unite a fractious nation in danger of collapsing into civil war. Also published as *Invictus*, the title of the Clint Eastwood film, which starred Matt Damon and Morgan Freeman.

Andrew Feinstein *After the Party: Corruption, the ANC and South Africa's Uncertain Future*. A personal account of where South Africa's government has lost its way, by a former ANC member of parliament. Feinstein resigned in 2001 in protest at the government's coverup of graft and corruption in negotiating the country's cripplingly expensive arms deal.

★ **Peter Harris** *In a Different Time: The Inside Story of the Delmas Four*. Brilliantly told true historical drama about four young South Africans sent on a mission by the ANC-in-exile, which ultimately led them to Death Row. As their defence lawyer, Harris had unique and sympathetic insight into their personalities and motivations. Also published as *A Just Defiance: The Bombmakers, the Insurgents and a Legendary Treason Trial*.

Hermann Giliomee and Bernard Mbenga *A New History of South Africa*. A comprehensive, reliable and entertaining account of South Africa's history, published in 2007, making it the first new major illustrated work on the topic in a decade.

★ **Antjie Krog** *Country of My Skull*. An unflinching and harrowing account of the Truth and Reconciliation Commission's investigations. Krog, a respected radio journalist and poet, covered the entire process, and skilfully merges private identity with national catharsis.

Hein Marais *Pushed to the Limit*. An assessment of why the privileged classes remain just that with a handful of conglomerates dominating the South African economy and how this relates to Jacob Zuma's rise to power.

Alan Mountain *An Unsung Heritage: Perspectives on Slavery*. An account of the nature of slavery in the Cape, and the contribution imported slaves made to the fabric of the area today. Best of all is the guide to slave heritage sites in the Cape Peninsula, Winelands and West Coast and along the Garden Route, with attractive photos and illustrations.

Mike Nicol *Sea-Mountain, Fire City: Living in Cape Town*. One of the most recent books in that rare category, a documentary on living in Cape Town at the beginning of the new millennium. Hinging his narrative on the apparently prosaic business of moving house from one part of the city to another, Nicol maps many of those fissures, not to say abysses, that make Cape Town the divided city that it is.

Nigel Penn *Rogues, Rebels and Runaways*. A hugely entertaining collection of essays on deviant types in the eighteenth-century Cape. Tragi-comic and written in a wry, engaging style.

Robert C-H Shell *Children of Bondage*. Definitive social history of Cape slavery in the eighteenth century – a compelling academic text that is accessible to the lay reader.

Allister Sparks *The Mind of South Africa*. An authoritative journalist and historian traces the rise and fall of the apartheid state; a lively, economical and serious work. *Beyond the Miracle: Inside The New South Africa* examines the prospects for South Africa, looking beyond the initial buoyancy of democracy to emerging patterns in its government.

Stephen Taylor *The Caliban Shore: The Fate of the Grosvenor Castaways*. Gripping account of the wreck of the *Grosvenor* in the eighteenth century along the Eastern Cape's aptly named Wild Coast. Meticulously researched history, it has the depth and pace of a well-crafted novel as it traces the fates of the survivors.

★ **Desmond Tutu** *No Future Without Forgiveness*. Tutu's gracious and honest assessment of the Truth Commission he guided. An important testimony from one of the country's most influential thinkers and leaders.

Frank Welsh *A History of South Africa*. Solid scholarship and a strong sense of overall narrative mark this publication as a much-needed addition to South African historiography.

BIOGRAPHY AND AUTOBIOGRAPHY

★ **J.M. Coetzee** *Boyhood*. A moving and courageous childhood memoir by South Africa's greatest novelist. Written in the third person, it depicts the thoughts of a young boy with profound attentiveness.

★ **Sindiwe Magoma** *To My Children's Children*. A fascinating autobiography – initially started so that her family would never forget their roots – that traces Magoma's life from the rural Transkei to the hard townships of Cape Town, and from political innocence to wisdom born of bitter experience.

Nelson Mandela *Long Walk to Freedom*. Superb best-selling autobiography of the former president and national icon, which is wonderfully evocative of his early years and intensely moving about his long years in prison. A little too diplomatic, perhaps, on his love life and on the inside story behind the negotiated settlement that spelt the end of apartheid.

William Plomer *Cecil Rhodes*. There are countless books on Rhodes and his huge influence on South Africa in the nineteenth century. Most feed the legend, though some

historians now regard him as a flawed colossus. Plomer, a South African poet-novelist, went against the grain several decades ago, when he pulled no punches in presenting Rhodes as an immature person driven by his weaknesses.

★ **Benjamin Pogrund** *How Can Man Die Better? The Life of Robert Sobukwe*. Story of one of the most important anti-apartheid liberation heroes, the late leader of the Pan Africanist Congress and a contemporary of Nelson Mandela, so feared by the white government that they passed a special law – The Sobukwe Clause – to keep him in solitary confinement on Robben Island after he'd served his sentence.

★ **Anthony Sampson** *Mandela, The Authorised Biography*. Released to coincide with Mandela's retirement from the presidency in 1999, Sampson's authoritative volume competes with *A Long Walk to Freedom* in both interest and sheer poundage. Firmly grounded in the author's long association with his subject, as well as exhaustive research and interviews, it offers a broader perspective and sharper analysis than the autobiography.

THE ARTS

Marion Arnold *Women and Art in South Africa*. Comprehensive, pioneering study of women artists from the early twentieth century to the present.

Thorsten Deckler, Anne Graupner, Henning Rasmuss *Contemporary South African Architecture in a Landscape of Transition*. Lavishly illustrated coverage of fifty outstanding architectural projects completed since 1994, all of which, the authors say, display a sense of South African identity.

S. Francis and Rico *Madam and Eve*. Various annual volumes of telling and witty cartoons conveying the daily struggle between an African domestic worker and her white madam in the northern suburbs of Johannesburg, these cartoons say more about post-apartheid society than countless academic tomes.

Steve Gordon *Beyond the Blues: Township Jazz of the Sixties and Seventies*. Portraits, in words and pictures, of the country's jazz greats such as Kippie Moeketsi, Basil Coetzee and Abdullah Ibrahim (Dollar Brand).

★ **Andy Mason** *What's so Funny Under the Skin of South African Cartooning*. Insightful, fascinating and thoroughly

collectable wade through the history of South African visual satire from the colonial period, through the apartheid years to the present.

Ralf-Peter Seippel *South African Photography: 1950– 2010*. South Africa's history has provided a rich vein of material for photographers and this volume covers the work of some of the country's most celebrated lensmen, whose work is divided into three periods: apartheid, struggle and freedom.

Sue Williamson *South African Art Now*. A survey of South African art from the "Resistance Art" of the 1960s to the present, covering movements, genres and leading artists such as Marlene Dumas and William Kentridge, by one of the country's most influential commentators and an accomplished artist in her own right.

Zapiro *Do You Know Who I am?* In a country where satire is in notoriously short supply, Zapiro is the leading cartoonist, consistently exposing what needs to be exposed. This book is the umpteenth in a series of annual collections, containing work originally published in a number of dailies as well as the *Mail & Guardian* and *Sunday Times*.

POETRY

Ingrid de Kok *Transfer* Technically adroit and always moving work from probably the most intelligent of South Africa's feminist poets.

Finuala Dowling *Notes from the Dementia Ward*. At once cynical, humorous and sad, Dowling's award-winning collection explores the death of her brother and mental decline of her mother against the clearly delineated backdrop of Cape Town.

★ **Denis Hirson** (ed) *The Lava of this Land: South African Poetry 1960–1996*. Comprehensive anthology of South African poetry that includes work from the oral period, as well as translations from Afrikaans and other languages. The most useful introduction to date.

Ingrid Jonker *Selected Poems*. One of the few Afrikaans-language poets to be in print in an English translation that does justice to her work. The poems display a remarkable rawness in depicting the outrage of 1960s apartheid, as well as a grief-stricken lyricism from a poet who drowned herself off Sea Point in 1965.

★ **Stephen Watson** *The Other City* and *The Light Echo*. No one better evokes Cape Town's changeable beauty, though Watson (who died of cancer in 2011) also writes of the heart and the great universal themes that make him a first-rate poet of the world, rather than just of his native city.

TRAVEL WRITING

Richard Dobson *Karoo Moons: A Photographic Journey*. If you need encouragement to explore the desert interior of South Africa, these enticing images should do the trick.

★ **Sihle Khumalo** *Dark Continent, My Black Arse*. Insightful and witty account by a black South African who quit his well-paid job to realize a dream of travelling from the Cape to Cairo by public transport.

★ **Ben Maclennan** *The Wind Makes Dust: Four Centuries of Travel in South Africa*. A remarkable anthology of fascinating travel pieces, meticulously unearthed and researched.

Julia Martin *A Millimetre of Dust: Visiting Ancestral Sites*. Sensitively crafted narrative that begins on the Cape Peninsula and takes the author, her husband and two children on a journey to important archeological sites in the Northern Cape, raising ethical, ecological and philosophical questions along the way.

Dervla Murphy *South from the Limpopo: Travels Through South Africa*. A fascinating and intrepid journey – by bicycle – through the new South Africa. The author isn't afraid to explore the complexities and paradoxes of this country.

Paul Theroux *Dark Star Safari: Overland from Cairo to Cape Town*. Theroux's powerful account of his overland trip from Cairo to Cape Town, with a couple of chapters on South Africa, including an account of meeting writer Nadine Gordimer.

Music

Cape Town's most proclaimed musical treasure is Cape jazz, whose greatest exponent is Abdullah Ibrahim, a supremely gifted pianist and composer, born in the Cape Flats, who for decades has produced a hypnotic fusion of African, American and Cape Muslim idioms. Other Cape Town jazz legends include saxophonists Robbie Jansen, Winston "Ngozi" Mankunku and the late Basil Coetzee, plus guitarist Errol Dyers, pianist Hotep Galata and bassist Spencer Mbadu. Two young stars stand out as heirs to the Cape jazz tradition, the astronomically cool guitarist Jimmy Dludlu and subtle, mellow pianist Paul Hanmer; catch them live if you can.

Among African township youth, much the biggest sound is **kwaito** and local hip-hop. In an accurate reflection of the depressed and nihilistic mood of township youth culture, *kwaito's* vibe tends to be downbeat, and the music frequently carries a strong association with gangsterism and explicit sexuality. Although the supporters of local **hip-hop** eagerly proclaim that it is now replacing *kwaito*, the reality is more nuanced, and the difference between the two isn't always clear-cut.

DJ-mixed South African **house** attracts practitioners and fans from all parts of the country's racial and cultural divisions, but it is black DJs such as **DJ Fresh**, **Glen Lewis**, **DJ Mbuso** and **Oskido** who garner by far the most attention from the local media, while South African **rap** has enjoyed sustained popularity since the early 1990s, but has remained almost completely ghettoized within the coloured community of the Western Cape. Heavily influenced by African American rappers, performers often exude a palpable sense of being "Americans trapped in Africa". Pioneers of the style were the heavily politicized **Prophets of Da City**, several members of which made names for themselves as solo artists after the group's break-up, most notably **Rahim**, **Junior Solela** and **Ishmael.** Other performers who have since come up are **Brasse vannie Kaap** (who rap in Afrikaans) and **Reddy D.** Less easy to confine under the rubric of rap is **E.J. von**

ENTER DIE ANTWOORD

Die Antwoord (meaning "the answer") was an overnight sensation – an unknown crew from Cape Town's northern suburbs rapping in Cape Flats slang – that stormed the internet in 2010. This was the true grit from the streets of the Mother City: a lowlife rap genre known as *zef* (from an Afrikaans word that denotes trashy style). That, at least, was the story.

Their success was real enough: in February 2010, internet traffic to their website (ⓦdieantwoord.com), which was streaming their debut album *o*, was so heavy (fifteen million hits) that it crashed and they had to move to a US server. Their signature foul-mouthed lyrics aside, there's nothing rough and ready about their output. If you aren't convinced, look at the tight machine-gun vocal style (likened by *Rolling Stone* to "Eminem's *Lose Yourself* on mescaline") the slick art-direction, the careful choreography and the cool Keith Haring-esque graphics on their *Enter the Ninja* video.

Far from being the band that came from nowhere, Die Antwoord (frontman Ninja, helium-voiced Yo-landi Vi$$er and DJ Hi-Tek) is the latest surreal vehicle for Watkin Tudor Jones (Ninja), whose previous excursions included hip-hop rig Max Normal and the Constructus Corporation. Jones's history of taking on personas has led detractors to express disappointment that Die Antwoord "aren't real" (whatever that means in show business), while fans declare him a creative genius. Does it matter? The fact is, Die Antwoord deliver an unmistakably Cape Town sound that really cooks.

Lyrik (of the hip-hop crew **Godessa**), who jams rap, reggae and funk influences into her sound, while **Die Antwoord** (see box), who rap in a style known as **zef**, which is a mixture of English, Afrikaans and Cape Flats slang.

English-speaking South Africans have successfully replicated virtually every popular Western musical style going back to the late nineteenth century, and some have found fame in the outside world, but there are still many gifted performers who have remained in the Mother City, including **Goldfish**, the **Parlotones**, string-maestro **Steve Newman** and **Tananas**, a string trio he plays with for a couple of months each year.

Afrikaans music, on the the other hand, is a world unto itself, but from the late 1920s until the 1960s American country was its greatest outside influence. Following the end of apartheid, a general concern about the future of the Afrikaans language and culture spurred a revival of interest in Afrikaans music. There is undoubtedly more stylistic variety now than ever before: witness the house/disco of **Juanita**, the heavy rock of Karen Zoid and Jackhammer, the Neil Diamond-esque songs of **Steve Hofmeyer** (the bestselling Afrikaans music artist), as well as the punk-rock riffs of **Fokofpolisiekar** and the studied banality of rapper **Jack Parow**, both of whom have collaborated with Die Antwoord.

Arguably the place where many contemporary South African artists sit most comfortably is the catch-all category known as **Afropop**. Characterized by a knack for combining various local African styles with Western popular influences, and the eschewing of computer-generated backing in favour of actual instruments, Afropop has the ability to attract a multiracial audience. Cape Town's most successful proponents of the style are **Freshlyground**, who, because of the their broad appeal and engaging sound, were chosen to accompany Shakira in jamming to a billion viewers at the opening and closing ceremonies of the 2010 Fifa World Cup.

ESSENTIAL CAPE TOWN SOUNDS

Basil Coetzee *Monwabisi* (Mountain). Smoky, intensely energetic jazz record from the greatest of Cape jazz saxophonists.

Dantai *Operation Lahlela* (Nebula BOS). R&B-flavoured *kwaito* from one of Cape Town's up-and-coming dance acts.

Die Antwoord *O* (Rhythm Records). The signature album of the zef rave rap style that brought the trio to the world's attention featuring their addictive and weird anthem track Enter the Ninja.

Jimmy Dludlu *Essence Of Rhythm* (Universal). Dludlu is the essence of smooth jazz, and is arguably the single most popular representative of what is in turn the most commercially successful jazz style in South Africa.

Brenda Fassie *African Princess Of Pop* and *Memeza* (CCP). The former is a posthumous survey covering the entire career of South Africa's very own Madonna; the latter, featuring the massive hit "Vul'Ndlela", was Brenda's most commercially successful effort.

Freshlyground *Ma'Cheri* (Freeground Records/Sony BMG). Voted Album of the Year at the 2008 SA Music Awards, *Ma'Cheri* sees the most enduring of South Africa's Afropopsters do to a tee what they're known for: crossing national and stylistic boundaries to deliver catchy hooks and accessible melodies.

Fokofpolisiekar *Swanesang* (Rhythm Records/The Orchard). One of South Africa's most successful live bands has helped redefine Afrikaner-identity for the post-apartheid generation with its punk-rock-influenced sound, while repeatedly outraging the conservative establishment, starting with their name which translates as "fuck off police car".

Goldfish *Perceptions of Pacha* (Pacha Recordings/ Finetunes). Cape Town-based jazz-boogie duo weave accoustic sounds into their predominantly electronica-based grooves to crank out one addictively upbeat track after the other.

Paul Hanmer *Trains To Taung* (Sheer Sound). This album is constructed around Hanmer's dreamy, piano-based compositions. Now considered a classic and one of the first expositions of the new jazz of the post-apartheid era.

Abdullah Ibrahim *African Marketplace* (Discovery/WEA). Ibrahim's best album – a wistful, nostalgic, other-worldly journey.

Robbie Jansen *Nomad Jez* (EMI). Great, if slightly flawed, album from veteran saxophonist Jansen, playing with other luminaries of the local jazz scene including Hilton Schilder and Errol Dyers.

Winston Mankunku *Crossroads* (Nkomo/Sheer). Sinuous, upbeat township jazz from the veteran Cape Town saxman.

Prophets of Da City *Ghetto Code* (Universal). South Africa's rap supremos' finest release, full of tough but articulate rhymes and some seriously heavy samples, all in true Cape Flats style.

Ringo *Sondelani* (CCP). A superb modern reworking of traditional Xhosa sounds by this bald Capetonian heart-throb, including the hit track "Sondela", which has become one of South Africa's most popular love songs.

Springbok Nude Girls *Afterlife Satisfaction* (Sony Music). One of South Africa's most popular white bands before they disbanded, here delivering a powerful, if not particularly original, belting rock set.

ESSENTIAL SOUTH AFRICAN SOUNDS

Bayete *Umkhaya-Lo* (Polygram). A seminal fusion of South African sounds with laidback soul and funk, blended by lead singer Jabu Khanyile's unique mixing talent and spiced with his beautifully soothing vocals.

Gloria Bosman *Tranquillity* (Sheer/Limelight*). A young and compelling jazz vocalist, Bosman juggles African and American styles with consummate ease. Paul Hanmer arranges and tickles the ivories.

Lucky Dube *Prisoner* (Gallo). Originally a township jive singer, the late Dube made a switch to reggae that was both artistically and commercially inspired. *Prisoner* was South Africa's second bestselling album ever, full of stirring Peter Tosh-style roots tunes.

Sibongile Khumalo *Ancient Evenings* (Sony Music). Though a classically trained opera singer, Khumalo takes on both jazz and a variety of traditional melodies on this wonderful album, demonstrating why she is currently one of South Africa's best-loved singers.

Ladysmith Black Mambazo *Heavenly* (Gallo/Spectrum*). An inspired and commercially successful foray into Afropop, featuring solo versions of various pop classics as well as vocal collaborations with Dolly Parton and Lou Rawls.

Vusi Mahlasela *Silang Mabele* (BMG). Lush harmonies and lilting melodies from this sweet-voiced township balladeer.

Mfaz'Omnyama *Ngisebenzile Mama* (Gallo). The title means "I have been working, Mum", and is amply justified by this superb set, featuring some of the best *maskanda* ever recorded.

Pops Mohamed *How Far Have We Come?* (Melt2000). An exciting celebration of traditional African instruments: mbiras, koras, mouthbows and various percussion instruments are supplemented by bass and brass in this ethereal but funky album.

Moses Taiwa Molelekwa *Genes and Spirits* (Melt2000). Fascinating jazz/drum'n'bass fusion by a talented young pianist, who died tragically in 2001.

Language

In Cape Town and along the Garden Route you'll rarely, if ever, need to use any other language than English. Forty percent of whites are mother-tongue English speakers, many of whom believe that they are (or at least should be) speaking standard British English. In fact, South African English has its own distinct character, and is as different from the Queen's English as Australian is. Its most notable characteristic is its unique words and usages, some drawn from Afrikaans and the indigenous African languages, of which Xhosa (see below) is one of the most widely spoken. The hefty *Oxford Dictionary of South African English* makes for an interesting browse.

Afrikaans, although a language you seldom need to speak, nevertheless remains very much in evidence and you will certainly encounter it on official forms and countless signs, particularly on the road (see p.275).

The other main language spoken in Cape Town is **Xhosa**, the predominant mother tongue of the city's African residents and easily distinguished by the clicks that form part of the words. It is also Nelson Mandela's mother tongue, which he shares with seven million other South Africans, predominantly in the Eastern Cape.

The glossary below is far from comprehensive, but it does include some of the more common words that are unique to South African English. Words whose spelling makes it hard to guess how to render them have their approximate pronunciation given in italics. Where *gh* occurs in the pronunciation, it denotes the **ch** sound in the Scottish word lo**ch**. Sometimes we've used the letter "r" in the pronunciation even though the word in question doesn't contain this letter; for example, we've given the pronunciation of "Egoli" as "*air-gaw-lee*". In these instances the syllable containing the "r" is meant to represent a familiar word or sound from English; the "r" itself shouldn't be pronounced.

GLOSSARY

African In the context of South Africa, an indigenous South African

Afrikaner Literally "African": a white person who speaks Afrikaans

Aloe Family of spiky indigenous succulents, often with dramatic orange flowers

Apartheid (apart-hate) Term used from the 1940s for the National Party's official policy of "racial separation"

Arvie Afternoon

Baai Afrikaans word meaning "bay"; also a common suffix in place names eg Stilbaai

Bakkie (bucky) Light truck or van

Bantu (bun-too) Unscientific apartheid term for indigenous black people; in linguistics, a group of indigenous southern African languages

Bantustan Term used under apartheid for the territories such as Transkei, reserved for Africans

Bergie A vagrant living on the slopes of Table Mountain; a hobo on the streets of Cape Town

Big Five A term derived from hunting that refers to the trophy animals hunters most want to bag: lion, leopard, buffalo, elephant and rhino; often now used generically to indicate top big game country (as opposed to game reserves that only have antelope and other small mammals)

Black Imprecise term that sometimes refers collectively to Africans, Indians and coloureds, but more usually is used to mean Africans

Boer (boor) Literally "farmer", but also refers to early Dutch colonists at the Cape and Afrikaners

Boland (boor-lunt) Southern part of the Western Cape

Bottle store Off-licence or liquor store

Boy Offensive term used to refer to an adult African man who is a servant

Bundu (approximately boon-doo, but with the vowels shortened) Wilderness or back country

Burgher Literally a citizen, but more specifically a member of the Dutch community at the Cape in the seventeenth and eighteenth centuries; free burghers were VOC employees released from contract to farm independently on the Cape Peninsula and surrounding areas

Bush See bundu

Bushman South Africa's earliest, but now almost extinct, inhabitants who lived by hunting and gathering

Cape Doctor The southeaster that brings cool winds during the summer months

Cape Dutch Nineteenth-century, whitewashed, gabled style of architecture

Cape Dutch Revival Twentieth-century style based on Cape Dutch architecture

CBD The Central Business District of Central Cape town.

Coloured People of mixed race

Dagga (dugh-a) Marijuana

Dagha (dah-ga) Mud used in indigenous construction

Dassie (dussy) Hyrax

Disa (die-za) One of twenty species of beautiful indigenous orchids, most famous of which is the red disa or "Pride of Table Mountain"

Dominee (dour-min-ee) Reverend (abbreviated to Ds)

Dorp Country town or village (Derived from Afrikaans)

Drostdy (dross-tea) Historically, the building of the landdrost or magistrate

Fundi Expert

Fynbos (fayn-boss) Term for vast range of fine-leafed species that predominate in the southern part of the Western Cape (see box, p.190)

Girl Offensive term used to refer to an African woman who is a servant

Gogga (gho-gha) Creepy-crawly or insect

Griqua Person of mixed white, Bushman and Hottentot descent

Group Areas Act Now-defunct law passed in 1950 that provided for the establishment of separate areas for each "racial group"

Homeland See bantustan

Hottentot Now unfashionable term for indigenous Khoisan herders encountered by the first settlers at the Cape

Indaba Zulu term meaning a group discussion and now used in South African English for any meeting or conference

Is it? Really?

Jislaaik! (yis-like) Exclamation equivalent to "Geez!" or "Crikey!"

Jol Party, celebration

Just now In a while

Kaffir Highly objectionable term of abuse for Africans

Karoo Arid plateau that occupies a large proportion of the South African interior

Khoikhoi (ghoy-ghoy) Self-styled name of South Africa's original herding inhabitants

Khoisan A conflation of the terms "Khoikhoi" and "San" used to collectively refer to South Africa's aboriginal inhabitants; the two were socially, but not ethnically, distinct, the Khoikhoi having been herders and the San hunter-gatherers

Kloof (klo-ef) Ravine or gorge

Knobkerrie Wooden club

Koppie Hillock

Kramat (crum-mutt) Shrine of a Muslim holy man

Krans (crunce) Sheer cliff face; plural kranse

Lapa Courtyard of group of Ndebele houses; also used to describe an enclosed area at safari camps, where braais are held

Lekker Nice

Lobola (la-ball-a) Bride price, paid by an African man to his wife's parents

Location Old-fashioned term for segregated African area on the outskirts of a town or farm

Madiba Mandela's clan name, used affectionately

Malay Misnomer for Cape Muslims of Asian descent

Mbira (m-beer-a) African thumb piano, often made with a gourd

MK Umkhonto we Sizwe (Spear of the Nation), the armed wing of the ANC, now incorporated into the national army

Mlungu (m-loon-goo) African term for a white person, equivalent to honkie

Moffie (mawf-ee) Gay person

Mother City Nickname for Cape Town

Muti (moo-tee) See umuthi

Nkosi Sikelel' iAfrika "God Bless Africa", anthem of the ANC and now of South Africa

Pass Document that Africans used to have to carry at all times, which essentially rendered them aliens in their own country

Pastorie (puss-tour-ee) Parsonage

Platteland (plutta-lunt) Country districts

Poort Narrow pass through mountains along river course

Protea National flower of South Africa

Raadsaal (the "d" is pronounced "t") Council or parliament building

Robot Traffic light

Rondavel (ron-daa-vil, with the stress on the middle syllable) Circular building based on traditional African huts

San A more common term for Bushmen (see above)

Sangoma (sun-gom-a) Traditional spirit medium and healer

Shebeen (sha-bean) Unlicensed township tavern

Southeaster Prevailing wind in the Western Cape

Spaza shops Small stall or kiosk

Stoep Veranda

Strandloper Literally "beach walkers"; Bushman or San social group who lived along the shores of the Western Cape and whose hunting and gathering consisted largely of shellfish and other seafood

Tackies Sneakers or plimsolls

Township Area set aside under apartheid for Africans

Transkei (trans-kye) Now-defunct homeland for Xhosa speakers

Trekboer (trek-boor) Nomadic Afrikaner farmers, usually in the eighteenth and nineteenth century

Umuthi (oo-moo-tee) Traditional herbal medicine

Vlei (flay) Swamp

VOC Verenigde Oostindische Compagnie, the Dutch East India Company

Voortrekkers (the first syllable rhymes with "boor") Dutch burghers who migrated inland in their ox wagons in the nineteenth century to escape British colonialism

FOOD AND DRINK

Amarula Liqueur made from the berries of the marula tree

Begrafnisrys (ba-ghruff-niss-race) Literally "funeral rice"; traditional Cape Muslim dish of yellow rice cooked with raisins

Biltong Sun-dried salted strip of meat, chewed as a snack

Blatjang (blutt-young) Cape Muslim chutney that has become a standard condiment on South African dinner tables

Bobotie (ba-boor-tea) Traditional Cape curried mince topped with a savoury custard and often cooked with apricots and almonds

Boerekos (boor-a-coss) Farm food, usually consisting of loads of meat and vegetables cooked using butter and sugar

Boerewors (boor-a-vorce) Spicy lengths of sausage that are de rigueur at braais

Bokkoms Dried fish, much like salt fish

Braai or **braaivleis** (bry-flace) Barbecue

Bredie Cape vegetable and meat stew

Cane or **cane spirit** A potent vodka-like spirit distilled from sugar cane and generally mixed with a soft drink such as Coke

Cap Classique Sparkling wine fermented in the bottle in exactly the same way as Champagne; also called Méthode Cap Classic

Cape gooseberry Fruit of the physalis; a sweet yellow berry

Cape salmon or **geelbek** (ghear-l-beck) Delicious firm-fleshed sea fish (unrelated to northern hemisphere salmon)

Cape Velvet A sweet liqueur-and-cream dessert beverage that resembles Irish Cream liqueur

Denningvleis (den-ning-flace) Spicy traditional Cape lamb stew

Frikkadel Fried onion and meatballs

Geelbek See Cape salmon

Hanepoort (harner-poort) Delicious sweet dessert grape

Kabeljou (cobble-yo) Common South African marine fish, also called kob

Kerrievis (kerry-fiss) See pickled fish

Kingklip Highly prized deepwater fish caught along the Atlantic and Indian ocean coasts

Kob See kabeljou

Koeksister (cook-sister) Deep-fried plaited doughnut, dripping with syrup

Maas or **amasi** or **amaas** Traditional African beverage consisting of naturally soured milk, available as a packaged dairy product in supermarkets

Maaskaas Cottage cheese made from maas

Mageu or **mahewu** or **maheu** (ma-gh-weh) Traditional African beer made from maize meal and water, now packaged and commercially available

Malva Very rich and very sweet traditional baked Cape dessert

Mampoer (mum-poor) Moonshine; home-distilled spirit made from soft fruit, commonly peaches

Mealie See mielie

Melktert (melk-tairt) Traditional Cape custard pie

Mielie Maize

Mielie pap (mealy pup) Maize porridge, varying from a thin mixture to a stiff one that can resemble polenta

Mqomboti (m-qom-booty) Traditional African beer made from fermented sorghum

Musselcracker Large-headed fish with powerful jaws and firm, white flesh

Naartjie (nar-chee) Tangerine or mandarin

Pap (pup) Porridge

Peri-peri Delicious hottish spice of Portuguese origin commonly used with grilled chicken

Perlemoen (pear-la-moon) Abalone

Pickled fish Traditional Cape dish of fish preserved with onions, vinegar and curry; available tinned in supermarkets

Pinotage A uniquely South African cultivar hybridized from Pinot Noir and Hermitage grapes and from which a wine of the same name is made

Potjiekos or potjie (poy-key-kos) Food cooked slowly over embers in a three-legged cast-iron pot

Putu (poo-too) Traditional African mielie pap (see above) prepared until it forms dry crumbs

Rooibos (roy-boss) **tea** Indigenous herbal tea, made from the leaves of a particular fynbos plant.

Rooti Chapati

Salmon trout Freshwater fish that is often smoked to create a cheaper and pretty good imitation of smoked salmon

Salomie Roti

Sambals (sam-bills) Accompaniments, such as chopped bananas, green peppers, desiccated coconut and chutney, served with Cape curries

Samp Traditional African dish of broken maize kernels, frequently cooked with beans

Skokiaan (skok-ee-yan) Potent home-brew

Smoorsnoek (smore-snook) Smoked snoek

Snoek (snook) Large fish that features in many traditional Cape recipes

Sosatie (so-sah-ti) Spicy skewered mince

Spanspek (spon-speck) A sweet melon

Steenbras (ste-en-bruss) A delicious white-fleshed fish

Van der Hum South African naartjie-flavoured liqueur

Vetkoek (fet-cook) Deep-fried doughnut-like cake

Waterblommetjiebredie (vata-blom-a-key-bree-dee) Cape meat stew made with waterlily rhizomes

Witblits (vit-blitz) Moonshine

Yellowtail Delicious darkish-fleshed marine fish

AFRIKAANS STREET SIGNS

Derde	Third	**Perron**	Station platform
Doeane	Customs	**Polisie**	Police
Drankwinkel	Liquor shop	**Poskantoor**	Post office
Eerste	First	**Regs**	Right
Geen ingang	No entry	**Ry**	Go
Gevaar	Danger	**Sentrum**	Centre
Goof	Main	**Singel**	Crescent
Hoog	High	**Stad**	City
Ingang	Entrance	**Stad sentrum**	City centre
Inligting	Information	**Stadig**	Slow
Kantoor	Office	**Stasie**	Station
Kerk	Church	**Strand**	Beach
Kort	Short	**Swembad**	Swimming pool
Links	Left	**Verbode**	Prohibited
Lughawe	Airport	**Verkeer**	Traffic
Mans	Men	**Versigtig**	Carefully
Mark	Market	**Vierde**	Fourth
Ompad	Detour	**Vrouens**	Women
Pad	Road	**Vyfde**	Fifth
Padwerke voor	Roadworks ahead		

Index and small print

A ROUGH GUIDE TO ROUGH GUIDES

Published in 1982, the first Rough Guide – to Greece – was a student scheme that became a publishing phenomenon. Mark Ellingham, a recent graduate in English from Bristol University, had been travelling in Greece the previous summer and couldn't find the right guidebook. With a small group of friends he wrote his own guide, combining a highly contemporary, journalistic style with a thoroughly practical approach to travellers' needs.

The immediate success of the book spawned a series that rapidly covered dozens of destinations. And, in addition to impecunious backpackers, Rough Guides soon acquired a much broader readership that relished the guides' wit and inquisitiveness as much as their enthusiastic, critical approach and value-for-money ethos.

These days, Rough Guides include recommendations from budget to luxury and cover more than 200 destinations around the globe, as well as producing an ever-growing range of eBooks and apps.

Visit **roughguides.com** to see our latest publications.

Rough Guide credits

Editors: Charlotte Melville, Emma Gibbs
Layout: Pradeep Thapliyal
Cartography: Katie Lloyd-Jones
Picture editor: Nicole Newman
Proofreader: Karen Parker
Managing editor: Kathryn Lane
Assitant editor: Jalpreen Kaur Chhatwal
Production: Rebecca Short
Cover design: Nicole Newman, Pradeep Thapliyal
Photographer: Alex Robinson
Editorial assistant: Lorna North

Senior pre-press designer: Dan May
Design director: Scott Stickland
Travel publisher: Joanna Kirby
Digital travel publisher: Peter Buckley
Reference director: Andrew Lockett
Operations coordinator: Becky Doyle
Operations assistant: Johanna Wurm
Publishing director (Travel): Clare Currie
Commercial manager: Gino Magnotta
Managing director: John Duhigg

Publishing information

This fourth edition published January 2012 by
Rough Guides Ltd,
80 Strand, London WC2R 0RL
11, Community Centre, Panchsheel Park,
New Delhi 110017, India
Distributed by the Penguin Group
Penguin Books Ltd,
80 Strand, London WC2R 0RL
Penguin Group (USA)
375 Hudson Street, NY 10014, USA
Penguin Group (Australia)
250 Camberwell Road, Camberwell,
Victoria 3124, Australia
Penguin Group (NZ)
67 Apollo Drive, Mairangi Bay, Auckland 1310, New
Zealand
Rough Guides is represented in Canada by Tourmaline
Editions Inc. 662 King Street West, Suite 304, Toronto,
Ontario M5V 1M7
Printed in Singapore
© Barbara McCrea and Tony Pinchuck 2012

Maps © Rough Guides
No part of this book may be reproduced in any form
without permission from the publisher except for the
quotation of brief passages in reviews.
296pp includes index
A catalogue record for this book is available from the
British Library
ISBN: 978-1-40538-968-6
The publishers and authors have done their best to
ensure the accuracy and currency of all the information in
The Rough Guide to Cape Town, however, they can accept
no responsibility for any loss, injury, or inconvenience
sustained by any traveller as a result of information or
advice contained in the guide.
1 3 5 7 9 8 6 4 2

Help us update

We've gone to a lot of effort to ensure that the fourth
edition of **The Rough Guide to Cape Town** is accurate
and up-to-date. However, things change – places get
"discovered", opening hours are notoriously fickle,
restaurants and rooms raise prices or lower standards. If
you feel we've got it wrong or left something out, we'd like
to know, and if you can remember the address, the price,
the hours, the phone number, so much the better.

Please send your comments with the subject line
"**Rough Guide Cape Town Update**" to ✉ mail@uk
.roughguides.com. We'll credit all contributions and send a
copy of the next edition (or any other Rough Guide if you
prefer) for the very best emails.

Find more travel information, connect with fellow
travellers and book your trip on ⓦ roughguides.com

ABOUT THE AUTHORS

Tony Pinchuck launched his travels as a schoolboy hitching around South Africa in the 1970s and his explorations of the subcontinent have continued ever since. Now resident in Cape Town, he is production editor on the investigative magazine *noseweek*.

Barbara McCrea was born in Zimbabwe and taught African literature at the University of Natal. She lived in London for fifteen years, working on Rough Guides to Zimbabwe, South Africa and Cape Town, before returning to Southern Africa. She lives with views of whales, surfers and mountains in Cape Town.

Acknowledgements

Barbara McCrea: Thanks to our cheerful editor Charlie who always remained upbeat during tricky times, to Tony Pinchuck without whom these books would never get started or finished, to our son Gabriel Pinchuck for putting up with the levels of obsessiveness and staying power which Rough Guides demand, to Lizzie and Ant and the many other people who have given us accommodation, meals and information. And thanks to everyone else in this network of help and support I haven't mentioned by name.

Tony Pinchuck: Thanks to our excellent editor Charlie Melville for making our words make sense and for steering us through the stormy seas of the redesign; to my co-author Barbara McCrea for her vital contribution to the book; to our picture editor Nicole Newman for her hard work and some inspired choices; to the City of Cape Town's Kylie Hatton for delivering the goods at a moment's notice; and to all the unmentioned people who had a part in producing this book.

Readers' letters

Thanks to all the readers who have taken the time to write in with comments and suggestions (and apologies if we've inadvertently omitted or misspelt anyone's name):

Christoph Baltzer, Elizabeth Brierley, Alex Crossman, Anthony Fenton-Wells, Jim Lambert, Keith & Diana Morgan, Chris Myburgh, Alichia Nortje, Emma Norton, Fannia Polet, John Tatam, William Timmermans, Ron Zuiderwijk and Paula

Photo credits

All photos © Rough Guides except the following:
(Key: t-top; b-bottom; c-centre; l-left; r-right)

p.1 Superstock, Yadid Levy
p.2 Axiom, Jenny Aceson
p.6 Almy, Photos 12
p.7 Getty, Allan Baxter
p.9 Axiom, Ian Cumming (t); Corbis, Theo Allofs
p.10 AWL, Danita Delimont
p.11 Gallo Images/Getty (t); Superstock (c)
p.12 Superstock (t)
p.13 Getty (t); 4Corners, Massimo Ripani (c)
p.14 Alamy, Danita Delimont (tl); Superstock (bl); Getty, Christopher Thomas (br)
p.15 Photolibrary (t); Superstock (c)
p.16 Superstock (t); Getty, Martin Harvey (c)
p.17 Getty, Nigel Dennis (t); Getty, Roger de la Harpe (cl)
p.18 Alamy, Robert Hollingworth
p.40 Superstock, Andrew McConnell
p.47 Superstock (t); 4Corners, Huber (b)
p.68 4Corners, Huber
p.75 Superstock
p.80 Getty, Neil Overy
p.85 Superstock
p.100 AWL, John Warburton-Lee
p.106 Alamy, John Warburton-Lee
p.111 DK Images (t); DK Images (c); Superstock (b)
p.115 Axiom, Jenny Acheson
p.124 DK Images
p.129 DK Images

p.130 Getty, Lavonne Bosman
p.132 Axiom, Jenny Acheson (tr); AWL, Ian Trower (bc); Superstock (bl)
p.137 Corbis, Nic Bothma
p.139 DK Images (t); Getty, Alistair Berg (m)
p.142 Gallo Images Alamy
p.144 Superstock
p.148 AWL, Ian Trower
p.161 Superstock, Masiant Ludovic (tr); Superstock, Walter Bibikow (b)
p.166 4Corners, Giovanni Simeone
p.179 Getty, Peter Chadwick (t); Photobank/Alamy (b)
p.186 Getty, Chris Bradley
p.193 Superstock (t); Alamy, Eric Nathan
p.199 Superstock, Rafaele Meucci
p.226 Alamy, Ariadne Van Zandbergen
p.231 Alamy, Ariadne Van Zandbergen (t); Superstock (c); Getty, Roger de la Harpe (b)
p.242 Getty, Ian Trower
p.251 Superstock (tl); AWL, Danita Delimont (tr); AWL, Josh Anon (b)

Front cover: Boulders Beach, Penguin Picture Colour Library
Back cover: St James Beach huts, Gavin Hellier/AWL Images (t); Lions at Addo, Superstock (l); Long Street, Cape Town, Getty Images/Axiom (r)

Index

Maps are marked in **grey**

Maps

Index

Listings key

- Accommodation
- Restaurant/café
- Bar/club
- Shop

City plan

The **city plan** on the pages that follow is divided as shown:

N

0		300

metres

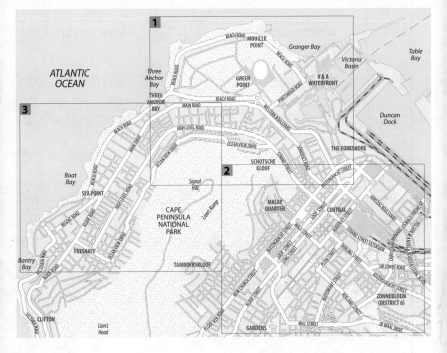

1

BEACH ROAD

MOUILLE POINT

Granger Bay

BEACH ROAD

Table Bay

Victoria Basin

V & A WATERFRONT

ATLANTIC OCEAN

Three Anchor Bay

BEACH ROAD

GREEN POINT

PORTSWOOD RD

THREE ANCHOR BAY

MAIN ROAD

BEACH ROAD

WESTERN BOULEVARD

Duncan Dock

3

HIGH LEVEL ROAD

OCEAN VIEW DRIVE

STRAND STREET

SOMERSET ROAD

THE FORESHORE

BEACH ROAD

BEACH ROAD

MAIN DRIVE

OCEAN VIEW DRIVE

Boat Bay

SCHOTSCHE KLOOF

STRAND STREET

BUITENGRACHT STREET

HIGH LEVEL ROAD

BEACH ROAD

Signal Hill

2

HERTZOG BOULEVARD

KLOOF ROAD

SEA POINT

REGENT ROAD

MALAY QUARTER

LOOP STREET

CENTRAL

ANDERSON STREET

STRAND STREET EXTENSION

Lion's Rump

CAPE PENINSULA NATIONAL PARK

OCEAN VIEW DRIVE

BUITENGRACHT STREET

WALE STREET

PLEIN STREET

DARLING STREET

KIZERS BEACH STREET

SIR LOWRY ROAD

FRESNAYE

LOOP STREET

LONG STREET

ZONNEBLOEM (DISTRICT 6)

VICTORIA ROAD

KLOOF ROAD

Bantry Bay

TAMBOERSKLOOF

NEW CHURCH STREET

KLOOF STREET

BUITENKANT STREET

ROELAND STREET

VICTORIA ROAD

CLIFTON

Lion's Head

KLOOF NEK ROAD

GARDENS

MILL STREET

DE WAAL DRIVE

Map symbols

✈	Airport	♦	Place of interest	⊠	Entrance gate	▦	Building
★	Bus/taxi	⊥	Garden	⋏⋏	Mountain range	▢	Market
P	Parking	🌺	Vineyard	▲	Mountain peak	⊡	Church
⊠	Post office	⛳	Golf course	⌒	Cave	⬯	Stadium
(i)	Information office	🏛	Monument	🎋	Picnic site	▢	Park
🏥	Hospital	🚢	Ship wreck	⚓	Swimming area	●‒●	Cable car
🕌	Mosque	🔦	Lighthouse			⊢⊢⊢⊢	Funicular
✡	Synagogue	🌾	Windmill				

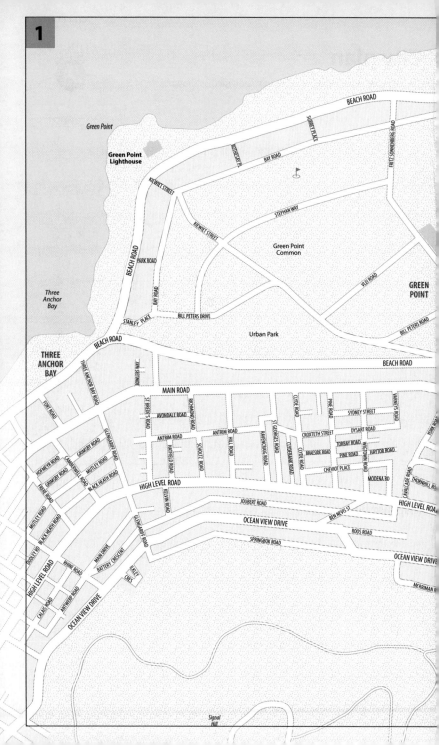

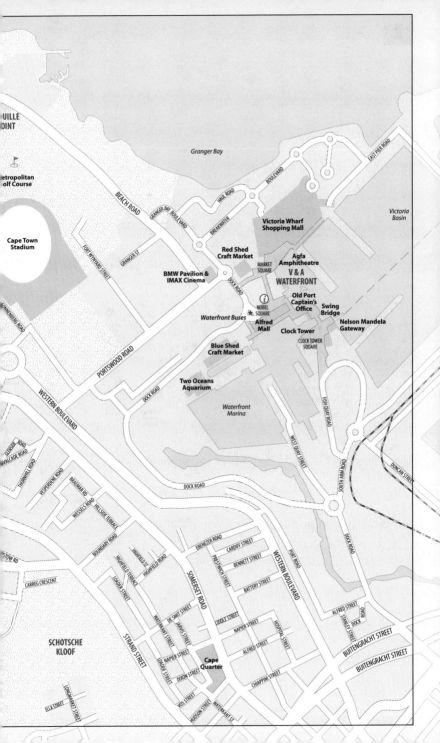

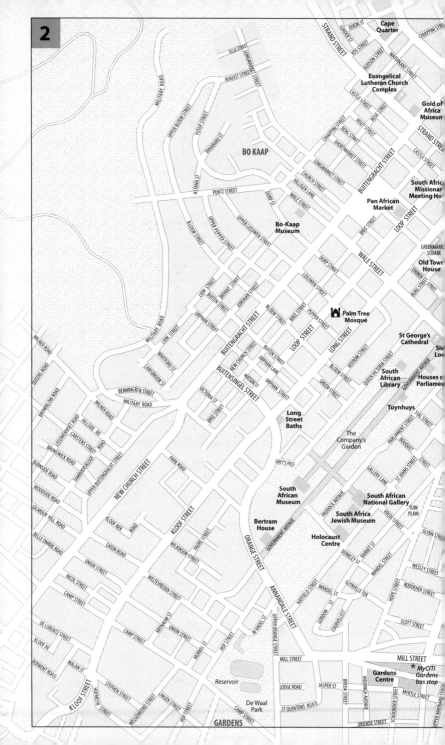

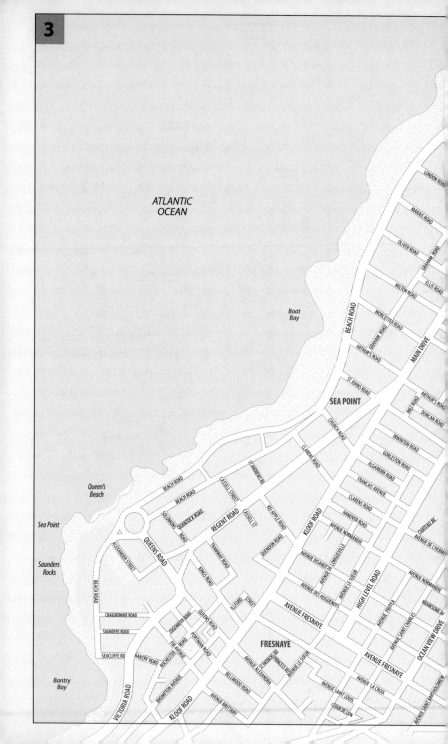

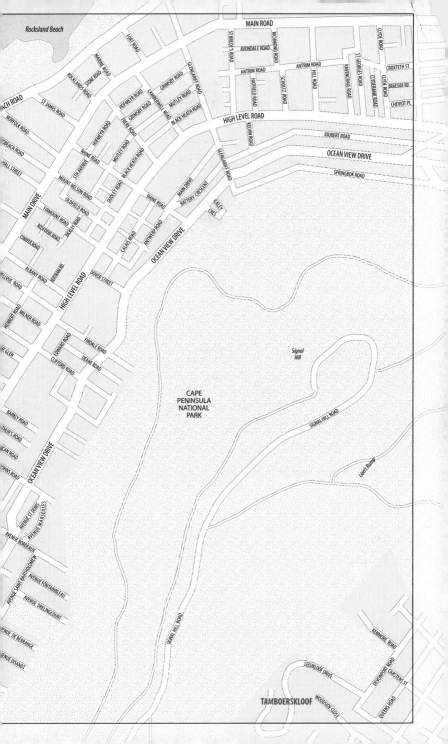

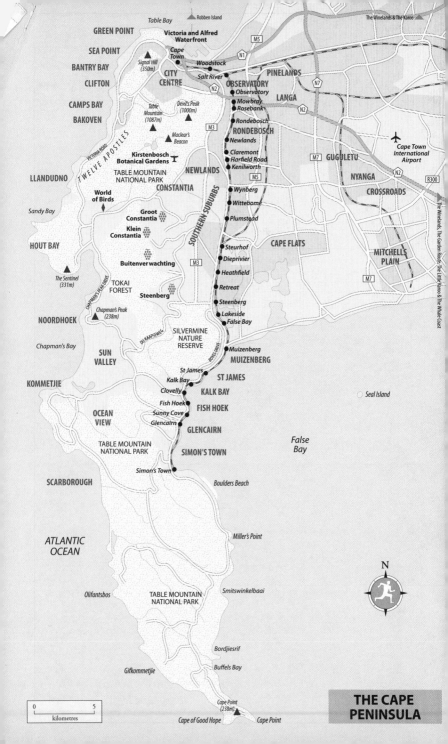

THE CAPE PENINSULA

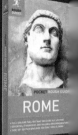